OXFORD AND EMPIRE

By the same author

THE MAKING OF PAKISTAN
THE BRITISH AND THEIR SUCCESSORS
INTERNATIONAL TARGETS FOR DEVELOPMENT (*editor*)
THE UNITED NATIONS AND THE POPULATION QUESTION (*with Michael Car*

OXFORD AND EMPIRE

The Last Lost Cause?

Richard Symonds

St. Martin's Press New York

St. Martin's Press, Inc., 175 Fifth Avenue, New York, NY 10010
Printed in Hong Kong
Published in the United Kingdom by The Macmillan Press Ltd.
First published in the United States of America in 1986
ISBN 0-312-59362-7

Library of Congress Cataloging in Publication Data
Symonds, Richard, 1918-
Oxford and empire - the last lost cause?
Bibliography: p.
Includes index.
1. University of Oxford - Faculty - Attitudes - History.
2. University of Oxford - Alumni - Attitudes - History.
3. Great Britain - Colonies. 4. Colonial administrators -
Great Britain - Attitudes - History. I. Title
LF509.S95 1985 378.425′74 85-11870
ISBN 0-312-59362-7

For Ann Spokes Symonds

Contents

List of Plates

The author and publishers should like to thank the following for permission to reproduce photographs:

Plates 1 and 7: the Master and Fellows of University College, Oxford; Plate 2: the Master and Fellows of Balliol College, Oxford; Plate 3: Lady Alexandra Metcalfe; Plates 4, 5, 21 and 24: the Warden of Rhodes House, Oxford; Plate 6: the Rhodes Trustees; Plate 8: the Editorial Committee of *The Round Table*; Plates 9 and 17: the Warden and Fellows of Merton College, Oxford; Plate 10: the Master and Fellows of St Peter's College, Oxford; Plates 13 and 15: the Indian Institute Library, Oxford; Plate 14: the Warden and Fellows of All Souls College, Oxford; Plates 16 and 25: the Bodleian Library; Plate 18: *Commonwealth Forestry Review*; Plate 19: the Oxford University School of Geography; Plate 20: the Pitt Rivers Museum, Oxford; Plates 22 and 23: the Royal Commonwealth Society; Plate 26: the Principal and Fellows of Somerville College, Oxford; Plate 27: the Imperial Forestry Institute, Oxford.

Photographs for Plates 1, 4, 5, 7, 10, 21 and 24 were provided by John Falconer; for Plates 2, 9, 14, 17 and 28 by Thomas Photos, Oxford (copyright); for Plates 11 and 12 by Oxford and County Newspapers (copyright); and for Plates 6, 13, 15, 16 and 25 by the Bodleian Library (copyright).

Preface and Acknowledgements

The materials for a study of Oxford University's connection with the British Empire are plentiful but scattered. The individual Colleges provide three main sources, namely the Registers of their former members, the papers of their former Heads and Fellows, and articles in the College periodical magazines or records. Only three of the former men's Colleges have published Registers containing information on the careers of their graduates over the whole period covered by this book, about 1870 to 1939. The former women's Colleges took more trouble to keep in touch with their alumnae. Three out of the five have published Registers, and information on the careers of women from the other two Colleges is available from unpublished records, although there are considerable gaps both in the published and unpublished Registers.

I should like to thank the librarians and archivists of all the Colleges who have helped in the research; and the Master and Fellows of Balliol College for access to the papers of three former Masters, Benjamin Jowett, J. L. Strachan Davidson and A. D. Lindsay as well as to the Jowett–Nightingale letters and the College Minutes; also the Provost and Fellows of Oriel College for access to the papers of L. R. Phelps.

Most of the Colleges published regularly or sporadically College magazines or records; on the whole those of the women's Colleges contain more articles about the work of their former members in the Empire than do those of the men's Colleges.

I should like to thank Mr Trevor Aston, Keeper of the University Archives, for access to the Archives and Miss Ruth Vyse for guidance in their use. In addition to the Minutes and Registers of the Hebdomadal Council, Congregation and Convocation, the retired University registry files are illuminating, particularly on Oxford's relationship with other universities in the Empire.

The Bodleian Library also contains the papers of a number of Oxford men who were in various ways concerned with the Empire. I should like to thank Lady MacAdam for permission to use the papers of Lionel Curtis; Dr Alexander Murray for those of Gilbert Murray; Mrs Mary Bennett for those of H. A. L. Fisher; and the Warden and Fellows of New College for those of Lord Milner, which are now kept in the Bodleian.

The Rhodes House Library contains much unpublished material about the careers of Oxford men who served in the Empire as officials, missionaries and in other capacities. I am grateful to Dr Alan Bell, Librarian of Rhodes House, for frequent guidance and to Dr Robin Fletcher, Secretary of the Rhodes Trust, for allowing me to consult the Minutes and files of the Trust, which contain fascinating glimpses of how the Oxford network operated in the Empire.

Several of the University Institutes and Departments contain important material. The Indian Institute has papers on its origins and some papers, or copies of them, of its founder, Sir Monier Monier Williams; I am grateful to the Librarian, Mr J. B. Katz, for frequent help, and to His Honour Judge E. F. Monier Williams for allowing me to borrow the Monier Williams papers which are in his possession. The School of Geography has the papers of its founder, Sir Halford Mackinder; the Hope Department in the Museum has the incoming, but not, alas, copies of the outgoing correspondence of Sir Edward Poulton. Other interesting material has been found in the libraries or archives of the Institute of Social Anthropology, the Department of Zoology, Pusey House, the Oxford University Appointments Committee, the Commonwealth Forestry Institute, the Pitt Rivers Museum, the Department of Educational Studies, the Oxford University Press, the Institute of Agricultural Economics, Queen Elizabeth House and the Institute of Commonwealth Studies. I am grateful to the Librarian of the last mentioned, Mr R. Townsend, for frequent advice and wish to express my appreciation for the help which I have received from the staff of all these institutions. I wish to thank the Committee for Commonwealth Studies and the Governing Body of Queen Elizabeth House for permission to see their papers.

Outside Oxford Dr Richard Bingle has been a kind guide in the India Office Library and Records Department of the British Library, which I would like to thank for permission to use the Cornelia Sorabji papers. I also wish to thank the Rt Hon. Viscount Scarsdale for access to the papers of Lord Curzon which are in that library. I owe much to the advice of Mr Donald Simpson not only on sources in the Royal Commonwealth Society of which he is Librarian but on those of missionary societies.

I also thank the librarians and archivists of the Church Missionary Society, the United Society for the Propagation of the Gospel and the Community of the Resurrection for help in studying the work of Oxford missionaries.

I should like to thank Mr N. Machin for letting me read his unpublished biography of R. S. Rattray; Dr A. Kadish for that on Arnold Toynbee; the late Sir Duncan Wilson for his then uncompleted biography of Gilbert Murray; Mrs Mona MacMillan for her unpublished book on W. M. MacMillan; Mrs Leonard Barnes for access to the unpublished autobiography of Leonard Barnes; Dr E. P. Thompson for access to the papers of Edward Thompson; Professor S. H. Frankel for letting me see papers concerning the origins of Queen Elizabeth House; and Professor K. Kirkwood for access to the Minutes of the Ralegh Club.

I am grateful to the following for permission to see their theses: Dr H. A. E. Ewing, 'The Indian Civil Service, 1919–42' (Cambridge University, Ph.D., 1980); Dr W. D. Meikle, 'And Gladly Teach: G. M. Wrong and the Department of History at the University of Toronto' (Ph.D. thesis, University of Michigan, 1977); Dr M. Warboys, 'Science and British Colonial Imperialism' (D. Phil. thesis, University of Sussex, 1979); also to the Rt Revd Bishop A. K. Warren for showing me the uncompleted thesis of Maurice C. Knight on the history of College House, Christchurch, New Zealand.

Amongst published material, the *Oxford Magazine* gives a useful impression of what senior members thought about the Empire over the whole period. Two ephemeral undergraduate magazines which illustrate particular points of view are the *Indian Magazine* and the *Blue Book*; the latter was largely inspired by Canadians. In addition to reports and histories of missions, schools and Universities and reports of Government commissions, numerous biographies and autobiographies of Oxford men at home or abroad have been used. There must be many others which I have not seen, for it is sometimes only by chance that I have come across such fascinating works as Cecil Headlam's *Ten Thousand Miles through India and Burma: An Account of the Oxford University Authentics' Cricket Tour in the Year of the Coronation, Durbar*, published in 1903, or G. K. Chettur's book *The Last Enchantment: Recollections of Oxford*, published in Mangalore in 1934 with the University's arms embossed on the cover.

A study which attempts to cover all aspects of Oxford's relationship with the Empire cannot be comprehensive. I have therefore concentrated on groups of people who may illustrate the various elements in the story, in so far as anyone can be considered to represent anything other than himself in such an individualistic and eccentric place as Oxford was in the Imperial period. I am aware that this approach may have led to omissions and perhaps lack of balance in some areas and shall be grateful to anyone who will point them out.

I should like to express my appreciation to the Oxford University Committee for Commonwealth Studies for appointing me as an Honorary Senior Research Officer and to the Director of its Institute, Mr Arthur Hazlewood, for much kindness; also to the Warden and Fellows of St Antony's College for appointing me as a Senior Associate Member and providing a delightful and stimulating base. I have benefited from discussion of draft chapters of the book with the Commonwealth History Seminar organised by Professor R. E. Robinson, Dr A. F. Madden and their colleagues, and in particular from collaboration in a series of papers delivered to this seminar in 1980, subsequently published in 1982 in honour of Sir Edgar Williams as *Oxford and the Idea of Commonwealth*, edited by David K. Fieldhouse and A. F. Madden. This series, though highly relevant to my theme, was more oriented towards the Commonwealth than to the Imperial period.

I am also grateful for similar discussions of ideas in the book in the African, South Asian and Race Relations Seminars organised by Professor K. Kirkwood, Mr A. Kirk-Greene and Dr T. Raychaudhury at St Antony's College and in a seminar organised by the Warden of Nuffield College, Mr Michael Brock, on the history of the University in the nineteenth century.

Certain passages in this book have appeared in the chapter on Oxford and India contributed by me to *Oxford and the Idea of the Commonwealth*, mentioned above; in an article, 'Powerhouse of Imperial Studies – the Early Search for a Role for Rhodes House', in *Round Table*, vol. 288 (1983) p. 284; and in an article, 'Some Early Oxford Women and the Empire', in *Oxford*, vol. 36, no. 4 (1984) p. 4.

I am particularly grateful to Michael Brock, Professor L. Gann, Dr A. F. Madden, Dr Gowher Rizvi and Professor K. E. Robinson for reading and criticising the whole book in draft and to Lord Beloff, the late Bishop Stephen Neill, the Revd Max Saint, Dr Ian Scargill,

Dr J. Beattie, Sir Edgar Williams and Mr J. Wyatt Smith for reading parts of it. I should also like to thank Mrs Anne Robinson and Mrs Rita Giwa for their excellent secretarial assistance and my son Peter for help in research.

Finally I should like to acknowledge the help of all those who have answered my questions in Britain, as well as in Canada, Australia, New Zealand, India and Jamaica on my travels. Some of those who have been most helpful have died before this book appears, including Dr Thomas Hodgkin, Bishop Stephen Neill, Dame Margery Perham, Lord Redcliffe-Maud, Sir George Schuster and Mr Lewis Wilcher. To those who are still alive I would wish to express warm appreciation for the way in which, however busy, they have found time to help in the advancement of knowledge on a subject which involves and cuts across many disciplines and areas of interest.

R.S.

Institute of Commonwealth Studies
Queen Elizabeth House
Oxford

List of Abbreviations

The following abbreviations are used:

Corpus	Corpus Christi College
D.N.B.	*Dictionary of National Biography*
E.H.R.	*English Historical Review*
I.C.S.	Indian Civil Service
J.I.C.S.	*Journal of Imperial and Commonwealth Studies*
L.C.C.	London County Council
L.M.H.	Lady Margaret Hall
O.H.S.	Society of Oxford Home Students (later St Anne's College)
O.U.P.	Oxford University Press
P.B.A.	*Proceedings of the British Academy*
P.P.	*Parliamentary Papers* (England)
R.G.S.	Royal Geographical Society
S.O.A.S.	School of Oriental and African Studies (London)

Note on Oxford Terminology

During the period covered by this book, from about 1870 to 1939, the Oxford Colleges were autonomous, with their own revenues, mainly from landed estates, and were each governed by a self-perpetuating Governing Body of the Fellows which elected the Head of the College, as well as new Fellows.

The Heads of the Colleges were variously called Principal, Warden, Master, Rector, President or Provost; they were collectively known as Heads of Houses and served in rotation as Vice-Chancellor of the University. Christ Church had a special position; its Head was also Dean of the Cathedral, and its Fellows were called Students.

The women's Halls, later to become Colleges, were established from 1878. Women were gradually allowed to sit for University examinations, but were not awarded degrees until 1920.

Congregation consisted of all resident M.A.s; after 1912 membership was confined to those who were teachers or administrators in the University; its members elected the Hebdomadal Council, which was the executive body, representative of Heads of Houses, University professors and other members of Congregation.

Convocation was the body of all M.A.s, whether living in or outside Oxford, who had left their names on the College books. Its members elected the Chancellor and certain of the professors, and it could be convened if a sufficient number of members of Congregation called for a meeting. In this period Convocation was usually dominated by country clergy and schoolmasters in Holy Orders and it tended to be more conservative than Congregation.

Matriculation was the procedure by which an undergraduate was admitted to the University, but he had first to be admitted to a College. University teachers were colloquially known as 'dons'.

To obtain the degree of B.A. an undergraduate had to pass a qualifying examination, Responsions, which until 1920 included Greek as well as Latin; a first public examination, either Moderations, colloquially known as 'Mods', or, in Natural Science and some Arts

Schools a preliminary examination; and a final examination leading either to an honours or pass degree.

In Classics after 'Mods' the final examination was taken in *Literae Humaniores*, colloquially known as 'Greats'. After the First World War a School of Philosophy, Politics and Economics was established which was sometimes referred to as 'Modern Greats'.

No examination was taken for the M.A., which could be obtained by leaving one's name on the books of one's College for a few years after graduation and then paying a small sum to the University.

The Oxford Union Society was a students' club best known for its debates. Its officers – President, Librarian, Treasurer and Secretary – were elected each term, mainly for their prowess in debates. To become an officer of the Union was regarded as an important first step in public life, particularly in politics.

A 'Blue' was someone who had represented the University in an important annual sporting event against Cambridge, such as cricket, rowing or football, and thus acquired the right to wear the dark blue colours of the University. A 'half blue' was awarded to those who represented the University in less prestigious sports.

Normally the Oxford University Press published books with its own imprint from its London office; those published in Oxford bore the imprint 'Clarendon Press'.

The Isis is the name of the stretch of the River Thames which passes through Oxford.

In this book the phrase 'Public Schools' is used in its English sense to describe schools such as Eton and Harrow, which were in fact private.

A Gaudy was a reception held by a College for its former Students.

Introduction

This book is about the influence of the University of Oxford on the British Empire and the influence of the Empire on Oxford between the middle of the nineteenth century and the Second World War. It is concerned with three broad questions.

The first is Oxford's contribution to the philosophy of, and national attitudes towards, Empire. In this the teaching of the Classics had an important place. The lessons of the history of the Greek city states were often applied to relations between Britain and the old Dominions, whilst in the government of dependent territories comparisons were frequently made with Rome. Not only candidates for honours degrees in Classics, but those who read for pass degrees, like Rhodes, and those who read for honours in other subjects were obliged to read Plato and Aristotle, Cicero and Tacitus. The critics of Empire whom Oxford produced throughout the period often conducted their arguments with the Imperialists in terms of classical precedents. The modern historians, together with the geographers, spread the Imperial message at a more popular level through the schools of the Empire, often by means of textbooks published by the Oxford University Press.

The second question is who wanted what in Oxford from, or in the name of, Empire and with what result. This leads to consideration of the motives of the classicists, which were mainly defensive and expressed through arguments that the study of Greats was the best possible preparation for a political or administrative career because it taught good judgement. The natural scientists, geographers and anthropologists, on the other hand, sought to use the needs of Empire to justify expansion in their fields. Those who were interested in religion saw the Empire as providing a framework within which the heirs to the Oxford Movement could advance their work from the slums of Britain to India, Africa and the Pacific. Jowett and many tutors were interested in the Empire as a provider of employment to their pupils in posts of responsibility and with potential for doing good.

Thirdly, an attempt is made to understand the influence which Oxford exerted in the one direction on her graduates who went out as administrators, teachers and missionaries and on the institutions which they founded; and in the other on those who came both from the dependent colonies and the old Dominions to study in the University.

The three questions cannot always be treated separately. Indian studies, for example, were variously affected by the desire to further Christian missionary work, the need to find jobs for pupils in the Indian Civil Service (I.C.S.), and the protection of classical studies by manipulation of the marking system of the I.C.S. entry Examination; there was also, of course, some genuine interest in Indian history and culture. Another example is that of the Oxford geographers, who not only climbed onto the Imperial bandwagon but helped to fuel and drive it.

In a final chapter these three main questions are brought together again and an attempt is made to assess Oxford's contribution to, and influence on, what Macaulay foresaw as the proudest day in English history, the end of Empire.

It may be asked why a book should be devoted to Oxford and Empire rather than, for example to Cambridge and Empire. A parallel study would indeed be of considerable interest. The Oxford relationship however had special characteristics. One was the preponderance of Oxford men in the posts in which Imperial policies were decided and implemented. During the high period of Empire between 1880 and 1914 the Prime Minister and Foreign Secretary were usually Oxford men; in the Indian Civil Service and Sudan Political Service Oxford men outnumbered Cambridge men by almost two to one. Over the whole period of British rule in India 15 Governors-General or Viceroys came from Oxford compared with five from Cambridge. Between 1888 and 1905 three Viceroys in succession were Balliol men. In the other direction the unique institution of the Rhodes Scholarships brought to Oxford hundreds of young men who had been selected as potential leaders from the colonies of settlement.

The difference between Oxford and Cambridge was not merely one of numbers. To Leslie Stephen, reviewing the life and letters of Benjamin Jowett in 1898, it appeared that 'Oxford has long been fertile in prophets; in men who cast a spell over a certain number of disciples, and not only propagate ideas, but exercise a personal sway. At Cambridge no such leader presented himself in my time; and, moreover, Cambridge men were generally inclined to regard their apparent barrenness with a certain complacency. . . . They did not deny the existence of the soul; but knew that it should be kept in its proper place.'[1] Looking at this difference from the other side, Sir Herbert Warren, President of Magdalen College, Oxford, told the Congress of Universities of the Empire in 1912 that Cambridge was more physical, Oxford more metaphysical. G. C. Brodrick, Warden of Wadham College, who had taught both at Oxford and Cambridge, observed in 1900 that at Cambridge studies were less speculative than those at Oxford and therefore more conducive to docility of mind. There was a greater disposition among Cambridge than among Oxford students, he concluded, to mind their own business, that of education and learning, rather than enlighten the world on theology and politics.[2]

No other University had a College such as Balliol between 1870 and 1914, devoted to selecting and preparing young men for high office and then, through the network of old Balliol men, ensuring that they secured it. Nor elsewhere was there an institution comparable to All Souls College, which had no undergraduates but appointed as its Fellows the most brilliant graduates of each year who, as one commentator said in the 1930s, thus joined a Committee which took upon itself no less a task than running the British Empire.[3]

Although this study is mainly focused on the period between about 1870 and 1939, the Oxford connection started much earlier and is as old as the Empire. It was always regarded as the duty of the University and the Colleges, as expressed in their official prayers, to breed up men for service in Church and State, and before the Reformation it was common for Oxford graduates to serve both. The story could start in the fifteenth century when the Lancastrian rulers of the English Empire in France, nervous of the influence of the University of Paris on their subjects, brought a scholar from Oxford to establish a University in their city of Caen[4] and become its first Rector. At about the same time Archbishop Chichele founded All Souls College at his old University in order that poor and indigent clerks should pray for the souls and the glorious memory of those who had fought and died in the wars with France. It may have been, now that the English Empire in France was crumbling, that the chantry was intended as an expiation by the aging Archbishop for his part in inspiring and supporting the aggressive military policies of Henry V and his brothers: but Chichele looked forward also; a high proportion of the College's members were required to study law, and this led to the tradition by which All Souls provided men for public service in later Empires.[5]

In the next century Queen Elizabeth I requested the Heads of Oxford Colleges to recommend men for her service; in her reign Walter Raleigh and his half-brother Humphrey Gilbert went from Oriel College to embark on discoveries and settlement in the Americas. Raleigh brought up to London, to instruct him in mathematics and astronomy, an Oxford tutor, Thomas Harriot (1560–1621); later this venturesome don sailed as a surveyor with Gilbert to Virginia and wrote a book on his experiences. At the same time Oxford's first geographer, Richard Hakluyt of Christ Church (1552–1616), was writing his great work on the voyages of the British mariners.

In the seventeenth century Archbishop Laud founded a Chair of Arabic, though this was intended more to promote theological studies than Empire. Its first holder, Edward Pococke of Corpus, lived in Aleppo as chaplain to the English merchants for five years and in Constantinople for four; he returned to Oxford as one of the foremost oriental scholars of his time. He and his successors were only allowed, however, to lecture in vacations, and to graduates, so as not to draw undergraduates from studies which were considered more important. Hence the Chair became devoted more to research than teaching. At the end of the century William III, through his Lord Almoner, endowed studentships in Oxford to provide men for the public service who were fluent in Arabic and Turkish and thus able to assist in negotiation of the ransom of the British seamen who were held captive by the Corsairs of the Barbary Coast.[6] The studentships were converted into the Lord Almoner's Professorship of Arabic in the eighteenth century, and this too became a research post. Another late-seventeenth-century initiative was that of Dr Fell, Dean of Christ Church, who persuaded the East India Company to support four or more scholars at Oxford who would become their future chaplains.[7]

It was usually from Oxford and Cambridge that men were sought for the service of the State abroad. Cromwell renewed Queen Elizabeth's request.[8] George I made a lavish benefaction to found the Regius Professorship in Modern History, together with lecturers in languages and support for King's scholars, in order to provide trained men for his diplomatic service; though the hostility towards the House of Hanover and the torpor of eighteenth-century Oxford caused the benefaction to be diverted to other purposes or to be used as a sinecure.[9] A little later Warren Hastings, Governor-General of

India, appealed in vain to Oxford to make provision for the teaching of Persian, which was the official language of the Mogul Empire, to the servants of the East India Company.[10]

Many sons of American and West Indian colonists came to study before American Independence. When the Americans established their own Universities, Oxford presented them with books. John Wesley, Fellow of Lincoln College, not only evangelised in America but founded Methodist Colleges there. After Raleigh founded the Colony of Virginia, the Quaker William Penn of Christ Church founded Pennsylvania, and General James Oglethorpe of Corpus founded Georgia as an asylum for insolvent Britons and oppressed European Protestants. John Locke combined the teaching of philosophy with the post of Secretary to the Proprietors of Carolina. Blackstone in his lectures as Professor of Jurisprudence provided the basis for the arguments of the revolutionaries in the debate on American Independence.[11]

The early nineteenth century was marked by a keen interest in the evangelisation of India which was to continue throughout the century. It was accompanied, after David Livingstone's visit to Oxford, by an equal interest in missionary work in Africa. Christ Church in this period provided a long succession of Governors-General of India. Christ Church men also played a main part in the founding of Christchurch, New Zealand, and its College in accordance with the principles of the Oxford Movement.

The story of Oxford's relationship with Empire is complicated by the fact that the Empire ended at different times in different places. In India the date was clearly 1947, when the King renounced his title as Emperor. Australia, Canada, South Africa and New Zealand effectively became independent under the Statute of Westminster of 1930, even though both the terms 'Empire' and 'Commonwealth' continued to be used until 1939. Oxford's main contribution to tropical Africa, however, came after the Second World War, within the Commonwealth period; a brief reference to this is therefore contained in an Epilogue in Chapter 14.

There is a constant risk in this kind of survey that the standards of the present may be applied to the past. Before starting to examine the questions which have been outlined, it may therefore be useful to see how the Empire appeared at various times to the senior members of the University, as they were recorded in a journal produced for dons by dons for most of the period under review, the *Oxford Magazine*.

Part I
The Perception of Empire

1 The View from the Senior Common Room

We are all Imperialists nowadays
Oxford Magazine, Editorial article (1895)

The British Empire – proud forlorn title!
Oxford Magazine, Editorial article (1926)

Apart from the *Oxford University Gazette*, which published official information, the main channel of communication between senior members of the University was the *Oxford Magazine*, which appeared weekly in term time from 1883 to 1970, died, was revived as a fortnightly, and finally ceased to be published in 1973. Its Editors changed frequently, often annually, and among them were some of the most talented members of the University. Before 1914 these included D. G. Hogarth, A. D. Godley, C. Grant Robertson, H. W. C. Davies, A. E. Zimmern, J. L. Stocks and G. S. Gordon. After 1914 some of the most distinguished were W. T. S. Stalleybrass, M. L. Jacks, M. R. Ridley, R. B. McCallum, D. W. Brogan, H. G. Nicholas and Max Beloff.

With such a rapid succession of strong-minded Editors it would be fruitless to try and trace a consistent editorial policy towards the Empire. Nevertheless from the magazine's articles, editorials, letters, and even verses, a pattern emerges of four phases. In the first period, from 1883 to 1895, there is a benign but mild interest in Empire; in the second, from 1895 to 1914, Empire becomes a matter of frequent, sometimes serious and sometimes sentimental, concern, and arguments about University policy and problems are often buttressed by references to Imperial welfare. In the third phase, between 1919 and 1939, interest gradually declines; by then the Empire seems to become something of a bore. For some years after the Second World War there is a revival of interest, not in Empire but in Commonwealth, when dons are teaching in new Universities in Africa and

Asia or in special courses in Oxford; this phase is outside the framework of this study but is discussed in the Epilogue.

1883 TO 1914: CRESCENDO

1883, the year in which the *Magazine* was first published, was also that in which Jowett became Vice-Chancellor. Jowett as Master of Balliol had already largely succeeded in leading the transformation of Oxford from being an Anglican and clerical University into one whose central purpose was to prepare, through the College tutorial system, an élite who would occupy the key positions of authority in a lay society. Ranged against him still were those who believed that teaching became stultified when it was not associated with research. They were led, unsuccessfully at the time, by Mark Pattison, the Rector of Lincoln College, looking, thought Mrs Humphry Ward, 'like a discontented lizard with a cold'.[1] The natural scientists continued the fight in the *Oxford Magazine* after Pattison's death. The scientists were also in conflict with the classicists on the allocation of marks in Civil Service Examinations, as well as on the question of whether teaching should be organised by the Colleges and their Fellows or by the University and its professoriate. Rumbling and occasionally erupting was the controversy regarding compulsory Latin and Greek. More gently conducted from about 1880 to 1920 was the debate on the status of women.

Elections to senior University posts were sometimes conducted along political lines. Whilst Convocation, when the clergy turned out in strength, was strongly Conservative, in Congregation Liberals were well represented until 1886 when the Liberal Party split over Irish Home Rule. The *Oxford Magazine* reported that there were only 17 supporters of Home Rule among senior members of the University at that time.[2] Those who opposed Home Rule for Ireland tended to oppose it elsewhere in the Empire. When Joseph Chamberlain started his campaign for tariff reform however a number of Oxford Liberal Unionists returned to the Liberal fold.

The Empire was of most interest to the University when it touched on, or was influenced by, domestic issues: apart from this the main attention which it received before 1914 concerned jobs; or what Bright had called the system of outdoor relief for the upper classes.

One of the *Oxford Magazine*'s main preoccupations at this time was with the entry of Oxford men into the I.C.S. Before 1892 candidates were recruited at the age of 19, so that Oxford graduates were not eligible, although many of the probationers came to study at Oxford after being recruited. When in 1892 the age limit was raised to 23, the *Oxford Magazine* published several articles drawing the attention of tutors to the advantages of the I.C.S. as a career in which the prospects far surpassed those of the Home Civil Service, and in which an officer might prudently even invite a girl without a penny to marry him. Every year from 1892 to 1914 the *Magazine* published a detailed table showing the proportion of places won by Oxford candidates and what degrees they had obtained. It would frequently quote Lord Dalhousie's remark that whilst in England civil servants were clerks, in India they were proconsuls. Throughout the period the tables showed that Oxford almost always won more places in the I.C.S. than any other University.[3]

This at first appeared eminently satisfactory to most tutors, but when the I.C.S. began to take a quarter of the men who had obtained Firsts in Greats, and when enrolment in the Modern History School dropped because the I.C.S. marking system favoured Greats men, there was some disquiet. Moreover some Greats men would leave before taking finals in order to fit in six months with a crammer who would prepare them for the I.C.S. Examination. Oxford disposed of this problem by persuading the Civil Service Commissioners to raise the maximum age of entry to 24 in 1906.

A number of the men who had read Greats went on to the highest positions in the Indian Government, such as Lord Hailey, a double First and twice Governor of a Province. Others literally came a cropper. An I.C.S. officer wrote to inform the *Magazine* in 1899 that two young colleagues from Oxford had been killed in riding accidents because they came from a background in which horsiness was considered vulgar; even worse, he continued, other Oxford men lowered their own and the race's prestige by the effeminate and despicable method of being carried in a palanquin.[4]

Before 1914 India received more attention than other parts of the Empire; in 1893 the *Magazine* stated that 'for every ten books which our fathers read about India we read 1000'.[5] Monier Williams was well supported in his efforts to obtain money and publicity for the Indian Institute; Oxford's role was generally seen as to present Western ideas to Eastern minds, not, as Max Mueller had suggested, to learn from India. In the early twentieth century the *Magazine* was prone to publish comical and condescending articles such as 'Baboos I Have Known' and 'Famine Frivolities'.[6]

For those who were not clever enough to enter the I.C.S., there was the possibility of the Colonial Service. For a time the entrants for some Eastern colonies were recruited through the same examinations as the I.C.S. and Home Civil Service, and they were almost always candidates who had failed to enter either of the other Services. Subsequently entry was by interview. The *Oxford Magazine* published a number of letters from Colonial Service officers in Malaya, Ceylon and Africa describing the unsatisfactory conditions of service and pointing out that in some territories no one had yet survived to draw a pension.[7]

In 1905 the Egypt and Sudan Services started to recruit from Oxford and train their probationers there. 'The man wanted for Egypt and the Sudan', the *Oxford Magazine* noted in 1910, 'is the good all round man who has played a creditable part in one honour school or another and at the same time, without being a pure athlete, has distinguished himself in college life.'[8]

Even in the 1880s a high proportion of dons were still in Holy Orders. Apart from jobs, the other continuous Imperial interest of the readers of the *Oxford Magazine* was in missionary work. As many as 1000 people, mostly members of the University, would attend the missionary breakfasts in the Town Hall organised by Canon Christopher, Rector of St Aldate's, when a well-known bush bishop was announced to speak. The *Magazine* referred to appeals for money to buy boats for missions in Africa and Melanesia and for volunteers to work in the Oxford and Cambridge hostel in Allahabad. The missions in which Oxford felt a particular involvement were the Oxford Mission to Calcutta and the Universities Mission to Central Africa (U.M.C.A.). The former appealed because it was felt to be Oxford's unique intellectual task to win over to Christianity Indian students in the University of Calcutta, India's capital city, and thus bring about the conversion of India from the top. The University Mission to Central Africa had a more emotional appeal as 'the Church's forlorn hope' in which missionaries from Oxford, preferably athletes, could look forward to an early death by martyrdom or fever.

Probably there were even more Oxford men working as teachers in the Empire than as administrators or evangelical missionaries. The *Magazine* often announced their appointment and observed in 1887 that in Australia Oxford men were coming to the top in education and politics.[9] In general, emigration did not receive much attention; indeed, it seemed that Oxford men were not always well received in the Antipodes. A correspondent in New Zealand in 1906 advised settlers from Oxford to 'drop their superior Oxford manner if they are fortunate enough to possess that indescribable gift, and remember that versatility and good nature are indispensable for getting on in the Colonies':[10] and what, it may be wondered, did the rugged Australians make of their future Metropolitan, Canon Barry, who shortly before his departure from Oxford in 1883 was quoted as describing Socialism as 'the caricature of Christianity'.[11]

The first intimations of Oxford's consciousness of patriotic Imperialism occur in 1895 when the *Magazine* announced 'We are all Imperialists nowadays' and published a poem by A. G. Butler, Rhodes's former tutor, which commenced

> The little Englander is dead and gone
> There lives a greater England far away
> Behind the rising of the Eastern day
> Beyond the setting of the Western sun[12]

and readers were urged to go and see the patriotic picture *Saving The Colours*[13] in Mr Ryman's shop in the High Street. Rhodes himself was the subject of a sonnet by Butler in 1895, beginning

> Deep voiced, broad fronted, with the Caesar's brow
> A dreamer with a diamond in his hand
> Musing on Empire . . . .[14]

Until the Boer War there was little participation in military service; nor did Lord Wolseley's remarks make an intellectual appeal when on a visit to Oxford in 1886 he was reported as saying 'he found book-reading overrated as a military accomplishment and when the time came for a storming party he would not choose a man with a large head and narrow chest, who needed spectacles to see the enemy'.[15]

When the Boer War broke out the *Oxford Magazine* found consolation in the fact that though Cambridge was providing more volunteers than Oxford, there were also more Cambridge men fighting on the other side including Generals Reitz, De Wet, Smuts and Villiers, all of whom had read Law there.[16] However it published lists of

Oxford volunteers, who were allowed to postpone their examinations, and the flow of patriotic verse increased, full of metaphors from organised games.

There was of course one on Mafeking:

> All is still well, but you must do the shouting
> We haven't time or heart indeed to stick it
> We've closed our innings and begun our outing
> Six to the over on a bowler's wicket.[17]

Mafeking night produced the editorial reflection that 'For an Oxford man to kick a policeman is quite shameful. One might as well be a bargee or a French gamin.'[18]

About the same time appeared *Nursery of Empire*, describing Oxford's contribution to bearing the 'White Man's Burden'.

> Sent forth as rulers from the banks of Thames
> They long for but one sight of midland trees;
> Amidst the sheen of Orient gold and gems
> Their swift souls pass the seas;
> In thought they watch the racing oars flash by
> Propelled by strenuous strength, or mark the cheer
> As towards the goal posts soars the ball on high
> And victory is near.[19]

Critics of Empire occasionally made themselves heard. Towards the end of the Boer War, the Dean and Chaplain of Trinity, Major the Reverend M. B. Furse, who was temporarily commanding the Oxford University Volunteer Regiment, wrote to the *Oxford Magazine* in February 1902 to stimulate recruitment at a time when patriotic zeal was flagging. He suggested that men who were about to be ordained as clergymen would particularly profit from the experience of service in the Army and was supported by the Editor.[20] This brought an indignant letter from Sir Arthur Quiller-Couch ('Q') recollecting that according to the *Book of Common Prayer* a clergyman's duty was 'to maintain quietness, peace and love' for which participation in hanging of rebels and burning of homesteads was an unsuitable preparation.[21]

The publication of Rhodes's Will in 1902 startled Oxford. Rhodes had not consulted the University. He had, as L. R. Phelps pointed out in the *Oxford Magazine*, no sympathy with the literary tradition or the scholarship or science of Oxford and he had never lived in College. The Editor regretted that he had given so much money for scholarships and so little for teaching.[22] Fellows of Colleges sensed that the Rhodes Scholars and their requirements were going to shake Oxford up and, in the custom of the time, expressed their apprehensions in verse. As A. D. Godley reflected gloomily in an *Ode on the Distant Prospect of Oriel College*

From Canada and New South Wales
Where'er the British tongue prevails
All, all alike our peace disturb
All, all assemble here . . . .
And who are we to grant degrees
To persons eminent as these
Whose marks are ninety five percent
For moral character? . . .
Not mine decanally to cope
With students from thy Cape, Good Hope,
Britannia's youth supplies a scope
Sufficient quite for me.[23]

An anonymous *Lament of An Old Oxonian* was even more lurid:

The married mussalman arrives
With 37 moon-eyed wives
And fills a quad at Oriel,
While Magdalen's classic avenues
Are occupied by shy Yahoos
Whose habits are arborial.

The Afghan hillsmen, knives in hands
Pursue the Proctor in his bands
From Folly Bridge to Johns;
And Dyak head collectors stalk
Behind the elms of Christ Church Walk
Decapitating Dons.

O – that such things should come to be
In my old University
But if some folk prefer 'em
And like a Barnum-Bailey show

Then Oxford's where they ought to go
My son shall go to Durham.[24]

Between the Boer War and 1914 the highest tide of Imperialism reached Oxford. So we find an appeal for 'children's books of a good patriotic tone for farm schools in Transvaal';[25] Raleigh's new edition of Hakluyt's *Voyages* was sold out immediately;[26] University officials joined with the Mayor and Corporation to celebrate Empire Day in the Cathedral, where 1000 children provided a chorus for the choir of the Gordon Boys' School, and the Duke of Marlborough spoke on 'The Swelling Act of the Imperial Theme'.[27] Sir Herbert Warren as Professor of Poetry devoted his lectures to a comparison of Virgil and Tennyson as Imperial poets, and to reading aloud patriotic and sentimental verses from the Australian Bush. The Hon. Mrs Gell taught Oxford Conservatives to sing *Oxford Stands for the Union* to the tune of *Marching Through Georgia*;[28] while Mrs L. K. Haldane made lists of Empire goods which the wives of dons should seek out at Elliston's and Grimbly Hughes, and sent out her son and daughter, J. B. S. Haldane and the future Naomi Mitchison, to enrol village children in the League of Empire.[29]

And yet, there still seemed considerable indifference. The Editor regretted that there was a very small attendance at a meeting to promote land settlement in the Transvaal,[30] and that the bicentenary of Pitt the Elder, described as the founder of the Empire and a Trinity man, was quite neglected.[31] The Rt Revd Mike Furse, by now Bishop of Pretoria, preaching in St Mary's in 1911 warned that unless Britain recognised her Imperial responsibilities a catastrophe would assuredly take place. If Englishmen realised their duties of citizenship, the Volunteer Movement would be eminently successful and their Christianity would be a reality. What, he asked sombrely, would St Paul have thought of the present attitude of England towards the colonies?[32]

Even in this period Oxford preserved a certain spirit of irony and detachment. Henry Newbolt, as a freshman at Corpus, was disappointed because there was nothing to take the place of the ardent and imaginative loyalty of his public school, Clifton. At Oxford games, he found, had not the same militant edge, and for military ardour there was no opportunity. There was plenty of partisanship but it was concerned with philosophy, politics and intellectual or artistic principles. He was delighted to return to visit Clifton where they roared out his patriotic poem *Drake's Drum* and told him how outside

Omdurman one of the boats had brought an individual message from the school to every Clifton man.[33]

Sometimes the Editor of the *Oxford Magazine* would dream that Oxford would become the leading school of national and Imperial politics. Every paper set by Oxford men on British history, he urged in 1911, whether for undergraduates or schoolboys, should give some opportunity of showing knowledge of the growth of Britain's naval power or of the foundation and government of the Dominions overseas.[34]

Milner at a New College Gaudy in 1905 paid tribute to the excellent practical service of his 'Kindergarten', all of whom were Oxford men; but the great question of the future relation of Great Britain to its colonies and dependencies, he said, was receiving little study, and he appealed to Oxford, whilst continuing to supply public servants, also to devote time to a constructive theory of Empire.[35]

This is just what Lionel Curtis and other members of the Round Table group which was established by Milner's former staff set out to do. The *Magazine* observed how Curtis, during the year he held the Beit Lectureship, gave a remarkable stimulus to scientific research into Imperial problems,[36] but on the whole the *Oxford Magazine* gave surprisingly little attention to the Round Tablers, in spite of its consistent admiration for Milner who was their patron. However many changes of Editor, no occasion seemed lost over 35 years to praise Milner, whose connections were both with Balliol and New College. He was noted in 1887 as 'very conspicuous in his generation, and marked out for success in the world'.[37] When he went to Egypt in 1889 'Oxford expected much of him'.[38] At the Palmerston Dinner in 1891 he gave 'An impressive defence of Liberal Imperialism'.[39] In 1892 the *Magazine*'s readers were 'strongly recommended to give themselves the pleasure of reading Mr Alfred Milner's "England in Egypt" '.[40] His lecture on Arnold Toynbee in 1894 was 'nobly done, with sympathy, sincerity and simplicity'.[41]

In 1901 a sonnet was devoted to his visit to Britain on leave from South Africa.

> Not as the Roman came from lands forlorn,
> Misgoverned for his own aggrandisement,
> But without pomp he comes, with labour worn
> For those he ruled . . . .[42]

In 1913 the *Magazine* maintained that 'If South Africa remains British his [Milner's] name will be associated with it, as that of

Warren Hastings is with India or of Lord Cromer in Egypt',[43] and in 1918 it recollected that 'It should never be forgotten that it was at the Oxford Union and from the lips of Milner and Parkin that the doctrine of Imperial Federation was first preached in England.'[44] In 1921 Milner's was described as 'the most important contribution which Oxford had made to extra-party politics. Above all, he has served, and twice done much to save the Empire.'[45] No one else in the *Oxford Magazine*'s history ever received such persistent support.

However great the admiration for Milner, and whilst the Editor from time to time repeated 'We are all Imperialists nowadays', there was a sharp reaction when the interests of Empire threatened Oxford's academic traditions and curriculum. When Lord Rosebery in his Rectorial Address to the University of Glasgow in 1900 stated that from the Imperial point of view it was not necessary, adequate or wise for Oxford or Cambridge to insist on compulsory Latin and Greek, the Editor commented:

> While French and German and chemistry, and the arts of brewing and stockbroking too for that matter, are probably more immediately useful to some people than the Classics, Latin and Greek are better instruments for training the individual mind . . . dunces and obscurantists are hard enough to deal with, without being allowed to masquerade in the guise of Imperialism.[46]

Some of the science professors, notably E. B. Poulton, Hope Professor of Zoology from 1893 to 1933, had visions of Oxford becoming the great scientific University of the Empire. They were encouraged by the transfer to Oxford of the Indian Forestry School, which by 1908 was also training probationers for Ceylon and Malaya; when, however, in 1910 it was proposed to raise the Forestry Diploma to degree status because the India Office wanted this, Christopher Cookson of Magdalen wrote 'I would rather see the University put bodily under a Minister of Education than have its educational policy dictated to by the action of the War Office, the India Office and the Board of Agriculture, acting independently.'[47]

In 1914 a proposal for a Business Diploma came before Congregation. This was favoured by the *Oxford Magazine* which urged breathlessly: 'If Oxford as yet refuses to recognise that training of her alumni to take their part in maintaining and enhancing the commercial supremacy on which Imperial supremacy leans for support is a function worthy of a great university, the process of educating our educators is still incomplete.' The Warden of New College, Dr

Spooner, carried more weight however in maintaining that 'it would be a pity if too much of the brains and vigour of the country were attracted into a business career, and the more important and more enobling careers of the clergyman, the student, the man of science, the teacher, the lawyer, the doctor and even the public servant be neglected'. Although the example of Cecil Rhodes's career was cited to show that a mastermind in commerce may be as potent a force in Empire building as a great proconsul, the proposal was rejected.[48]

In its first issue of the academic year 1914–15, the *Oxford Magazine* observed that 'only a few individual Oxford scholars had joined the unintelligent shrieks against war'.[49] It was obvious, the Editor continued, that Oxford could best serve the Empire by 'business as usual'. This proved hardly possible. By 1917 there were only 369 students in residence, including Serbian refugees; and 167 out of 208 Rhodes Scholars from the Empire had taken commissions.[50] Only the Indian students profited from the undivided attention of their tutors.

In the week when the First World War ended, the Editor reflected on the way in which Oxford should best discharge its duty to the Empire, in a fashion which so typically mingled pride and apprehension that it may be quoted at length.

> Oxford is a national and Imperial asset, and has Imperial responsibilities . . . we have received a great heritage which we hold in trust for mankind. To spread that inheritance more widely is the task laid upon us. . . . Our traditions are based on freedom. And from this material freedom comes a freedom of the spirit: truth is valued for its own sake, not as the road to material gain. . . . Classics may be, if wrongly taught, a most illiberal study; Natural Science as taught at Oxford is, and must be, a humane education. It is not the nature of the subject but the spirit in which it is taught that determines its educational value.

Again and again in this study we shall find Oxford's fears expressed that to become a great Imperial University would open the door to vocational education.

1919 to 1939: DIMINUENDO

The students who came up at the end of the First World War were mostly ex-servicemen, many of them disillusioned with appeals from

King, Country and Empire. At this time the League of Nations aroused much more idealistic support than Empire. In 1919 O.U.P. published several widely circulated 3*d*. pamphlets on the League by Viscount Grey, Gilbert Murray, Sidney Olivier and other Oxford men.[51] The Union voted by 251 to 166 in May 1919 for a resolution deploring any departure from President Wilson's Principles in the Peace Treaty, and later in the same year, by perhaps the largest majority in its history to date (924 to 99), voted in favour of immediate and actual establishment of a League of Nations.[52]

The *Magazine* noted that 1920 was remarkable for decisions on three important questions with which the University had long been preoccupied: the abolition of compulsory Greek, the admission of women as full members of the University and acceptance of grants from the Government.[53] The abolition of compulsory Greek greatly widened the field for selection of Rhodes Scholars and for admission of natural scientists. Success in the long-fought battle for admission of women as full members of the University led to an unsuccessful appeal for women to share in the advantages of Rhodes Scholarships. In 1921 St Hilda's College offered to reserve places for women of the Dominions,[54] if funds were raised for new buildings, but they were not forthcoming; it was not until after the Second World War that Rhodes's Will was adapted to allow women to become Rhodes Scholars. In the long run the decision to accept Government grants was the most important of all and perhaps fatal to the old Imperial connection; eventually it enabled the Government to instruct the reluctant University to raise the fees paid by students from Australian, Canadian and New Zealand families, who had come to Oxford for three generations, to a level which many of them could no longer afford.

There was less enthusiasm now for missionary work. Bishop Gore announced in 1922 that no Oxford man had joined the Oxford Mission to Calcutta for 12 years. 'It will be a peculiar disgrace to us', he said, 'if the presence and name of Oxford in the Mission's title becomes no more than a record of its origin.'[55] Bishop Weston of Zanzibar was perhaps more in tune with undergraduate sympathies when he was reported as stating that his whole aim was to prepare native candidates for the Ministry to work with, not under, the English missionaries and eventually to replace them.[56]

Now, too, the self-confident assumption of the previous generation in the export of Oxford's educational system to the colonies was being questioned. An article on 'The Soul of an Empire' in 1925 suggested that education by Englishmen had too often led to taking away the natives' souls and to giving them in exchange in India, West Africa and Egypt a superficial culture, a false copy of English political ideas. Before it was too late, the Editor urged, we must teach our colonial administrators the meaning of the souls of the peoples whose destinies they were to control; this might be done by bringing them to Oxford when they returned to Britain on leave.[57]

In the twenties the League of Nations continued to receive as much attention as the Empire. Undergraduates on Sunday afternoons were invited to walk out to have tea or a beer with John Buchan at his home in Elsfield, where T. E. Lawrence was likely to arrive on his motorcycle; alternatively, however, a more austere visit could be made to Boars Hill to visit Professor Gilbert and Lady Mary Murray, critics of Empire, teetotallers and enthusiasts for many good causes, whether those of the League of Nations or of private societies, such as that which later found posts in Britain for intellectual refugees from Hitler.

Lionel Curtis was becoming preoccupied with world government. The standard of the Empire, and subsequently Commonwealth, was now carried by Reginald Coupland, the second Beit Professor of Colonial History, who already in 1920 in his Inaugural Lecture saw race as the most serious problem of the Commonwealth. He reinvigorated the Ralegh Club, bringing in people with quite unofficial views such as Gandhi to address it, and, though an eloquent defender of Britain's colonial record, looked forward to the prospect of Indian self-government.

Enthusiasts for various Imperial causes sought to use Oxford's name. Sir Thomas Beecham, at a meeting in Rhodes House in 1929, asked Oxford's support for an Imperial League of Opera. 'There are hundreds of opera houses in Europe and the U.S.A.', he said, 'We have none.'[58] The *Daily Express* in the following year announced that Oxford supported Empire free trade, proclaiming 'We shall have a great Oxford Movement – something to eclipse the one of 100 years ago, and something comparable to the intellectual light which shone from Oxford all over Europe in the Middle Ages.'[59]

'The British Empire – proud, forlorn title!', commenced an editorial in the *Oxford Magazine* during the Imperial Conference of 1926, criticising the Dominions as unwilling to give themselves heart and soul to Britain's two greatest problems, industrial decline and surplus population, which only a vast system of emigration and Empire protection could solve.[60] When the ineffectiveness of sanctions was demonstrated over Ethiopia in 1936 the disillusioned supporters of the League did not turn to Empire, nor did the new concept of Commonwealth seem to mean much to students from its subject races. In the late thirties Fascism became the important issue and the Oxford men who joined the International Brigade in Spain included a Fellow of All Souls who had been an Australian Rhodes Scholar.[61] Oxford's moment of drama came when the Master of Balliol fought Quintin Hogg in a by-election for the City seat on the question of appeasement, on which the Imperialists of All Souls were divided.

Despite the elegant writing of Coupland and the forceful controversies conducted by Margery Perham, most younger dons and students in the University by the thirties seemed to find the contemporary Empire a boring topic. As D. W. Brogan, one of the liveliest younger historians, wrote in reviewing the *Cambridge History of the British Empire* in 1937:

> It is idle to deny that the history of the Overseas Dominions has for many persons a very faint attraction. The importance and interest of the new societies may be admitted; there may be full agreement that someone ought to know about them, but the normal attitude is that the someone is always someone else.[62]

No picture of how Empire looked to the Senior Common Room would be complete without some reference to organised games, whose cult coincided with that of Empire. The early success of the Rhodes Scholarship scheme, despite initial misgivings, was due as much to the prowess of Australians and South Africans in cricket, rowing and rugby football as to the fact that several of the scholars obtained First Class degrees. Oxford, however, before 1914 never had an Indian cricketer as attractive as Ranjitsinhji who perhaps did as much for India's reputation at Cambridge as the brilliant mathematicians and scientists who studied there.

An interesting example of how the dependent Empire appeared to sporting Oxford dons and men of letters is contained in an account of the Oxford University Authentics' Cricket tour of India in 1903 by Cecil Headlam. Cricket, he wrote, 'unites the ruler and the ruled. It also provides a moral training, an education in pluck and nerve and self-restraint far more valuable to the character of the ordinary native than the mere learning by heart of a play by Shakespeare or an essay of Macaulay.' He included some tips for future teams in light of his three months' experience. 'The upper class babu is swollen with good living and a sense of his own importance . . . and requires to be dealt with in a tone of authority.' On the other hand 'You must be very careful how you hit a man in India. Nearly every native suffers from an enlarged spleen and any blow on the body is very likely to be fatal. . . . It is best to carry a cane and administer rebuke upon the calves and shins, which are tender and not usually mortal.'[63]

Note: *The Oxford Magazine* resumed publication in October 1985 whilst this book was in proof.

2 Prophets, Classics and Philosopher Kings

I should like to govern the world through my pupils.
Benjamin Jowett to Florence Nightingale (1873)[1]

It is only possible to understand the kind of Imperialism which grew up in the late nineteenth century in light of two earlier and, as it seemed to many Oxonians, cataclysmic events. The first was the Tractarian or Oxford Movement of the 1830s and 1840s. The bitter theological feuds, the refusal of Christ Church to pay Jowett's salary as Professor of Greek because of his religious unorthodoxy, the suspension of Pusey from preaching in the Cathedral, and finally the secession of Newman to Rome led to a reaction against institutional religion. Secondly, the publication of Darwin's *Origin of Species* and *Descent of Man* caused a general questioning of the truths of the Bible.

The loss of faith is vividly described in one of the many accounts which survive of undergraduate life at Jowett's Balliol, the memoirs of John MacMillan Brown, who came up to Balliol in 1871 and later went out to teach in New Zealand. Most of his contemporaries at Balliol, he recalled, had broken loose from their religious moorings and were adrift on a great ocean of belief in search, as a rule hopelessly, of some fixed point from which they could take their bearings. Like spiritual dynamite, he said, was the problem of evolution which Darwin had flung into the debates of the time with the *Descent of Man*. All the undergraduates in Brown's circle were reading ethnological books and had been struck by the extraordinary hints of the fundamental doctrines of the Christian creed that were found in the customs and beliefs of primitive peoples, and which seemed to dispose of the idea that Christianity was a revelation from heaven. More directly damaging to religious belief was *The Martyrdom of Man* published in 1872 by Winwoode Reade, an Oxford man whose quest to prove or disprove the theories of evolution took him to West Africa to study the habits of gorillas. His book, which had no favourable reviews but a wide circulation, was militantly atheistic. 'Christianity is false. God worship is idolatry. Prayer is useless. The soul is not immortal. There are no rewards and punishments in a future state.' The book was to have a permanent influence on Rhodes.[2] For a number of Oxford men of this generation the stoicism of the classics and the mysticism of an Imperial faith were to replace the lost faith in Christianity. From Brown's memoirs it seems that he never regained his faith. Fascinated by the story of Greek expansion in the Mediterranean and by Alexander's conquests, as well as by the accounts in Livy and Tacitus of the expansion of the Roman Empire, he determined to work in the British Empire; and after considering teaching posts in India and Canada, he obtained through Jowett's influence a professorship in the new University College of Canterbury, New Zealand.

Between Newman's departure in 1845 and the emergence of Gore in the 1880s the message of Oxford prophets was secular. Those whose names recur again and again as formative influences in the memoirs both of the Imperialists and critics of Empire are Ruskin, Jowett and T. H. Green.

RUSKIN

Ruskin was Slade Professor of Fine Art at Oxford from 1869 to 1879 and again from 1883 to 1884. He used this position to lecture on whatever interested him in art, history, politics or economics. In earlier years his lectures were packed and his prophetic influence on the University was great. In his Inaugural Lecture in 1870, a copy of which was cherished by Rhodes, he declared:

> There is a destiny now possible to us, the highest ever set before a nation to be accepted or refused. We are still undegenerate in race; a race mingled of the best northern blood. We are not dissolute in temper, but still have the firmness to govern and the grace to obey. We have a religion of pure mercy.
>
> This is what England must do or perish. She must found Colonies as fast and as far as she is able, formed of her most energetic and worthiest men, seizing every piece she can get her feet on and teaching these Colonists that their chief virtue is to be fidelity to

their country, and that, though they live in a distant plot of land, they are no more to consider themselves therefore disenfranchised from their native land than the sailors of her fleet do.[3]

Ruskin also expressed his admiration for the authoritarian style of the rulers of the dependent Empire. In *A Knight's Faith* in 1885 he praised the heroes of the Punjab, Havelock, Lawrence and Edwardes. Their success, he proclaimed, was not owed to Parliamentary or any kind of collective wisdom. 'It is not by a majority of votes that Bunnoochees throw down their forts . . . in every vital matter the right opinion is in the majority of one.'[4]

During his professorship the focus of Ruskin's interest moved from art to social and economic questions. He preached the dignity of labour and attacked the ugliness and squalor which the policy of *laissez-faire* had brought about. An eloquent opponent of the Manchester School, he proclaimed that the anarchism in modern society was due to people minding their own business and not acting as their brothers' keepers. He advocated a national education policy, old age pensions and council houses, but abhorred the notion of natural equality and believed in an aristocracy in an ordered society. In 1874, describing Oxford's favourite exercise of rowing as 'Eight fools on a toothpick', he recruited undergraduates to work on constructing a road between North and South Hinksey. The project turned out to be quite useless, but the workers were admitted to breakfast with the Master. A remarkable variety of men participated; among them were Milner, Parkin, Arnold Toynbee, E. B. Poulton the zoologist and Oscar Wilde.[5]

Ruskin's social and economic ideas made themselves felt in the Empire in diverse ways. Though by no means uncritically accepted by Milner, Parkin and Toynbee, they contributed to their belief in a more positive role for the state in the development of the Empire than was prevalent either in Conservative or Liberal contemporary circles. Ruskin's teaching on the dignity of manual labour and on the revival of handicrafts such as spinning was to become an important element in the philosophy of M. K. Gandhi, as he recollected in his visit to Ruskin College at Oxford in 1931. J. A. Hobson of Lincoln College, whose attacks on Imperialism Lenin was to admire, said that his own economic theories owed more to Ruskin than to anyone who taught him at Oxford, and he wrote a book on Ruskin as a social reformer.[6]

JOWETT

Whilst Ruskin's influence was exercised through his lectures and writing, that of Jowett was through direct contact with his pupils. Benjamin Jowett (1817–93), the son of a Methodist printer, came to Balliol from St Paul's School as a scholar and remained there all his life, being Master from 1870 to 1893. As a young don he had been prominent among the group who sought to reform and emancipate the University, to strike off the fetters of mediaeval statutes from it and from its Colleges, set it free from the predominance of ecclesiasticism, recall it to its proper work and restore it to the nation.[7] As a result of the Parliamentary Commission on the State, Discipline, Studies and Revenues of Oxford University of 1850 these objects were largely achieved, and at Balliol a tradition was established by which brilliant young men of whatever origins and religious denominations were brought to the College and educated for service to the State: Jowett was prepared to take infinite trouble over pupils who were likely to occupy positions of influence in Britain and in the Empire; he continued to be devoted to their interests throughout their careers. Under Jowett it became fashionable for undergraduates to work hard, and the spirit of fierce competition for University prizes and for First Class degrees was carried on by them into the battle of life. He excelled in spotting young men of talent, inspiring them with a sense of duty and ambition, and giving them an education which enabled them to perform brilliantly in the new system which he had helped to devise by which written competition replaced patronage as the means of entry to Government Service. At the same time he gave parties, 'Jowett's Jumbles', at which carefully selected undergraduates were introduced to people who were eminent in their intended professions.

One example of Jowett's success was Lord Lansdowne who might otherwise have occupied himself with his great estates, but instead was goaded and inspired to become Governor-General of Canada, Viceroy of India and Foreign Secretary. 'There is more great and permanent good to be done in India than in any department of administration in England',[8] Jowett wrote to him when he accepted the Viceroyalty, as one of three of Jowett's pupils who held it in succession.

Margot Asquith observed that although with undergraduates Jowett was a prickly porcupine, with women he was like a soft and fluffy owl.[9] He revealed himself much more openly in his unpublished correspondence with Florence Nightingale than in the official life and letters. For many years Jowett worked closely with Miss Nightingale, particularly on Indian questions, 'like', he said, 'pickpockets in a crowd, not known to be confederates'.[10] Whilst his admission to her that he would like to govern the world through his pupils (as he suggested she would also like to do) was a humorous exaggeration, the Balliol network was remarkably pervasive. In addition to the three Viceroys, there was Asquith who became Prime Minister; Lansdowne and Sir Edward Grey who, as well as Curzon, became Foreign Secretary; St John Brodrick, Secretary of State for India, Milner in Egypt and South Africa; and numerous Balliol men at other sources of power such as the Civil Service, the I.C.S. and the Civil Service Commission. Jowett also encouraged men from the Empire to come to Balliol. In his time far more Indians studied there than at any other College, and there were also Australians and Canadians. The College offered places to all I.C.S. probationers at a time when no other College wanted them. Although he was the greatest authority on Plato of his time, Jowett was much less of a purist than some of his classical colleagues about the exclusion of vocational education from Oxford. His correspondence with Florence Nightingale shows a detailed interest in Indian irrigation, agriculture, land tenure, sanitation and economics and in the need for these subjects to be taught to the Indian probationers.

He had, for his time, little race-consciousness. He would walk around the Meadow with Indians, Japanese and Siamese, whom he had encouraged to come to Balliol, discussing the religion and ethics of their countries. He observed, however, that most Englishmen could not govern without asserting their superiority, and that they always had a latent consciousness of the sense of colour; one of the reasons why he wanted I.C.S. officials to have an Oxford education was that this might provide them with a courtesy of manner in dealing with Indians. The difficulty of India, he wrote, was social rather than political. If the natives of India were treated with greater kindness and civility, if we could be regarded as friends and not merely masters, the dangers to the Indian Empire would be sensibly diminished.[11]

Although he was in Holy Orders and preached in Balliol Chapel, Jowett's private view of the Church was critical. He had suffered severe humiliation in his early years, being accused of heresy and made to sign the Thirty-nine Articles in the presence of the Vice-

Chancellor. To Florence Nightingale he wrote of the Church of England: 'I wonder how long this organised hypocrisy will last' and 'I gain an increasing conviction that the established Church must come down. It is so extremely unjust to those who are not members of it, socially, educationally and in every way.'[12] 'How seldom', he reflected, 'you meet with a religious man who is quite sensible – as politicians most are almost insane.'[13]

In brief, Jowett's influence encouraged the recruitment, not only from the aristocracy but from the middle class, of Imperial administrators who would govern the Empire in a humanist rather than a religious spirit, and would concern themselves meticulously with the details of administration in such fields as health, education, agriculture and irrigation. It was a paternalistic philosophy; he opposed Irish Home Rule, though not violently. He had a good opinion of the Indians who came to study as I.C.S. probationers. His attitude to increased political responsibility for Indians was open. Just as he believed that it was wrong to bring clever but poor men to Oxford unless they could be helped to find fulfilment afterwards, there are hints in his correspondence that he perceived that educated natives would have to be given posts in Imperial administrations, though his preoccupation was more with good government than with self-government.

T. H. GREEN AND ARNOLD TOYNBEE

T. H. Green (1836–82) was a tutor and later Professor of Philosophy, the first layman to be a Fellow of Balliol, and, if Ruskin may be regarded as a Visiting Professor, he was the earliest academic exponent in Oxford of social reform. He taught that the State should be regarded as a positive moral good and he appealed to men with privileges to sacrifice personal pleasures in order that weaker members of society should not be left to sink or swim in the stream of unrelenting competition. He was the first Oxford don to enter the City Council by popular election, and he and his school sent out into public life men who carried the conviction that the philosophy they had learned at Oxford had a practical application. H. H. Asquith, who was Green's pupil, considered that he was the greatest moral force in Oxford of his time. His influence was at its zenith between the posthumous publication of his lectures in 1885 and 1914.[14] Closely associated with Green was his pupil Arnold Toynbee, who was tutor to the I.C.S. probationers at Balliol. Toynbee went even further than Green in attacking the social consequences of the Industrial Revolution. In a passionate speech which he made to a working-class meeting just before his death, he said: 'We, the middle classes, have neglected you. Instead of justice we have offered you charity, and instead of sympathy we have offered you hard and unreal advice . . . You have . . . to forgive us. We will devote our lives to your service.'[15]

Milner was one of Toynbee's closest friends, and wrote a memoir of him. The *Oxford Magazine*, after suggesting that Toynbee's early death should serve as a warning against excess enthusiasm, asked 'Is the new Oxford movement to be a Socialistic one?' Oxford, it said, 'has turned from playing at the Middle Ages in churches and at a re-renaissance in cupboards; and a new faith, with Professor Green for its founder, and Arnold Toynbee for its martyr and various societies for its propaganda, are among us'.[16] 'Socialistic' rather than 'Socialist' was correct. What Ruskin, Jowett (who taught what he called 'the new economics'), Green and Toynbee had in common was a detestation for the consequences of the economic policies of *laissez-faire*, and their pupils carried this out into the Empire.

THOMAS ARNOLD

Another prophet who deserves mention, even though his influence on Oxford came more through his disciples than from himself, is Thomas Arnold. Jowett once wrote to Florence Nightingale: 'I take the students out to walk and talk, and they behave very well to me. Yet I doubt whether they are inspired with the real educational spirit. I can avoid some of the mistakes of Dr Arnold but I cannot do what he did';[17] and on another occasion he said that there had been no one in modern times like Thomas Arnold in inspiring ideas.[18]

Arnold was a Fellow of Oriel from 1815 to 1819, and in the last year of his life in 1841–2 was Regius Professor of Modern History at Oxford. In his Inaugural Lecture and in his writings he described the social progress of States as following a pattern analogous to that of individuals. Thus there was an ancient and modern period in the life of every people, and classical studies provided two complete cycles of history, through the childhood, youth, maturity and decline of Greece and Rome.[19]

To this philosophy of history was added the lofty and religious estimate of duty which he inculcated into his pupils as Headmaster of Rugby. *Tom Brown's Schooldays* was followed by *Tom Brown at Oxford*. Earnest Oxford Rugbeians will be recurring figures in this study, often puzzled and never relaxed – T. H. Green wearing himself out on social reform; Congreve and Bridges resigning their Fellowships to lead the Wadham Positivists in their attacks on Empire; T. V. French, the retired bishop, dying of sunstroke whilst preaching to unconvertible Arabs. The Doctor's own sons will be among them, despairing of frivolous Oxford, Tom going as an Inspector of Schools in Tasmania and William to raise the tone of the East India Company's Army and then becoming Director of Public Instruction in the Punjab. The Arnold tradition was not without its critics. Leslie Stephen from Cambridge was appalled by the Rugbeians and by Arnold's influence on Oxford. 'A conscience,' he wrote, 'is no doubt a very useful possession in early years, but when a man had kept one until middle years, he ought to have established a *modus vivendi* with it.' The Rugby conscience, he said, had become unpleasantly obtrusive and self-assertive and Rugbeians were decidedly apt to become moral prigs.[20]

GREECE AND ROME

Most of the Oxford men who ruled the Empire in London and India had read Classics, though later in the Colonial Service, which was appointed by interview rather than by written competition, more had read Modern History; History too was recommended by Jowett as the best course for prospective diplomats who, he said, needed more money than intellect.

To the American, Logan Pearsall Smith, coming up to Jowett's Balliol, the course of Classical Moderations, followed by Literae Humaniores (better known as Greats) seemed the best system of education imaginable. It was based on accurate knowledge of the texts of Greek and Latin history, philosophy and literature, and the subjects studied were the eternal problems of thought and of conduct, translated back into another world and another language.[21]

Later Americans were to be more critical of the tradition of the omnicompetent generalist and of ignorance of science and modern languages which they found in the highest ranks of British and British Imperial administration as a consequence of the supremacy of Oxford Classics.[22]

Gilbert Murray considered that 'at home England is Greek. In the Empire she is Roman'.[23] Yet on future Oxford proconsuls, Aristotle, study of whose *Ethics* was obligatory at the University whether one read Classics or not, was perhaps as great an influence as any. Sir George Schuster even at the age of 100 would recollect how when he was an undergraduate a lecture by W. H. Hadow on Aristotle's *Ethics* in 1901 made him see in a flash what should be the purpose of his life, and how later the pursuit of Aristotle's principles of Excellence took him into a career as Finance Minister in India and Africa in which he would often fight Whitehall on behalf of the local people whom it was his duty to serve.[24] Rhodes, though he only took a pass degree, carried Aristotle as well as Marcus Aurelius with him on the veld, pondering the question 'How can a man do greatest good?'

Both from Aristotle and Plato there was comfortable support for rule by an élite, by that tiny proportion of the British population who passed from Public Schools through Oxford or Cambridge. Philip Woodruff, in his elegant history of the I.C.S., likened its members to Plato's Guardians.[25] The Platonic virtues of loyalty, courage, responsibility and truthfulness were admirably suited to Imperial administration; from Plato too, however, derived the dangerous belief that unexpert intelligence alone was the best qualification for the highest posts of Government.

Often, the rulers of Empire would see themselves and their contemporaries in classical roles. So Milner, as he went out to South Africa and precipitated the Boer War, felt himself to be a character in a Greek tragedy, whilst to John Buchan, a member of his staff, he seemed a Philosopher King. To Elinor Glyn, with whom he walked in the woods whilst taking the waters at a German spa, talking of nothing but the Greek poets and philosophers, he appeared like Socrates.[26] The Greats men everywhere lived with their beloved classics. Sir Cecil Clementi, whilst Chief Secretary of Hong Kong, produced two volumes on the *Pervigilium Veneris*. Sir Arthur Hertzel, Permanent Under Secretary for India, would work on his edition of Virgil at his desk in the India Office. When I.C.S. officials came on leave they would discuss the lessons of Roman provincial policy for Indian frontier policy with W. T. Arnold, grandson of the great doctor, lecturer at Oxford and Assistant Editor of the *Manchester Guardian*, who was haunted lest the tragedy of the Roman Empire, whose extremities grew at the expense of its heart, should repeat itself.[27]

Whilst study of Aristotle and Plato inspired principles of conduct, practical lessons of history emerged from that of Thucydides. Policy-makers and professors of colonial history would constantly return to the brief Athenian Empire. To some it showed the results of democracy run mad. To others the loose links between the Greek city state and its overseas settlements provided a model to be emulated by the evolving British Empire. The Liberal Unionist Goschen, addressing the young men of the Canning and Chatham Clubs in Oxford in 1889, used Thucydides to demonstrate that no Imperial nation in the plenitude of its powers had ever loosened its grasp on its dependencies.[28]

Two important studies which compared Roman and British Rule were written by Oxford men during the high Imperial period. Sir Charles Lucas, who was both a senior official in the Colonial Office and a Fellow of All Souls, wrote *Greater Rome and Greater Britain* in 1912. Lord Bryce, former Cabinet Minister, Ambassador and Professor of Jurisprudence, wrote *The Ancient Roman Empire and the British Empire in India* in 1914. Both writers reflected on the contrast between attitudes to race in the two Empires. To Lucas it seemed that whereas Roman Rule was based on class distinction between freemen and slaves, British Rule was based on race distinction. He noted that whereas under Rome anyone of any nationality could rise to almost any position – even to be Emperor – the British Imperial and Colonial Services were reserved for nationals of pure British descent. He urged that room should be found in them for men from the Dominions.[29] As the Dominions were then all white, his proposal, later to be implemented in the colonies by L. S. Amery, accentuated the distinction by race.

Bryce too pondered on the fact that all freemen in the Roman Empire who spoke Latin and Greek could become civil servants anywhere; but he hesitated to suggest that the same practice be introduced in India because 'The Indian does not as a rule . . . possess the qualities which the English deem to be needed for leadership in war or for the higher posts of administration in peace.'[30]

Bryce thought that the British feeling of separation from brown and black peoples was Teutonic in character: it had not existed in the Mediterranean-based Roman Empire. It might be unreasonable or unChristian, but it was too deeply rooted to be effaceable within any foreseeable time.[31] He observed that British rule in India in 1914 was essentially despotic, like that of Rome; whatever might be done for the people, nothing was done by them. Wrongly he prophesied that European ways of living and forms of thought and even the Christian religion would prevail everywhere in India; rightly, however, he saw that whereas the Roman system of roads had united the Empire, in India the railway system might serve to unite the people against the rulers.[32]

In the brief Edwardian period of self-confidence which preceded the First World War the style of Homer seemed to predominate. The Edwardians loved to shine in company with their kind and to receive adulatory deference from their inferiors; there was a preoccupation with honour rather than with morality. Perhaps the last of these Homeric heroes was T. E. Lawrence, a graduate of Jesus College, as seen in the *Seven Pillars of Wisdom* and in his translation of the *Odyssey*.[33]

The classical education was defended by the proconsuls until the end. Sir George Cunningham, the last British Governor of the North West Frontier Province of India, who had read Classics at Magdalen, told the students of St Andrews University in his Rectorial Address in 1947 that Latin, with its hard logicality and economy of words, was the best training for public life; he suggested that use of imprecise language might have been the cause of the great difficulties which then faced Britain in India and Palestine.[34]

The most eminent critic of the effect on the Empire of Oxford's obsession with the classics was the former Prime Minister, Lord Rosebery, who himself had left Christ Church without taking a degree. In his Rectorial Address to Glasgow University in 1900 he deplored the shortage of first-class men to run the Empire. 'Oxford and Cambridge', he said, 'still exact their dole of Latin and Greek. I cannot believe from the Imperial point of view, having regard to the changed conditions of the world, that this is necessary or adequate or wise . . . when our national ignorance of foreign languages has become not only a by-word but a national disaster. All those wasted years represent a dead loss to the Empire.' These remarks caused such fury in Oxford Senior Common Rooms that they may have cost Rosebery the Chancellorship; he compounded the offence in the same speech, and alienated the Public School men, many of whom regarded Rugby football as an almost religious rite, by singling out Association football for its contribution to Empire.[35]

For the Empire an unfortunate consequence of the predominance of the classics in Oxford was the refusal of the University to countenance any teaching which could be regarded as vocational. 'Modern languages' were only admitted to the curriculum on condition that they were not modern, so that Cromer's Government in Egypt complained that the probationers who came out from Oxford were more familiar with classical French literature than with the common language used by newspapers, Government and business.[36]

When the Royal Commission on the Public Services in India in 1913 was discussing the re-establishment of an Honours School of Indian Studies at Oxford, the Master of Balliol, Strachan-Davidson, told them that the kind of education which purists of the University would allow such a school to provide would necessarily be so classical and academic as to be unacceptable to the Indian Government. When questioned by the Commission as to whether men intended for the I.C.S. should study anthropology and economics at Oxford, he replied that if a man had a good education he would have learnt how to learn these things later. By 'a good education' he meant the Oxford Greats School.[37] About the same time, as we have seen, Warden Spooner of New College successfully led the opposition in Congregation to a proposal for a postgraduate course in Business Training.[38]

PHILOSOPHER KINGS

It is sometimes hard to distinguish whether it was the tradition of Oxford or of the Public Schools which was reflected in the style of government of the Empire. For the Governors-General of India who were at Christ Church in the first half of the nineteenth century, Lord Amherst, Lord Auckland, Lord Elgin and Lord Dalhousie, Oxford was a finishing school after Eton. There were two great proconsuls at the end of the century, however, who made an eloquent contribution to the philosophy of Empire and whom Oxford felt particularly to be her own, so much so that each was elected Chancellor of the University. Lord Curzon and Lord Milner were near contemporaries and had much in common. Both were undergraduates at Balliol, read Classics and won many prizes. Both became President of the Union and were recognised by their contemporaries as destined for great Imperial careers. Curzon in India was surrounded by Balliol men, just as Milner's staff in South Africa was almost exclusively selected from New College, where he had been a Fellow, and from All Souls. Both received a serious check in mid-career for which the Oxford connection was partly responsible. Each recovered from this and became a senior Cabinet Minister.

CURZON

Curzon, as the son of Lord Scarsdale, naturally went to Eton, where he already felt the fascination of the Indian Empire in a lecture by Fitzjames Stephen, 'the philosopher of the I.C.S.'.[39] Coming up with a scholarship to Balliol, he confided to his fellow undergraduate, Rennell Rodd, 'There has never been anything so great in the world's history as the British Empire, so great an instrument for the good of humanity. We must devote all our energies to maintaining it.'[40] Looking back later he was to say that he could not understand how anyone educated at Oxford in his time could fail to be an Imperialist.[41]

Whilst an undergraduate, his personal ambition was undisguised. He won the Lothian and Arnold Prizes and effortlessly became President of the Union. He lost no opportunity of becoming known, whether it was by giving a recital in Balliol Hall of the *Burial March of Dundee* for the Oxford University Branch of the Church of England Temperance Society, or by presiding during the vacation in his prospective Parliamentary Constituency at the Annual Meeting of the Society for the Propagation of the Gospel, at which he spoke of the unscrupulousness of the heathen tribes, the perfidy of coloured races and the obstinacy of caste.[42] Yet, with all this, he had, for an aspiring Oxford classicist, one weakness; he was not interested in philosophy and thus failed to obtain a First in Greats. This failure, and the competitive spirit which was Balliol's mark, made him resolve to devote the rest of his life to proving the examiners to be wrong. He started on this course by winning an All Souls Fellowship and by obtaining the post of Assistant Private Secretary to the Prime Minister, Lord Salisbury, who was Chancellor of the University. With Salisbury's help he entered Parliament and served as Under Secretary for India in 1892 and Under Secretary for Foreign Affairs in 1895. He used the interval, whilst the Liberals were in office, to carry out a remarkable series of journeys in Central Asia which provided material for three books. His qualifications thus inexorably established, and his financial position assured by marriage to the daughter of an American millionaire, he asked for and obtained from Salisbury the positon of Viceroy of India at the age of 39.

Curzon dedicated his book on *Problems of the Far East* in 1894 'to those who believe that the British Empire is, under Providence, the greatest instrument for good the world has seen'.[43] He went out to India believing that British rule in India was 'the noble work which has been placed by the inscrutable decrees of Providence upon the shoulders of the British race'.[44] Much of what was admirable in the Oxford tradition was reflected in his Indian reforms. Almost alone, he succeeded in making archaeology fashionable, and his restoration of the Taj Mahal and other monuments are gratefully remembered in India whilst the controversies in which he was involved are largely forgotten. In his speech at the opening of the Calcutta Public Library he announced that his desire was to collect there every book that had been written in an intelligible language in the continent: as he spoke of readers at Oxford who blessed the name of Humphrey, Duke of Gloucester every time they entered the Bodleian Library, his audience must have been intended to have in mind those future Indian readers who would bless the name of George, Lord Curzon.[45]

This was a harmless parallel, but in Curzon's approach to educational reform the Oxford precedents which he invoked were often inept. There was no question to which he devoted greater attention with less positive result. In each of the years of his Viceroyalty, he addressed the Convocation of the University of Calcutta as its Chancellor. In the first year, 1899, 'His Excellency was attired in the new robe recently presented by himself to the University for the use of future Chancellors and made on the model of the robe worn by the Chancellors of Oxford University.' 'I am a University man to the core of my being', he declared, and went on condescendingly to compliment Calcutta University on the quality and number of its successes. 'I am struck by the extent to which within less than fifty years the science and learning of the Western world have penetrated into the oriental mind, teaching it independence of judgement and liberty of thought and familiarising it with the conceptions of politics and law and society to which it had for centuries been a complete stranger.'[46]

Some of his Indian audience may have been bewildered by the facetious style of the Oxford Union when he concluded that if he did not think that benefits were being obtained by higher education 'I should be ready to proscribe your examinations, burn your diplomas and to carry off in some old hulk all your teaching staff, your Syndicate, your Senate, your Vice-Chancellor, and even your Chancellor himself and to scuttle it in the Bay of Bengal.'[47]

By 1901 however, his annual Address to the University had become not only critical but almost petulant in complaining how far Calcutta fell short of Oxford practice. He complained that whereas he himself had held a Fellowship at All Souls College which was terminable and charged with a definite obligation, in Calcutta the number of permanent Fellows had grown to immoderate dimensions; and that whilst in Oxford a graduate must come to the University to vote, in Calcutta he was allowed to do so by post. 'My one ambition', he announced, 'is to make this University capable of following in the footsteps of its European prototypes.'[48]

In 1901 he held a conference at Simla to discuss India's educational problems. At this he observed that the University of Oxford 'above all swayed the life of the College undergraduate by the memory of its past, by the influence of its public buildings, by its common institutions, and by the cosmopolitan field of interest and emulation which it offers. . . . An undergraduate in England goes to college in many cases for the moral and social influences which result from a University career and which are entirely lacking in this country.'[49] But to compare Calcutta with Oxford was meaningless without comparing the earlier formation given by Curzon's Eton with that of Colleges where hungry boys were huddled together in the slums of Calcutta, memorising texts in a barely comprehended language.

The Nationalist leader, G. K. Gokhale, complained that no Indians were invited to the Simla Education Conference, and that Curzon's Universities Act was more French than British in its spirit of centralisation.[50] Curzon admitted that 'We are bound to some extent to take the charge of higher education into our hands.' There had been scarcely a week in the past five years when the matter had not been in his mind. 'I should have left India ashamed had I looked on helplessly at the great mass of intellectual energy being misspent or flowing into improper channels.'[51] 'Education,' he said in one of his last speeches in India, 'is nothing if it is not a moral force'; and he ended his last Address to the University by reciting Say Not the Struggle Nought Availeth.[52]

How little was achieved by Curzon's attempt to reform Indian higher education was seen by the National Education Commission which was appointed shortly after Indian Independence under the Chairmanship of S. Radhakrishnan, himself Spalding Professor of Eastern Religions at Oxford; the Commission still found a huge failure rate in the B.A. examinations and a teaching staff demoralised by low salaries and student indiscipline.[53]

A remarkable feature of Curzon's Viceroyalty was the part which Balliol played in it. To the key post of Private Secretary he appointed Sir Walter Lawrence, a former I.C.S. officer and Balliol man of great tact and charm who had left the Service to go into business; Curzon and Lawrence were known as the Iron Hand and the Velvet Glove. Lawrence's return to England at the end of Curzon's first term removed an invaluable check on his intemperate despatches. The Law Member of the Viceroy's Council, who also served as Vice-Chancellor of Calcutta University, was Sir Thomas Raleigh, a Fellow of Balliol and All Souls. The Finance Member, another Balliol man, was Sir Clinton Dawkins, who left India to succeed his close friend Milner in Egypt.

At the London end, as Secretary of State for India, was St John Brodrick, Curzon's exact contemporary and one of his intimate friends at Balliol, but who backed Kitchener against him and brought about his resignation as Viceroy. Curzon believed that it was 'latent jealousy of my superior successes in life' which led Broderick to treat him so shabbily.[54] In this Brodrick was abetted by the Permanent Under Secretary of the India Office, Sir Arthur Godley, a Balliol man of an earlier generation, who had little sympathy for the Viceroy's grandiose and sometimes arrogant style.

In conducting India's foreign policy, Curzon had to deal with Lord Lansdowne, who had preceded him both at Balliol and as Viceroy, and was now Foreign Secretary; whilst Sir Arthur Hardinge, Ambassador in Persia, and Cecil Spring Rice, Chargé-d'affaires at St Petersburg, were also from his old College. Spring Rice was the author of the celebrated rhyme in the Balliol Masque beginning:

> My name is George Nathaniel Curzon
> I am a most superior person.

which, Curzon said bitterly, had followed him around all his life and perhaps prevented him from becoming Prime Minister.[55]

Curzon's caution, in Jowett's tradition, about enthusiasm in religion is seen in his treatment of his old Eton friend, J. E. C. Welldon, whom he had caused to be appointed as Metropolitan of India and Bishop of Calcutta. Welldon had seemed to have the appropriate qualities as Headmaster of Harrow where he had, he said, 'tried to excite in his pupils a living interest in the British Empire . . . and the solemnity of the duties imposed upon it'.[56] In India, however, he alarmed Curzon by attempting to force upon the country a policy of introducing the Bible in education and of proselytising among Indians instead of ministering to the Europeans, which Curzon considered to be his proper duty. Curzon had him sent back to Britain.

Curzon combined earnestness, fluency and occasional facetiousness in a way which was not unusual in the Oxford of his time. His deep and detailed interest in the mechanics of administration was a characteristic of many Balliol men. This absorption caused him to exaggerate the unique administrative ability of the English race and led him into sweeping and hurtful statements, such as that no Indian was capable of serving as a member of his Council,[57] and that 'The millions I manage are less than schoolchildren';[58] but he was insistent that the British should be kindly and virtuous rulers. On racial issues he was therefore firmly paternalistic, and incurred considerable unpopularity with the Army when he punished a regiment which treated Indian civilians brutally. He saw serious dangers due to racial pride. 'We need', he said, 'to build bridges over that racial chasm in our midst, and which, if it becomes wider, and there are no means of getting across it, will one day split the Empire asunder.'[59] His refusal to send 10,000 Indian coolies to the Transvaal in 1905 contributed to his unpopularity with the Conservative Government, whose introduction of Chinese labour into South Africa instead helped to bring about their downfall in the General Election of 1906 and Parliament's subsequent vote of censure on Milner.

Curzon's administrative achievements were very considerable in, for example, the irrigation survey of the whole country, the Punjab canal system, and the improvement of railways. His failures were in understanding and working with the emerging anglicised Indian middle class. As Bishop Welldon observed: 'He met opposition, and almost always met it effectively, by putting his finger on its intellectual weakness; but the supreme leaders of men, in the East as in the West, have appealed to their hearts.'[60] Emotional, enormously hard-working, autocratic, contemptuous of unimaginative bureaucracy, the thought can hardly have occurred to him whilst Viceroy that India might become independent within his children's lifetime.

MILNER

By contrast with Curzon's aristocratic background, Alfred (later Viscount) Milner (1854–1925) used to say that he was born with a copper spoon in his mouth. He was the son of an unsuccessful physician who earned his living as an English language teacher abroad, and he spent much of his childhood in Germany. Returning to England at the age of 15, he obtained a scholarship from Kings College School, London, to Balliol. Here he won a spectacular series of Prizes, the Craven, the Eldon, the Derby and the Hertford, and obtained a First in Mods and Greats. He became interested in the Empire through the influence of the Canadian George Parkin who was Secretary of the Oxford Union in the year in which Milner was its President. His only failure at Oxford was in the competition for the Ireland Prize. How seriously these prize competitions were taken is shown in a letter which he received at that time from Arnold Toynbee who wrote 'For the last three or four nights I have dreamt of nothing but you and your examination, and now that I know the result I feel positively sick.'[61] When he won the Hertford Prize, his tutor, Paravacini, was 'in a state of crazy exultation'.[62] Milner himself wrote of this success: 'I feel that . . . once more there is reposed on me a great trust . . . One can only hope that with the practical realisation of success may come also a profounder feeling of duty.'[63] All his life, it has been pointed out, Milner's letters were Balliol essays, parading the arguments against the policy he thought proper, then refuting them as a prelude to arguing what ought to be done.[64]

From his tutor, T. H. Green, and from Arnold Toynbee, he derived a philosophy of social service, which brought him to work on Ruskin's road and to teach in evening schools. Jowett took him on reading parties and arranged for him to earn money in the vacation by coaching the sons of influential families. After graduating he won an Open Fellowship at New College worth £200 a year which he held until he married 40 years later.

Feeling little inclination for the Bar, he earned a living writing for the *Pall Mall Gazette* and the *Fortnightly*, both edited by John Morley, an Oxford man. Jowett however put him on the first rung of the political ladder by arranging for him to become Private Secretary to the Liberal politician, G. J. Goschen, himself a former President of the Oxford Union, who had been impressed by Milner whilst attending Union debates. Milner followed Goschen into Liberal Unionism in 1886 and was his Principal Private Secretary when he became Chancellor of the Exchequer.

Milner planned each step in his career with great care. He always wanted to believe that the work on which he was engaged was a great work. Through the Senior Bursar of New College, Alfred Robinson, he received, but declined, an offer to become Private Secretary to the Viceroy, Lord Lansdowne, a Balliol man. He preferred to go out to Egypt as Director General of Accounts, seeing this as a step towards proceeding to India as Finance Member of the Viceroy's Council and then coming back to Egypt to succeed Cromer as its virtual ruler.

Milner remained in Egypt for two years, being promoted to Under Secretary for Finance. Margot Tennant on the Nile broke down his resolution not to marry lest marriage might interfere with his career; but she refused his proposal and he was able to continue to devote himself entirely to duty. He was always aware of the need to cultivate the press. 'Egypt', he said, 'must be saved in Grub Street not on the banks of the Nile.'[65] He wrote a eulogistic book about Cromer's administration, *England in Egypt*, which was well received in Government circles and in Oxford.

The next step on the ladder was to return to England to become, through Goschen's influence, Chairman of the Board of Inland Revenue, refusing the post of Permanent Under Secretary of the Home Office, which was offered to him by his Balliol contemporary, Asquith, who was Home Secretary; he also declined the same post in the Colonial Office, where another Oxford friend, Lord Selborne, was Under Secretary. In 1897, however, at the age of 43 he accepted the post of High Commissioner in South Africa and Governor of Cape Colony. At a farewell party given for him at Cafe Monico, 16 former Presidents of the Oxford Union were present, including 11 from Balliol.

Often in Milner's South African career echoes of Oxford can be heard. His famous 'Helot' despatch describing the grievances of the Uitlanders was, as Gilbert Murray pointed out, a false analogy from his classical studies. When he announced at the Diamond Jubilee that everyone should dig a hole and plant a tree without the help of native labour, he was spreading Ruskin's message of the dignity of manual labour.

Milner's great object in South Africa was to create a united State under the British Crown in which the British race and English language would predominate. His background gave him neither sympathy nor patience with the Boer leaders. As John Buchan, one of his disciples and admirers, admitted, 'He was the last man likely to obtain a settlement with Kruger: there was a gnarled magnificence in the old Transvaal President, but he saw only a snuffy, mendacious savage. He detested lies, and diplomacy demands something less than the plain truth.'[66]

Milner had his war: after the fright of the initial military reversals his popularity in England rose high as Roberts easily occupied the Boer capitals. When Milner returned on leave in 1901 most of the Cabinet met him at the railway station. He went back to South Africa knowing that E. T. Cook of Balliol, for whom he had obtained a post on the *Pall Mall Gazette*, was writing a book championing his policies, and also believing that he had persuaded his Balliol friends in the Liberal Party, H. H. Asquith and Sir Edward Grey, that it was essential to import Chinese labour into South Africa in order to increase the output of the gold mines, upon which the financing of reconstruction depended. Asquith and Grey continued to be his admirers; indeed, the leader of their Party, Campbell Bannerman, complained that his colleagues suffered from 'The Religio Milneriana, a psychological infirmity of the Balliol mind'.[67] However, neither in the General Election of 1906, when he was attacked because of the iniquities of Chinese 'slave labour', nor in the subsequent debate in the House of Commons on a motion censuring Milner, were Asquith or Grey to defend him.

Milner's administrative genius found its fullest scope in the rapid reconstruction of South Africa after the war, as he directed his admiring Oxford young men in 'Milner's Fads' – reafforestation, application of scientific methods to agriculture, integration of railway systems and the organisation of a national system of education. Yet he made little progress towards his essential objective, immigration from Britain. When he left South Africa, only 700 of the English-speaking settlers whom he had tried to settle on the land remained: his Kindergarten were to help to create a Union, but one which came to be controlled not by the English speakers but by the Afrikaaners.

Despite Milner's philosophy of race, he was much more sympathetic to the black Africans than were most of those around him. Shortly after he arrived in South Africa he wrote that the press had reported 'nothing except that Mrs Hanbury Williams [the wife of his Military Secretary, who acted as his hostess] had kissed a black child as well as a white one. But that really is the most important thing that has happened since I came here – at least it has created the greatest amount of general public interest and controversy. I think she was right. Most white people in South Africa think she was wrong. There you have the great South African problem posed at once. It is the native question. The Anglo-Dutch friction is bad enough but it is child's play compared with the antagonism of white and black.'[68] For the civilised native, he wrote towards the end of his stay in South

Africa, all colour disabilities, political or other, should be cancelled. Property and a high education test would be essential conditions.[69]

After his return to Britain in 1905, Milner spent ten years out of favour or sympathy with the Liberal Government, but earning enough in business to become financially independent. He returned to office to become a member of Lloyd George's War Cabinet in 1916 and subsequently Secretary of State for the Colonies. In his papers at his death was found a document called 'Key to My Position' in which he reaffirmed that he was a Nationalist and not a Cosmopolitan, and believed that competition between nations was the Divine order of the world. As a British race patriot he felt himself to be a citizen of the Empire, of Canada, of Australia, of New Zealand, of South Africa, just as much as of Surrey or Yorkshire. The first great principle for the British State, he urged, was to follow the race and comprehend it wherever it settled abroad. 'The work of British Imperialists in my lifetime', he concluded,

> has been to hold the fort, to keep alive the sentiments which made against disruption, which delayed it against the time when its insanity became generally apparent. This business has been, and still is, to get over the dangerous interval during which Imperialism, which for long appealed only to the far-seeing few, should become an accepted faith of the whole nation.

He recalled that in his young days the gradual dissolution of the Empire had been regarded as an inevitable, almost a desirable, eventuality. 'This view is no longer anything like so general, anything like so potent, as it was. In another twenty years it is reasonable to hope that it may be altogether extinct – that all Britons, alike in the Motherland or overseas, will be Imperialists, that it will be the happier fate of those who come after us to create that State which it has been our duty to preserve for them the possibility of creating.'[70] This was a remarkable miscalculation. Even when he wrote this in 1925, the current was flowing fast in the opposite direction. Oxford, however, which loves a lost cause, elected Milner as its Chancellor the day before he died.

Curzon and Milner, as Oxford's greatest proconsuls, were in a category of their own. Indeed, their only contemporary of equal fame was Cromer in Egypt. Cromer was educated at Woolwich which produced many Army engineers who had distinguished careers in Imperial administration. He did not attend a University, but was exceptionally well-read and, after his retirement, became President of the British Classical Association. Where he differed notably from Curzon and Milner was in his lack of interest, even at times hostility, towards education whilst he was in Egypt.[71]

There were important differences between the philosophy of Empire of Milner and Curzon. Milner's was the clearer. His idea of Empire was of a Union of British peoples to which the non-white dependencies were a temporary excrescence. That is how, when he was Secretary of State for the Colonies, he could view the end of British Rule in Egypt with equanimity, and why, in later years, he gave so much of his time to the Chairmanship of the Rhodes Trust in an attempt to make the founder's vision a reality. If it ever came to the choice, he said, he would prefer an effective Union of the self-governing States to the retention of the dependent States, accompanied by separation from the communities of our own blood and language.[72]

Curzon's philosophy whilst Viceroy was succinctly stated by Sir Harcourt Butler who worked under him and had been an I.C.S. probationer at Balliol. 'Our duty, in the words of the Te Deum, is to govern them and lift them up for ever.'[73] Curzon could not envisage an Empire deprived of India's markets and fighting strength, but, though he strained the idea of race to comprehend both British and Indians as brother Aryans, he would sometimes admit, as Milner never did, that an Empire built on race must eventually give way to broader concepts.[74] After he left India he sought without much success to define those concepts. Thus in a speech in 1914 to the Victoria League he reflected on the ties which might hold together a multiracial Empire. He examined and rejected in turn the Crown, Parliament and the Judicial Committee of the Privy Council as fulfilling this purpose, and concluded vaguely that 'The cement of Empire' was 'brotherhood . . . no Roman wall of military defence, no Chinese wall of selfish exclusiveness, but a wall of human hearts.'[75]

Milner considered that the burden of ruling the dependent countries, though it strengthened the national character, could not be borne by Britain alone and should be shared with the white Dominions.[76] Curzon, however, opposed the opening of the I.C.S. to white colonials because men of an inferior class, with contemptuous attitudes to coloured races, might be selected.[77] Milner, as an assimilationist, stated that 'We have gone too far when we have allowed languages of incorporated races to be put on a footing with

English.'[78] Curzon in India, on the other hand, tried to extend the use of vernacular languages in order to counteract excessive centralisation.

The differences should not be exaggerated. Curzon would have agreed with Milner that 'Imperialism has all the depth and significance of a religious faith. Its significance is moral more than material.'[79] Both had a profound belief in the genius of the British race as rulers and in the moral benefits which being an Imperial power brought to Britain. Yet in their later writings and speeches can be found hints of the divergence which was to emerge in the next Oxford generation, notably among Milner's former Kindergarten, between those who worked for an Empire which would be a Federation or Union of white and predominantly Anglo-Saxon races and those who came to advocate a loose Commonwealth of self-governing, and ultimately independent, States of white, brown and black races.

Before moving on to the next generation of Imperialists, however, it may be useful to examine the influence on them of the Oxford historians, for by the turn of the century as many Oxford men were reading Modern History as Classics.

3 Historians and Sentinels of Empire

Every school building is a citadel of Empire and every teacher its sentinel.
H. E. Egerton, Beit Professor of Colonial History (*c.* 1910)

Although the classicists exercised an important influence on the philosophy and style of Empire, it was the historians who were more prone to become involved in current Imperial issues from the middle of the nineteenth century. Earlier the Regius Professorship of Modern History had been largely a sinecure. When the Chair was founded by King George I in 1724 with the object of training loyal servants for the House of Hanover, the University, according to Bishop Stubbs, not only acknowledged the King's letter in a most contemptuous way by forwarding their letter of thanks by a bedell, but clothed their reply in such words as to show that the introduction of the new study was an unwarranted interference with the educational government of the place. Stubbs did not find that his predecessors as Regius Professor before the nineteenth century were men to whom the study of history was in any way indebted.[1]

The first Regius Professor to make much impact was Thomas Arnold, whose influence has been noted in the previous chapter. His importance in the Oxford History School lies in the insistence in his Inaugural Lecture that history should be studied for its moral lessons. This message was spread by a stream of earnest Rugbeians who came to Oxford and dominated the Oxford Union in the mid-nineteenth century, and was to be echoed by succeeding Oxford historians who dealt with Empire.

Arnold had intended to settle in Oxford as a full-time professor. It would be interesting to speculate what the influence on Oxford, and on the administrators, teachers and clergymen who went out to the Empire would have been if the Doctor, instead of dying in 1842 at an early age after holding the Chair for a year, had been in residence for 20 years, forming the consciences of a higher grade of prefect.

The next Regius Professor to influence attitudes to Empire was Goldwin Smith who held the Chair from 1858 to 1866 and whose profession is described in the *Dictionary of National Biography* not as historian but as 'controversialist'. His role as a critic of Empire is discussed in Chapter 4.

Goldwin Smith was succeeded by William (later Bishop) Stubbs, the great medievalist who was Regius Professor from 1866 to 1884. Stubbs's only direct expression of interest in Empire was to urge, unsuccessfully, that the University should appoint a Professor of Indian History. He was, however, much influenced by the new German School of History and insisted on the purely Teutonic origins of English freedom. The enthusiasm of Stubbs, Freeman and the popular Oxford historian J. R. Green for Teutonic institutions made a significant contribution to Oxford's ideas about race in the later part of the century.

E. A. FREEMAN

The belief in Germanic origins was carried by Stubbs's friend and successor, E. A. Freeman (1823–92), to the point of arguing that the Norman (whose influence on English institutions he could hardly disregard) 'was a Dane whose brief sojourn in Gaul had put on a slight French varnish, and who came to England to be washed clean again'.[2] It also often caused him to express contempt for other races. Freeman, who held the Chair from 1884 to 1892, was appointed to it by Gladstone, had stood for Parliament as a Liberal, and regarded himself as a Republican. From Athenian history he drew the lesson that the British Empire should be a unity of scattered kinsfolk, 'Englishmen everywhere, but Englishmen free from the beginning'. The unity of the scattered kinsfolk was a thought dearer to him than any idea of an Empire in which English was a foreign tongue for the vast majority of its subjects.[3] This view caused him to describe the Jubilee celebrations and processions as 'unutterable folly',[4] and to oppose Imperial Federation on the grounds that English-speaking electors would be outnumbered by Tamils and Telegus. His one great doctrine, he said, was the right of every nation to govern or misgovern itself.[5] So alarmed was Queen Victoria about a speech in which he appeared to suggest that Britain withdraw from India, that she held up his appointment to the Regius Professorship until an explanation was given.[6]

Freeman combined Home Rule principles with racial sentiments which he expressed with vehemence and eccentricity. Whilst in America he wrote of the negroes:

> I feel like a creep when I think that one of these great black apes may (in theory) be President. I told a man here my ideas on citizenship which were these –
> 1. Dutchmen, high and low, at once.
> 2. Other aryans in the third generation.
> 3. Non-aryans not at all.

His impression of the United States was that 'this would be a great land if only every Irishman would kill a negro and be hanged for it'.[7]

His anti-Semitism was also strident. Of Disraeli's Government he wrote 'They need not lie, but I suppose with a Jew at their head they really cannot help it.'[8] When asked to sign a protest against pogroms in Russia, he replied that every nation had the right to wallop its own Jews.[9]

In one of his essays Freeman made an observation which may help to explain the development of racial attitudes in the nineteenth century, including his own. One hundred years ago, he said, a man's political likes seldom went beyond the range which was suggested by the place of his birth or immediate descent. Ethnological and philological research, however, had opened up the way for new national sympathies and antipathies, founded on race, as distinct from feelings of community in religion and of nationality.[10] How far Oxford took Freeman seriously is not clear. The *Oxford Magazine* wrote of him in 1883 'the only people to whom he is distinctly unkind are the negroes, Irish, the Chinese and Mr Oscar Wilde', and it went on to quote with distaste his remark that 'we should have thought little of Russian persecution of Jews but for Jewish control over the press in European countries'.[11]

J. A. FROUDE

On Freeman's death, by an irony appreciated in Oxford, Lord

Salisbury appointed to succeed him an enthusiastic Imperialist, J. A. Froude (1818–94), whose scholarship Freeman had savagely attacked; by convention Froude had to pay tribute to his persecutor in his Inaugural Lecture. Whatever might be said of Froude's careless use of sources, his easily flowing prose brought him a wide public. He was only Regius Professor from 1892 to 1894, though this was a triumphant return after his experiences many years earlier as a Fellow of Oriel, a position which he had resigned when one of his books was publicly burned by a colleague as heretical.

As with many other academic champions of Empire, Froude's Imperialism started with Ireland, but he went further than most in maintaining that Cromwell 'was the best friend in the best sense to all that was good in Ireland'.[12] He was an advocate of Imperial Federation, and Lord Carnarvon, the Conservative Secretary of State for the Colonies, had sent him on a mission to South Africa in 1874–5 to promote Confederation; there Froude showed much sympathy with the Boers and little with black Africans. Later he visited and wrote about the West Indies, showing the influence of Carlyle, whose biographer he was. In many instances, perhaps in most, he said, the slave trade had been innocent and even beneficial. The indigenous population, 'the enormous majority of whom are of an inferior race', needed a century or two of wise paternal British administration and were totally unfitted for British institutions. 'Give them independence and in a few generations they will peel off such civilisation as they may have learnt as easily and as willingly as their coats and trousers.'[13]

During his professorship Froude lectured on English seamen in the sixteenth century. His lectures, unlike those of Stubbs and Freeman, were packed. Because he had travelled widely overseas; because of the elegance of his style and the consistency of his romantic, racial concept of Empire, he probably had more influence on Oxford than Freeman. To the young ladies from North Oxford who thronged his lectures there was a gratifying, if illusory, sense of security in hearing that the Authorised Version of the Bible and the British Navy were the twin symbols of Britain's greatness; and the professor could forget that he had once been dismissed by Disraeli as 'a desultory and theoretical *litterateur* who wrote more rot on the reign of Elizabeth than Gibbon required for all the *Decline and Fall*, and who, when sent out to reform the Cape, had brought about a Kaffir war'.[14]

York Powell, who followed Froude, held the Chair from 1894 to

1904; he was appointed on the recommendation of Lord Rosebery and described himself as 'a decent heathen aryan, a socialist and a jingo'.[15] He favoured Irish Home Rule, was an advocate of the Boer War and President of the Tariff Reform League. His great interest was in Nordic, particularly Icelandic, history and literature, and he did not take an active part in the debate on Empire.

In 1904 it occurred to L. S. Amery that the first Rhodes Scholars would find practically no provision at Oxford for the teaching of the history of the British Empire or anything like an adequate supply of books on the subject. He managed to get himself placed next to the South African diamond magnate, Alfred Beit, at a dinner and persuaded him to endow a professorship, lectureships, the purchase of books and a prize essay for colonial history – all in the course of the soup.[16] From this time the Regius Professor was usually content to leave pronouncements about Empire to his colleague, the Beit Professor of Colonial History. Moreover, of York Powell's successors, Sir Charles Firth, who held the Chair from 1904 to 1925, specialised in the seventeenth century, and Sir Maurice Powicke, who held it from 1928 to 1947, was a medievalist; neither showed much interest in Empire.

H. E. EGERTON

H. E. Egerton, the first Beit Professor, who held the Chair from 1905 to 1920, was a graduate of Corpus and a former Colonial Office official who had published an early study of colonial policy. He brought to his task the earnestness of a Rugby education, but resolved that the new Chair should not be used for propaganda, a resolution which he sometimes failed to keep. He lectured comprehensively on most periods of British colonial history but left little that was memorable. In his Inaugural Lecture Egerton echoed Arnold in stating that colonial history had to be justified as a branch of study making for practical edification. Britain's colonial history, he said, was largely a record of failures and blunders, and it should be taught in such a way as to cultivate a historical imagination in order to recognise the point of view of those from whom we may fundamentally differ.[17] Egerton distinguished between two Empires, one which was, or would become, self-governing, and one which was inevitably despotic. Whilst the first was a forcing-house for political and economic experiments, the other was an estate, to be managed wisely and liberally after the fashion of every other estate.[18]

'Important as are the demands of commerce,' he said in a subsequent lecture, 'the final justification for every Colonial empire, must ultimately be the moral one. Does it or does it not promote the welfare of the persons over whom it has assumed the control?'[19] This moral tone and concern for the welfare of the colonies was to become a hallmark of Oxford Imperial historians and was to be repeated again and again in the lectures of Coupland, Harlow and Margery Perham.

'Ultimately', Egerton suggested,

> the good or badness of an Empire depends upon the character of the men who administer it. Because of the improvement in the character of the individual (administrator) we can honestly say that the permanence of British expansion is in the interests not only of the trade and population of this island, but is in the interests of those who come under her influence, and in the interests of the world at large.[20]

The special genius of the British race, he considered, had shown itself in Egypt and the Sudan.

Although he believed in closer Imperial union, Egerton did not favour an Imperial Parliament. At times he became mystical about Empire; in one Oxford lecture he described the 'sense of an unseen providence controlling the development of the Anglo-Saxon race', and ended by reciting Blake's *Jerusalem*.[21] As late as 1924 he expressed 'a desire to bow down with reverence before the majestic fabric of British imperial development'.[22] Both Egerton and his former colleague in the Colonial Office, C. P. Lucas, who was also to leave it to become a Fellow of All Souls and to write works on history, considered themselves to be disciples of the Cambridge historian, J. R. Seeley: but whilst Seeley used dispassionate, scientific methods to account for the expansion of England, Egerton and Lucas adopted an emotional, almost religious approach to the way in which the successive racial virtues of Romans, Danes, Saxons and Normans had combined to launch the British Empire.[23]

Egerton urged the need for a school of training at Oxford in the practical work of colonial administration, a suggestion which was to be carried further by his successors. He was also interested in the popularisation of the Empire, proclaiming that 'Every school building is a citadel of Empire and every teacher its sentinel.'[24] His own lectures, however, attracted few members of the University. Among them was Miss Wordsworth, the Principal of Lady Margaret Hall, who attended his Inaugural Lecture and deplored the way in which he twice misquoted the Bible. 'He can't really be educated,' she wrote, 'I suppose he's some London man – but it shows a sloppy mind. Well, one must not be uncharitable, perhaps his bark is worse than his Beit.'[25]

SIR REGINALD COUPLAND

Egerton was succeeded in the Chair by R. (later Sir Reginald) Coupland (1884–1952), a Fellow in Classics of Trinity who had been persuaded by Curtis to turn to colonial history. His tenure of the Chair from 1920 to 1948 spanned the transition from Empire to Commonwealth, and indeed to the beginning of decolonisation.

In his far-sighted Inaugural Lecture Coupland dealt with two main questions, nationality and colour. He saw the British Empire as constantly adapting itself by the quiet process of discussion and agreement, by evolution and not revolution. In his three elegant books on East Africa and his *Life of Wilberforce* he dwelt proudly on the contribution of Britain to the abolition of the slave trade. He was perhaps the last Oxford Professor of History to dare to write, even privately, that 'Personality is the really interesting thing in history. Damn the economists!'[26]

Although the Beit Professor was not expected to teach about India, Coupland involved himself deeply in Indian questions as a member of the Lee Commission on the Indian Public Services, and later in a massive survey of the problem of India's constitution. In 1942 he was on the staff of Cripps's mission to India. As a member of the Peel Commission on Palestine, his influence was decisive in the recommendation of partition and independence.

In his Inaugural Lecture he expressed the hope that Oxford, which had taken a notable part in the training of cadets for the Indian, Egyptian and Sudanese Civil Services, might also be associated with the Colonial Service;[27] he had much to do with implementing this recommendation and also served as an unofficial talent spotter for the I.C.S. His somewhat bland attitude to constitutional and humanitarian progress could be an irritant to Nationalists. When he tried to persuade M. K. Gandhi, on the latter's visit to Oxford in 1931, that all that was required for India's constitutional progress was patience and cooperation, the Mahatma commented that whilst he was only a peasant, not a professor, this was not how he read the lessons of the way in which American and Irish Independence were obtained.[28] Eric Williams, later President of Trinidad, who held Coupland responsible because he was not elected to a Fellowship of All Souls, later wrote about him venomously as 'the most tedious of British historians'.[29]

Both Coupland's imaginative liberalism and his complacent, even patronising manner can be illustrated from his Address to the Oxford Indian Majlis Society during the Round Table Conference in 1931.

> I am proud of what England on the whole has done in India in the last hundred years. But that is nothing to what my pride will be if England can help to bring that connexion to its natural and noble climax, help to set India in her true place as a Dominion in our Commonwealth of nations, linking east and west in the service of mankind. . . . After the Round Table Conference there is no going back. You are the first generation of Indians to be called on to determine the destiny of India. Democratic government of India is the hardest task that any nation has ever attempted. What is the message that the spirit of Oxford, our common mother, so old and wise, has whispered to generations of her scholars in their hours of weariness and disappointment? What is it but this 'Nothing is worth doing that is not difficult to do.'[30]

Reviewing Lugard's *Dual Mandate* in 1922 he was also prescient about Indirect Rule in Africa –

> Can the status quo be maintained for ever? Will not the Chiefs, as time goes on and the educated class increases, however wise their education, be compelled to introduce, as indeed the rulers of Indian states have done, some substantial measure of self-government? And would it not be well, with the example of India before us, to think out betimes some scheme of gradual transition, lest in the end self-government, coming with such a rush, finds the African to his own undoing, ignorant of its meaning and inexperienced in its responsibilities?[31]

Coupland gave the highest priority in his teaching to the needs of the Colonial Service probationers, whom he had helped to bring to

Oxford. On a wider stage between the First and Second World Wars he was the inspiration of the Ralegh Club which introduced a remarkable range of distinguished speakers from all over the world to discuss the affairs of the Empire and Commonwealth with senior and junior members of the University. To address the Club's dinners came the great proconsuls, Lord Milner, Lord Lugard, Lord Chelmsford and Lord Lloyd, as well as political leaders such as Winston Churchill, L. S. Amery and Ramsay MacDonald. Commonwealth statesmen including Smuts, Hofmeyer, R. G. Menzies and General Hertzog, were glad to be invited when they visited London. The critics of Empire such as Leonard Barnes, J. H. Oldham, Alek Frazer and, perhaps most remarkable of all, M. K. Gandhi, were also heard. Membership of the Club was by election. Many of its members went on to careers in the Empire and Commonwealth. Vincent Harlow, who succeeded Coupland as Beit Professor, said that he learnt more about the Commonwealth from the Ralegh Club than from any other source.[32]

Vincent Harlow held the Beit Chair from 1948 until his death in 1961. Though his book *The Founding of the Second British Empire* established his reputation as an outstanding scholar, his influence was not as wide as that of Coupland, nor was he as involved in the practical problems of Empire. In his Inaugural Lecture he was more detached in his judgements of British achievement. Whilst he saw a Roman sense of justice and something of a Christian ethic in the attitudes of the British colonial administrators, he also considered that in their social contacts they had inherited some of the arrogance of the Greeks towards the Barbarians. He suggested that colonial policy needed to be seen against the changing social, religious and economic background of Britain itself, so that future historians would treat the development of social services in Britain and the projects of the Commonwealth Development and Welfare Acts in the same chapter. His peroration was in the high (and somewhat vague) moral tradition established by his predecessors. Quoting Burke's exhortation to the British not to make themselves too little for the sphere of their duty, he concluded 'the compass of our object today is more than status, more even than fulfilling a Commonwealth task without dishonour. It is nothing less than the vindication in corporate action of the spirit of man.'[33] Like Coupland, Harlow attached great importance to his lectures to the probationers of the Colonial Service, whom he sometimes embarrassed in the final lecture of their course by bursting into tears as he spoke of their noble mission of trusteeship for the people of backward races.

DAME MARGERY PERHAM

If Coupland exercised a discreet background influence on Imperial policy, Dame Margery Perham (1895–1982) not only discerned the moral lessons of history, but regarded it as her public duty, from her base in Oxford, to see that they were applied. A graduate with First Class honours in Modern History, she returned from her first visit to Africa to St Hugh's College in 1924 as a tutor in Modern History and Modern Greats. Her principal interest became African administration. With the aid of the Rhodes Trust she made long visits to Nigeria and Kenya. The life which she wrote of her friend Lord Lugard, and her book *Native Administration in Nigeria*[34] caused her to be regarded by colonial administrators, as well as in academic circles, as the greatest authority on Indirect Rule. In Oxford she became the first Reader in Colonial Administration and Director of the Institute of Commonwealth Studies.

Dame Margery drew her strength from her ability to sympathise with all parties in the colonial situation – administrators, missionaries, settlers, Nationalists and tribal peoples. Much of her life was spent in courteous controversy, mainly carried out through *The Times* and on the BBC. She conducted a public dispute with Lionel Curtis on whether the High Commission territories should be returned to South Africa, and another with Elspeth Huxley on the future of Kenya. She protested publicly against the deportation of Seretse and Tsekhedi Khama from Bechuanaland. She successfully opposed the return to Hitler's Germany of her former colonies and unsuccessfully the creation of the Central African Federation.[35]

Her strong emotions were both a strength and a weakness. Sometimes she made mistakes, which she often acknowledged later. She should not, she admitted, have broadcast a message from Lagos to her old pupil Colonel Ojukwo urging the surrender of Biafra. More seriously her enthusiasm for Indirect Rule led her to oppose the admission of Africans to the Colonial Administrative Service, so that she had a responsibility for the situation in which many of the former colonies were inadequately staffed by local people after Independence. She wrote in 1947 'The day when Nigeria becomes a true federation, still more a nation, is far away.'[36] But if, as she later realised, she misjudged the time-scale of decolonisation in the thirties, in the 1950s she would admonish the colonial officials who came to Oxford courses that they should spend less time in administration, more in teaching Africans how to administer.

She never lost sight of the duties of trusteeship. Curtis, in their correspondence, urged that the High Commission territories should be returned to South Africa because this would encourage young South African liberals. 'Little by little, South Africa will listen and wipe the colour bar sinister from its shield. South Africa will listen to its own countrymen, but not so long as they see us standing over them with uplifted forefingers.' Margery Perham replied firmly to this inept prophecy – 'It is men and women we are asked to give, and that against their will.'[37]

Dame Margery was responsible, in whole or in part, for many Oxford initiatives in relation to Empire. She set up the Institute of Commonwealth Studies and during the Second World War, when the new Nuffield College was seeking a role, she steered it towards colonial research. Later she helped to start the Oxford Colonial Records Project. When decolonisation was in full swing in 1961, she gave the Reith Lectures on the BBC under the title of *The Colonial Reckoning*. It was an eminently fair reckoning. She reminded her listeners of the poverty, ignorance, disease and cruelty of the Africa which the British had taken over. She believed that Britain was on the whole the most humane and considerate of modern colonial rulers, but was sometimes slow, neglectful and unimaginative. She could understand that Nationalists had to paint a black and exaggerated picture of the evils of colonial rule, for 'the crushed mind and the wounded dignity have to recover'.[38] She concluded that 'we must try to keep, indeed to increase, our two main assets, . . . our great knowledge of the peoples of the former Empire and the measure of understanding and good will we share with them':[39] but she lived to see the decline of the British Government's interest both in bringing Africans to study in Oxford and in sending British nationals out to teach in Africa.

IMPERIAL HISTORY FOR SCHOOL-CHILDREN

Most of the historians who have been mentioned exercised influence in a limited if influential circle. At the same time, however, some of the Oxford historians were reaching a far wider audience by providing textbooks as ammunition for the schoolmasters, whom Egerton had called the Sentinels of Empire. By far the most successful of these textbooks was the *History of England* by C. R. L. Fletcher and

Rudyard Kipling, published by the Clarendon Press in 1911 and remaining in print for 40 years.

C. R. L. Fletcher (1857–1934) was a Fellow of Magdalen and All Souls. As he nursed the College cat through tutorials he would exercise a mesmeric influence on his pupils through the highly individual Anglo-Saxon, Protestant and Erastian prejudices which he eloquently expressed. He was violently hostile to Liberalism and Socialism and no woman was ever admitted to his lectures. *The Times* called him the greatest writer of short history since J. R. Green.[40]

Fletcher had already written a four-volume history of Britain for secondary schools. As this ended in 1880 it gave little opportunity to deal with the contemporary Empire, except in a reference to 'the vain dreams of democracy that India could ever be left at the mercy of Jews, Baboos and Madrassee lawyers'.[41] Although he was a delegate of the University Press, his prejudices were so well known that O.U.P. had misgivings when he offered himself as potential author of an Oxford history for primary schools. The offer, however, became irresistible when Fletcher introduced Kipling as his partner, with a promised contribution of 23 new poems. The success of their book was immediate. The *History* was described in reviews as the most popular book and chief literary event of the Coronation year. Only the *Manchester Guardian* protested that 'as a work designed to influence the minds of children, it is the most pernicious we have seen'.[42]

The horror of the liberal *Guardian* is understandable. In the early part of the book some European characteristics are described, such as the 'vindictiveness' of Spaniards, and arguments are introduced into most chapters in favour of naval expansion. There follows a comprehensive section of the Empire. In this Fletcher first disposed of Irish Home Rule, explaining that the unsatisfactory character of the Irish was due to the fact that they were not conquered by the Romans. 'So Ireland never went to school and has been a spoilt child ever since.'[43] 'Most people fear', he continued,

> that a separate Irish Parliament would be followed by a complete separation between Ireland and Great Britain, by the establishment of an Irish Republic and by the oppression of the well to do and intelligent classes of Irishman, who are certainly loyal to the British Crown. All British politicians, on both sides, have, during the last seventy years, made haste to remove any real, and indeed

> every imaginary, grievance of the Irish people, though they have earned no gratitude by doing so.[44]

In general the situation in the Empire was described with satisfaction. 'In Canada we had really little difficulty in making good friends with our new French subjects, for they hated and feared the pushing Americans. . . . In Australia we had nothing to fear but a few miserable blacks who could hardly use even bows and arrows in a fight.' In New Zealand 'we had a more warlike race, the Maoris', but in South Africa 'the hatred between British and Dutch is now almost a thing of the past. . . . In other African colonies the natives everywhere welcome the mercy and justice of our rule . . . most of the rest are Crown Colonies who do not enjoy any form of parliamentary government or need it.'[45] But the West Indians attracted Fletcher's particular disdain. 'Lazy, vicious and incapable of any serious improvement, or of work except under compulsion. In such a climate, a few bananas will sustain the life of a Negro quite sufficiently; why should he want to get more than this? He is quite happy and quite useless, and spends any extra wages which he may earn upon finery.'[46]

Towards India he was more restrained but had no doubts as to what would happen should the paternal administration end. 'Our rule has been infinitely to the good of all the 330 millions of the different races. . . and if our rule was taken away for a moment the Afghans would swoop down and slay and enslave them. . . . Egypt and the Sudan also enjoy justice and mercy which they have not known since the fall of the Roman Empire.'[47] As for the future of the self-governing colonies, perhaps the best thing that could happen, Fletcher considered, would be a Federation of the whole British Empire, with a central Parliament, in which all the colonies should get representatives, with perfect free trade between the whole, and with an Imperial Army and Navy, to which all should contribute payments. But where and when, he mused, should we find the statesman great and bold enough to propose it?[48]

In explaining the meaning of Parliamentary democracy at home (still stated to be 'on trial') Fletcher gave his young readers an extraordinary view of the constitution.

> Any very revolutionary proposal . . . such as the surrender of India or the Colonies or the reduction of the Navy far behind the

> strength necessary to defend the Empire might quite conceivably obtain for a moment a majority in the House of Commons, and, though it is unlikely, it is just possible that the House of Lords might be terrified into accepting it. But THEN it would be the duty of the King to interfere, and to dismiss, at all costs, the Ministry which was rash enough to make such a proposal.

At the end, brooding over the lessons of history, Fletcher urged boys to become more brave and manly, and girls to become more affectionate and home loving. He concluded that 'the only safe thing for all of us who love our country is to learn soldiering at once and be prepared to fight at any moment'.[49] Two of his sons were to be killed in the First World War.

The *History* sold 134,000 copies, was reprinted ten times, and remained in print until 1954. It was banned by the Government of Guiana, to Fletcher's bewilderment, for, he said, he had not mentioned Guiana.

None of the other O.U.P. school histories rose to Fletcher's heights of impassioned prejudice. In 1921 the Clarendon Press, however, published *The British Empire, A Short History* intended for secondary schools throughout the Empire, by J. W. Bulkeley, M. A. Oxon, of the Indian Educational Service and formerly of the Educational Service of Natal. Bulkeley referred to 'the unnecessary blotting out of the Tasmanians as perhaps the saddest and blackest story in our Empire's history',[50] though he considered (as many would not today) that the Australian natives had on the whole met with fair treatment from the settlers. He prudently omitted any account of the Indian Mutiny, but wrote that the Boer War[51] had been a conflict between racialism and democracy. His main message was that the British Empire was an 'adventurous attempt to educate the world in self-government'. 'The middle and upper classes', he asserted, 'realise that progress must be gradual and safeguarded by proper precautions; but the working classes, represented in Parliament by the powerful Labour Party, do not understand this,' lacking 'enough historical and local knowledge to admit the need for delay and caution in establishing democracy all over the world.'[52]

The Oxford historians of India are discussed in Chapter 6. Most of them were uninspired and uninspiring. What they have in common with many of those mentioned in this chapter is a sense of involvement in current events – Sidney Owen with the evangelisation of India, Vincent Smith with the iniquity of Indian Home Rule, Edward

Thompson with Indian independence. Again and again the Oxford historians proclaimed that history was to be studied for its moral lessons, and asserted on the Imperial stage how those lessons should be put into practice. The influence of the Oxford historians as well as the classics on the heirs to Milner and Curzon will be seen in the next chapter.

4 The Round Table and their Friends

Haply we are but tools in the Hand
Of a Power we do not know
And not for ourselves we plough the waste
And not for ourselves we sow;
Yet by the Vision that leads us on
To the goal of a single state
We are blessed that our great weal is woofed
With strands of Eternal Fate.

Programme of the Oxford Pageant of the Allies and Empire (1919)

In 1919 Oxford held a Pageant of Victory on the Iffley Road Football Ground to honour the Allies and Empire. The Mayor of Oxford felt himself too old and busy, so the Sheriff organised the Pageant with the assistance of two eminent historians from the University, Sir Charles Oman and Sir John Marriott, M.P. for Oxford. Sir John comfortably referred to 'the spirit of proud humility, of high and inspiring responsibility which shall animate those who possess the priceless privilege of Oxford citizenship; a citizenship in the Empire of which Oxford is a microcosm'. But as they waited for those actors who represented the Dominions to group round the throne and pay homage to the Imperial Crown, the spectators who studied the printed programme found that it started with the short poem quoted above which seemed to strike a curiously uncertain note.

Even as the representative of India in the Pageant was advancing to swear allegiance under the Imperial Umbrella, in India itself the massacre of Amritsar was leading to Gandhi's civil disobedience campaign: some of those present may have recollected the occasion in future years, as the strands of Eternal Fate were unwoofed and the vision of Empire as a single State slowly faded away.[1]

That the Pageant of 1919 should have taken the unity of the Empire as its theme was mainly due to the work of the Round Table whose roots were in Oxford, and whose story begins in South Africa.

MILNER'S KINDERGARTEN

Even before the Boer War ended Lord Milner moved his office from Cape Town to Johannesburg to become Governor of the occupied Transvaal and Orange Free State, whilst also remaining the British High Commissioner in South Africa. He faced urgent problems in the resettlement of Boer families from the concentration camps and in the revival of agriculture. In the longer run his great object was to bring in British settlers in such numbers as to ensure British predominance in South Africa; in order to finance this development the production of gold mines was to be increased by introducing Chinese labour. His programme was a race against the time when the Liberal Party might come into power in Britain and restore self-government to the Transvaal and the Orange Free State.

That Milner recruited the celebrated Kindergarten from Oxford to assist in this task was something of an accident. He would have preferred more mature men like his Balliol contemporary Lyttelton Gell who was then working with O.U.P.; but the British Government would not sanction adequate salaries. 'So I must begin to run my Empire on second division clerks', Milner grumbled. The dissatisfaction which he expressed led to funds from an anonymous source being placed at his disposal with which he recruited, instead of second division clerks, a staff of young Oxford graduates, each of whom was directly responsible to himself, with no rank in the official hierarchy.[2] The term 'Milner's Kindergarten' was first used derisively in a newspaper article, but the group were delighted to use the title. Of the 11 members who regarded themselves as comprising the Kindergarten, nine were graduates of New College, of which Milner was a Fellow, and four were Fellows of All Souls: the oldest member was 31 and the youngest 23. The method by which they were selected from amongst the many enthusiastic applicants who wished to work with Milner in the reconstruction of South Africa throws an interesting light on Oxford's informal network of influence at the time.

J. F. Perry of New College and All Souls, who was to handle relations with Swaziland, Basutoland, Bechuanaland and Rhodesia, came from the Colonial Office, as did Geoffrey Robinson (later Dawson), of Magdalen and All Souls, who became Milner's Private Secretary and closest confidant. Patrick Duncan of Balliol, who was the oldest member and became Colonial Secretary, had worked with Milner in the Inland Revenue Department. Perry brought in his New College contemporary, the Hon. R. H. Brand, another Fellow of All Souls, who became Secretary of the Intercolonial Council; Brand in turn engaged as his assistant the Hon. Philip Kerr of New College who had come out to South Africa as Secretary to the Lieutenant Governor of the Transvaal, a former member of his father's regiment.

Lionel Curtis of New College had taken part in the Boer War and was made Town Clerk of Johannesburg by Milner on the basis of a letter of introduction from the Chairman of the London County Council, with which he had briefly served. When a Treasurer was needed for the Johannesburg Council, Curtis brought in his New College friend Lionel Hichens from the Egyptian Finance Department. He also sent for a New College contemporary with legal experience, Richard Feetham, to be his deputy. Another New College man in his office was John Dove who was recommended by the Warden of All Souls, Sir William Anson. Of the other members, Milner himself engaged Hugh Wyndham of New College at the request of his uncle George Wyndham who was a member of the Cabinet; Basil Williams of Brasenose, who handled education in the Transvaal, had come out with the Army. Dougal Malcolm of New College and All Souls arrived later as Secretary to Lord Selborne, Milner's successor, who had himself obtained a First in Modern History at University College, Oxford.

Among those who were not regarded as members of the inner circle of the Kindergarten but who were closely associated was John Buchan of Brasenose College, the novelist, who worked on the resettlement of Boer families from the concentration camps; and William Marris of Christ Church, a New Zealander, who was seconded from the I.C.S. to organise the Civil Service. L. S. Amery of Balliol and All Souls, the correspondent of *The Times* in South Africa, also liked to consider himself a member.[3]

The Kindergarten, mostly bachelors, and living closely together in or around the 'Moot House' built for them by Herbert Baker, became a laboratory for the working out of the ideas which they had absorbed at Oxford, and they held fortnightly meetings modelled on those of New College Essay Society. From their study of Aristotle they believed that it was in government that man found his noblest form of activity. The philosophic idealism of T. H. Green caused them to view the State as a positive moral good and to see social improvement and reform as a duty. From Stubbs and Freeman came the concept of the progression of self-government from the Anglo-Saxon Moot through to the English Parliamentary system. From the constitutional lawyer, A. V. Dicey, came the belief that religion and politics were inseparable.[4] The group contained young men of great ability but their prejudices and priggishness can be seen in letters which they wrote back to Oxford, often to their former tutor at New College, H. A. L. Fisher.

Thus Philip Kerr in 1905 expressed the shock for 'a son of Oxford' on

> being plunged into a society where heartiness and familiarity take the place of urbanity. This sort of soil is difficult to cultivate the Imperial ideal upon. What England can really give to her colonies [is] not preferential tariffs, nor representative assemblies, but a measure of savoir faire. . . . Unless we lucky Englishmen can teach them a little *savoir faire* they'll end in the condition that the most Colonial of all Colonies is in – Australia. South Africa little knows what her social comfort owes to Lord Milner and his gang. I am afraid that this is going to be as difficult a country to govern as Ireland. People are just as irresponsible and politically just as immoral.[5]

How fortunate he was, in this cultural desert, he told his old tutor, to live in an oasis of old Oxford men.

A year later Kerr still found the Boers 'worse than the Irish . . . they cannot understand, and cannot be expected to understand, the advantages of civilisation'.[6] Curtis also wrote to Fisher that 'the special weakness of the South African character is . . . that they profess and mean more than they have the stamina to carry out'. Brand wrote complacently of the Contitutional Conference, surrounded though he was by crafty Boers, 'No one of them could draft. We had to do it all.'[7]

Curtis was almost always optimistic 'We have got the new (Municipal) council to throw over all the old rules and traditions, after which their soul hankered, to adopt an abridgement of the LCC's – isn't it splendid?' he wrote from the Office of the Mayor, Johannesburg; and when a representative of the *The Times of Natal* said to this young

Solon 'You are making a new Johannesburg', he replied 'Yes but we have got to make citizens first.'[8] By contrast the gloomy Geoffrey Robinson wrote, after the Liberals came into office in Britain, 'It really is an exasperating place, what with the poisonous government at home and the rotters out here.'[9]

Although Milner returned to England in 1905, the Kindergarten stayed on after the Liberal Government which came into office in that year restored self-government to the Transvaal and the Orange Free State. So far from sharing Milner's disgust because this precipitate step ended the hope that there would be a British South Africa, under a British flag and using the English language, his disciples enthusiastically embarked upon a campaign to bring about a political union of the Cape, Natal, Transvaal and Orange River Colony. Originally they thought in terms of a Federation, but they were converted to the idea of a Union by coming across F. S. Oliver's *Life of Alexander Hamilton: An Essay on the American Revolution*, with its account of the debate which led to the establishment of the United States after the War of Independence. Several of the Kindergarten had opportunities to raise the question of unity in a practical form through participation in interterritorial committees on railways and communications; but as they were replaced in their posts by South Africans, they came to conduct the propaganda by other means. Curtis set up Closer Union Committees and drafted a proposal for union which was submitted first to the 'Moot' of Kindergarten members for criticism and then to the Governor-General, Lord Selborne, who circulated it in a more discreet form to the four Governments. Geoffrey Robinson spread the message as Editor of the *Johannesburg Star* and South African correspondent of *The Times* (London), and Philip Kerr set up a weekly paper, the *State*, specifically to discuss the idea of union. The Boer leaders overcame their original dislike of Milner's young men and cooperated with them, seeing that the Union would not lead to Milner's British South Africa but to one which, if the constituencies were arranged in favour of the rural areas, would be dominated by themselves. When the Union came into being in 1910, Selborne wrote to Curtis that this was largely due to the Kindergarten.[10] Curtis characteristically wrote to his mother 'This is the Lord's doing and marvellous in his eyes.'[11] The Afrikaaners, however, as Milner observed, immediately self-government was obtained set about dismissing British officials and restoring the use of their own language.

THE FORMATION OF THE ROUND TABLE

After the Union was created, some of the Kindergarten remained in South Africa. Feetham and Duncan practised law and went into politics, Duncan ending as Governor-General. Wyndham became a farmer. Those who returned to England, elated by their success, decided to apply the lessons and methods of their South African experience in the broader field of Imperial unity. The problem which they saw was that the whole burden of Imperial defence, in light of the naval threat from Germany, could no longer be carried by Britain alone: on the other hand, decisions vital for the Dominions, determining issues of peace and war in which they were inevitably involved, were being settled by a British Government responsible only to a national Parliament and electorate. While the Dominions had virtually assumed autonomy in internal matters, externally they remained dependencies. The solution seen by the former members of the Kindergarten, as an unescapable alternative to weakness and stagnation, was to create an Imperial Parliament, which would be directly elected by the peoples of Britain and the Dominions, with responsibility for defence and foreign policy and power to levy taxes.

In order to stimulate discussion of this issue, Milner's former staff, under his patronage, formed themselves into a loose association which they called the 'Round Table', partly to denote its informality and perhaps also with a romantic echo of King Arthur and his knights. They published a journal by the same name whose articles were unsigned and were discussed in draft in a 'Moot' of the members. Curtis and Kerr became full-time agents, paid by the Rhodes Trust, and visited Canada, South Africa, Australia and New Zealand to establish branches there.

In 1912 Curtis, who had been commissioned by the Round Table to prepare a report on Imperial Federation in light of the constitutional history of the components of the Empire, came to Oxford as Beit Lecturer in Colonial History. Deborah Lavin has written a vivid account of how he brought dons and students into colonial studies, and used them to help him draft his report, and how he made Egerton, the Beit Professor of Colonial History, feel like a country rector with the Prophet Isaiah as his curate. He pressed into service the Canadian Murray Wrong and the young L. S. Namier to investigate the lessons of American history. W. G. S. Adams and Charles Grant Robertson worked on the British chapters. Keith Feiling and Reginald Coupland were also drawn in. The participants in the weekly Colonial History seminar were induced to act out the roles of Ministers of an Imperial Cabinet: Curtis opened the doors of Whitehall for them to be briefed: he also formed the Ralegh Club which served as the Oxford branch of the Round Table, where the new concept of 'Commonwealth' in place of Empire was spread. Among Oxford men recruited to the Round Table at this time were Alfred Zimmern, Edward Grigg, W. G. S. Adams and Reginald Coupland, whom Curtis established as his successor as Lecturer in Colonial History.[12]

OXFORD AND IMPERIAL FEDERATION

Curtis was not breaking new ground entirely in Oxford. A number of Oxford men had been involved in the Imperial Federation League in the 1880s. Lord Rosebery had been its President and Parkin its travelling salesman. Bryce, though a Liberal, had been Chairman of the Oxford branch, whom he told in 1886 that Oxford might perform a useful and effective part in realising the dream of a federalised 'Oceania'.[13] Oxford historians and lawyers in the late nineteenth and early twentieth centuries were fascinated by Federations, Confederations and Constitutions. Freeman delighted in watching the Swiss Constitution in action in the primitive cantons. His successor as Regius Professor, Froude, as has been seen, had an unsuccessful experience in trying to introduce a Confederation in South Africa. James Bryce, who was Regius Professor of Law from 1870 to 1893, first made his reputation with his prize essay on the Holy Roman Empire and consolidated it with his book on the working of the American Constitution.

Whereas Bryce's studies turned him into a Home Ruler, and indeed a Minister in three Liberal Governments, those of his friend and contemporary A. V. Dicey (1835–1922), who was Vinerian Professor of Law at Oxford from 1882 to 1909, made him a passionate opponent of Home Rule for Ireland or of any kind of Imperial Federation, because this would diminish the powers of the British Parliament. The most famous constitutional lawyer of his time, Dicey brought to bear on the Empire the enthusiasm of an evangelical upbringing and the elevated view of the role of the State which he had acquired from T. H. Green whilst an undergraduate at Balliol. He believed that religion and politics were inseparable and that the

British Empire had a historic mission as a positive force for good in a deteriorating world. Harold Laski considered that he had more influence on the outside world than any Oxford teacher since Green.[14]

Oxford men were also leading figures in the political dining clubs which were a feature of the Edwardian age. The Coefficients Club, founded by Sydney and Beatrice Webb with the object of discussing national efficiency, included Mackinder, Hewins, Clinton Dawkins, recently Finance Member of the Government of India, and Sir Edward Grey, with L. S. Amery to remind them continually of the Imperial theme. The Compatriots Club was founded in 1904 by Mackinder, Hewins and Amery as a forum for strengthening each other in the Imperial faith.[15] Perhaps most influential of all was the Pollock Committee which met as an informal dining club under the Chairmanship of Sir Frederick Pollock (1845–1937), Corpus Professor of Jurisprudence at Oxford; it included politicians from both Parties and discussed ways of improving Imperial cooperation. The Pollock Committee, despite the membership of Milner and Parkin, rejected Imperial Federation; in memoranda published in *The Times* between 1904 and 1905 it proposed instead that the Colonial Conference be made permanent with its own Secretariat, a solution which became the basis for the policies of the Conservative Government of the time.

The Oxford academics who visited the Empire to discuss ideas of Imperial Federation had a varied reception: the scholarly humility of Bryce and Dicey was well received but when Pollock went to Canada to try out his Committee's ideas, the Oxford professorial manner made a disastrous impression. Lord Grey, the Governor-General, described him as 'the ill-mannered Pollock' who had succeeded in establishing a record in the number of people anxious to be friendly whom he had succeeded in alienating.[16]

Thus the Round Table were by no means raising a new issue in discussion of Imperial Federation. What distinguished them from other groups was that they looked at Imperial issues not simply in terms of British interests but with what Curtis called 'the Dominion perspective'.[17] They were also careful to avoid the issue of tariffs, on which the Imperial Federation League had foundered, though this caution annoyed Amery and others. Another characteristic was that they spread their message very largely through the network of Oxford men in positions of influence.

Whilst they started by considering an Imperial Federation of white races, very soon they were confronted with the question which none of the other groups had faced – what would be the place of India in relation to an Imperial Parliament? Initially they suggested that India and other dependencies should have representatives without votes, but this could hardly be a permanent solution.

Kerr returned from visits to India in 1911 and 1912 convinced that India and other dependencies should progressively become independent in internal affairs but must for all time remain in the Empire. He became an eloquent defender, particularly against American critics, of Britain's trusteeship role, explaining how in Africa, Asia and the Pacific peoples had proved incapable of governing themselves, not from inherent deficiencies but because of their inability to withstand the drink merchants, arms dealers and capitalists from outside, to which Satanic list he added after 1918 the Bolsheviks.[18]

It is an irony of history that the period of the Round Table's greatest influence in the British Government marked the quiet abandonment of the dream of Imperial Federation. In Lloyd George's administration of 1916–18 Milner was a member of the War Cabinet, and Kerr, W. G. S. Adams, Grigg and Amery were members of the Prime Minister's staff. Close Imperial cooperation was achieved through the Imperial War Conference of 1917 and through attendance by Dominion representatives at the War Cabinet, but the Imperial War Conference flatly rejected the Federal idea, describing the Dominions as 'autonomous nations of an Imperial Commonwealth';[19] nor was its recommendation that there should be an Imperial Constitutional Conference after the war ever implemented. Instead the separate membership of the Dominions in the League of Nations emphasized their independence in foreign relations which was formalised in subsequent declarations. Indeed the ideas in Curtis's book, which was published in 1915, with its proposal for a Federal Parliament with powers of taxation, were seen as quite unacceptable at the time by other members of the Round Table who insisted that it should be issued in Curtis's own name and not in that of the group as a whole.

CURTIS AND KERR

After the First World War the Round Table remained in being, held together as an editorial committee for its journal. As the dream of Imperial Federation faded, some, though not all of its members came to enlarge their vision to contemplate a Commonwealth which would include brown and black races. Curtis and Kerr in their different ways continued between the First and Second World Wars to exercise considerable influence in Oxford and the nation, Curtis from All Souls and Kerr from the Rhodes Trust.

Curtis, known to his friends as 'the Prophet' was an idealist, influenced by an evangelical background and by the philosophy of T. H. Green. His practical thought had the nature of a religion. His intellectual ability was questionable; he had obtained a double Third. The honesty of his tactics was criticised, as when he pretended to be a South African on his Australian visit, because this obtained more sympathy for his ideas than if he had come as an Englishman. He was accused of having a talent for prostituting history for propagandist purposes.[20] His lack of discretion when visiting India caused the Viceroy, Lord Chelmsford, who had been a good friend of the Round Table whilst Governor of New South Wales, to forbid members of the I.C.S. to associate with the group; he simultaneously alienated the Indian National Congress who suspected him of being an agent of the British Government. Yet in spite of these defects he was able to mesmerise people into working for his current causes, Lord Hailey for example, into undertaking the African Survey, and Hancock the Chatham House Survey of the Commonwealth. He worked behind the scenes in the introduction of Dyarchy into the Indian Constitution, in the Irish Settlement of 1921 and in setting up institutions such as the Royal Institute of International Affairs, the Oxford Society and the Oxford Preservation Trust. Kerr observed that Curtis saw only one thing at a time but that with marvellous clearness. Arnold Toynbee, who knew him well, summed him up as a great man and a monomaniac, who wanted a Federal Union of Empire, but in effect helped to turn it into a congeries of independent States; who neglected Indian and African interests in South Africa and paved the way for a police State there; and whose concern with constitutional reform in India caused a political avalanche.[21]

Curtis once wrote to Kerr 'I am only one blade of the scissors and can cut nothing unless I am hinged with you.' Kerr was also an idealist but more pragmatic than Curtis. 'The Empire', he once wrote to Curtis, 'is a noble thing, but not fit to be a God.'[22] Kerr obtained a First in Mods and Greats at Oxford and his early experience in editing the *State* in South Africa set him on the path of journalism; he wrote frequently for *The Times* and the *Observer* whilst Secretary of the Rhodes Trust. He has been described as 'having a mind like a pat of fresh butter, which would take any impression and record it sharply and accurately'.[23] This led him into enthusiasms and superlatives. Generally these were only mildly ridiculous. Christian Science, to which he was converted from Roman Catholicism, was 'the real key to all our problems, political, and economic, no less than personal'.[24] The General Strike of 1926 was 'the greatest danger to the country since the Armada', and the financial crisis of 1931 was 'the most serious crisis in our country's history'.[25]

Sometimes his enthusiasms were dangerous, as in his repeated assertions that Hitler did not want war. Whilst he was Secretary of the Rhodes Trust the brooding personality of the founder made the impression on the pat of butter. Rhodes had believed intensely in Anglo-American union as well as in cooperation with Germany. Kerr more and more diverged from the Round Table's original idea of organic union of the Empire and preached instead organic union of the English-speaking peoples. He was also a fervent supporter of Chamberlain's policy of appeasement of Germany. His finest moment, for which the long service with the Rhodes Trust had been a superb preparation, came at the beginning of the Second World War as Ambassador to the United States at a time when American aid meant the difference between survival and defeat in Britain. He died in the post before he was 60, described by Churchill as the best Ambassador that Britain had ever sent to Washington. Curtis lived on in Oxford, as the Ancient Mariner of All Souls, meandering from the organic union of the Empire to the organic union of the world in *Civitas Dei* (a book which few of his colleagues read but referred to as *Civitas Mei*), and buttonholing visitors in the quad to help him draft a constitution for the world.

ALL SOULS

Thanks to Curtis and others All Souls became an important base for the Round Table and the Imperial cause. Under its Warden, Sir William Anson, a constitutional lawyer and M. P. for the University from 1899 to 1914, the college had emerged from long years of torpor, during which the only duties of its members had been to pray for the souls of those who died in the Hundred Years' War against France. Its system of Open Fellowships, awarded by competition and carrying a salary for several years without statutory duties, now attracted the most brilliant of Oxford's graduates and enabled them to start on political careers. When they no longer received stipends, as Quondam Fellows they continued to visit and stay in College.

Among them at the end of the nineteenth century were Rochefort Maguire, the business associate of Rhodes, and Dougal Malcolm, a future member of the Kindergarten, who was celebrated for his Greek epigrams and likened to Alciabades. Amery and the other All Souls men from the Kindergarten were able to strengthen the College's interest in Empire by obtaining the election as Fellows not only of Curtis but of Coupland and T. E. Lawrence. When Amery proposed an Australian for election, one of his colleagues remarked that in his devotion to Empire he was capable of electing even an emu or a giraffe.[26]

Three Fellows in the early twentieth century were Viceroys of India, Curzon, Chelmsford and Irwin, Chelmsford becoming Warden of All Souls on his return from India, and both Curzon and Irwin later serving as Foreign Secretary. Among other contemporary Fellows were another Foreign Secretary, Sir John Simon, Cosmo Lang, the Archbishop of Canterbury, and, of course, Geoffrey Dawson, the Editor of *The Times*.

At the height of its influence in 1932 All Souls was depicted in an anonymous pamphlet by a staff member of *The Times*:

> There is no set of men, bound together by similar ties, which exerts a comparable influence on the world where things have got to get done. . . . Having representatives in all Departments of State, in every profession and in all branches of knowledge (except possibly the physical sciences) and being a body of diligent travellers, familiar with all languages, constitutions and legal systems, at home equally in Europe, the Dominions and America, and being able from their own body to give themselves the necessary introductions to almost any potentate in the world, they have an extraordinarily rich and deep common fund of information and intelligence, which they are always pooling at their dinners. . . . Having at the same time a natural genius for management, since it is one of the unwritten laws of their society never to let theory outrun the limits of the practical, they have taken upon themselves no less a task than forming a committee for running or helping to run the British Empire. Consciously or unconsciously they have taken almost all political, economic and administrative life into their province.[27]

OTHER CHANNELS OF INFLUENCE

Another important instrument of the Imperial cause was *The Times*, where Amery was Colonial Editor from 1901 to 1909. He was succeeded in this post by Edward Grigg who was also Editor of the *Round Table*. Amery got Geoffrey Dawson on to the staff of *The Times* where his devotion to Empire delighted the proprietor, Lord Northcliffe, who made him Editor from 1912 to 1919. When Dawson could no longer tolerate Lord Northcliffe's megalomania he resigned and then served for a short time simultaneously as Secretary to the Rhodes Trust, Editor of the *Round Table* and Estates Bursar of All Souls. Dawson, who again became editor of *The Times* in 1923, believed that the maintenance of Empire was by far the greatest contribution which British statesmanship could make to mankind. Like most of the Round Table, he distrusted European entanglements and strongly supported appeasement. He seldom neglected an opportunity to make Oxford's influence apparent in *The Times*, through letters to the Editor and commissioned articles, many of them on Imperial issues.

In the House of Commons Amery was the outstanding Imperialist. He had become one whilst still a schoolboy at Harrow, inspired by a powerful lecture from Parkin on Imperial Federation. A Balliol man, he regarded Milner as his spiritual leader and became his Parliamentary Under Secretary when Milner was Colonial Secretary from 1919 to 1921. Amery later became Colonial and Dominions Secretary and Secretary of State for India. Although he was critical of the Round Table for not coming out in favour of Imperial Preference, he worked closely with many of its members. None of the other Oxford Imperialists had particularly distinguished Parliamentary careers. The geographer Halford Mackinder was an M.P. from 1910 to 1922 but, though a brilliant lecturer, seldom caught the mood of the House. W. A. S. Hewins, like Amery, was a strong advocate of Imperial Preference, whose devotion to Imperialism came to replace his Roman Catholic faith. He read Mathematics at Oxford and was one of the founders of the Oxford Economics Society. He later became Secretary of Joseph Chamberlain's Tariff Commission and Director of the London School of Economics before serving as Parliamentary Secretary for the Colonies, in which post he was caricatured by cartoonists as the Mad Hatter. John Buchan was M.P. for the Scottish Universities but his influence on Oxford came rather through his Sunday open house for undergraduates at his home in Elsfield. Sir Edward Grigg interrupted a Parliamentary career to become Governor of Kenya;

although on his return he served briefly as a Parliamentary Secretary, he was happier as a proconsul. Kerr, after he entered the House of Lords as Marquess of Lothian, served briefly in the National Government of 1931.

Several of the former Kindergarten members were prominent in the City and could be relied on to stimulate private funds for the Round Table and sometimes to find jobs for promising supporters of Empire. Hichens became Head of Cammell Laird, the shipbuilders; Malcolm was Chairman of the British South Africa Company; Brand was Managing Director of Lazard Brothers.

The Round Table was not without its critics. An acute and effective opponent in the early years was Richard Jebb of New College (1874–1937) who, in his book *Studies in Colonial Nationalism* in 1905, pointed out that the people of the colonies were by no means 'ten million Englishmen living abroad' as Seeley had said, and as the Round Table later seemed to believe. He strongly disagreed with Curtis's proposal for an Imperial Parliament, proposing instead a 'Britannic Alliance' of sovereign Dominions held together by an Imperial Conference with a permanent Secretariat. Jebb also believed that the colonies should have independent Navies. He considered that the Round Table were wrong in any case in asserting that Imperial defence was the first priority. The first duty of a State, he argued from Plato and Aristotle, was to provide food for its citizens and enable them to live well. Jebb, who travelled widely in the Empire and wrote for the *Morning Post*, had considerable influence before 1914.[28] The Commonwealth which was to emerge after the Second World War, though it bore a name popularised by Curtis, was closer to the system foreseen by Jebb.

The Round Table and their circle were much involved, either overtly or behind the scenes, in constitution making. For Lothian this was mainly in India, for Curtis both in India and Ireland. Amery, whilst Colonial Secretary, sent Grigg as Governor of Kenya to bring about a closer union between Kenya, Uganda and Tanganyika. He planned that this union would be recommended by a Royal Commission which was also sent out with Sir Hilton Young as Chairman; but the Chairman was left in a minority, outvoted by Oxford men of a different character, the missionary J. H. Oldham and the Imperial financial expert Sir George Schuster, who were not prepared to allow the white settlers to have predominant positions over Africans and Asians.[29] In the next generation Oxford academics continued to collaborate enthusiastically in the planning of Federations of various regions of the Empire – Commonwealth. These were usually inspired by a book by K. C. Wheare, *Federal Government* published in 1946, although Wheare himself was 'dubious, amused and somewhat embarrassed by the subsequent decade of fashionable federation'.[30] Almost everywhere the Federations collapsed, as in the Caribbean and Central Africa, or were never formed, as in East Africa.

RACIAL ATTITUDES

The young men who went out to South Africa had carried with them the fundamental belief, shared by most of their Oxford contemporaries, in the inherent superiority of British civilisation and in Britain's duty to carry the forms of that civilisation throughout the world. Their attitudes to race had been simply expressed. Curtis in his diary in 1901 noted that 'it would be a blessed thing for us if the negro, like the Red Indian, tended to die out before us'.[31] At the farewell reception given to him by the Johannesburg Municipal Council in 1906 he said that its most important department was that of Asiatic Affairs which would keep this a white man's country and save it from the fate of Mauritius and Jamaica.[32] John Dove in 1907 wrote that mixing of race was a deadly danger. 'The almost brutal contempt and dislike of most white men for the kaffir is said to be a healthy sign. It marks the determination of the white South African not to allow his race to become mongrel. It is at all events better than the friendliness which you find in Portuguese Territory.'[33] Later the views of Curtis and Kerr evolved considerably as they contemplated a Commonwealth which included brown and black races; Kerr stayed with Gandhi in his village when he visited India. They never quite seemed to be realistic however about the situation in South Africa. Thus Curtis in 1935 as has been seen tried to persuade Margery Perham that there was 'a passionate feeling among young Afrikaaners that the present treatment of natives and coloured persons was wrong and that little by little South Africa would wipe the colour bar sinister from its shield'. Kerr told a South African correspondent in 1937 that 'the Americans have found the right solution, retention of complete political power in the hands of the white, coupled with the grant of real economic power to the negro'.[34]

Among those who disagreed with Curtis and Kerr in the latter years of the Round Table was Grigg who in 1936 in a book called *Faith of an Englishman* boldly asserted that 'patriotism is the only sure foundation for a political faith', and 'internationalism with its misty enthusiasms and perverted sense of duty is a treacherous mirage'.[35] This was published shortly after the Oxford Union passed its famous 'King and Country' Resolution and at a time when Low's cartoons of Colonel Blimp were ridiculing this kind of expression.

Another issue with which the Round Table were faced after 1919 was how to reconcile membership of the Commonwealth with that of the League of Nations. They often did so by suggesting that the ideals and methods of the Commonwealth should be extended throughout the world. Curtis saw this as an evangelistic task and told Toynbee that if Christ came back to earth he would find that his precepts were being better practised in the Commonwealth than anywhere else.[36]

APPEASEMENT

The Round Table has been accused of being a main source of support for Neville Chamberlain's policy of appeasement of Hitler. Neither Curtis nor Kerr spoke any European language, and the Round Table as a whole opposed European entanglements. Kerr was a leading exponent of appeasement, though he later admitted he had been wrong. On this, Brand, whose banking interests took him to Europe, differed strongly with him and with the Astors, into whose family he had married. Amery, who had been *The Times* Correspondent in the Balkans as a young man, was one of the fiercest of Chamberlain's opponents. Defenders of the Round Table have argued that the Munich Agreement enabled a united Empire to be brought into the Second World War in 1939, as it would not have been in 1938. Similarly the apparently ingenuous policies of the Kindergarten, by which political influence over the whole of South Africa was handed over to the defeated Boers, could be defended because they brought South Africa into both the First and Second World Wars on the side of the Empire.

LATER ROUND TABLERS

Between the First and Second World Wars Curtis and Coupland in Oxford recruited a new generation to the Round Table, often through the Ralegh Club, among them being John Maud, who visited South Africa on a Rhodes Trust Fellowship and acquired there his interest in Local Government as well in the Commonwealth, and H. V. Hodson, a Fellow of All Souls who became Editor of the *Round Table* at the age of 25. Malcolm MacDonald, who was an undergraduate at Queen's whilst his father was Prime Minister, was gathered into the Ralegh Club, and when he left Oxford Curtis got him appointed as secretary of the British delegation to two conferences on Pacific affairs. The investment was rewarded. When Macdonald became Secretary of State for the Colonies, among those with Oxford connections whom he appointed to a consultative committee of non-officials were Coupland, Margery Perham, J. H. Oldham and W. M. MacMillan.[37]

ACHIEVEMENTS OF THE ROUND TABLE

What in the end, it may be asked, did the Round Table achieve? Their early objective of an Imperial Parliament, levying its own taxes and responsible for the Empire's foreign and defence policies, was very soon seen by all except Curtis as quite unpractical in light of the attitude of Canada and Australia. They could claim some credit for the improved informal consultative methods which operated between Britain and the Dominions between the First and Second World Wars. They made a notable contribution to Constitutional development in India where their various channels of interest converged. Marris, the I.C.S. official who had worked with the Kindergarten in South Africa, drafted the Montagu Chelmsford reforms. Curtis thought of the name and perhaps the scheme of Dyarchy. When the next round of reforms was opposed by Churchill and the Right wing of the Conservative Party, Geoffrey Dawson kept The Times behind the Government which was also supported by Amery. Lothian (the former Kerr) agreed to serve as Parliamentary Secretary for India and Chairman of the Indian Franchise Committee only because of his sense of commitment to Indian self-government. H. V. Hodson, the last Editor of the old *Round Table*, became Indian Reforms Commissioner. When India became a Republic she could remain in the 'Commonwealth' of Curtis, though it would have been politically impossible to remain in an 'Empire'. Yet even on this question there was no unanimity. Some members of the Round Table would have preferred to let India and other new-born nations go into an outer orbit, in order to keep closer defensive and foreign policy arrangements with the old Dominions.[38]

The Round Table, or at least Curtis, were led by their experience of India to suggest that the Commonwealth existed for the purpose of extending self-government as rapidly as possible to all communities within its circle.[39] Perhaps their most important contribution was to stimulate interest in the Empire through their journal and almost imperceptibly over a long period to prepare the way for the concept of a multiracial Commonwealth of self-governing nations. Their basic premise that the Commonwealth would be united in belief in and practice of democracy among its members proved, however, unsound. By the end of their lives both Curtis and Kerr ceased to be primarily interested in the Empire–Commonwealth. Curtis saw it as transcended by a system of world government, whilst Kerr was more interested in a Union with the United States.

In Oxford Curtis and Coupland through the Ralegh Club kept interest in the Empire alive in the minds of some of the brightest students from Britain and the Dominions at a time when the Empire – Commonwealth was generally unfashionable in the University. It was Curtis's tragedy that many of these young men later escaped from his intense control, and that, demanding complete loyalty he usually ended by quarrelling with them.[40]

5 Professors, Prigs and Pedants – the Critics of Empire

Professors and rhetoricians find a system for every contingency and a principle for every chance; but you are not going, I hope, to leave the destinies of the British Empire to prigs and pedants.

Benjamin Disraeli (1863)

Whilst Oxford made an important contribution to the Imperial philosophy, at the same time it produced a continuous line of anti-Imperialists and critics of Empire; among them one of the earliest and best known was Goldwin Smith, who was Disraeli's principal target in the remark quoted above. This was made in a debate in the House of Commons on the Queen's Speech, in which he was attacking the Government of Lord Palmerston for proposing Britain's very first act of decolonisation, the cession of the Ionian Islands to the Greek Government. 'There can be no question either in or out of this House', he continued, 'that the best mode of preserving wealth is power. A country, and especially a maritime power, must get possession of the strong places of the world.'[1]

GOLDWIN SMITH

Goldwin Smith (1823–1910) was, at the time of this debate, Regius Professor of Modern History at Oxford; on another occasion he was described by Disraeli as 'an itinerant spouter of stale sedition, a wild man of the cloisters going around the country maligning men and things'. Goldwin Smith, on the other hand, wrote about Disraeli that 'the Tories, being rather more stupid than the Whigs, have been rather more often obliged to take adventurers into their pay'.[2] Disraeli's reference in the debate was to a series of letters to the *Daily News* written by Goldwin Smith in 1862–3 and subsequently published under the title *The Empire*. In these letters he had put forward policies for what he distinguished respectively as strong points, colonies and dependencies.

The value of the existing strong points should, he suggested, be periodically examined. Such an examination would show that Gibraltar, the Ionian Islands and perhaps Malta were no longer necessary, now that there was a revived Spain, a revived Italy and a revived Greece to balance French power in the Mediterranean. Corfu was indefensible, and the possession of Gibraltar caused the implacable enmity of Spain. As for guarding the way to India, the overland route across Egypt would probably be unusable in time of war in any case.

The colonies of settlement Goldwin Smith saw as a general source of weakness because the need to defend them dissipated Britain's strength and enfeebled her diplomacy. 'We are keeping the Colonies', he said, 'in a perpetual state of infancy and preventing the gristle of their frames from being matured into bone.'[3] Canada and Australia should become independent and responsible for their own defence, though under new treaties their citizens might also acquire British citizenship. The relationship between Britain and the colonies of settlement should resemble the purely parental links which the Greek city states used to maintain with the territories colonised by their citizens. Such new relationships, he argued, should not adversely affect either emigration or commerce, for, at the time, for every one British emigrant to the colonies two went to the United States, and Britain's export trade was increasing less with the colonies than with other countries.

There remained the dependencies. India Goldwin Smith saw as a splendid curse. 'When we come to the advantages, a perennial supply of old Indians spending Indian pensions at Bath and Cheltenham is the main item on the side of profit.' On the other side was 'the paralysing sense of our weak point and the loss of dignity and force thence resulting to our diplomacy in Europe.'[4] But there would be anarchy, he admitted, if the British were to leave India; for the present it should be governed autocratically by a Governor-General with widely delegated powers. Similarly he considered that in the West Indies, where Democracy had failed, the negroes should be treated as wards of the British Government. He was sceptical of the prospects of converting India to Christianity, especially in light of the

Mutiny, for the religion of the conqueror was seldom a welcome gift.[5]

These articles were attacked not only by Disraeli but by *The Times* which advised foreigners to note that 'in this country Professors of History do not count for statesmen'.[6]

The career of Goldwin Smith was unusual. After winning many distinctions as an undergraduate at Christ Church he became a Fellow of University College where he was identified with the University party who opposed religious tests and exclusive teaching by the clergy. He served as Secretary of the Commission on University Reform of 1850. He also became associated with the Manchester School of economists and a friend of Cobden and Bright.

In his Inaugural Lecture as Regius Professor he described Oxford's task as the education of the future ruling class of Britain in their duties, and Modern History as an integral part of that education.[7] Whether he came to feel that this task was impossible, or that America was more fertile ground for a publicist, he resigned his Chair for personal reasons at the age of 43, and moved to Cornell University in the United States. When Cornell decided to admit women, he moved on to Toronto, where his advocacy of Canadian union with the United States gained him considerable unpopularity. He frequently returned to Oxford to lecture. Thus in 1886, for example, the *Oxford Magazine* in the same week reported a meeting in New College to form an Oxford branch of the Imperial Federation League and a lecture by Goldwin Smith in the New Schools, in which he stated that Imperial Federation in Canada was a dream, because there was not the slightest willingness to accept the two necessary conditions, namely colonial contribution to Imperial armaments and acceptance of an Imperial tariff.[8]

Throughout 50 years Goldwin Smith wrote articles and letters in some 200 journals in Britain, the United States and Canada. He attacked Carlyle for the cult of the hero and Tennyson for the militarism of *Maud*. He aired his prejudices against Catholics and the Irish, and opposed Home Rule in 1886. In his old age he described the Boer War as inhuman folly, and expressed his dislike of Oxford being made a pedestal for Rhodes and his Scholarships.[9] In 1902 he also fiercely criticised American Imperialism in the Philippines, and predicted that the lack of continuity under the U.S. constitution would mean that the thread of an American Imperial policy would be broken every four years.[10]

Jowett thought Goldwin Smith not altogether right in his mind, though sometimes a great instrument in politics and education.[11]

Lord Selborne compared him to Milton, with the same mixture of liberalism and prejudice.[12] Sometimes his jibes stung Conservative Oxford into retaliation. His portrait was removed from the Senior Common Room by University College; and an *Oxford Magazine* review in 1891 described one of his books as 'a farrago of history, polemic and prophecy . . . every chapter marked by an exaggeration and inaccuracy and by unworthy political prejudice'.[13]

University College repented and in 1881 invited him, without success, to return to Oxford as their Master. Among Canadians resentment lasted longer. Vincent Massey in his Romanes Lecture of 1961 declared that 'If Oxford is a home of lost causes, she has to thank Goldwin Smith for his part in creating that reputation.'[14] What Goldwin Smith wrote in the sixties was not much different from the views of other members of the Manchester School. Merivale, in his lectures as Professor of Political Economy in Oxford, had also expressed separatist ideas. Goldwin Smith was unusual, however, in the violence with which he expressed his opinions about Empire and the fact that he never changed them over 50 years. Later anti-Imperialists in Oxford regarded themselves as following in his footsteps.

THE WADHAM POSITIVISTS

Goldwin Smith might be described by Disraeli as a professor and pedant but hardly as a Prig, for his arguments for decolonisation were on practical, not on moral, grounds. The professorial prigs whom he had in mind were probably the Positivists from Wadham College or, as they called themselves, the 'Mumbo Jumbo Club'. Their leader Richard Congreve (1818–99) had tutored Goldwin Smith at Oxford. Congreve, who had studied and taught at Rugby, brought to Wadham the high-minded earnestness and taste for new ideas which Arnold inspired in many of his pupils. He was one of the most successful and influential Oxford tutors of the 1840s and a leading evangelical. 'The one burden of his method', one of his pupils wrote, 'was self improvement, the cultivation of right judgement and high thinking, the making of enlightened citizens. Everything was brought to the social and moral test.'[15] In 1855 he abandoned his evangelical Christianity to become a Positivist.

Positivism was the philosophy taught by the French educationalist

Auguste Comte with the object of reconciling science and religion in what he called 'the religion of humanity'. Among its tenets was that nations, like individuals, should subordinate self-love to the general good of society. It followed from this that no nation should rule over another, and to this effect Comte hoped that large nation states such as France and Britain would be divided into smaller sovereign units. When Congreve forsook his evangelical Christianity to become a Positivist, Comte asked him, as his most important follower in Britain, to take up the question of the relinquishment of the colonies, starting with Gibraltar. As a consequence Congreve wrote a pamphlet in 1857 entitled *Gibraltar or the Foreign Policy of England*. In this he suggested that Britain should restore Gibraltar to Spain in order to inaugurate a new policy in her relations with other nations and as an example to Europe; he proceeded to assert a general concept that no single nation could be trusted to rule over another, and that any guardianship over backward races should be exercised by West European nations collectively.[16]

He followed this with a book on India published in 1857, after the outbreak of the Mutiny, in which he stated that there was no moral justification for retaining our dominion in the East and recommended withdrawal as early as practicable. Other European nations should, he suggested, be associated in a mixed Commission to settle Britain's relations with India. Although this policy was primarily based on moral considerations, he considered that politically India was more of a liability than an asset and that commerce could be as successfully conducted with an independent India as it was with the United States. Congreve dealt sharply with the argument of the Bishop of Oxford, Samuel Wilberforce, that 'God has entrusted India to us to hold it for Him, and we have no right to give it up.'[17] He observed that at a time when the Empire was tottering to its fall in India it was a very questionable course to advance Christian motives for holding it which had never influenced our previous policy.

Every Sunday in term Congreve's pupils would meet over breakfast in Wadham College for discussions on questions of philosophy, religion and literature which sometimes lasted for 12 or 14 hours. Because they breakfasted on cold duck, the duck was described as their 'totem' by less serious members of the College, and they themselves as the 'Mumbo Jumbo Club'. Three out of the four members of the Club were to follow Congreve into the Positivist movement. Congreve himself resigned his Fellowship and Holy Orders in 1855 and qualified as a doctor of medicine. Of his pupils,

Frederic Harrison (1838–1923), after a period as Fellow of Wadham, became a prolific writer of biography and politics; E. H. Beesly (1831–1915) was Professor of History at University College London from 1860 to 1893; J. H. Bridges (1832–1906) held a Fellowship at Oriel for a few years before resigning, like Congreve, to qualify in medicine. The only member of the Club who did not become a Positivist and thus did not have to abandon an Oxford career was G. F. Thorley who stayed on to become Warden of Wadham. The other 'Mumbos', as they continued to call themselves, remained associated over many causes for half a century.

In 1866 Congreve and his Oxford disciples combined to write a book on *International Policy* based on Positivist principles. In this E. H. Pember, a former Student of Christ Church, elaborated Congreve's case for quitting India. As a step towards independence he urged that Indians be admitted to the I.C.S. and to the Governor-General's Council, and preferred to Europeans for judicial and magisterial appointments. He called for the restoration of Princes whose States had been annexed, and for the revival of village *panchayats*. He was particularly critical of the Christian missionaries whom he described as 'for the most part rash and ignorant men . . . with the scantiest knowledge of Hindoo society', and of the Government officials whose Christian zeal had been a cause of the Mutiny; he pointed out how unlikely it was in any case that British Rule could achieve a conversion which the Muhammaden conquerors had found it impossible to effect.[18] Pember presumably did not remain a Positivist, for in 1897 he was counsel for Cecil Rhodes before the Parliamentary Committee appointed to investigate the Jameson Raid.

The Positivists' philosophy caused them not only to advocate decolonisation but to rewrite colonial history. Thus Beesly in a chapter on 'England and the Sea' in *International Policy* maintained that Britain's cherished maritime supremacy was based on violence and injustice; the war with France of 1792 was caused by our monstrous claim to close the Rhine to commerce; and the shameless thirst for gain of the commercial classes had brought about the seizure of the colonies of our Dutch allies. Britain's claim to capture commercial vessels, he said, was resented by the rest of the world, and he proposed that Malta should be turned into an international police station.[19]

The most prolific of the Wadham Positivists was Frederic Harrison who wrote about Imperial questions for 50 years, and whose friendship with John Morley gave him access to influential periodicals such as the *Fortnightly Review* and the *Contemporary Review*. He opposed the Crimean War, and the Indian Mutiny, he said, aroused his ingrained enthusiasm for real nationalities; he likened the mutineers to Cromwell's Ironsides, as the élite yeomen of the rural areas, and expressed his disgust with English clergymen who demanded that every Hindu in the Army should be put to death. In 1866 he was a member of the Jamaica Committee which called for the trial of Governor Eyre. In 1867 he protested against the war with Abyssinia. He opposed the Afghan war of 1879–80, on which he wrote a pamphlet, attacking General Roberts for executing prisoners. He helped to form an anti-aggression league which included 36 M.P.s, though this fell to pieces when Gladstone's Government occupied Egypt. When Harrison visited Egypt he admired the benefits brought to the peasants by Cromer's administration, but pointed out the impossibility for a regenerated Egypt to be permanently governed by any Christian power. He lived not only to oppose the Boer War but to observe that it had resulted in South Africa becoming a solid Afrikaaner State. Harrison believed that the Oxford legacy of the study of the *Ethics* of Aristotle and the *Republic* of Plato could not be absorbed by a superior mind without leaving it a soil fertile of good thought: but for himself the influence of Comte was far more important; every other occupation was secondary to the teaching of Positivism.[20]

The other 'Mumbo', Bridges, like Congreve, had studied at Rugby where, his friends observed, 'he acquired the power of directing the most trivial subjects into lines which led to earnest and worthy discussion'.[21] When he resigned his Fellowship and left 'the dusty college rustiness which has been my bread and butter for the last four years',[22] he emigrated to Australia, but returned after the death of his wife to serve as medical adviser and inspector to the Poor Law Board. This allowed him time for writing. In his chapter on 'England and China' in *International Policy* he attacked the opium trade. Thoughout his life he was a vigorous foe of Imperialism. On Uganda he wrote in 1893 'The Positivists stand almost alone in our protest against the combination of Christianity and commerce to force western civilisation on negro tribes by Bibles and Maxim guns.'[23] In the Boer War he protested against the 'wholesale infanticide in concentration camps'.[24] He lived on to collaborate as earnestly as ever with a new generation of critics of Empire, among whom was L. T. Hobhouse who wrote of him 'he winced if subjects to him serious and important were treated lightly or dragged into drawing room conversation'.[25]

The influence of the Wadham Positivists in promoting anti-Imperialism perhaps deserves rather more attention than it has received. Their writings and teachings consistently followed Comte's dictum that international relations should be based on an acceptance of duties, not on an assertion of rights, and should have a moral, not a political, foundation. They rejected Sir Robert Peel's assertion in the House of Commons that the lower races must disappear in contact with the higher, as well as the Social Darwinists' concept of the inherent right of the white man to dominate over black. Distrusting national Governments, they were pioneers of the idea of international trusteeship. Because they were not in a formal sense Christians, their assumptions regarding the Christian civilising mission were very different to those of their contemporaries. As Congreve wrote in relation to the Ashantee War, 'Let the missionary go at his own work, take his life in hand and, if it so happen, perish in the cause';[26] it was not the duty of the Government to protect or avenge him. The Wadham Positivists were among the most gifted students and teachers of their generation. In the Oxford Union, of which Congreve, Beesly, Harrison and Bridges were officers, their influence was preponderant in the middle years of the century. In the history of Oxford they were a link between Goldwin Smith, who used to go picnicking with the young 'Mumbos', and the Oxford Liberals, centred on the *Manchester Guardian* under C. P. Scott, who were to join them in their old age in opposing the Boer War.

THE MANCHESTER GUARDIAN CIRCLE

In 1865 a Unitarian soap manufacturer wrote to Jowett for advice on admission to Oxford of his son C. P. Scott (1846–1932) who had been rejected by Queen's College and Christ Church because he had no certificate of baptism. There was no spare place at Balliol but Jowett passed Scott on to Corpus, where he found that whilst the dons were mostly 'Jowettites and freethinkers', those undergraduates who were interested in religion were High Church men and unsympathetic to a nonconformist. The Dean harrassed him over Chapel attendance and he felt coerced and bullied. He wrote home, 'With the whole influence of the place bearing against the opinions I hold, I am forced to define them to myself more clearly and to hold them more tightly.' He considered trying to move to Balliol, the most liberal College of all, but eventually came to terms with Corpus, rowing in the College Eight and obtaining a First in Greats. 'The very fact of being in a minority', he wrote to his parents, 'is so likely to awaken one's combativeness as to make one perhaps zealous for truths which are felt to be by others unjustly and hastily rejected.'[27]

Scott was to carry this zeal for minority causes into journalism, when shortly after leaving Oxford he became Editor of the *Manchester Guardian*, a post which he held for 57 years. He championed Irish Home Rule, opposed the Boer War and criticised Grey's foreign policies as likely to involve Britain unnecessarily in a world war. Under him the *Manchester Guardian* became not only the most respected liberal newspaper of the time, but acquired a great moral influence abroad, so that Nansen, for example, wrote to Scott in 1922 that the *Guardian*'s support would make all the difference between failure and success in his Russian relief operation.[28] Although Scott bought the ownership of the paper, he paid himself a modest salary and refused many offers of Honours. Whilst his contemporary editors became press Lords he continued to ride to his office on a bicycle. From 1895 to 1905 he was a Liberal Member of Parliament where with John Morley and with R. T. Reid, who had read Greats at Balliol, he opposed the Liberal Imperialists, led by Asquith and Grey, both of Balliol. Scott had a strong preference for Oxford men, especially those with Firsts in Greats, and assembled a remarkable group of them as his leader writers. Among them was L. T. Hobhouse (1864–1929), who came from a notable Liberal family, being a descendent of Byron's friend, the Radical M. P. John Cam Hobhouse, and brother of Emily Hobhouse who became famous for her exposure of the conditions in which Boer women and children were kept in concentration camps in the war. His uncle, Lord Hobhouse, a Balliol man whose life he wrote, resigned as Law Member of the Viceroy's Council in order to attack the Conservative forward policy in Afghanistan.

Leonard Hobhouse's father, a clergyman, distrusted the unorthodox atmosphere of Balliol, the family College, and sent him to Corpus where, after taking a First in Mods and Greats, he became a Fellow, and taught the *Ethics* of Aristotle. Hobhouse was influenced by Comte through Bridges, and his passions and conscience were profoundly stirred by the good and evil he discovered in current history. Barbara Hammond, whom he taught, observed that a pupil likely to do badly in the Schools but to whom the wrongs of the Armenians or Russian revolutionaries were real, was infinitely preferred to any brilliant scholar who cared for none of these things, Striding disgustedly through an Oxford which was in a reactionary and Imperialist phase, dressed in a homespun suit with a red tie, Hobhouse became restive and was glad to move to Manchester in 1897 when C. P. Scott, through Arthur Sidgwick, offered him a post with the *Guardian*. There the New Imperialism became his central theme. He wrote on China, India, Bechuanaland and Crete; his attacks on mortality in the concentration camps in South Africa, on the suspension of State Constitutions, and on the effects of the Government's native policies there, were considered by Morley as being among the most acute and powerful journalism of the time.[29]

Hobhouse moved to London in 1902 and became the first Professor of Sociology in Britain. His sociology was nourished on living history, and his book, *Democracy and Reaction* (1904), contained a trenchant attack on Imperialism. In the Transvaal, he said, the result of a campaign for equal rights for all civilised men had resulted in a despotism as absolute as that of Russia, in which any act or word supposed to bring Milner into contempt might be punished by five years' penal servitude, and under which Africans were flogged and refused their pay in the mines. More broadly he analysed the current literature of Imperialism as contemptuous of coloured races and scornful of the old liberal concept of opening to them the road to self-government. In India the tendency, he said, was to curtail measures of freedom already granted and to restrict opportunities which had been opened to Indians in the last generation of taking part in the government of the country. In short, he proclaimed, 'The central principle of Liberalism is self-government. The central principle of Imperialism is the subordination of self-government to Empire. The one stands for autonomy and the other for ascendancy.'[30]

It was this preoccupation with the iniquities of the Empire that led Hobhouse in 1899 to persuade Scott to send out to South Africa J. A. Hobson (1858–1940) whose well-known book on *Imperialism* was based on his observations as the *Manchester Guardian*'s Correspondent in South Africa. Hobson had read Mods and Greats at Lincoln College. These studies contributed, he considered, not a little towards the rationalism and humanism which he later strove to apply to economics. 'The contributions which Plato and Aristotle made to the permanent possessions of the human mind, what to feel and what to think about man's inner nature and his place in the universe and the methods of testing and achieving knowledge, were of immense service in liberating me from the easy acceptance of current ideas and feelings in an age rightly described as materialistic and narrowly utilitarian.'[31] Those who influenced him most at Oxford were Ruskin, Jowett and T. H. Green.

In South Africa Hobson observed 'the dominant power of a particularly crude form of Capitalism operating in a mixed political field, as well as the wildly exaggerated grievances of the Uitlanders'. In *Imperialism* he linked the rising struggle for Empire with the pressure for investment of surplus profits in the development of backward countries.[32] Lenin's tribute to this book, though qualified, made Hobson famous. Marxism however repelled him and he was unhappy in the Labour Party. He was an extension lecturer from Oxford and London, but neither University ever invited him to lecture on political economy which was his main interest.

Perhaps the most trusted of all Scott's Oxford men was J. L. Hammond (1872–1949) of St John's College, who would usually deputise for him whilst he was on holiday. Hammond and his wife Barbara are best known as social historians, but for some years J. L. Hammond edited the *Speaker*, a Liberal weekly set up to combat Jingoism, before returning to the *Guardian*. Hammond saw the great issue in politics at the turn of the century as between the Gladstonian principle of 'Public right as the common law of Europe' on the one hand, and on the other, both the '*civis romanus sum*' of Palmerston and the colonial expansionism of Chamberlain.[33]

Another of Scott's intimate friends was his son-in-law, C. E. Montague of Balliol (1867–1928) who did much of the leader writing whilst Scott was in Parliament. After the First World War Montague became one of the most elegant and influential writers about disillusionment with King, Country and Empire; in his book *Disenchantment* he bitterly attacked Andrew Lang, another Oxford man, for his praise of the romantic Imperialism of Haggard, Kipling and W. E. Henley.[34]

Almost inevitably in a team as serious minded as Scott's there was an old Rugbeian and grandson of Dr Arnold. This was W. T. Arnold (1852–1904) of University college, who was a lecturer and coach in Oxford before being recruited by Scott through Humphrey Ward. Arnold's great interest was in the Roman Empire and its provincial administration. So he would compare the chief princes of the Roman Empire with the protected rulers of India; and the abolition of suttee and juggernaut would remind him of the abolition by the Romans of the religion of the Druids. Arnold welcomed the colonisation and settlement by Britain of the waste places of the earth. He admired the I.C.S., but, even when British Rule was just, he considered that by depriving our fellow men of self-government we deprived them of their manhood. He was an ardent Home Ruler for Ireland and pro-Boer, whose test of nationality, he said, was the consciousness of it.[35]

GILBERT MURRAY

One of Hobhouse's closest friends at Oxford was the Australian Gilbert Murray (1866–1957) of St John's College, who was to become Regius Professor of Greek and the best-known Greek scholar of his time. Murray came from an Irish Catholic family which took pride in ancestors who had fought at the Battle of the Boyne and in 1798. The family, he recollected in his memoirs, were all Home Rulers who suspected British Governments of behaving elsewhere as they had behaved to the Catholics in Ireland, and championed the protection of animals, children, foreigners, heretics and unpopular minorities.

In his youth Murray attended Congreve's Positivist Church and found there, he said, a fairly clear explanation and justification of the moral law and the ultimate duty of man. He wrote several articles for the *Positivist Review* during the Boer War. Disappointed by the Imperialism of Oxford, Murray and Hobhouse as young men found a more congenial circle in their vacations at Castle Howard with the Carlisle family, where they all had very low opinions of Tories, Jingoes, Protectionism and anti-Suffragettes. Above all, at Castle Howard, Murray recollected, there were causes to work for – the protection of all who were or were likely to be oppressed – Russians Egyptians, subject nations and coloured races.[36]

In a book on Liberalism and the Empire published in 1900, in which he collaborated with J. L. Hammond, Murray brought his classical expertise to the anti-imperialist cause, comparing forced labour in Rhodesia with that in Ancient Greece. He rebuked Milner for the false analogy in the famous despatch in which he describe the Uitlanders as 'Helots'. The Helots in Greece, Murray pointed out, were in fact an indigenous primitive agricultural community held down by outlanders.[37] On a later occasion, addressing the Oxford

Indian Majlis Club, Murray spoke of himself as an Irish Nationalist who sympathised with Indian Nationalism and warned the Indian students to be on their guard against the flatteries of Englishmen.[38]

Murray's criticisms of Empire were effective because of their fairness. The greatest crimes and the greatest miseries, he told the Conference on Nationalities and Subject Races in 1910, had been inflicted by man upon the weakest and lowest peoples – the blacks in Australia, the New Hebrides, the Congo and the Camerouns, and the slaves in the West Indies; but these, he said, were the deeds of traders and adventurers; now, however, we sent out the best men we possessed as Governors and officials; such as his brother Sir Hubert Murray, a graduate of Magdalen College who was for many years Governor of New Guinea, and his lifelong friend from undergraduate days, Sir John Maynard, who in a regular correspondence over 30 years kept him informed of the point of view of the I.C.S.[39] Murray indeed believed that the British were the only people in the world who attempted to be really just towards inferior races; but he was haunted by the lessons of Greek history and the memory of how Athens had forsaken democracy, had become corrupted by Imperialism, and gone to its friendless doom. He feared that Britain too would be overcome by hubris. As he wrote in 1903 to his former pupil, John Buchan, who was working with Milner in South Africa –

> The consciousness of belonging to a very great nation with a high and peculiar task or destiny acts in two ways, first a sort of noblesse oblige; an Athenian or Englishman is bound in self respect to be in various ways better than his neighbours, worthy of his country; secondly there is a perversion of this. 'An Englishman never tells a lie'; 'an Englishman always likes fair play', which are really statements of ideals taken as statements of facts. Thirdly, I cannot help seeing in modern England as in ancient Athens a dangerous extension of this: an argument that because Englishmen are superior creatures therefore they should be allowed a little extra latitude.[40]

In his Address to the Conference on Nationalities and Subject Races he attacked his friend Rudyard Kipling and various writers in *Punch* for stirring up in the minds of hundreds of thousands of Englishmen a blind and savage contempt for the Bengali. 'Year after year', he said,

> clever natives of India come over to England at great sacrifice of money and trouble, to study at our universities and satisfy our tests

> for obtaining positions in their own countries. They compete with us well and with all the odds against them. And year after year they have found in our greatest newspapers caricatures of themselves – ridiculous baboos, cowardly, vain, untruthful, in every way absurd, talking bad and bombastic language. This is not fair play nor decent policy. You cannot govern the man and insult him too. This incessant girding at the Bengali, the most intellectual and progressive of the peoples of India, has an ugly look. It goes along with much irritable hostility to the Congress, to the students, to almost every Indian Society that professes high aims. If ever in a ruling race there creeps in a tendency to be jealous of its subjects, to keep them out of power, not because they are unfit, but because they are too obviously fit, such a tendency is disastrous to an Empire.[41]

Although Murray was generally recognised to be the most brilliant classical lecturer of his time, his openly expressed Home Rule and anti-Imperialist views, combined with his failure to support the cause of retaining compulsory Greek, so antagonised Conservative Oxford that in 1910, as he recalled, only New College, Balliol and Jesus continued to send pupils to his lectures; the absence of undergraduates from Christ Church, to which his Chair was attached, was particularly noticeable.[42]

OTHER CRITICS OF EMPIRE

There were other Oxford allies of the Positivists, who, like Murray, had been to some extent affected by their philosophy. John Morley (1838–1923), who had been at Lincoln College where he became an agnostic and left prematurely, was for a time a disciple of Comte, and, although he later criticised the Master, he remained close to Harrison and Congreve and opened the way to publication of their articles. One of the few Positivists to have a career in the Government of the Empire was Sydney Olivier (1859–1943) who read Classics at Corpus; his fellow Fabian, George Bernard Shaw, considered that it was his Huguenot ancestry rather than his Positivism which gave Olivier the invaluable power of taking an objective view of his employer, the Colonial Office.[43] Although Olivier had a distinguished career in the Colonial Office, as Governor of Jamaica, and as Secretary of State for India in the first Labour Government, he is perhaps most likely to be remembered for his books and articles which championed the qualities of people of mixed blood in the West Indies and in India at a time when they had few friends. In Eric Williams's savage attack on the Oxford historians who wrote on the West Indies Olivier's enlightened views on race make him the shining exception.[44]

One of the few anti-Imperialists who remained in Oxford during the High Imperial period was the Fabian, Sydney Ball, Fellow of St John's, who would often remark that Imperialism was the last refuge of a scoundrel.[45] Arthur Sidgwick of Corpus, President of the Oxford Liberal Association for 28 politically unsuccessful years, was another member of both the Positivist and *Manchester Guardian* groups. The position of James Bryce is more difficult to define. He was a leading Home Ruler, but, as was seen in the previous chapter, was also the first President of the Oxford branch of the Imperial Federation League. He opposed the Boer War and regretted the deep-rooted feelings about colour which gave the British Empire such a different character from that of Rome. The *Oxford Magazine* used to tease him as believing in an 'Unholy British Empire'. But he should perhaps be regarded as an observer and critic of institutions rather than as an anti-Imperialist.

THE CRITICS AFTER 1918

In the period after the First World War Imperialism began to be on the defensive and it became fashionable in the Round Table and in the Ralegh Club to speak of Commonwealth rather than Empire. Yet there remained the two great problems identified by Coupland in his Inaugural Lecture in 1921 – nationality and colour.[46] Murray, in an Introduction to Norman Leys's book on Kenya in 1924, described the problem of race 'as presenting a violent and bloody challenge, which we must needs master, or it will master us'. He saw the doctrine of Article 22 of the League Covenant on mandates as presenting a basis for solving the problem, but admitted that most English people accepted the doctrine 'with the same mental reservations such as they are in the habit of applying to all fine language, whether in political programmes or sermons or the New Testament'.[47]

There were still causes to be fought for by the Oxford anti-Imperialists therefore in the period between the First and Second

World Wars. The role of critics of Empire was largely taken over by members of the Labour Party from the declining Liberals. One of the most influential critics within the Labour Party was Leonard Barnes who was typical of many of the last generation of anti-Imperialists in that he had utterly lost confidence in established authority whilst serving in the First World War. 'Never believe anything until it has been denied' became his motto.

Returning to University College Oxford in 1918 to read Mods and Greats, he was fascinated by the contrast to life in the trenches of one in which consecutive lectures were devoted to 'The Nature of Truth', 'The Theory of Beauty' and 'The Meaning of Meaning'. From his tutor E. F. Carritt he learnt that the prime essential in life was to grasp the ideas which you are minded to oppose. 'My time at Oxford', he wrote in his unpublished memoirs, 'was basically concerned with one particular phase of my life-long search for wholesome and efficacious ways of using one's mental powers. The worst obstacle was the terrifying power of the establishment.' His classical studies at Oxford, particularly of Plato and Thucydides, confirmed him in his hatred of what he called 'the schoolmaster sophist', his symbol of authority.[48]

After graduating he worked in the Colonial Office for several years before resigning to take up farming in South Africa. On learning that the land cleared for ex-servicemen had been forcibly stolen from Zulus, he disposed of his farm to become a journalist and a trenchant critic of the South African Government's native policies. Contact with Afrikaanerdom convinced him that the great enemy of the human cause was racism. He compared its moral corruption with that of the Athenians after the destruction of Melos, as described by Euripides. He broadened his attacks to include the British Empire in several books published in the 1930s, when he returned to Britain. Among his targets was the type of colonial administrator recruited mainly from Oxford and Cambridge, of good intelligence and general ability but ill-equipped to deal with the complex problems of race, culture contact, applied anthropology, economics, politics and administration. In contrast to the French these Oxbridge officials, he said, were far better at getting on with tribal folk than with the rising intelligentsia.[49]

Barnes in 1939 called for a colonial Magna Carta providing for compulsory free education, freedom of speech, movement and association, and a minimum level of labour and social legislation in the colonies. India, Burma and Ceylon, he urged, should be given independence and the other colonies internationalised.[50] He played an important part in the Imperial Policy Committee of the Labour Party. By the time he returned to Oxford as Director of the Oxford Delegacy of Social Training in 1947 much of what he had advocated was being implemented under a Labour Government. Instead of resting on his not inconsiderable contributions to decolonisation, he wrote sadly of the corruption and maladministration in the new African States and embarked on one more crusade, against the pollution of the environment.[51]

A close associate of Barnes was W. M. MacMillan (1885–1974) who had been one of the first South African Rhodes Scholars. From 1917 to 1934 he was Professor of History at Witwatersrand, where his historical researches resulted in a new interpretation of South African frontier policies which was favourable to the missionaries who had championed native interests. His enquiries into contemporary economic questions then caused him to enter into a spirited correspondence with Oswald Pirow, Minister of Native Affairs, about Pass Laws and control of squatters. When rebuked by the Minister as a negrophilist, prig and crank, he appealed to the right given to the subject by the British Bill of Rights to petition the King and his Ministers. Government pressure was put on the University to curb him and though it did not do so, he left for England where Curtis arranged for him to be an Associate Fellow of All Souls.

From there between 1936 and 1939 with Barnes, Winifred Holtby and others, MacMillan constituted a group which was concerned to prevent the cession of Bechuanaland, Swaziland and Basutoland to South Africa, the extension of discriminatory legislation from South Africa to Rhodesia, and land demarcation unfavourable to Africans in Kenya. On the first issue he parted with Curtis. Encouraged by Olivier he also turned his attention to the West Indies where he urged the planned control of economic and social development.

MacMillan's activities as a journalist and propagandist probably prevented him from being appointed to a Chair in Britain though in his later days he became Director of Colonial Studies at Aberdeen University. His immediate political influence in South Africa was small at a time when the current was moving strongly in a contrary direction. In Britain, however, it was considerable, particularly in helping to bring about a positive attitude towards colonial development and in checking the extension of South African discriminatory racial policies to British colonies. The Oxford connection was important through the network of Rhodes Scholars and of the Round Table, with which he had an ambivalent relationship; it also facilitated access to the Colonial Office, particularly when Malcolm MacDonald was Secretary of State. Oxford made MacMillan an Honorary D. Litt. in 1957.[52]

A more effective anti-Imperialist than any of his colleagues in the Labour Party was, Barnes considered, R. Palme Dutt of the Communist Party. Palme Dutt a Balliol man, was half Swedish, half Bengali. He was Editor of the *Daily Worker* and author of a polemical Marxist analysis of British Rule in India. He was a frequent lecturer to the Oxford University Labour Club and largely responsible for its interest in and commitment to Indian independence in the late thirties. A number of the Club's members of this generation became Members of the Parliament of 1945 which gave independence to India, Pakistan, Burma and Ceylon.

Last in the line of Oxford critics of Empire was Thomas Hodgkin. Hodgkin came from a Quaker family and read Classics at Balliol. After working as an archaeologist, he joined the colonial administration in Palestine, from which he resigned and was expelled from the country. He subsequently organised Oxford's extra-mural work in West Africa. In Oxford in the fifties he was teaching and writing about African Nationalism when few other teachers knew or cared about it. What was the purpose, he asked in 1956, of discussing how you ought to administer territories when the day after tomorrow you would cease to administer them? It was necessary, he urged, to study African political institutions in precisely the same way as British, French or American institutions were studied.[53]

The granting of Independence to Burma in 1946 and to India in 1947 under a Labour Government, headed by C. R. Attlee, an Oxford man, led on inevitably to a general process of decolonisation. Though they still were occasionally involved in debates on the future of Kenya and Central Africa, the critics of Empire could fold up their tents or move over to different causes: the eradication of poverty in the Third World and the protection of the environment.

In conclusion, some characteristics of the Oxford critics of Empire may be noted. Most of them had read Classics and it will have been seen how often they illustrated their arguments by reference to the history of Greece and Rome. A high proportion of them were nonconformists or agnostics, although, as will be seen in Chapter 9, there were also trenchant critics of Empire among both Anglo-Catholic and evangelical missionaries from Oxford.

Of the Colleges, Balliol and Corpus as the most liberal were most likely to produce anti-Imperialists. Wadham at the time of the conversion of the Positivists was an evangelical College. St John's, though generally conservative, produced some anti-Imperialist pupils of Sydney Ball. Coming from Rugby School to Oxford, a number of Dr Arnold's pupils in various Colleges found an outlet for their earnestness in the cause. In general – with the exception of the eccentric Goldwin Smith – the Oxford critics of Empire were also in favour of Home Rule for Ireland. It was not only because of ideology that the anti-Imperialists were numerically weak in the high Imperial period. The Empire brought to Oxford the substantial benefactions of Rhodes, Beit, Sir Abe Bailey and others. It also provided jobs for pupils with no clear vocation.

The impact of the Oxford anti-Imperialists is not easy to assess. Whatever influence Goldwin Smith had in the 1860s, he had little later. He was, as he said, the last member of the Manchester School. Positivism as an organised Church or group had virtually disappeared when Frederic Harrison died in 1923 at the age of 93. A movement whose members divided the calendar into 13 months, each named after great men such as Caesar and Archimedes; whose festivals commemorated both the Virgin Mother and the Post Office, and whose temples were built to face Paris as the home of the High Priest of Humanity, eventually provided too rich a diet to be sustained by British intellectuals. When Harrison's ashes were deposited in Wadham Chapel, Gilbert Murray was somewhat incongruously harnessed with Lord Birkenhead to give an Obituary Address. He stated with the stoic frankness of a humanist that all the main causes for which Harrison fought had been lost in his lifetime. But, he concluded, 'The others for whom we live need not be those that we see, try to help and perhaps utterly fail to help. A good life serves always something greater than it knows'.[54] In this sense the Positivists made a not insignificant contribution to the ideas of international trusteeship, and ultimately to peaceful and voluntary relinquishment of colonial rule.

The group of Oxford men with Firsts in classics, many of them conscious heirs of the Positivists, who worked or wrote for the *Manchester Guardian* were as brilliant as Geoffrey Dawson and his Oxford friends who wrote about Empire for *The Times*. When the dust settles it may appear that their work was in its different way as important as that of Curtis and the Round Tablers in helping to bring about the transformation of the Empire into a loose association of fully independent States.

Part II
A Great Imperial University?

6 Benares on the Isis – Indian Studies and the Indian Institute

The Indian Institute will, we hope and believe, like the sacred Indian fig tree, send many fresh stems downwards: . . . Oxford should thus constitute herself the Benares of the Isis.
Daily Telegraph, Editorial article (2 May 1883)

EARLY LINKS WITH INDIA

When the Canadian George Parkin, as first Organising Secretary of the Rhodes Scholarships, exhorted Oxford to rise to its responsibilities as 'a great Imperial University', there was already a long history of association with Britain's Indian Empire, going back to the time of the East India Company. Hamayun Kabir, returning in 1960 as Indian Minister of Culture to give the Marett Lecture at his old University, described Oxford as 'the most important single factor in bringing Britain and India nearer to each other in the field of knowledge over a period of two centuries'.[1] There was perhaps some courteous exaggeration in this. Of the early links with Oxford cited by Kabir, Father Thomas Stephens of New College, 'the first Englishman in India', is a shadowy figure; for College authorities in Elizabethan Oxford were reluctant to record Jesuit priests among their alumni. Stephens went from Oxford to Rome, where he became a priest, and from Rome to Goa in 1579. He stayed in India for the remaining 30 years of his life and is best remembered for the epic poem which he wrote in Mahratti to convey the lessons of the Old and New Testaments.[2]

The evidence of Oxford's connection with India becomes firmer in the next century when two Oxford graduates who became chaplains to the East India Company wrote books about their travels. Edward Terry of Christ Church accompanied Thomas Roe, himself an Oxford man, when he visited the Mogul Emperor Jehangir on an Embassy from King James I in 1617. The modest Introduction to Terry's *Voyage to East India* published in 1655 might profitably have been heeded by future Oxford travellers who wrote about India —

> There never was an age more guilty than this present of the great expense and waste of paper: whose fair innocence hath been extremely slubbered by errors, heresies and blasphemies and what-not, in these bold times. Certainly there hath been of late abundantly more printed than ought, and if what follows in this discourse lay under the guilt of any such exceptions, it should feel the fire, not the press.[3]

Terry may have had in mind his contemporary Henry Lord of Magdalen Hall, who was chaplain of the English factory at Surat in 1624, where he learned Hindustani and Persian, and on his return published in 1636 a book called *Discovery of Two Foreign Sects in the East Indies*, a not very accurate account of religions and customs. For whilst Terry attempted to describe faithfully the societies which he encountered, Lord's observations of the Banians and Parsees were intended to show 'How Sathan leadeth those who are out of the pale of the Church around in the maze of errour' and 'to beget in good Christians the greater detestation of these heresies and the more abundant thanksgiving of our calling'.[4]

These travellers' tales were isolated individual contributions. Oxford's connection with India may more seriously be reckoned from the work of Sir William Jones, who has two memorials. That in University College massively shows him translating or codifying the Laws of Hindus and Muslims; in the Church of St Mary the Virgin a more modest memorial, ambiguously surmounted by what may either be an Oxford ox or a Brahmini bull, is placed immediately under a boss depicting Mahatma Gandhi, who did more than anyone to bring the Indian Empire to an end.

Jones, who lived from 1747 to 1794, had the broad interests of the Age of Enlightenment; whilst an undergraduate at University College he brought in a Syrian to share his rooms and teach him Arabic, and he used manuscripts in the Bodleian to study Persian. In London he became a friend of Johnson and Burke and a member of 'The Club'. He went out to India as a Judge of the Supreme Court with the objects of studying Sanskrit and of saving enough money to be able to devote his life to scholarship. In his 11 years in India he saved £50,000 but died just as he was about to re-embark for England. His range of interests in India could only have been attempted by a man of his time. He made digests of both Hindu and Muslim law. He investigated Indian botany, astrology and music. His greatest achievement was to demonstrate the genetic relationship of Sanskrit to the major European languages. It would be hard to overestimate the importance of this for the Indian cultural renaissance and for the future of Oriental Studies in Oxford and elsewhere.[5]

One of Jones's Oxford friends was Nathaniel Halhed (1751–1830) of Christ Church, whom he persuaded to learn Arabic. Jilted by a girl who married R. B. Sheridan instead, Halhed went out to Calcutta as a writer in the East India Company where he published the first grammar in the Bengali language in 1778.[6]

THE BODEN CHAIR OF SANSKRIT

In the early nineteenth century the evangelicals, having achieved the abolition of the slave trade, turned to the conversion of India to Christianity as the next great cause. In 1813 the East India Company was obliged by Parliament in its renewed Charter to admit missionaries to its territories. In Oxford prizes were offered for essays on the best refutation of Hinduism. It was in this context that Colonel Boden of the East India Company endowed a Chair of Sanskrit in 1832 with an annual stipend of £1000 a year and tenable for life, 'being of opinion that a more general and critical knowledge of that language will be a means of enabling my countrymen to proceed in the conversion of the natives of India to the Christian religion, by disseminating a knowledge of the Sacred Scriptures amongst them more effectually than all other means together'.[7] The early elections for the Boden Chair took place in an unusual manner. The electors were the members of Convocation, that is, all the M.A.s of the University, whether in residence or not; in order to enable applications to be received from India, nine months' notice of election was given, thus opening the way to a long period of campaigning and lobbying. This was the first Chair of Sanskrit to be established in Britain, and the stipend was larger than that of any other professorial post in Oxford. The competition therefore was keen, and the first two elections were fiercely contested on the question of whether it was more important to elect the best Sanskrit scholar or the candidate who was most likely to aid in the diffusion of Christianity in India.

In the first election in 1832 the two main protagonists were Horace Hayman Wilson, Secretary of the Royal Asiatic Society in Calcutta, and Revd W. H. Mill, Principal of Bishops College, Calcutta. There was no question that Wilson was a far more distinguished scholar than Mill. His opponents, however, maintained that he was irreligious; and although Wilson was able to produce a letter from the Bishop of Calcutta supporting both candidates, they circulated a letter alleging that he had seven or eight illegitimate children, a contention indignantly denied by his supporters, who only admitted that there were two.[8] Wilson defeated Mill by 208 votes to 200, to the great benefit of the University. In a different way he was as versatile as Jones. Whilst he was qualifying as a surgeon, he had spent some of his leisure hours with an uncle who worked in the Government Mint in London. Although he went out to India as an Assistant Surgeon of the East India Company, he was soon appointed as Assay Master of the Mint in Calcutta, a post which gave him leisure to study Sanskrit, 'excited', as he said, by the example and biography of Sir William Jones'.[9] He was Secretary of the Asiatic Society of Bengal, which had been founded by Jones, and published the first Sanskrit–English dictionary. He served for a time as Secretary of Public Instruction and introduced European science and literature into the curriculum of schools whose programmes had hitherto been confined to the qualifications needed by Indian clerks. Nevertheless he maintained that India's improvement would come from a renewed and vigorous study of her own learning; and at the time he left India he was a leader of the Orientalist Party in their losing battle against the Anglicists, Macaulay and Trevelyan, over whether Government funds should be devoted to education in the English or local languages.[10]

Wilson's zest for occupying several posts at once continued on his return to England. In addition to holding the Boden Professorship, he was simultaneously librarian to the East India Company and Director of the Royal Asiatic Society. He crammed the 42 University lectures, which he was obliged to deliver annually, into nine weeks of the year. Nevertheless he firmly established Sanskrit studies in Oxford not only by his publications but by laying the foundations of Oxford's collection of Sanskrit manuscripts. He also caused the Clarendon Press to set up a Devanagari type, and he brought Max Mueller to Oxford to work with the Press on his edition of the *Rig Veda*.

On Wilson's death in 1860 a celebrated and uninhibited contest for the Boden Chair of Sanskrit took place between two of his pupils, Max Mueller, broadly supported by the Liberals and reformers, and Monier Williams, supported by the Conservatives. *The Times* commented that whilst Monier Williams was a competent Sanskrit scholar, Max Mueller was 'simply the greatest scholar alive.'[11] The protagonists of Max Mueller spread rumours that Monier Williams did not understand Sanskrit; Monier William's supporters on the other hand suggested that Max Mueller's nomination was part of a plan of the Prince Consort to 'place a whole array of German professors, spectacles on nose and pipe in mouth, in possession of our cloisters'.[12] This proved an effective argument with the Tory country clergy, to whom German scholarship was identified with questioning the Divine inspiration of the Bible, and their vote carried the day for Monier Williams by 833 votes to 610. The consequence was a tragedy for Indian Studies at Oxford. Max Mueller, bitterly wounded, turned from Sanskrit to Philology and Comparative Religion. His contribution to these fields was great: but his enmity to Monier Williams was to encompass the Indian Institute.

MAX MUELLER AND MONIER WILLIAMS

Max Mueller and Monier Williams were the dominant figures in Indian Studies in Oxford in the second half of the nineteenth century. They were almost exact contemporaries. Friedrich Max Mueller (1823–1900) was the son of a court librarian and poet in Dessau, Germany. He studied Sanskrit in Berlin and Paris. Wilson then persuaded the East India Company to finance, and the Clarendon Press to publish, Max Mueller's edition of the *Rig Veda*. He came to Oxford to supervise this work in 1848 and never left. He lectured on Modern Languages and Comparative Philology, was naturalised and became a Fellow of All Souls. After his defeat in the election for the Boden Professorship, a Chair in Comparative Philology was created for him by the University.

Max Mueller's influence went far beyond Oxford. He did much to establish Sanskrit as a third classical language. He introduced both the study of Comparative Philology and of Comparative Religion in Britain. He was a frequent lecturer to the British Royal Family at Windsor. A thousand copies of his lectures would be sold on the day of publication. He was in fact a brilliant populariser who made the study of the origins of languages and religions fashionable. He enjoyed the honours and decorations which he received from all over the world, and would refer to Kaiser Wilhelm II of Germany, who used to send him a congratulatory telegram whenever Oxford won the boat race, as 'my favourite Emperor'. Oxford even believed that Mrs Max Mueller had received from the Sultan of Turkey the Order of Chastity (Third Class).

Max Mueller was a Lutheran and uninvolved in the controversies within the Church of England. One of his main achievements was to persuade O.U.P. to publish at the expense of the India Office a series of Sacred Books of the East. Because of his oecumenical philosophy he had to defend himself against charges of being lukewarm to missionaries; in doing so he argued that it was necessary for Christians to study other religions in order to understand their own. He also proposed that the University give financial support to missionaries who would serve as correspondents or 'Cultural Vice-Consuls'.[13] He never altogether shook off the suspicions of Oxford High Churchmen; the *Oxford Magazine* in 1892 commented that he preferred to lecture on religion in Scotland rather than in Oxford 'where orthodoxy lay in ambush for him'.[14] This was hardly surprising, for he maintained that 'there has yet been no religion in the world which the Priests, the Brahmans, the Shaimans, the Bonzes, the Lamas, the Pharisees and the Scribes have not corrupted and destroyed'.[15]

In India, which he never visited, Max Mueller was held in high respect, particularly for his defence of the Indian character in his book *India – What Can It Teach Us*, though there were many in Oxford who agreed with an anonymous protest in the *Oxford Magazine* that 'As Oxford men we should be much more interested in what we can teach India than in what India can teach us.'[16] Indians also admired his enthusiastic assertion that Anglo-Saxons, Teutons and Indians were all members of the 'Aryan race', though by race it was not altogether clear whether he meant common ancestry or common language. This assertion was to have curious consequences; it was used by Imperialists to justify British Rule in India as a 'family reunion', that is a return of the more vigorous branch of the Aryan family to govern the branch whose energies had been sapped by an unfavourable climate. The achievements of the Aryans also came to be contrasted with the backwardness of other races in the Empire, particularly the Africans.[17]

Max Mueller had many Indian friends, including members of the Tagore family and of the Brahmo Samaj. He was not enthusiastic, however, about the increasing number of Indians who came to study in Oxford in the 1880s. He considered that they often went home with inappropriate and Anglicised values. He cared more for the fostering of an Indian renaissance and wrote 'By encouraging a study of their own ancient literature, as part of their education, a natural feeling of pride and self respect will be reawakened. Among those who influence large masses of people a new national literature may spring up, impregnated with Western ideas, yet retaining its native spirit and character.'[18] Oxford's role as he saw it, rather than shaping Indian students to the model of English Public School gentlemen, was to train Englishmen to go out to India and help in the creation of Indian institutions. To do this he continually argued for the strengthening of the study of Indian languages, neglect of which he regarded as an important factor in the Indian Mutiny of 1857.

Overshadowed by Max Mueller, the reputation of Monier Williams (1819–99) has not stood high in recent years. His unpublished memoirs are the portrait of a nervous, unhappy man, who felt his life to have been dogged by misfortune, and whose achievements were the result of 'plodding perseverence'.[19] He was born in Bombay where his father was Surveyor General, but returned to England as a child when his father died. Because of poor health he was educated privately. Entering Balliol he felt the social disadvantage of not coming from a Public School, as well as the practical handicap of being disqualified for scholarships which were mostly reserved for men born in Britain. Feeling no vocation for the Church, for which his family intended him, he left Balliol before taking a degree in order to enter Haileybury College and be prepared for service with the East India Company. His brother's death in action in India however caused him for family reasons to decide to remain in England. He returned to Oxford but Balliol would not take him back. At University College he read Classics but continued the Sanskrit Studies which he had commenced at Haileybury. He overworked and obtained a double Fourth Class degree.

He went back to Haileybury as Professor of Sanskrit. When Haileybury closed, the Boden Professorship of Sanskrit was a providential opening, and he admitted to spending £1000 on the election. At the victory dinner which was held at University College Monier Williams said that 'I had not prayed for success but only that the will of God be done, and that whether Mr Max Mueller or I myself were chosen, the choice might make for the promotion of the glory of the great dispenser of human events.'[20]

Disgusted by the manner of his defeat and by this apparent sanctimoniousness, Max Mueller, normally an open and genial character, was never reconciled. Writing in 1895, Monier Williams noted that for the past 35 years they had not been invited to the same dinner party. 'The irreconcilability and implacable hostility of a man of great power and influence . . . was to be a thorn in the flesh during my whole Oxford career; it was a serious hindrance to the carrying out of every important work which I tried to accomplish.'[21]

A visitor to Oxford may be puzzled at the origin of a large building at the corner of Broad Street, whose outside walls are decorated with tigers and Hindu gods, surmounted by a golden elephant, whose apparent function is to indicate which way the wind is blowing, though it lamentably failed to do so. This was Monier Williams's Indian Institute, to the establishment of which, together with that of an Honours School of Oriental Languages, he devoted the best part of 20 years.

Monier Williams was concerned by the fact that the probationers of the I.C.S. spent a year or two after their selection studying languages without supervision, mostly in London but occasionally in Oxford. In 1875 he persuaded Congregation to pass three Resolutions: first, that arrangements should be made for I.C.S. probationers to reside at the University; second, that University teachers should be appointed in certain branches of training required by them: and third, that the B.A. degree should be brought within their reach.

These Resolutions were eventually implemented. Jowett offered every candidate who passed the I.C.S. Examination a place at Balliol, where by 1884 half of the probationers in the whole country were studying. In 1886 the University established a degree course in Oriental Studies, one of whose options was Indian Studies, which it was hoped that missionaries and others contemplating Indian careers would take as an alternative to classical Greats. Until this course was established, as Monier Williams pointed out, an undergraduate who interested himself in Oriental Studies was likely to imperil his place in the classical class list, and his prospects in life.[22]

There was, however, a further problem; that of the Indian students who in the 1870s began to come to England in considerable numbers, mostly studying without supervision. Of those in Oxford about half had no College attachments. Monier Williams declared that no young

Indian was fit to stand alone; cast adrift during six months of vacation, the Indian students would return to India deteriorated in character rather than improved.[23]

THE INDIAN INSTITUTE

The Indian Institute which he planned in Oxford was intended to provide a centre for union and intercourse for all engaged in Indian and Oriental Studies. It would restore among the I.C.S. probationers the old *esprit de corps* of the East India Company's College at Haileybury and would promote the welfare of Indians at Oxford. The Institute should, he said, have two wings: one would teach Europeans about India, and the other would further studies of the West by Indians.[24] But his imagination did not stop there. He saw it as the University's duty to instil some general knowledge of India into its ordinary students, reading other subjects, some of whom would one day exercise supreme control over the destinies of India in Parliament, at a time when about a quarter of the members of the House of Commons and perhaps a higher proportion of the House of Lords were Oxford men.[25]

The Institute was intended to have lecture rooms, staff rooms, a library and museum and accommodation for Indian students and visitors. In 1875 and 1876 Monier Williams travelled in India obtaining official support, money and gifts for the library and the museum from the Government, from princely rulers and businessmen. He was strongly supported by Jowett both in the creation of the Indian Institute and in that of the degree course in Oriental Studies. Initially indeed it was planned that the Institute should have been part of Balliol College.[26] It might have had a better chance of development had it been so; however at the time Jowett had incurred unpopularity for attaching too many of the staff appointed by the University to Balliol, and when he became Vice-Chancellor he found it more prudent to establish the Institute as a University institution. Jowett was sometimes, but not always successful in restraining Max Mueller's attacks on Monier Williams's projects.[27]

In 1880 Convocation approved the plan for an Indian Institute and granted a site in the Parks; there was so much subsequent opposition to building in the Parks, however, that a site in Broad Street was obtained instead. The Queen and the Prince of Wales headed the subscription list along with Maharajahs and Bishops. In Oxford not everyone who was approached subscribed. Freeman replied that he was not interested in anything east of Trebizond. Ruskin wrote 'I energetically dissent from the proposition unless accompanied by proposals to found an Athenian Institute, Roman Institute and Italian, German, French and Spanish Institutes. Oxford, as I understand its position, has to educate English gentlemen in the elements of noble human knowledge – not to prepare them for clerks in foreign counting houses.'[28]

Max Mueller circulated a flyleaf to Congregation urging that the funds which had been collected for the Institute should be spent on research and fellowships rather than buildings. It was a great mistake, he said, to imagine that orientals care for show and display only. He suggested that modest premises could be found on existing University property.[29] Privately he was caustic. 'What all the Indians say', he wrote later, 'is that the rich Oxford University went round with a hat, promised to help Indian students, and all the money they subscribed in India was spent on bricks and stuffed animals.'[30]

The foundation stone was laid in 1883 by the Prince of Wales. When the Institute was opened, Jowett, as Vice-Chancellor, described the Institute as 'a sign of mutual interest and affection between Oxford and India for many centuries'. We could only safely govern India if we knew it, he said, 'there was a great debt which England and Europe owed to India, though it might be one to be paid in the far distance'.[31]

The Institute started work in temporary premises; completion of the building was delayed until 13 years later, when the Maharajah of Gondal provided the additional money required. At the formal opening in 1896 Lord George Hamilton, the Secretary of State for India, expressed qualms that the I.C.S., which was so admirably performing its work, was not increasing in popularity on the scene of its labours. The Institute could constantly remind the I.C.S. probationers, he said, of the great Indian civilisations; that when their ancestors were unclothed savages there was a literature and architecture in India well worthy of being preserved; and that there was a need for closer and more sympathetic relations between English and Indian peoples.[32]

Monier Williams by now was an old man who had long since turned over his teaching duties to a deputy. His hope that the Institute would be residential and provide accommodation for the non-collegiate Indians in Oxford had not been fulfilled. Even more grievous was the fact that whereas he had obtained a promise from the Viceroy that the Government of India would provide six scholarships annually to Oxford from the Indian Universities, this had been overruled by the Secretary for India, who was not prepared to favour Oxford more than any other British University. At the opening ceremony he lamented the lack of money for research or for paying salaries to staff.

In his last years he became more evangelical, and gave several Addresses to missionary societies attacking the 'limp jellyfish tolerance of other religions' and in particular Max Mueller's project of the publication of the Sacred Books of the East by O.U.P. Every library, he said, 'teems with infidel publications; false criticism and carping scepticism are in the air. The divine purpose has entrusted India to Britain's care not for the increase of our trade or wealth or imperial prestige but so that the Gospel message might be presented to them in their own vernacular language.'[33]

Monier Williams had been knighted in 1886, becoming Sir Monier Monier Williams. Max Mueller by contrast refused a knighthood but became a Privy Councillor, and thus Right Honourable – a very rare prefix for an academic who was never in Parliament. When Monier Williams planned his first visit to India he asked the University to give him a Doctorate of Civil Law, in order that his pleas for contributions to the Indian Institute should carry more weight. This scandalised Bryce, the Professor of Jurisprudence; Max Mueller added to the unfavourable publicity by threatening to resign his Chair and leave Oxford if Monier Williams were given the Doctorate.

Cornelia Sorabji when she met Monier Williams in 1890 found him 'soured, discontented and austere' in contrast to the 'genial and delightful' Max Mueller. 'There could be no more opposed natures than these two great oriental scholars, the one imaginative, friendly, poetic, romantic; the other melancholy, shrivelled up, cynical, discontented and uninteresting. They might have stood for pendants of success and failure.' Later, however, when she dined with Monier Williams he told her of the woes of his life at Oxford and persuaded her that Oxford had treated him shamefully. 'He only wants someone to appreciate him, poor old man', she concluded.[34]

Monier Williams's second great object, an Honour School of Oriental Studies, came into existence in 1886, with two divisions, one of Semitic Studies, and one of Indian Studies. That of Indian Studies, however, came to an end in Monier Williams's own lifetime, after a change in the age limits of the I.C.S. made it no longer possible for the I.C.S. probationers, who were practically the only people to take the degree in Indian Studies, to stay in Oxford for more than a year.

Ten years after Monier Williams' death, when Lord Curzon visited the Institute as Chancellor of the University in 1909, his report was scathing. The social gatherings which were among the purpose of the Institute, he said, had fallen into disuse: even more regrettable was the disappearance of lectures by writers and public men who knew India. The whole concept of the founders, he considered, was too grandiose in relation to the funds available from the University, the Secretary of State and the Boden Fund. As for the museum, it was of no service whatever to education and equally useless to art and science. 'That the collection is visited annually by more women than men', he concluded 'is a sufficient condemnation of its retention here.'[35]

Despite Lord Curzon's severe observations, the Curators of the Institute remained too courteous to refuse a steady flow of gifts, often presented by former proconsuls and their widows as they moved into modest retirement homes. To receive a bust of H. H. Wilson and a miniature of Sir William Jones was gratifying, but some embarrassment may have been felt at the arrival of an alabaster model of the Taj Mahal and another of Calcutta Cathedral; or of a carved board for the game called Pallangui, with shells and printed instructions; or even the watercolours of Lady Markby.[36]

The fine art objects in the museum were eventually transferred to the Ashmolean Museum. The Pitt Rivers Museum, however, had no room for the models illustrating crafts and anthropology. The stuffed animals decayed. The library, used mainly by I.C.S. probationers, came under the control of the Bodleian in 1927. The rest of the rooms were used by the Boden Professor of Sanskrit and by those who lectured to the I.C.S.

INDIAN HISTORY

The Institute might have been more successful if the teaching of Indian History at Oxford with which it was associated had been more scholarly and imaginative. The first Reader of Indian History was Sidney Owen, who had spent two years as Professor of History at Elphinstone College, Bombay. He held the Readerhip for 48 years from 1864, and for a time combined it with that of Indian Law. The

Reader was by Statute required only to lecture on the History of British Rule and not on the earlier History of India. Owen believed that British Rule would provide the framework for the evangelisation of India, just as Roman Government and Greek philosophy had provided the means of converting the ancient world to Christianity.[37] He regarded education not as an intellectual but a moral process. When he was imparting knowledge he seemed always to be at a white heat, and the torrent of his eloquence at times reduced his hearers almost to stupefaction.[38] In his book, *India on the Eve of the British Conquest*, he frankly admitted that he had used no original sources, but this did not prevent him from generalising about 'the moral turpitude of most of the prominent personages that occupy these sheets'.[39] Wisely, in later years he concentrated on editing the despatches of the Indian Governor-General Lord Wellesley and of his brother the Duke of Wellington's Indian campaigns, which became established as set textbooks.

Owen's successor as Reader in Indian History, Revd W. H. Hutton, a Fellow and History tutor of St John's, was a prolific writer of biographies and textbooks but before his appointment had no special interest in India. In his Inaugural Lecture he deplored the fact that under the Statutes the Reader was required to teach only about British Rule in India. He recollected that Stubbs in 1876 had called for the appointment of a Professor of Indian History who could take a broader view; he pointed out the need for the University to provide teaching in Indian literature, philosophy, geography and archaeology in view of her Imperial responsibilities.[40] He also made a plea for the training of, and cooperation with, Indian historians. Hutton's tenure of the Readership, however, was only from 1913 to 1920, which included the lost war years, and for most of this time he was simultaneously Archdeacon of Peterborough or Dean of Winchester; thus he had no chance to set a new tradition. Instead the posts in Indian History now became a perquisite of the I.C.S.

Vincent Smith, who retired from the I.C.S. in 1900 and deputised for the aged Owen, but failed to obtain the Readership, had serious qualifications. Whilst in the Service he had published articles on the coinage of the Gupta Dynasty and on Indian art and archaeology which broke new ground. The massive *Oxford History of India* which he wrote after retirement became the most widely used textbook on the subject in India and in Britain; but it has been criticised because 'the imaginative and intellectual effort demanded in order to see the world through the eyes of a people not nurtured on the Bible and the

Classics was too much for him'.[41] Further, his Irish Protestant origins caused him to abandon any objectivity when steps towards Home Rule – whether in India or Ireland – came under discussion. He lost no opportunity to lambast Gladstone and Ripon and devoted a book to an attack on the Indian Constitutional Reforms of 1919 which indicated how out of touch with India he had become.[42]

Sir Verney Lovett, who became Reader in Indian History in 1920 on his retirement from the I.C.S., had recently served as a member of the Rowlatt Committee whose recommendations that Indians might be jailed without trial had sparked Gandhi's civil disobedience campaign. Lovett's claim to be a historian was precariously based on his *History of the Indian Nationalist Movement* which was written from an official point of view and in which Gandhi was dismissed as 'an elderly man', when he was only 50 and had nearly 30 years of political life ahead of him.[43]

Lovett's Inaugural Lecture as Reader, speaking against the background of Civil Disobedience, the Khilafat Movement and the Amritsar massacre, confidently concluded 'We may found our hopes for the future in deep seated loyalty to his Majesty the King Emperor, on memories of a past which goes back far beyond all recent troubles, on the prospective entry into politics of the landed classes, on the generally sensible and orderly character of the people, and on a consciousness of need on their side and on ours.'[44] The I.C.S. probationers who were to be Sir Verney's captive audience for the next 12 years found his lectures almost unbearably tedious. His main written contributions during his Readership were chapters on administration in the *Cambridge History of India*.

Lovett's successor as Reader, appointed in 1932, Sir Geoffrey Corbett, had neither taught nor written any published work, but had been Secretary of Commerce to the Government of India. For the first two years of his appointment he even remained a member of the I.C.S. The most active historian of India at this time was P. E. Roberts of Worcester College, who taught Indian History as a special subject for 30 years and wrote a lengthy history of British India. Roberts' predelictions may be illustrated from his observation that Vincent Smith had 'lightened and simplified the whole dreary and repellent subject of the Hindu and early Muhammedan periods'.[45]

The only historian at Oxford at this time who was much concerned with the history of India itself as opposed to that of the British in India was Edward Thompson, who held no University appointment. Thompson had been a Methodist missionary in India, and was a novelist and poet who had come to Oxford to teach Bengali to the

I.C.S. probationers. Henry Spalding financed a Research Fellowship for him at Oriel and he wrote a number of books such as *The Other Side of the Medal* which took into account the Indian Nationalist point of view. He was also a friend of Tagore and Nehru.

Apart from the professional teachers of Indian History, a wealth of knowledge of India existed in Oxford. Sir Henry Maine used his experience as Law Member of the Viceroy's Council in his lectures on village communities while he was Corpus Professor of Jurisprudence between 1869 and 1877, and introduced the idea that Europe's past could be studied in India's present. A little later W. W. Hunter (1840–1900), who had organised the *Indian Gazetteer* and the first Census of India, came to live in Oxford on retirement from the I.C.S. He became a Curator of the Indian Institute and promoted and edited the O.U.P. series of books on Rulers of Empire. Sir William Markby (1829–1917) who had been a High Court Judge in India and Vice-Chancellor of Calcutta University, became Reader in Indian Law, supervisor of the I.C.S. probationers and one of Jowett's closest friends. Markby, who was a graduate of Merton, was a notable accession to the Liberals in Oxford. In light of Queen Victoria's proclamation in 1857 that colour, religion or birth were not to be disqualifications from any office under the Crown of India, he believed that Indians should be prepared for high office; he had devoted much time in India to training Indian lawyers, and in Oxford gave a special welcome to Indian students. He was a supporter of the Indian National Congress and also considered that not only Indians but negroes could aspire to equal positions with Europeans, if given equal opportunities. Markby became an influential figure in the University as Fellow and Bursar of Balliol, Member of the Hebdomadal Council, Curator of the University Chest and of the Indian Institute, Treasurer of Ruskin College and delegate of the University Press.[46] Jowett also brought to Balliol as its chaplain G. U. Pope, a former missionary and teacher in India and the greatest Tamil scholar of the time.

These scholarly men with Indian experience were able to exercise an influence in late-nineteenth-century Oxford because Indian studies were fashionable. Even Queen Victoria had her Munshee. Jowett was inspired to work for India because two of his brothers died there and by the enthusiasm for Indian social and economic reforms of his close friend Florence Nightingale. Max Mueller, even if he would have nothing to do with the Indian Institute, made Indian studies entertaining. Between 1892 and 1914 as will be seen in Chapter 11 many of the best classical graduates joined the I.C.S.

There were Oxford men of equal distinction with Indian experience in the next generation. Sir Michael Sadler, Master of University College, had been Chairman of the Calcutta University Commission, whose Report was a massive analysis of India's educational problems. H. A. L. Fisher, Warden of New College, had been a Member of the Royal Commission on the Public Services in India from 1913 to 1917, and married the daughter of Sir Courtney Ilbert, the author of the famous 'Ilbert Bill' of Ripon's Viceroyalty. A. D. Lindsay, Master of Balliol, made a lengthy visit to India to advise on the future of Christian missions. All Souls had as Fellows not only the three former Viceroys, but Sir John Simon, L. S. Amery, Sir Reginald Coupland, Lionel Curtis and H. V. Hodson, all of whom were to be involved at one time or another with Indian reforms. In the period after the First World War, however, Indian studies were no longer fashionable or interesting. Few British candidates now came forward for the I.C.S. The Indian Empire and officially inspired teaching and writing about it bored Oxford. As D. W. Brogan, the Editor of the *Oxford Magazine*, wrote in 1933 in a review of the first volume of the *Cambridge History of India*, to which several chapters were contributed by Oxford men, 'The problem of India is psychological and it is the great weakness of the Volume that sympathetic understanding of the problems involved in any nationalist movement is available in small quantity.'[47]

The only time that India came into prominence in Oxford at this period was when M. K. Gandhi stayed with A. D. Lindsay, the Master of Balliol, during the Round Table constitutional discussions in 1931. Lindsay organised informal weekend discussions for Gandhi with a group of Oxford men which included Lord Lothian, Under Secretary of State for India, Malcolm Macdonald, representing the Prime Minister who was his father, and Reginald Coupland. For an exciting 24 hours a formula seemed to have been found which could have led to a breakthrough in the Conference and to India's progress to Dominion status by peaceful constitutional means: but the hope vanished in the formal atmosphere of London next day.[48]

THE ATTEMPT TO BROADEN INDIAN STUDIES

One important critic of the fossilisation of the Indian Institute and the failure of Oxford to concern itself with the history of India instead of that of the British administration of India was Lord Lothian, who remained Secretary of the Rhodes Trust, whilst he was Parliamentary Under Secretary for India in 1931–2, a Liberal representative at the Round Table Conference, and Chairman of the Indian Franchise Committee. Both Lothian and his successor as Secretary of the Rhodes Trust, Lord Elton, were considerably influenced on Indian questions by Edward Thompson.

The Rhodes Trust financed several visits by Thompson to India. He returned from one of these visits in 1932 to suggest that the Trust establish prizes for Indian writers as well as Fellowships which would bring distinguished Indian writers to lecture at Oxford, and that O.U.P. be encouraged to publish works by Indians. 'The tragedy of this Indian business', he wrote to Lothian, 'is that the Indians like us better than they like any other nation, and they admire us. A very small gift of serious study from our side would lighten the political burden immeasurably.'[49]

The Rhodes Trustees in 1932 offered the University to finance a visiting lectureship for a distinguished Indian who would lecture on Indian History, Literature and Art; Lothian saw this only as a first step, and suggested that an Indian should also be appointed as administrator or deputy administrator of the Indian Institute whose main function would be to bring a series of eminent Indian scholars to lecture in Oxford.

Lothian suggested that Thompson consult with Curtis about a rejuvenation of the Indian Institute, as a base for some of his new projects. To this Thompson replied that the Indian Institute was 'lost, damned beyond redemption. Our alleged Indian studies are solely utilitarian and governmental, the appointments being mainly political.' Describing Corbett's appointment as Reader as 'a ramp', he exclaimed 'you leave Indian History in the hands of the men who copy and compile, always nervously resolved not to give any peephole for sedition'.[50]

He was adamantly opposed to any attempt to revitalise the Indian Institute. No Indian, he said, would ever regard this jail-like structure with anything but horror and aversion, whilst scholarship was subordinated to administrative requirements and culture was expected to walk hand-in-hand with a Knight Commander of the Indian Empire (Corbett). The whole system was based on perquisites. Language lecturers were employed who only had two or three pupils. The lecturers should be sacked and the I.C.S. probationers concentrated in London, which had much better facilities for Indian Studies.

The building should be sold to a College and a new 'Irwin House' built to house an Indian library, offer rooms to distinguished visiting Indians and provide lectures and entertainments without the stigma of the I.C.S.[51] A new Irwin House, named after the Viceroy who had earned the esteem of Indians when he negotiated with Gandhi as an equal, was a costly proposition. Lothian and Curtis therefore turned to Henry Spalding.

Henry Spalding (1877–1953) was a New College man who inherited a fortune made in sports goods. He lived in Oxford and endowed the Chair of Eastern Religions and Ethics, as well as lectureships in Chinese Philosophy and Religion, and paid for various gifts which Oxford made to other Universities. His overriding interest was the mutual understanding which could be brought about by a study of the spiritual content of Eastern and Western thought and culture. He dreamed that Oxford might become the centre of a new renaissance based on an Honour School of Religions and Ethics.[52] What emerged therefore from a dinner at All Souls of Lothian, Curtis, A. D. Lindsay (the Vice-Chancellor) and Spalding was a project not for an Indian 'Irwin House' but an 'Asia House', modelled on Rhodes House, with all the books from the Bodleian on the living East, a Warden, a library, a theatre and a museum. Spalding was left to raise the funds.[53] He had a profound admiration for Thompson, the imagery of whose novels he compared with that of Shakespeare and Aeschylus, and saw him as the 'kingpin' of the enterprise.[54]

Nothing happened. Not even the Indian lectureship materialised. First the correspondence was lost by the University in a change of Vice-Chancellors;[55] then Lothian, with his many other preoccupations, failed to follow the matter up. When Lothian left as Ambassador to the United States in 1939, his successor Lord Elton was baffled by the misadventures which had prevented the Trust from doing anything useful for India in Oxford in the past seven years though, as he wrote to Curtis, 'an immense improvement might have been – and still might be – made in British Indian relations by public recognition in Oxford of the current intellectual movement in India. Successful though the British Commonwealth has been politically and administratively and even in a sense socially, it has all too seldom established sufficient intellectual contacts with the subject peoples.'[56]

Elton, acting mainly on Thompson's advice, proved more pertinacious than his predecessor. Rhodes Scholarships were created for Indians. The University was persuaded to confer a degree on Rabindranath Tagore at his home in Santiniketan in a colourful ceremony conducted in Latin, English, Bengali and Sanskrit.[57] The Trustees also proposed to invite to Oxford in 1940 as Rhodes visiting lecturer Jawarharlal Nehru, who Thompson percipiently saw might one day become a second Smuts. The Viceroy, Lord Linlithgrow, however, advised against this visit.[58]

Elton, like Lothian, was influenced in his attitude to the Indian Institute by Thompson's contempt for almost everyone connected with Indian Studies in Oxford; this had become even more ferocious after he had failed in 1935 to obtain the Readership in Indian History, for which A. D. Lindsay had urged him to apply. He described the Oriental Faculty to Elton in 1942 as 'Nearly all of them ex. I.C.S. . . . this criminal tribe . . . as long as North Oxford remains unbombed the wicked will continue to prosper and to earn their ill gotten pensions.'[59] Elton told Amery, the Secretary of State for India, that the Indian Institute performed scarcely any function as such, and was clearly not in a position to contribute to Indian studies.[60]

No more I.C.S. probationers came to Oxford after 1939. One last attempt to revive the Indian Institute was made by H. A. R. Gibb, the Professor of Arabic, in 1945 in a memorandum to the Board of Oriental Studies. It had long been recognised, he said, that the Institute had not fulfilled the expectations entertained at the time of its foundation: now, with the new demand for specialists in Eastern Studies brought about by the Second World War, there was an opportunity for the Institute to become the centre of Indian Studies in England. This should grow out of the links with related studies in the University, such as history, archaeology and sociology. Modern Indian languages should be taught, and postgraduate scholarships should be provided which would include the cost of visits to India.[61]

When the I.C.S. courses ended shortly before India became independent in 1947, there were two possibilities for the Institute. One was to turn it into a new Centre for Indian or South Asian Studies as proposed by Professor Gibb, a proposal supported by the Curators. The other, adopted by the Hebdomadal Council, was to allow it to expire, leaving its library to be integrated into the Bodleian and any other functions absorbed in the new Oriental Institute.

When Council in 1965 proposed to dismantle the building and put University offices on the site, there were a series of spectacular debates in Congregation and Convocation in which the opponents of the proposal alleged bad faith towards the Indian Princes who had contributed much of the money for the building, and towards the memory of Monier Williams who had collected it. Council's representatives replied that they had High Court approval for taking over the site on condition that £20,000 was provided by the University for Indian Studies elsewhere. Eventually the issue went to Convocation – the body of all the M.A.s of the University – which supported Council's proposals by 288 votes to 270; it was believed that the narrow victory was due to Hertford College which, hoping to acquire a share in the site, invited all its M.A.s to come and vote in return for a free lunch.[62]

Bodley's Librarian and the Reader in Indian History resigned in protest. But there was irony in the epilogue. The University, once having taken over the building, decided that it would not after all be suitable for administrative offices. It was therefore used to house a new library, that of the History Faculty, although a main argument which had been used by Council to evict the Indian Institute was that it was in danger of collapsing under the weight of its books.

As for Sanskrit Studies, Monier Williams's successor, A. A. MacDonell, secured manuscripts for the Bodleian which made it the largest collection of Sanskrit material outside India. They remained mostly uncatalogued, however, for lack of staff. By 1928, when MacDonell ceased to be Professor, there had been a notable decline of interest in Sanskrit. His successor, F. W. Thomas, noted that between 1921 and 1930 only four candidates sat for honours in Sanskrit, whereas 30 years earlier MacDonell had 18 students in his Elementary Sanskrit class. In 1931 there had been no candidate for the Boden Scholarship in six out of the previous eight years. Whilst a main reason for the decline was that I.C.S. probationers no longer studied the subject, it was also associated with the simultaneous decline in classical studies; for classical scholars of an earlier generation had been attracted to Sanskrit by its affinity to Latin and Greek. In addition Thomas attributed the lessened interest to the fact that recent archaeological studies in the Near East had deprived India of the palm of antiquity.[63] Thomas was succeeded by a retired I.C.S. officer, E. H. Johnstone, which added to the official atmosphere of the Indian Institute.

R. H. Gombrich in his Inaugural Lecture as Boden Professor in 1977 – the first to be given since that of Monier Williams more than 100 years earlier – paid the usual tributes to his predecessors but concluded that 'We have three problems: we are not very good at English; we are not very good at Sanskrit; and we are not very good at anything else.' He was appalled to find out that no Indian had ever been employed in a permanent capacity to teach Sanskrit at a British University.[64]

Thus in the end few of Monier Williams's objectives were permanently achieved. An insufficient number of undergraduates enrolled in Indian Studies to enable the course to continue after the I.C.S. probationers' residence in Oxford was curtailed. Future legislators remained as ignorant as ever about India; most of the Oxford men who continued to fill the highest posts in the Government of the Empire had read Classics. Even when modern History began to overtake Classics, only a handful of those who read it acquired any knowledge of India, through taking an optional special subject on Lord Wellesley's administration or, later, on Warren Hastings.

Sir Thomas Brassey, one of the Institute's principal benefactors, had expressed the hope when the foundation stone was laid that it might 'be a means of giving to the people of India a capacity for self government'.[65] The Indian students went in to the Institute to read the newspapers, but they came to regard those who worked there as spies of the India Office. A major error was to place all the eggs in the I.C.S. basket. There were some 50 I.C.S. probationers at Oxford when the Institute was founded. Their numbers fell even in Monier Williams's lifetime. After 1919 sometimes the lecturers had no pupils; moreover when the probationary course was reduced to nine months it ceased to be taken very seriously. Eventually, when the I.C.S. ceased to exist and the India Office financial support was withdrawn, the Institute disappeared because it had no other orientation. Yet as those who tried to save it pointed out, the library was being used by more readers than ever before, and in other Universities, including Cambridge, there was more interest in Indian Studies after Independence than in the days of the Empire.

The fundamental cause of the Institute's failure was that except from 1886 to 1895 Indian Studies never obtained the requisite place in the undergraduate curriculum, and postgraduate studies were slow to develop in Oxford in any field. The Boden Professor of Sanskrit, who was *ex officio* Keeper of the Institute, was likely, after Monier Williams's time, to have a narrow view of Indian Studies. The Beit Professor of Colonial Studies who might, and indeed in Coupland's time did, have a broader view was debarred by Statute from teaching about India, whilst the former I.C.S. officers who occupied the post of Reader in Indian History were too unskilled in University politics to obtain a better representation of Indian Studies in the curriculum, even if they wanted it.

There remains perhaps the best open-shelf library in Britain on India. When the pictures and busts of benefactors, Maharajas and scholars were rudely dispersed, the devoted staff brought from their old building to the new premises only a plaque to the Revd Solomon Caesar Malan and the portrait of Monier Williams. Malan was the son of a Protestant in Geneva who became engaged to an English girl whose parents insisted that he could not marry her unless he obtained an Oxford degree. When he had done so he served as a missionary in India and succeeded Wilson as Secretary of the Asiatic Society of Bengal. He was considered by MacDonell to be the most accomplished oriental linguist in England, but he refused all academic appointments which were offered to him and concentrated the best energies of his life to writing *A Vindication of the Authorised Version of the English Bible*. Having no further use for his oriental books and manuscripts he presented them, 4000 volumes in all, to the Indian Institute in 1886. This, said Monier Williams in a letter to *The Times* 'elevated the library of the Indian Institute to a unique position among the Oriental libraries of Europe'.[66]

As for the Founder himself, his portrait hangs facing what remains of his Institute, wearing through all time the cherished Doctor's robes so begrudged him by Max Mueller.*

*It is only fair to add that since 1984 the Librarian of the Institute has recovered and put on display a number of the portraits and busts of its former worthies.

7 Muzzled Lions – the Scientists and Empire

Nero was probably a musician of taste and training, and it was artistic and high class music which he played while Rome was burning: so too the studies of the past carried on in Oxford have been charming and full of beauty, whilst England has been, and lies in, mortal peril for lack of knowledge of nature.

Sir E. Ray Lankester, Romanes Lecture (1905)[1]

THE CLAIMS OF THE SCIENTISTS

The complacent view of Oxford's influence on Empire which was so often expressed by classicists and historians was not shared by natural scientists. The scientists in the period before the First World War used the needs of the Empire to strengthen their arguments that the University should devote far more attention not only to their own disciplines but to research in general. Their idea of a Great Imperial University was one in which the University and the professors which it appointed would have a much stronger position in conducting teaching and research in central institutes, departments and laboratories than they enjoyed at the time in relation to the Colleges and their tutors.

The study of science in Oxford had declined sadly after the brief Golden Age when Willis, Boyle, Wren and other founders of the Royal Society worked together in the Oxford of Cromwell and Charles II. In the mid-nineteenth century, however, there was a revival when the University Museum was built under the inspiration of Acland and Ruskin to be a centre, it was hoped, like that in ancient Alexandria, where men from all branches of science would work together for its advancement.[2] New departments of physiology, pathology and zoology were founded.

The most articulate of Oxford's scientists during the high period of Empire were George Rolleston (1829–81), H. V. Moseley (1844–91) and Sir E. Ray Lankester (1847–1929), each of whom held the Linacre Chair of Comparative Anatomy, and Sir Edward Poulton (1856–1944) who was Hope Professor of Zoology from 1893 to 1933.

The Oxford scientists tended to be more versatile and more widely travelled than the contemporary classicists, many of whom had entered a College as undergraduates and stayed on as Fellows for the rest of their lives. Rolleston, Moseley and Lankester undertook post-graduate studies abroad after graduating at Oxford; Rolleston took a First in Classics, had a medical degree, and served as an Army surgeon in the Crimea; Moseley spent four years as a naturalist with the Challenger Expedition; Poulton started as a geologist before turning to entomology. In the early twentieth century the Oxford scientists strengthened their Imperial connections by making extended visits to Canada, South Africa and Australia, when the British Association for the Advancement of Science frequently held its Annual Conferences outside Britain.

Most of the Oxford scientists in the late nineteenth and early twentieth centuries were fervent Darwinites. Some of them were influenced by Social Darwinism. Rolleston and Moseley were craniologists and great collectors of human skulls for the Museum; W. J. Sollas, the Professor of Geology, commented in 1911 on the extinction of the Tasmanians – 'It is a sad story, and we can only hope that the replacement of a people with a cranial capacity of only about 1200 cc by one with a capacity nearly one third greater may prove ultimately of advantage in the evolution of mankind. The world certainly needs all the brains it can get.'[3]

In their time only a small minority of students studied Natural Sciences; in 1887 of those entering for honours examinations only 5.3 per cent were studying the subject. The proportion rose to 13.5 per cent by 1912, but this was still far lower than at Cambridge where the figures were 20.9 per cent in 1887 and 24.3 per cent in 1912.[4] In general, the professors of science believed that Oxford's excessively classical orientation, its system of examinations and its lack of support for research caused the leadership of the nation and Empire, which it so largely supplied, to be dangerously illiterate in science.

Rolleston in 1881 likened the examination system to the Casino in Monte Carlo, with its excitement, its gambling, its power to dull aspiration of every better kind, and its all but entire monopoly of the place.[5] Moseley was reminded of Oxford when he visited the Examination Halls of Pekin on his voyage as naturalist to the *Challenger*; in both cases, he noted, the main energies had been devoted to the study and reiterated translation of the mouldy and worm-eaten lore of a bygone age.[6]

LANKESTER AND POULTON

Lankester and Poulton developed the attack more broadly. Lankester was not only the most notable British zoologist of his time but wrote a great number of popular articles on science. Poulton was one of the few students of Natural Sciences in the nineteenth century to be elected President of the Oxford Union. He was a man of wide contacts and one of the best popular lecturers in England;[7] under him the Hope Department in the Museum became the entomological centre of the Empire at a time when entomological research and fieldwork had a crucial role in finding solutions to human and animal diseases in new territories brought under British Rule. From all over the Empire his correspondents sent him specimens to classify and articles to correct. He had a more stable character than his friend Lankester, who twice quit Oxford in disgust with 'this grave, this sepulchre, this dead man's paradise, with its rotten system of teaching'.[8]

In 1890 Lankester criticised 'the effort which has been made to throw the Indian and other civil service appointments into the hands of the upper classes by favouring in examinations the subjects taught at the Public Schools'.[9] He devoted much of his Romanes Lecture of 1905 to an attack on Oxford's system of education for the injurious influence which it exercised by imposing classical studies both directly on the future leaders of Empire who studied in Oxford and indirectly through the Universities and Colleges which Oxford men were helping to set up all over the Empire. He admitted that several hundred years earlier it had been necessary for scholars to learn Latin and Greek as the key to the knowledge of science; now, however, this key was no longer required and study of the classics should therefore be replaced by study of nature and of modern languages. The ablest youth of the country should be encouraged to proceed to the extreme limit of knowledge in physics, chemistry, geology and botany.[10]

He pursued the theme in his Presidential Address to the British Association for the Advancement of Science in the following year, describing whole departments of the British Government in which scientific knowledge was the one thing needful, but in which the entire staff from Minister and Permanent Secretary down to the clerks were not only wholly ignorant of science but had a fear and dislike of scientific knowledge.[11] By contrast, he pointed out, in Germany everyone from the Emperor downwards had a real understanding of the danger of allowing people ignorant of science to act as administrators.[12]

Poulton, perhaps with more tactical sense, stated that the issue was not so much what was taught but how it was taught. The Imperial importance of the conflict, he wrote in two articles on 'The Empire and Oxford' in 1905, was not between science and classics but between those on the one hand who believed that the intellectual inspiration of our youth could only be received in an atmosphere of learning, and given by men who were themselves students; and on the other hand those who upheld the ancient Chinese and modern British educational methods by which young men were instructed by purveyors of second-hand knowledge. He warned that 'When once the critical period of intellectual growth has been devoted solely to the collection and recollection of material for the examiner, any awakening of original power is rare indeed.'[13]

The whole power of influencing passing generations of young men was left to the Colleges, he said, who spent their endowments on scholarships to attract the men most likely to do best in examinations, and on engaging as Fellows and tutors the most successful purveyors of the knowledge which would be useful in examinations. The example of All Souls was most harmful of all; this College which had no undergraduates, and which with its great riches could have done so much to encourage learning, instead discouraged it by awarding the most prestigious Fellowships in the University to men who knew best what would pay in examinations, instead of to those who showed evidence of research and latent imagination and power. The infatuation with examinations, Poulton maintained, had a disastrous effect on the imagination, the initiative and resourcefulness of the nation and Empire. The supreme interests of Empire required that the whole of the teaching should be taken over by the University, and that College Fellowships should be given in part for University teaching and in part for original work and should be held only during the continuance of research. Because of the influence which they exerted on the curriculum and teaching methods of the Universities, competitive examinations for the I.C.S. and Home Civil Service should be abolished and candidates should be nominated instead by the Universities through a committee which collected all available information on them.[14]

The scientists deplored the situation in which the University professors had few pupils, because most teaching was done in the colleges. Poulton described the professors as 'muzzled lions, tied by the leg',[15] compelled to lecture in accordance with an examination system over which they had no influence. Oxford scientists who had pursued their postgraduate work in Germany compared Oxford's system unfavourably with that designed by Fichte who saw the University 'not as a place where instruction is given, but an institution for the training of experts in making knowledge, by the association of the pupil with his professor in the enquiry which the latter initiates and pursues'.[16]

Among Poulton's contemporaries in the Oxford Union had been Alfred Milner and George Parkin. When Parkin came to Oxford in 1903 to set up the Rhodes Scholarship scheme, Poulton was among those he consulted; as a consequence Poulton wrote to Milner, who was a Rhodes Trustee, but still in South Africa, to expand on Parkin's idea that, in order to fulfil Rhodes's intentions, Oxford needed to become a great Imperial University. Many of the Rhodes Scholars, he predicted, would want to come to take research degrees, and Oxford was not adequately equipped to receive them. A million pounds, he suggested, would be needed from the Rhodes Trust to increase the efficiency of the scientific departments and realise the dream of making Oxford the Imperial centre of University education and research.

Milner was sympathetic. 'The Boers,' he said, 'ignorant as they are, have been much quicker in application of science to war than we have.' He entirely agreed that considerable expenditure on scientific equipment was necessary before the ideal of Oxford as an Imperial University could be realised, but he felt unable to be active as a Rhodes Trustee whilst still High Commissioner in South Africa.[17]

In 1916, Lankester took the lead in organising a conference on 'The Neglect of Science' which was attended not only by scientists, including Poulton and Osler, but by educationists from other disciplines, retired colonial proconsuls and Robert Bridges, the Poet Laureate, who was a doctor of medicine. Now the scientists were no longer in the wilderness, preaching that Britain should emulate Germany and give to science adequate resources for research and a larger place in education and the public services. German technical superiority had cruelly and effectively been demonstrated in battle; the sons of some of the participants in the conference were dead as a consequence. Even then indeed admirers of classical education were saying that the study of Greek and Latin had taught men how to die; but the message of the conference was that study of science might have taught them how to live. Among the unanimous recommendations was that capital importance be attached to the natural sciences in competitive examinations for the Home and Indian Civil Services and as part of the entry qualification for the Colonial Administrative and Forestry Services.[18]

MEDICINE

Rhodes, in his Will, stated that he would have liked to have established Scholarships in Medicine at Edinburgh, where many South Africans studied the subject, but refrained from doing so because that University had no residential system. Instead he expressed the hope that Oxford would extend its scope to make its Medical School at least as good as that of Edinburgh. Although there was some resentment in Oxford at this observation,[19] it was true that only preliminary medical studies took place in Oxford, mainly because it was believed that the city was too small to provide the number and variety of patients required for practical teaching. In 1878 Lankester had pointed out that the Regius Professor of Medicine gave no lectures, and that Medicine had an insignificant place in contemporary Oxford compared with the mediaeval University, in which Theology, Law and Medicine were the three Queens of the sciences.[20] Right up until 1940, although medical students continued to do their preliminary studies in Oxford and were finally examined there, their practical work was done in London hospitals.

In 1904 Sir Herbert Warren, the President of Magdalen Colllege, wrote to the Prime Minister, Arthur Balfour, to suggest that the Canadian William Osler be appointed as Regius Professor of Medicine. 'He is a philosophic and a cultivated man, a student and lover of Locke and Burton, and so far the kind of man whom Oxford generally, I believe would welcome. It would also, I think, be a very interesting and pleasing thing from the Imperial point of view just now to appoint a Professor to Oxford who is a Canadian by birth and a Professor in the United States.'[21]

Although the President of Magdalen may have considered this a less important qualification, Osler (later Sir William, 1849–1919) was also the best-known physician of his time, whose textbook on *Principles and Practice of Medicine* had sold over 100,000 copies. The son of an Anglican clergyman who had migrated from England to Canada, he had studied in Vienna and Berlin as well as in London and Toronto, and had revolutionised medical education in the United States and Canada by combining the British system of bedside teaching with the German system, in which wards and laboratories cooperated closely under a single Director. He accepted the Oxford professorship because the pressures of combining teaching and practice at Johns Hopkins University in the United States had become unbearable. His prestige and his personality did much to encourage medical studies in Oxford, where, as Jowett had complained, it had been difficult to get able men to go into the profession.[22]

Osler's appointment to the Regius Professorship, which he held from 1905 to 1919, proved a notable success. His range of interests was remarkable. He collected books for the Bodleian so energetically that its Librarian said he deserved a statue in the Bodleian quadrangle. He became President of the Classical Association, to which he gave a Presidential Address on 'The Old Humanities and the New Science'. He was an Imperialist, a tariff reformer and a liberal whose genial manner won him friends on all sides. 'The way he would slap you on the back and pick your tail pockets as you read the telegrams was delightful.'[23] Both Liberals and Conservatives asked him to stand for Parliament as Member for the University. He was mainly responsible for the establishment of the Radcliffe Infirmary as the most complete clinical and pathology unit yet attached to a county hospital, and he delighted to give informal teaching on its wards, not only to future medical students but to future missionaries.

Osler, like Poulton and Lankester, deplored the English examination system. 'To replace the Chinese by the Greek spirit', he said, 'would enable the student to seek knowledge for itself without thought of the end, tested and taught day by day, the pupil and teacher working together in the same lines, only one ahead of the other.'[24] In his Presidential speech to the Classical Association in 1919 he also gently but boldly deplored the effect on the Empire of the predominance of Greats, in which those who had obtained First Class degrees 'could be recognised by that altogether superior expression, that self-consciousness of having reached life's goal'. As a discipline of mind for the few, he considered, the system was excellent, but there was a holocaust of students for whom the course was unsuitable and who were sacrificed each year to produce one scholar, just as it cost thousands of eggs and fry to produce one salmon.[25]

Osler's pupil and biographer was Harvey Cushing of Boston; Cushing, in turn, taught Hugh Cairns, who perhaps with Osler did more than anyone else from the Empire to advance the study of Medicine in Oxford. Sir Hugh Cairns (1896–1952) was a Rhodes Scholar from Adelaide. At Balliol he won a rowing Blue and married one of the daughters of the Master, A. L. Smith. After studying under Cushing, he became the pioneer of brain surgery in Britain and had a busy London practice. He remained, however, in touch with Oxford, in particular with A. D. Lindsay, the Master of Balliol, and Veale, the Registrar; in consultation with them he prepared in 1934 a memorandum to the Regius Professor of Medicine on the desirability of establishing a complete School of Medicine at Oxford. The Regius Professor, Sir Farquhar Buzzard, slipped a copy of the memorandum into the pocket of Lord Nuffield, for whom medicine was a favourite object of philanthropy. Nuffield, a shy man, with little formal education, was attracted by the direct Australian approach of Cairns in the discussions leading to the great Nuffield benefactions which established a medical research school in the University; Cairns was appointed as the first Professor of Surgery under the new arrangements. His overall design was, in the tradition of Osler, that the Oxford clinical school should be closely linked with strengthened scientific departments in the University, and that a new and more scientifically trained doctor should emerge. That considerable progress was achieved towards this before his premature death was largely due to the unconventional approaches which he used and his refusal to accept negative replies through regular channels. His Australian nationality and his membership of the Balliol network enabled him to circumvent normal procedures in a way which would hardly have been permitted otherwise.[26] He thought Imperially; in his office was a map of the world, on which the attention of his former pupils would be drawn to Commonwealth countries in which their skills were needed. Lord Nuffield, perhaps on his advice, endowed Fellowships to enable South Africans, Australians and New Zealanders to come to Oxford for postgraduate medical studies.

Shortly after Cairns another Rhodes Scholar from Adelaide, Howard Florey, the first to win a Nobel Prize, came to Magdalen as a graduate student. It is curious that it was Cairns, coming from a poor family, who so quickly became accepted as a charming and urbane member of the Oxford establishment, whereas Florey, who had grown up in comfortable circumstances, was caustic, unself-confident and mistrustful of the English. He found the 'typical Englishmen without a spark of imagination, and with a conviction of English superiority in everything: they have a habit of getting angry when challenged in their beliefs'.[27] Magdalen was perhaps an unfortunate choice of College; three-quarters of its undergraduates came from three great Public Schools: Eton, Harrow and Winchester.[28] 'It is a fact', he wrote home in his first year, 'that one tends to meet only Colonials. The Englishmen are a queer lot . . . the majority preserve a frigid silence.'[29] As for the dons, 'they conceal a great amount of ignorance under a noble exterior'.[30] The aesthetes he found nauseating, and the few people he liked played games. Fortunately he received much kindness from Sir Charles Sherrington, whose laboratory, when Florey joined it, was providing the best neurophysiological training in the world, and he made friends with the socialist scientist J. B. S. Haldane.

Florey's work with Sherrington led to appointments in Cambridge and Sheffield Universities before he returned to Oxford as Professor of Pathology in 1935. In this post it would seem, he wrote in 1939, that the University almost wished to make it as difficult as possible for him to carry out his experiments. Starved of funds by the University and the Medical Research Council, he circumvented established channels and obtained a grant from the Rockefeller Foundation which enabled him and his team to demonstrate that penicillin was able to overcome otherwise hopeless infection. Florey's normal indication of satisfaction was 'We don't seem to be going backwards', but when this notable breakthrough came he is recorded as saying 'It looks promising.'[31]

Florey never spoke in Congregation, never served on the Hebdomadal Council and had little interest in University administration except when it impinged on his work. Yet this laconic, shy Australian became Baron Florey of Adelaide and Marston, President of the Royal Society and Provost of Queen's College, Oxford. He was elected to the latter positions because he had a genius not only for research but for organisation; he told the Fellows of Queen's at his first College meeting that not one of them was fit to run a fish and chip shop.[32] Australia tried to entice him back as Director of the School of Medicine at the new National University, but he preferred to remain in Britain at the centre of the scientific world.

The ambition of Poulton and Lankester that Oxford should become a University in which science and research had an important place was eventually largely realised and many of the causes for which they fought were won in their lifetime. The presence of the Rhodes Scholars hastened the abolition of compulsory Greek and the development of postgraduate work. After the First World War, when the University began to receive substantial grants from the Government, a considerable proportion of the money was allocated for the natural sciences. New science buildings advanced into the area of the Parks despite the apprehension expressed in Congregation lest syphilitic goats, used in unthinkable experiments in the Pathology Department, might escape and infect the undergraduates at play.[33] Poulton, Lankester and Parkin had been concerned that the University should be reformed in the interest of the Empire; it had, however, been men from the Empire, unfettered by too much respect for tradition, who had played a leading part in the revival of science and medicine, and in transmitting the new discoveries throughout the Empire, not only as returning Rhodes Scholars but under the Nuffield scheme through which research students from the Empire were brought to the new medical school.

FORESTRY

Among the most majestic of the new science buildings was the Imperial Forestry Institute. The establishment of Forestry Studies in Oxford was initially impeded within the University by dislike of what was regarded as vocational training, and outside it by inconsistent Government policies which erratically reflected pressures from Oxford, Cambridge and Edinburgh. The teaching of Forestry in Oxford started in response to the needs of India. In the mid-nineteenth century, Indian teak was needed to replace Britain's exhausted stocks of oak for naval construction. Other woods were also required to supply the new railways and steamers with fuel. Britain, however, had no experience in the scientific management of State forests; thus the first three Inspectors General who headed India's Forest Department from 1864 to 1900 all came from Germany. Under them the earliest forest officers were British, selected from the Army, Public Works and Survey Departments, and they were sent to France and Germany for training. The suspension of this training during the Franco-Prussian War of 1870 eventually caused the Indian Government to set up a Forestry School at their engineering College at Coopers Hill near Windsor, under the direction of Wilhelm (later Sir William) Schlich (1840–1925).

Schlich had gone out to India in 1866 after taking a doctorate in Forestry in his native Germany. He served in Burma in the teak forests, and as Conservator of Forests successively in Sind, Bengal and the Punjab, before becoming Inspector General of Forests. This exceptionally wide experience had long convinced him of the need on the one hand for men with a University education in the Indian Forest Service, and on the other, for an understanding of modern principles of scientific forestry in Britain itself. Whilst he was at Coopers Hill, he wrote his great *Manual of Forestry* which was to become a standard book of reference throughout the Empire, and he became naturalised as a British citizen.

Although the school at Coopers Hill lasted for 20 years, Schlich considered that it suffered through isolation from the scientific departments which would have reinforced it in a University. He also believed that Indian Forest Officers needed the prestige of a University degree in order to hold their own with the officers of the I.C.S., whose ignorance of science was a major obstacle to the development of forestry management. The Government committees which considered the question recommended the transfer of the Coopers Hill School to Cambridge, whose science teaching was generally agreed to be more advanced than that at Oxford. The India Office, however, on Schlich's advice, moved the school instead to Oxford in 1905, apparently because St John's College offered Bagley Wood for experimental work.[34] In future, it was decided, the Indian Forest Service probationers were to take a diploma course in a School of Forestry to be established by Oxford Universtiy. The reaction in Cambridge was furious, and led to an unusual debate in the House of Lords in March 1905, when the Earl of Lytton put down a motion:

> to call attention to the scheme at present under the consideration of the India Office for the removal of the Forest Department, now at Coopers Hill, to the University of Oxford and to move to resolve 'that in the opinion of this House the Indian Forest Service should be open to all the universities of the United Kingdom.

Lytton maintained that the new arrangements would shut out the other Universities from the Indian and Colonial Forest Services, and he called on Parliament to refuse to sanction a scheme 'so unprecedented in its character and which in its operation would be manifestly unjust'. The Marquess of Bath, Under Secretary of State for India, defended the Government's decision on the grounds that there were no forests near Cambridge. At this, Lord Spencer caustically observed that he had often passed through Oxford but had never noticed that it was situated in the centre of a great forest.

Lord Lansdowne, the Secretary of State for Foreign Affairs, had to be brought down to point out, with all the authority of a former Viceroy, that only ten probationers a year were appointed and that they could hardly be scattered among several Universities, each staffed by professors with Indian experience. Lord Goschen, Chancellor of Oxford University, tried to conciliate by suggesting that Cambridge would probably get most of the engineers who had formerly gone to Coopers Hill; but the resolution was pressed to a division, with the Archbishop of Canterbury's name at the head of the Oxford supporters and that of the Archbishop of York at the head of those of Cambridge.[35]

The motion was lost by 24 votes to 30, but it was a Pyrrhic victory for Oxford. The probationers at Coopers Hill had been recruited at school-leaving age on the basis of an examination in subjects which were taught by public schools and grammar schools; there were usually twice as many candidates as vacancies. Under the new scheme, however, the probationers were to be recruited from among men who had already passed the preliminary Oxford examination of Responsions or its equivalent elsewhere, and thus had a knowledge of Latin and Greek; they were then to be selected on the basis of a highly specialised written entry examination in mechanics, physics, chemistry, zoology and botany; they also had to show a knowledge of German. Whether the University, or Schlich, or the India Office was responsible for these unrealistic requirements, the result was ludicrous. In 1905, 13 vacancies were advertised; four candidates applied, of whom two were appointed. In 1906, 24 vacancies were advertised for which there were only two candidates, of whom one was appointed. As a temporary measure the examinations had to be waived and probationers appointed who had 'a good general education and if possible a knowledge of mechanics and physics'.[36] The India Office set up a committee to examine the situation. On its recommendation probationers were no longer to be obliged to obtain a diploma at Oxford after 1911. Support was withdrawn from Oxford, including the financing of the two teaching posts which had been transferred from Coopers Hill. In future probationers could be recruited by examination from science graduates of any British University and would then take a two-year diploma course at any approved University (effectively Oxford, Cambridge or Edinburgh) whose teaching included Forestry fieldwork in France or Germany.[37]

One of the posts from which Government support was withdrawn was that of Schlich who in any case reached the retirement age from the Indian Forest Service in 1911. The crisis brought out his qualities of courage and generosity. He set up a fund to endow a professorship in Forestry at Oxford, starting it off with a gift of the money which he had received from his old pupils on his retirement. Meanwhile he offered, at the age of 70, to continue to teach without remuneration; in fact, the University appointed him on a Reader's salary with the personal title of Professor, and found money for the Assistant Professorship.[38] Schlich's endowment fund received donations from most of the Oxford Colleges, from the Indian and colonial Governments and from various Indian and Asian Princes. In 1919 he was finally able to retire, leaving a fully-funded professorship to be occupied by his former pupil, R. S. Troup.

Schlich had saved the Oxford Forestry School, in which by 1914 there were 35 students, of whom only five were Indian probationers. His objection to a dispersal of the probationers proved to be justified. In the three years between 1911 and 1913 there was an average of only two probationers at Cambridge and three at Oxford, whilst Edinburgh was preparing to insist on a further subdivision: but the controversy had been focused on the wrong issue.[39] The real question by now was not the training of future British Forest Officers but that of their Indian successors.

Under Indian Nationalist pressure a Royal Commission on the Public Services was appointed in 1913 whose main attention was focused on the proportions of British and Indian Officers in the Services. One volume of its massive report was devoted to Forestry. Indian witnesses pointed out that the requirement of a degree in Natural Sciences from a British University, in addition to a knowledge of Latin and German, made it practically impossible for Indians to enter the Imperial Forest Service.[40] Schlich in his evidence ignored this aspect; he continued to insist in 1914 that Latin and German were necessary and preferably Greek as well. The Indian Forest Service, he said, had to manage a quarter of the total area of India in places which were rarely or never visited by an I.C.S. officer. 'If

Great Britain was to keep India she would have to send out men of a certain class, and if she did not do that, the greater the danger of her not holding India for ever.'[41]

The Commission's report and the Montagu Chelmsford reforms, however, caused more than half the places in the Indian Forest Service to be reserved for Indian nationals. Indian Nationalists now pressed for future training of probationers to be carried out in India. Schlich protested that this would be unsatisfactory because India, unlike France and Germany, did not possess long-established records of forest measurements; but from about the time of his death in 1925 the Indian probationers of the Indian Forest Service were trained at Dehra Doon, although for a few years more the British probationers sometimes continued to study in Britain.

In the First World War the suddenly increased demand for timber caused a crisis in Britain, where Schlich's warnings at last were heeded and a permanent Forestry Commission was set up. The Commission inaugurated a series of Empire Forestry Conferences at which in 1920, and again in 1923, Resolutions were passed calling for the establishment of an Imperial Forestry Institute to conduct advanced training, carry out research and circulate information.

It is remarkable that Oxford, after the embarrassment of 1905, should have been chosen as host for this Institute. More than anyone, Major R. D. (later Sir Ralph) Furse was responsible. Furse was for many years the official in the Colonial Office who recruited officers for the Colonial Services.[42] He became keenly interested in forest problems, and, because the Colonial Office had no forestry adviser, he unofficially took over that role. He was Chairman of the Educational Committee of the Empire Forestry Conference of 1923 and, as a very loyal Oxford man and skillful committee man, was not only largely responsible for funds being made available from the Colonial Office for the new Institute but for bringing it to Oxford.[43] This time the procedures were more sophisticated and the claims of Cambridge and Edinburgh were formally examined. Edinburgh was excluded because it could not offer residential accommodation; Cambridge felt unable to accept the measure of control upon which the Colonial Office, as the principal source of funds, insisted; Oxford farsightedly accepted the controls and gradually whittled them away.[44] Although the Institute started with an outside governing body, eventually in 1938 it was merged with the undergraduate school in a University Department of Forestry under the supervision of a University Committee, of which Furse became a member.

Although India did not for long send its probationers to the Institute, whose main task was to train men for the Colonial Services, the Indian tradition remained strong. Not only R. S. Troup but his successors as Directors of the Institute and Professors of Forestry, Sir Harry Champion and M. V. Laurie, were former members of the Indian Forest Service. Thus, for 63 years, from the arrival of Schlich in 1905, Oxford's Forestry teaching was largely based on Indian experience, though the field visits to the great State forest enterprises of France and Germany continued.

The work of the undergraduate school, financed by the University, and that of the Institute, financed mainly by contributions from the Governments of the Empire, were closely integrated, even before the amalgamation. Until 1930 most of the School's graduates obtained posts in Government Services. Their numbers fluctuated considerably, with a sharp drop during the Depression of 1929–32. After the Second World War, undergraduate enrolment greatly increased, only to drop again as decolonisation and the replacement of British by local officers took place in the colonial territories.

The Colonial Office recruited by interview men with degrees in Natural Sciences from any British University and then sent them on the Oxford diploma course. The Institute, in addition to running the diploma course, conducted very successful refresher courses in the long vacations. Under Laurie's directorship (1959–68) it adapted imaginatively to training foresters from Commonwealth countries in place of the British officers who previously went abroad. Between 1958 and 1968, a total of 468 students studied at the Department. Of these, 97 were undergraduates, half of whom were British. Of the remaining 371 who were doing postgraduate work or on special courses only 12 per cent were British.[45]

One of the main purposes in the creation of the Institute had been dissemination of information within the Empire: but science could hardly be confined within a political framework. By 1935 the Institute's *Annual Report* defined the role as making it the centre 'for world information in relation to Commonwealth forestry problems', and also accepted that senior officers from the Commonwealth would come as much to teach as to learn.[46] The information activities, though still within the overall supervision of the Director, were taken over and financed by the Imperial Forestry Bureau, one of the Imperial Agricultural Bureaux.

Quite soon the need for a substantial building to house all the activities of the Institute, School and Bureau became apparent. In

1934 Congregation, by 122 votes to 91, approved the allocation of a site in South Parks Road, in the face of strong opposition from those who maintained that forestry, which was not a true science, did not deserve a place in the science area. Only appeals to patriotism in response to the needs of the Empire carried the day.[47]

The Second World War and lack of funds delayed construction. The Raja of Sarawak contributed £25,000 and the passing of the Colonial Development and Welfare Act made possible a substantial grant from the British Government. In one respect, the delay was fortunate, for instead of a museum, as originally contemplated, the building incorporated timbers which were presented by 28 Governments as permanent examples of how different kinds of wood could be used with skill and imagination. The Imperial Forestry Institute was formally opened by Princess Margaret in 1950, after the King–Emperor had relinquished his Imperial title. Eleven years later the name was changed to Commonwealth Forestry Institute. Prudently at this point, in order to provide not only for further political change but for fluctuations in the Institute's own ambivalent relationship with the University, only the word 'Forestry' was left on the stone face of the building.

The foresters had a long, hard fight to fulfil Schlich's ambition that Forestry should become a degree subject. In 1910, though Congregation approved, Convocation refused a proposal that Forestry become an honours degree subject. In 1919 a pass degree was approved. A proposal that this become an honours degree was defeated in 1938 and only approved in 1944. In 1969 the Forestry degree course was absorbed into a joint course in Agricultural Sciences and Forestry.

At the postgraduate level, the Commonwealth Forestry Institute proved flexible and successful. It frequently adapted its postgraduate and special courses to meet changing needs and increasingly extended its perspectives to take in students from outside the Commonwealth and to carry out work, whether in the Commonwealth or elsewhere, financed by international organisations. In 1969 a Tropical Silviculture Unit was set up to concentrate on work for the Commonwealth.

To a visitor, entering the imposing building, passing through the hall of Canadian yellow birch and red cedar to the library, with its floor of African olive, or to the Meeting Room of Rhodesian teak, the portraits of Schlich and Furse might seem to look down with legitimate satisfaction. Here, at least, it might be felt, is a solid contribution made by Oxford to the Empire and Commonwealth.

And yet, if the situation at Independence is considered, some doubts may arise. Of all the 272 Indian Forest probationers trained by Schlich in 35 years only two were Indian nationals; it was not until India broke free from Oxford that substantial numbers of Indians (no longer required to know Latin and German) were trained for the Service in India itself. At Independence even Britain's largest African colony – Nigeria – had no department for training in forestry at its Universities.[48] In Malawi an Africanisation Commission in 1960 suggested that Africans with School Certificates should be sent to Universities in the United States and Canada to obtain degrees in Forestry because the entry requirements of British Universities were too exigent and irrelevant.[49] Perhaps Schlich and his successors, in order to win the long battle for recognition by the University, set standards which were not altogether appropriate for the needs and budgets of colonial territories. And if this was an Imperial Institute, why were the staff all British – and why indeed, if the visitor dared to repeat the observation of Lord Spencer, was the Institute anyhow in Oxford, or even in Britain, which had no great forests or traditions of forest management, rather than, for example, in Canada? A suspicion might arise that in the creation of this splendid institution the best to some extent had been the enemy of the good: and the melancholy reflection might also cross the visitor's mind that the scorn of Oxford's academic legislators for a 'vocational' subject had been doomed to be repeated in the Universities which Oxford had helped to establish overseas.

8 Suburbs of the Celestial City – Geopoliticians, Anthropologists and Others

The serious mistakes made and the risks of war incurred by geographical ignorance have often been referred to; with the establishment of this school there will be no excuse for such ignorance among those who have the conduct of the Empire's affairs.

The Times, leading article on the Oxford School of Geography (29 March 1899)[1]

At the celebrations at Christchurch, New Zealand, of the centenary of the University of Canterbury in 1973 the representative of Christ Church, Oxford, recollected how in medieval Oxford the down-to-earth subjects of medicine and law were overshadowed and affected by theology and grew up 'not in an ivory tower, but in the suburbs of the celestial city'.[2] So too in late-nineteenth-century Oxford anthropology, geography and economics had to attach themselves modestly to the Schools of Greats and Modern History until the needs of Empire enabled them to justify their expansion into independent diploma, if not honours, subjects.

GEOGRAPHY

Oxford's Imperial geographers derived considerable inspiration from their famous predecessor, Richard Hakluyt of Christ Church (1533–1616), though he lived in a less modest age. 'In my public lectures', he wrote, 'I was the first that produced and showed both the olde imperfectly composed and the newly reformed mappes, globes, spheares and other instruments of this art for demonstration in the common schooles, to the singular pleasure and general contentment of my auditor.' He described also the weary work of the researcher whose materials 'lay so dispersed, scattered and hidden in several hucksters' hands, that I wonder at myself to see how I was able to endure the delayes, curiosity and backwardness of many from whom I was to receive originals'. More important than his teaching and research methods was the tradition he established and which was revived 300 years later, that it was the business of the geographer to apply the lessons of his studies to contemporary problems. His great work, *Principal Navigations, Voyages, Traffiques and Discoveries of the English Nation*, was written with the purpose of encouraging his countrymen in their journeys of discovery. In his *Particular Discourse Concerning Western Discoveries* he urged that colonies be established in North America to relieve unemployment,[3] and in general he argued that geographical knowledge could benefit the State. From 1583 to 1587 his post in Paris as Embassy Chaplain furnished a cover for gathering information for Burghley and Walsingham; thus he was perhaps the first in a distinguished line of dons, such as D. G. Hogarth in the First World War and J. C. Masterman in the Second, to be engaged in intelligence work.[4]

Some practical interest in geography continued to be taken in Oxford throughout the seventeenth and eighteenth centuries but in the examination reforms of the early nineteenth century its importance was overlooked. In 1885, in Europe there were 45 professors of geography, which was well-established in Germany and in France had been a subject of fervent interest since the defeat of 1870; there was no full-time geography teacher however in a British University.[5]

The revival of Oxford geography was largely due to the concern of the Royal Geographical Society (R.G.S.) because those responsible for the destinies of the Empire had so little knowledge of the subject. In 1874 Sir Bartle Frere, President of the R.G.S. and among the most experienced proconsuls of his time, proposed that University posts be established to promote the study of scientific geography, and eventually in 1886 Oxford accepted the Society's offer to finance a Readership.

Modern geography, and indeed Imperial geography, was largely the creation of H. J. (later Sir Halford) Mackinder (1861–1947) who, as the originator of geopolitics, was the best-known geographer of his time. His career as an undergraduate at Christ Church was remarkably versatile. He first took a degree in Natural Sciences, working with H. N. Moseley on animal morphology at a time when the focus of scientific interest lay in the theory of evolution. This led him on to take a degree in Modern History in order to see how the theory of evolution would appear in human development. Simultaneously he obtained the Burdett Coutts Scholarship in Geology and read Anthropology with Tyler. He found time to be called to the Bar and to be President of the Union, where he made lasting friendships with Milner and Curzon. He was also an enthusiastic participant in military training. As a young extension worker he lectured widely on the 'New Geography' and startled the Royal Geographical Society with a paper which insisted that geography was a subject in its own right which could build a bridge between the natural sciences and the study of humanity. When Oxford finally accepted the R.G.S.'s offer of a Readership, Mackinder was appointed to it at the age of 26 by a reluctant University on the suggestion of the Society.

In the two most important works which he published whilst at Oxford, *Britain and the British Seas* (1902) and 'The Geographical Pivot of History' (1904), Mackinder warned that Britain should not be complacent about her Empire. Her seapower could not suffice unless it were expanded into an Imperial Navy to which the colonies would contribute.[6] Later, in his famous theory of the Heartland, he foresaw the nature of the German challenge: 'Who rules Eastern Europe commands the Heartland. Who rules the Heartland commands the World Island. Who rules the World Island commands the World.'[7] Mackinder held the Readership from 1887 to 1904, during which time he established the Oxford School of Geography, the first in any British University to offer a diploma course.

Mackinder was admirably equipped to obtain the cooperation both of historians and natural scientists, though he found the historians more ready to include geography in their curriculum. This was supported by the Chancellor of the University, Lord Curzon, who in his Romanes Lecture in 1907 emphasised the importance of political geography and Oxford's responsibility to teach it.[8]

Mackinder was also a skilled propagandist and organiser. He admitted women to the diploma course; he succeeded in placing many of those who took the diploma in key positions in other Universities, and spread the 'New Geography' through the secondary schools in the first vacation summer schools for teachers ever to be held in Oxford. He believed that if the Empire was to develop any cohesion, then education must play a vital role in bringing citizens of many parts of the world to some understanding of the Imperial ideal. Through his courses at Oxford, through the 'Mackindergarten' which he organised for senior Army officers, and through his books, he taught that the world had become one of closed systems in which Britain's task was not to expand, but to survive, and that this would only be possible within a Federated Empire, centred upon an Imperial Parliament.

Whilst Reader and Director of the Oxford School, Mackinder was simultaneously the first Director of the Extension College at Reading; during a long vacation he led the first expedition to climb Mount Kenya; but despite these additional activities the Oxford stage was too small for him. He moved on to be Director of the London School of Economics, an M.P. and Privy Councillor, and Chairman of the Imperial Shipping Committee and of the Imperial Economic Committee. Friends such as Beatrice Webb and Sir Michael Sadler had expected him to achieve even higher positions, but he was unfortunate in moving from the Liberal Party to the Conservative Party just as the Conservatives were going out of office for ten years. In Oxford he was lamented as the lost leader of geography, but, to his own dismay in old age, he was popularly known to the world at large as the prophet whose Heartland theory had been absorbed by the German geographer Haushoffer and by Rudolph Hess, and through them had influenced Hitler in writing *Mein Kampf* and in his subsequent politics of German expansion.[9]

Mackinder was succeeded as Reader by A. J. Herbertson, whom he had brought to Oxford from Edinburgh as a lecturer and whose qualities were somewhat complementary; whilst Mackinder was an inspiring speaker, Herbertson was the patient tutor. Even more than Mackinder, Herbertson considered that geography was concerned with the future, and with the future of Empire. It should be utilised, he wrote, to foster first a local patriotism, then an affection for country and Empire, and ultimately the loyalty of a citizen of the world.[10] In his time the Geography School organised lectures for the I.C.S. probationers and taught surveying to those from Egypt and the Sudan. With money from Sir Abe Bailey, the South African magnate, he established a library and reading room for students of Colonial Geography and History, and the School provided special facilities for colonial civil servants on furlough.

Even so the geographers had to overcome considerable prejudice. When O. G. S. Crawford in 1909 informed his tutor that he had decided to give up Greats to take the diploma in Geography, it was like telling his father he had decided to marry a barmaid. Going from Greats to Geography, he wrote, was like leaving the parlour for the basement; one lost caste but one did see life.[11]

Whilst Lankester and Poulton were proclaiming that the Empire was in mortal danger because of the scientific illiteracy of its rulers, Herbertson at about the same time pointed out the serious consequences of the lack of geographical knowledge in high places. In his Presidential Address to the Geographical section of the British Association in 1910 he suggested that each colonial Government should have a Geographical–Statistical Department which would supply information to a central Imperial Intelligence Department. 'Thinking in continents . . . might then become part of the necessary equipment of a statesman instead of merely an after dinner aspiration. The country which first gives this training to its statesmen will have an immeasurable advantage in the struggle for existence. Our universities will naturally be the places where the men fit to constitute such an intelligence department will be found.' He concluded by comparing the great investment which Germany made in her Institutes of Geography with the three rooms which were all that was provided for Oxford's School of Geography.[12]

Herbertson's dream was to establish an Institute of Imperial Geography and History in Oxford, but the outbreak of war in 1914 and his own death at the age of 49 in 1915 put an end to this.[13] Between the First and Second World Wars, although the Oxford School continued to devote considerable attention to Empire and colonisation, its influence diminished because it was unable to persuade the University to agree to an honours degree course until 1932, whilst Cambridge and other Universities developed such courses from 1919 onwards. In 1932 Major Kenneth Mason, Director of the Indian Government Survey, was, however, appointed as the first Professor of Geography; until then the post had been a Readership, although Herbertson was given the personal title of Professor. By 1937 100 students were reading for degrees and Mason reported that all but one Geography graduate who applied to join the Colonial Administrative Service had been accepted.[14] Geography had become established as a flourishing school, but no longer had a political message.

The popular interest in Empire and the scope for specialised teaching under the Education Acts of 1902 led to a great demand for textbooks not only on the history but on the geography of Empire. To this demand the Oxford geographers responded with zest. Mackinder and Herbertson were both highly successful popularisers. The Clarendon Press sold 1.4 million copies of geographical textbooks by Herbertson and his wife, while George Philips sold half a million copies of Mackinder's works.

The introduction of geography into the school curriculum was opposed by some Liberals on the grounds that its study lent itself to the growth of militarism and Jingoism. Mackinder and Herbertson took pains to avoid such charges. Mackinder disliked geography taught by maps on which the Empire was coloured red and said that 'the essentially provincial contempt for other races is a vice to be fought in the education of an Imperial race';[15] Mackinder and Herbertson, however, were by no means alone in the textbook field. Between 1899 and 1910 the Clarendon Press published a *Historical Geography of the British Colonies* in several volumes by C. P. Lucas, described as 'of Balliol and the Colonial Office', and later to become Sir Charles Lucas and Fellow of All Souls. In this series, the Colonial Office approach seemed to prevail over that of Balliol. Thus, Cyprus was described as held by the British Government 'for the benefit of the Cypriot people'[16] and Ceylon as 'entitled to the continuance of the good government which it enjoys under the British supremacy'.[17] Of West Africa it was observed that 'the English would not be justified in withdrawing their law and justice or in transferring to some other less trained European nation the burden which history has given them to bear'.[18] The Balliol man's historical conscience may have suffered a twinge at the statement regarding the Jameson Raid – 'The redeeming feature in the disastrous episode was that the good faith of the British Government was kept beyond reproach.'[19]

When Mackinder arrived in Oxford, the only lectures on geography, for one hour a week, were given by Hereford George, Fellow of New College, who wrote a *Historical Geography of the British Empire* in 1904. In this book, the robust style reflected the author's position as Chairman of the Oxford University War Games Club, a society of dons which met alternately in All Souls and New College.

'The enemies of England abroad are in the habit of sneering at her greed for territories, fulminating against her endless intrigues, threatening her with the vengeance of outraged humanity and so forth.' After enquiring 'what is the basis of such ill will and whether our attitude justifies or excuses it', he concluded that 'Englishmen know that their country has a clearer conscience than most others and that the last thing their Government would dream of doing is to intrigue. . . . Our empire is not unfair to the other nations, as England stands alone in the favourable treatment which she offers to foreigners. The wealthy landowner must expect to be envied by his less fortunate neighbour; but his conscience need not be uneasy at this unless he treats them unfairly.'[20]

The magnum opus of the Oxford Geography School was the publication of the six-volume *Oxford Survey of the British Empire* in 1914, edited by Herbertson and his colleague, O. J. R. Howarth. 'It is a necessary preliminary to imperial organisation', Howarth explained, 'in whatever department, that those on whom the task falls (and it may fall not on individuals only but on generations) should possess some organised knowledge of the Empire. To supply such knowledge has been the object of this survey, first physical; then natural wealth; and then . . . in regard to its inhabitants.'[21] In dealing with the inhabitants, the contributors were allowed full scope for generalisations.

Thus, writing on India, Sir Richard Temple (formerly of the I.C.S.) contrasted the disloyalty of the Indian National Congress with the attitude of the native ruling Princes, who were 'practically English gentlemen', although he considered that there was no danger in the situation if it were handled with discernment. After some observations on mixed marriages (almost always a mistake, in his opinion), he declared that the criticism of the attitude of Europeans towards natives as 'cold superciliousness' was a shallow observation. 'Europeans in India are for the practical purposes of society willy-nilly a caste, and as a caste they have the same business and general social relations towards all the other castes as they have towards each other. . . . Free intercourse is impossible when men cannot dine together.'[22] Vincent Smith, in another chapter on India, was more worried. His main concern was 'how to reconcile the just claims of the Indians with the imperious necessity of maintaining the British political supremacy and the conduct of the government on principles approved by the British nation'.[23]

As for Ceylon, J. C. Willis wrote that 'the average Ceylonese (except members of the highest castes) dislikes responsibility and does not readily rise to it as does a capable European. For the same reason, the native being as yet incapable of satisfactory self government, there is no elective legislative council.'[24] As it turned out, Ceylon was to become the first of Britain's Asian colonies to be given a form of internal self-government.

West Africans were the subject of more favourable assessment. 'Speaking generally,' wrote T. J. Allridge, 'both Sierra Leoneans (often called Creoles) and natives are capable of considerable intellectural development.' In South Africa, however, the *Survey* was 'baffled' by the consequences of the failure of the natives to die out. 'Elsewhere in the Empire', wrote Basil Worsfield, 'the aboriginal races when brought into contact with European colonists have dwindled or disappeared: but in South Africa the Bantu have multiplied and thriven under European administration. . . . The presence of the preponderant dark skinned population, unable or unwilling to provide manual labour sufficient to satisfy completely the industrial needs of the country . . . prevents the Union of South Africa from offering a livelihood to a class of European immigrants who, as in the other dominions, would otherwise have contributed most effectively to build up its European population.'[25]

As for our kith and kin, Australians were described as more apt than the British to regard their own State or city as of greater importance than it really is, more ready to misunderstand and resent criticism.[26] It may have been a relief to readers on the other hand to learn that 'those born in New Zealand become immensely patriotic New Zealanders and Imperialists, even if not of British stock',[27] whilst in Canada 'immigrants from the United Kingdom are specially desired, not only for their inherent qualities, but to balance the foreign element, and to help the Canadians to preserve the traditions and characteristics of the British race, and maintain that spirit of loyalty to the Empire which pervades the country in such a marked degree today'.[28] The *Survey* provides a fascinating picture of Oxford's perception of the Empire at its highest tide.

ANTHROPOLOGISTS AND SCHOLAR ADMINISTRATORS

In Oxford geography has for many years shared a Faculty with anthropology. The establishment of anthropology resulted from General Pitt Rivers's ruminations on the historical collection of firearms which he made after the Crimean War. He observed that the evolution of firearms had progressed by successful minute variations rather than by sudden jumps. To enlarge his observations he proceeded to collect ethnological and archaeological materials in order to investigate whether the phenomena of development associated with firearms might apply more widely. The result was a museum of comparative technology, including examples of the principal appliances and basic industries and arts of mankind from the earliest times to the age of mass production.

In 1883 Pitt Rivers gave this collection to Oxford University on condition that a separate building should be provided for it and that a person be appointed to teach the subject. On the initiative of H. N. Mosely, E. B. Tylor was appointed as Reader in Anthropology to fulfil the latter condition, despite the protest of the *Oxford Magazine* against the appointment of 'a foreigner to Oxford' to a post in a subject which did not form part of any honours School of the University.[29]

Sir Edward Tylor (1832–1917) was the founder of anthropology in Britain. He never took a competitive examination in his life. He left school at 16 to work in the family brass foundry, but because of lung trouble was sent to travel abroad at the age of 23. In his travels he studied ethnology, and, virtually self-taught, established his reputation with his book *Primitive Culture* in 1871. Oxford appointed him Keeper of the Museum in 1883 and Reader in 1884, a post which he held until 1909 with the personal title of Professor.

Tylor's interest was in the unity of mankind. He was preoccupied with questions of coincidences of customs, of beliefs, of arts and crafts, of proverbs and riddles. Using objects from the Museum, he would lecture on flint implements, on gestures and language, the origins of weights and measures, on marriage, counting, and the decline in the belief in ghosts. Initially, at least, his lectures were something of a social event; a number of Oxford men who were to serve the Empire had their curiosity aroused by them, and would recollect how the professor's beard caught alight when he was demonstrating how to manufacture fire with a bow and a piece of wood.

Tylor failed to obtain the status of a degree course for anthropology. This was opposed, he said, by an alliance of Scribes, Pharisees and Sadducees. The theologians would not countenance teaching about false gods; the classicists knew no culture other than that of Greece and Rome; and the Museum people maintained that the study of man was not a science.[30]

Despite Tylor's remark there was, however, a considerable interest in anthropology among Oxford classicists at the turn of the century. The great achievement of Marett, who was to succeed Tylor as Reader, was to mobilise this interest in support of a diploma course in Anthropology which could be related to the needs of Empire. R. R. Marett (1866–1943), who eventually became Rector of Exeter

College, was far more adept in University politics and in touch with the outside world than Tylor. After obtaining a First in Mods and Greats from Balliol he had been a philosophy tutor at Exeter College and moved into anthropology through his interest in early religions.

In 1905 Marett and J. L. Myres were instrumental in obtaining approval for a one-year diploma course in Anthropology, which was justified by the needs for instruction of I.C.S. probationers and Rhodes Scholars; its curriculum was also aimed at missionaries, administrators and Census officials. The first probationers to study anthropology were those of the Sudan Political Service. About the same time Marett obtained the sympathy of the classicists by involving them in a series of lectures on 'Classics and Anthropology' given by distinguished scholars including Sir Arthur Evans, Gilbert Murray, J. L. Myres and Andrew Lang. Several of the classicists subsequently taught on the diploma course together with the natural scientists. Marett was also co-founder with G. C. Robson in 1909 of the Oxford University Anthropological Society, whose meetings were often concerned with the contribution of anthropology to colonial administration.

Marett held the Readership from 1908 until 1937. For many years, he and Henry Balfour were a constant source of encouragement not only to those who had taken the diploma, but to other Oxford men throughout the Empire, particularly administrators who became interested in anthropology.

Henry Balfour (1862–1939) was Curator of the Pitt Rivers Museum from 1891 to 1939. He was trained as a biologist and taught technology as well as archaeology on the diploma course. Once his pupils, the colonial administrators remained his pupils for life. They would return to him on leave with objects for his collection and he would visit them, from the Zambesi to Manipur, to interpret their local findings in light of his unequalled knowledge of the culture of primitive peoples.

There was, however, a tradition of anthropological studies among Oxford scholar administrators which, although encouraged by Marett and Balfour, anticipated the diploma course and owed much on the one hand to classical studies and on the other to scientific studies of evolution. It was in India that this tradition first became established by the Oxford-educated members of the I.C.S. Among the most notable were Sir Herbert Risley (1851–1911), J. H. Hutton (1885–1968), J. P. Mills (1890–1960) and Sir Wilfred Grigson (1896–1949). All of them became interested in anthropology through their work with primitive tribes; and Risley and Hutton were able to express this on a broad canvas as Census Commissioners.

Risley was the archetypal scholar administrator. After working on the *Gazetteer of Bengal* with W. W. Hunter, he went on to be Commissioner for the Indian Census of 1901 whose Report set a new style in Indian official literature. His book on *Tribes and Castes of Bengal*[31] was a pioneer classic which established a pattern for similar studies in other parts of India. Yet he was also at the centre of political decisions. As Curzon's Home Secretary he was involved in the partition of Bengal; later he played an important part in drafting the Morley–Minto reforms. On retirement he became President of the Royal Anthropological Institute, and revealed how much his classical studies at Winchester and Oxford had influenced him. Just off the beaten track of the regular duties of the I.C.S. officer, he explained, and overlapping it at many points, there lay a wide field of research for the classical scholar, the study of custom, myth, ritual, religion and social structure. Indian society offered a version of the daily life of Greeks and Romans. In it could be seen how ancestor worship determined laws of inheritance; how minor gods presided over boundaries, rocks and trees. Departmental deities responsible for cholera and smallpox had to be kept in good humour. Even the shape of a village courtyard would remind the observer how Penelope's suitors were trapped by Odysseus.[32] Characteristically, Risley's major work on *The People of India* begins with a quotation from Homer's *Iliad*[33]

Hutton and Mills worked among, and wrote books about, tribes in Assam. Hutton only obtained a Third in Modern History at Worcester College before entering the I.C.S. As Census Commissioner of the Government of India in 1931, however, he wrote a Census Report which advanced novel theories on migrations and cultural patterns, and is regarded by demographers and anthropologists as the most scholarly of all the Reports in this decennial series. It ended with a quotation in the original Greek from Thucydides. Even if this was not understood by the majority of the Census Report's users, the reputation which Hutton gained by the Report, and by his book on *Caste in India* which was drawn from it, led to his appointment as Professor of Social Anthropology at Cambridge. Hutton made himself the advocate of the tribal peoples during discussions on constitutional reforms and was mainly responsible for the special status of excluded areas in the Government of India Act of 1935.[34]

J. P. Mills of Winchester and Corpus spent most of his service in

Assam where he was adviser to the Governor for Tribal Areas and States. Like Hutton, he was visited by Balfour, and contributed important collections to the Pitt Rivers Museum. He wrote two books on the Nagas, and so gained their confidence that the headhunters would ask him to settle small wars whenever their digestions were sufficiently ruined by the deliberately bad cooking of their wives, whose relatives they were hunting. On his retirement he became a Reader at the London School of Oriental and African Studies and President of the Royal Anthropological Institute. He called his Presidential Address 'Anthropology as a Hobby', and commenced it with a Latin tag '*homo sum*; *humanum nil a me alienum puto*'. What the amateur anthropologist needed most, he said, was training and encouragement and above all someone to answer letters and give a welcome and patient hearing when he came on leave. This was exactly what Balfour and Marett provided.[35]

Sir Wilfred Grigson was a classical scholar of Christ Church who whilst Administrator of Bastar State from 1927 to 1931 wrote a remarkable book on the Maria Gonds as well as an official report on the aboriginal problems in the Central Provinces. In these he showed the misery caused by the imposition on a primitive People of criminal, civil and revenue laws framed for districts in British India which were some centuries more advanced. He was able to restore village *panchayats*, to restrict the alienation of land to outsiders, and to end the harassment of the Gonds by petty officials. Hutton wrote of Grigson's work: 'It is the very high privilege of that altogether rare individual, the anthropologically minded administrative officer, that he can often bring practical benefits to the subjects of his studies as well as informative benefits to the reader he instructs.'[36] 'For nearly 20 years', wrote Verrier Elwin, on Grigson's death whilst in the service of Pakistan, 'the administration of Bastar proceeded on lines laid down by him, to the infinite benefit of the state. I have often thought how wonderful it must have been to feel that one has been responsible for so much happiness of half a million tribesmen over a period of two decades.'[37]

In addition to the administrators, some of the earliest anthropologists or ethnologists were missionaries. One of the most remarkable was R. H. Codrington (1830–1922), a Fellow of Wadham, who worked with Bishop Patteson in Melanesia. When Patteson was killed, Codrington refused the Bishopric because he considered that he could be more useful in studying and making known as much as possible what natives said about themselves, not what Europeans said about them. He wrote the grammar and vocabularies of 34 languages. When his book, *The Melanesians, A Study in their Anthropology and Folklore*, was published in 1891 as a result of 24 years' fieldwork, he apologised for its insufficiency.[38] His modesty and wide interests charmed Oxford, where he returned to produce a translation of the Bible in the Mota language, and where his friends were as various as Ruskin, Max Mueller, Samuel Wilberforce and Charles Dodgson. He maintained his Fellowship of Wadham throughout his time in Melanesia and sent many gifts to the Pitt Rivers Museum. He was described as resembling the Venerable Bede in his powers of teaching and learning, never meeting error by direct contradiction; whenever he heard something said which was quite wrong, he simply asked a few questions and by the method used by Socrates led the mistaken person to admit his error.[39]

A later missionary who had a very different career was Verrier Elwin, a friend and protégé of Grigson. The Empire was in his blood. His father was Bishop of Sierra Leone; he had two uncles in the I.C.S. and another in the Bengal Lancers. After taking Firsts in English and Theology at Merton, he was ordained and became Vice-Principal of Wycliffe Hall. From Oxford, he went out to India to work with the Christa Seva Sangha Mission, whose members lived in Indian style and aimed to re-orientalise Christian religion. There Elwin became closely associated with Gandhi, hoisted the Congress flag on the Mission, and vowed never to wear shoes again until India became independent. This made him *persona non grata* both with the Bishop and with the British administration, within which Oxford friends saved him from deportation on condition that he confined himself to non-political work.

He settled among the Gonds, marrying a tribal girl, setting up schools and dispensaries and a leper home and cottage industries. At the same time, he published several books about their customs and translations of their poems. Merton College gave him a research grant, and the Oxford University Anthropological Society helped to finance publication of his books. His experience caused him to disagree with Gandhi, whose ideas on spinning, sex relations and diet seemed inapplicable to Gond society. His books, however, charmed and impressed Jawarharlal Nehru, who made him Adviser for Tribal Affairs after Independence when he took Indian nationality. Thus this gentle rebel became the last in the line of Oxford scholar administrators in India, with an office in the Secretariat.

In his memoirs, Elwin expressed his debt to Oxford. His interest in human beings began with his study of literature there, and his studies in theology developed his interest in man. 'For me anthropology did not mean field work; it meant my whole life . . . at Oxford I developed the habit of thinking in Neoplatonic terms by which one can build up a store of inner strength that will be independent of outside circumstances. Without this, I do not think I could have endured the isolation and the tragedies of village life.'[40]

There were also early Oxford anthropologists whose initial interest derived from studies in zoology and botany. Among them was Mackinder's closest friend as an undergraduate, Baldwin (later Sir Baldwin, 1860–1929) Spencer of Exeter College who attended H. N. Moseley's zoology classes with him. Whilst the fascination of evolution was to carry Mackinder into history and geography, it led Spencer into anthropology. After graduating he worked as an assistant to Moseley and helped him and Tylor to arrange the Pitt Rivers collection. He became a Fellow of Lincoln College and made his scientific reputation with a paper to the Royal Society which, from study of the vestigial eye in lizards, explained the presence of a mysterious part of the brain in all higher mammals. On the strength of this he was appointed Professor of Biology in Melbourne.

With Frank Gillen, an administrator in Alice Springs who had come to know the aborigines through having to control their depredations on the telegraph lines, Spencer made a study of the Arunta tribe which J. G. Frazer, who incorporated much of it in *The Golden Bough*, described as 'taking the scientific world by storm'.[41] Among his conclusions was that the aborigines were unaware of the role of the male in reproduction: each man's totem was the insect, tree or animal in which the spirit which impregnated his mother had concealed itself. This belief, though no odder perhaps than those held at that time on the subject by some of the young ladies of Oxford, was considered by anthropologists to be of outstanding importance in the study of a Stone Age civilisation.

Spencer corresponded frequently with Marett and Balfour and sent back many objects to the Pitt Rivers Museum. His Oxford colleagues considered that his success as an anthropologist was due to the powers of observation which he had acquired as a biologist, as well as his genial disposition. In 1911 he became Special Commissioner and Chief Protector of the Tribes in the Northern Territory of Australia. Despite his academic interest in their culture he was realistic as administrator and recommended that stations be set up for the aborigines where they would be taught to abandon their wandering habits and to practise agriculture. When Spencer died at the age of 69 whilst on an expedition to complete Darwin's observations of the Indians of Terra del Fuego, Marett suggested that his epitaph should be the name which the aborigines had given him – 'Him Goodfellow: Him Talk True'.[42]

The Colonial Office showed more interest in the teaching of anthropology to its probationers than did the India Office, a fact deplored by Risley, Temple and other former I.C.S. officials. In 1913 of 41 students enrolled for the Oxford diploma, 20 were officers serving under the Colonial Office in various parts of Africa and ten others were seeking similar posts.[43] The best-known and earliest of the colonial administrators who took the diploma was R. S. Rattray (1881–1938). Rattray had run away from school in Scotland to fight in the Boer War and then worked for the African Lakes Corporation from 1902 to 1907. Alone in a trading post or shooting big game, he found that he had a talent for African languages and the collection of folklore. He joined the Gold Coast Administrative Service in 1907 and whilst on leave took the Oxford Anthropology diploma in 1909. Marett recognised his talent in spite of his limited academic background; so did Sir Gordon Guggisberg, most far-sighted of African Governors, who made him the first head of the Anthropological Department of the Gold Coast Government. In this capacity he not only wrote several books on the Ashanti but played an invaluable part in tranquilising the inflamed situation which arose when the Ashanti Stool was desecrated: thirty years earlier, a Governor of the Gold Coast had lost his life because the significance of the Stool had not been understood. Oxford gave Rattray an honorary D.Sc., and he taught Hausa to colonial probationers there after a somewhat early and perhaps unwilling retirement: but he was sensitive about his lack of formal qualifications and had the reputation of being a rude and difficult colleague, although infinitely patient with Africans. He lacked the assurance of the scholar administrators of the 'Heaven-born' I.C.S.[44]

A Colonial Service official whose career was more similar to those of the scholar administrators of the I.C.S. was C. K. Meek (1885–1965). An exhibitioner of Brasenose College, he graduated in Theology before entering the Colonial Service, in which his career was in Nigeria. There he played an important part in the extension of Indirect Rule to the South. Through his work as Census Commissioner he became a largely self-taught anthropologist, with encouragement from Marett. On his retirement he returned to Oxford to lecture to the colonial services' courses.[45]

By the 1930s the importance of anthropology in relation to colonial administration was widely accepted. Whilst some colonial Governors appointed members of their services as anthropological officers, others brought in anthropologists from Universities to advise on particular problems. Among the latter was Evans-Pritchard, whose study of the Nuer was carried out at the request of the Sudan Government in an attempt to understand why they were on the verge of rebellion. After the time of Marett and Balfour however the collaboration of anthropologists and colonial administrators became less close, partly because of the more theoretical approach of Marett's successor as Reader, A. R. Radcliffe-Brown (1881–1955), who became the first occupant of the University Chair in Anthropology and Director of the new Institute of Social Anthropology.

He had indeed a much broader experience than Marett. He had been Director of Education in Tonga, ethnologist in the Transvaal Museum, and Professor of Anthropology in Capetown, Sydney and Chicago. In Australia he had also organised training of administrators who were to work in New Guinea, though this was criticised as being too theoretical. Wherever he went, however, he was mainly interested in grand schemes for systematic research. He told his students that they must not expect anthropology to be of direct practical use. He argued that the anthropologist's job was to provide a 'scientific appraisal of the situation which the administrator faced and that he should not advocate any particular policy.[46]

Perhaps the greatest of all Oxford's scholar administrators was Lord Hailey (1872–1969), a classical scholar of Corpus who, after occupying the highest posts in the I.C.S., started on an even more influential career as author of the massive *African Survey* and other comparative studies in African administration, and as Adviser to the Colonial Office. In this second stage, he took a keen interest in anthropology and gave a magisterial lecture to the Royal Anthropological Institute in 1944 on 'The Role of Anthropology in Colonial Development'. Though praising the work of Rattray in the Gold Coast, Meek in Nigeria, and Evans-Pritchard in the Sudan, he suggested that colonial Governments still needed to make more use of anthropologists and that University departments of anthropology could be more helpful in investigation of how societies worked rather than how they originated. Whilst the study of native institutions in relation to Indirect Rule continued to be useful, he considered that unfortunately British Universities were less interested than those in the Netherlands in such practical questions as social effects of migration, food habits in relation to nutrition, systems of landholding in relation to agricultural production and the effect of educational policies. In short, there was a need for anthropologists to give special attention to the reaction of native life to the administration's programme of social and political progress, rather than concentrating on the survival at any cost of traditional institutions.[47]

In India, though Risley's work was admired by Indian intellectuals, later Hutton and Grigson were attacked by Nationalist politicians as wanting to keep the primitive races of India 'uncivilised' and in a state of barbarism, as raw material for their science.[48] Such observations were to some extent debating points, for on coming to power Congress readers learnt to appreciate the advice of anthropologists such as Elwin on problems of tribal areas. There may have been more justice in the allegation in Africa where the enthusiasm of academics for the policies of Indirect Rule shocked Hailey who saw this system as a temporary stage which by 1938 was out of date except as a form of Local Government.[49]

Hailey's pleas seem to have had little effect on Oxford anthropology which became more individualistic and academic. Sir Edward Evans-Pritchard (1902–73), Radcliffe Brown's successor as Professor, enjoyed a considerable reputation as guerrilla leader of Ethiopian tribes in the Second World War; under him the number of anthropology students at Oxford, now mostly taking doctoral degrees, and a third of them American, greatly increased. Godfrey Lienhart, however, in an obituary of Evans-Pritchard in 1974, expressed surprise that an 'Oxford School of Anthropology' was claimed to exist, for there had never been a staff meeting during the directorship of Evans-Pritchard, who felt physically sick at the thought of meetings of any kind. No one had any idea, or indeed took any interest in what his colleagues were lecturing about.[50]

Whilst it might be admitted that there was never an Oxford School, it can be concluded that there was an Oxford influence. Most of the earlier Oxford scholar administrators had read Mods and Greats. What they brought to the study of primitive people was knowledge of ancient Greek and Roman societies. It appeared not a bad preparation for understanding and governing them. Even the colonial officials like Rattray who were taught by Marett on the diploma course were exposed to the classical approach at second hand.

The other approach was through the study of evolution and the natural sciences. Of this, Spencer was the most notable of Oxford anthropologists in the field and Balfour in Oxford. One of the happiest features was the combination of the two approaches provided by Marett and Balfour. In the end this may have been one of Oxford's most useful if modest contributions to the anthropological problems of Empire: it provided, in Mills's words, 'Someone who will always answer letters and give a welcome and patient hearing when one comes on leave.'[51]

ECONOMICS

By contrast with geography and anthropology, the interest of Oxford economists was, with the brief exception of Merivale, very late to develop. The Sibthorpian Chair in Rural Economy was founded in 1798 but for many years the only duties of the Professor were to give one lecture a year and allow his garden to be used for growing plants. The Drummond Chair in Political Economy was founded in 1825 and one of its early incumbents, Herman Merivale, a Fellow of Balliol, devoted his lectures between 1839 and 1841 to the subject of 'Colonies and Colonisation'. These gave critical support to Wakefield's theory of colonisation and advocated free trade and colonial self-government. When published, they were so much appreciated that Merivale became Permanent Under Secretary to the Colonial Office, and later held the same post in the India Office.[52]

Whilst the founding of the Drummond Professorship was under discussion, Sydney Smith observed that 'when a University has been doing useless things for a long time, it appears at first degrading for them to be useful. A set of lectures upon Political Economy would be discouraged at Oxford, possibly despised, probably not admitted.'[53] Although this was proved to be an exaggeration, it took another 100 years for economics to become firmly established in Oxford. Apart from the Drummond Professor, who was often not resident in Oxford, economics continued to be taught as part of Greats or Modern History, usually by tutors like Jowett or Phelps, who had no methodical grounding in the subject. During the 1880s and 1890s a number of young dons formed the Oxford Economics Society in which there was a strong religious influence linked with an interest in the amelioration of the lot of the working-class, in contrast to Cambridge where the subject was dominated by Marshall and *laissez-faire*.[54] Among them was Arnold Toynbee. Some of these young men became professional economists at the London School of Economics and took part in the new extension work organised from Oxford by Sadler and Mackinder. One of them, W. A. S. Hewins, was to become a prominent Imperialist. After starting as a diploma subject, economics obtained a regular place in the undergraduate curriculum when the School of Philosophy, Politics and Economics (P.P.E.) was established after the First World War. In the 1930s a number of Oxford historians, notably Keith Hancock, wrote about the economics of Empire. It was only at the end of Empire in 1946 however that the importance of economic problems of the dependent territories was recognised by the appointment – financed by the United Africa Company – of the South African S. H. Frankel as Professor of Colonial Economic Affairs.

The long neglect of economics at Oxford was often criticised. In 1920 Edwin Cannan, a Balliol man who was Professor of Political Science at the University of London, told the Royal Commission on Oxford and Cambridge Universities that Oxford had fallen immensely behind other Universities and 'has only been providing a smattering of economics and that for the most part of the bad kind of smattering which makes them think they know when they do not, rather than the good kind of smattering which makes them know they do not know'. He deplored the fact that public finance was being left to amateurs with disastrous results.[55]

There was, however, one institution in Oxford, largely financed by the Government, which did give attention to the economic problems of the Empire, and this emanated, as might be expected, from Jowett's Balliol where A. D. (later Sir Daniel) Hall had taken his degree in Chemistry. Hall went on to become Director of Wye Agricultural College and then of the Rothamsted Agricultural Experimental Station and was the founder of the profession of Agricultural Economics in England. In 1913, whilst he was a member of the Development Commission, he persuaded Oxford to establish an Institute for Research into Agricultural Economics which would both carry out work on specific projects for the Government and train agricultural economists. Its first Director, C. S. Orwin, who held the post from 1913 to 1945, had been one of Hall's students at Wye and under him the Institute made a considerable contribution through its research into the expansion of British agricultural production and consequently to survival in the Second World War.

The Institute dropped the word 'Research' from its title and from 1925 at the request of the Colonial Office, trained men who were destined for administrative posts in the agricultural services of the Crown Colonies. These spent two terms at Oxford and one at Cambridge (later changed to three terms at Oxford and vacation work in Cambridge) before going on for a second year to the Imperial College of Tropical Agriculture in the West Indies. There was thus no controversy with Cambridge, such as had exploded over forestry.

Orwin's influence in the University was firmly based on his position as Fellow and Estates Bursar of Balliol, and a diploma course was introduced which the colonial probationers were able to take. At the same time in Whitehall in the early days support was assured by Sir Daniel Hall who was Chief Scientific Adviser at the Ministry of Agriculture from 1920 to 1927; later the Colonial Office also gave financial support.[56]

LAW

The only part of the Empire for which special provision was made in the study of law in the nineteenth century was India. In 1868 the Readership in Indian Law and History was created, occupied by the long-lived historian, S. J. Owen. In 1878 a separate Readership in Indian Law was financed by All Souls. This was held in early years by a succession of former British judges from India, often men of considerable distinction, such as Sir William Markby, Sir Thomas Raleigh and Sir C. J. Trevelyan. The Reader's main duties were in teaching I.C.S. probationers, whose numbers declined so that the Readership was abolished in 1938. It never seems to have had the kind of research orientation desired by Max Mueller rather than Monier Williams.

Early in the twentieth century, partly in connection with the Rhodes Scholarship scheme, there was a general feeling that Oxford should do more to meet the needs of the Empire in this area. In 1908 and again in 1909 Parkin made an earnest appeal to Oxford to become a great centre for the study of the legal systems of all parts of the Empire.[57] Lord Curzon about the same time, addressing the Imperial Press Conference at All Souls in his capacity as Chancellor, asked 'What is there in the whole history of Imperial expansion that has done so much to mould your Institutions as English law? What in future is more required for peaceful progress of nations than the evolution, harmonization and codification of international law?[58] Some of Oxford's Professors of Law, indeed, including Bryce, Dicey and Pollock, took a considerable interest in the problems of Empire, as has been seen, but this was expressed more through their extra-curricular activities than through the teaching of law within the University.

A Chair of Roman Dutch Law was endowed by the Rhodes Trustees in 1919. Its first incumbent, R. W. Lee, had been a civil servant in Ceylon which, because it had formerly been a colony of the Netherlands, used Roman Dutch Law. The Chair attracted Ceylonese to Oxford and served the needs of South African Rhodes Scholars. It was downgraded to become a Readership in 1956.

In no other area did the Rhodes Scholars make such an impact as in law. Many of them came from countries where legal education had a more important place than at Oxford and they tended to be more mature than the British undergraduates. They thus raised the standards in the final examinations and became the backbone of the Bachelor of Civil Law course. A substantial number stayed on to teach in Oxford. In 1965 18 of those who had taught law in Oxford had received their early education in Commonwealth countries. Seven of these were Australians.[59]

9 Rhodes and the Imperial Athens

If Oxford ever became a self-conscious intellectual metropolis, inculcating an Imperial culture, she would very quickly degenerate and stiffen into a cold and pedantic conceit, as Athens stiffened under the Romans, when men flocked thither for culture and Greece herself was dying.

Sir Alfred Zimmern in 'The Third British Empire' (1926)

RHODES AND OXFORD

No one has more memorials in Oxford than Cecil Rhodes (1853–1902). There are two busts and a portrait in Rhodes House, a portrait in Oriel College, a plaque in the Examination Schools, and another on his lodgings in King Edward Street. In the High Street, on top of the building which Oriel erected with his money, his statue is poised above those of Edward VII and George V, Rhodes in his rumpled suit and the King–Emperors in their Coronation robes. He would have appreciated all this, for he was obsessed by a desire for posthumous fame, and liked to be told that his bust resembled that of a Roman Emperor.

The story of how Rhodes came to Oxford has so often been told that it is hard to disentangle fact from legend. Fifth son of a clergyman and educated at grammar school, he was sent to South Africa to save his health at the age of 17. He came back to Oxford from South Africa in 1873 because he wanted to qualify as a lawyer, in order to have a profession to fall back on should his diamond interests fail. The Master of University College refused to accept a man who wanted to read only for a pass degree, but recommended him to

Oriel, whose Provost gloomily took him in with the comment 'All the Colleges send me their failures.'[1]

Rhodes kept his terms at Oxford intermittently over an eight-year period, between 1873 and 1881, instead of over the normal three years. He came whenever his interests in South Africa, his finances and state of health permitted, and simultaneously read for the Bar. He belonged, according to his tutor, A. G. Butler, 'to a set of men like himself, not caring for distinction in Schools and not working for them, but of refined tastes, dining and living for the most part together and doubtless discussing passing events in life and politics with interest and ability'.[2]

During this time Rhodes became an Imperialist and resolved, as can be seen from his first Will, that his overall object in life was to bring about the governance of the world by the British race. How much was due to his experiences in South Africa and how much to what he learnt and heard in Oxford is disputed. He does not seem to have participated in the debates on Empire in the Oxford Union led by Parkin and Milner, nor is it known whether he attended Ruskin's Inaugural Lecture, but his biographers tell us that its text became one of his most cherished possessions, with its message that Englishmen should go out and colonise every piece of fruitful land on which they could set foot.[3]

Rhodes was at Oxford when the influence of religion was on the decline and that of Darwin on the ascendant. He studied Latin, Greek, Political Economy and Law. He carried from Oxford the constant inspiration of the pursuit of excellence derived from Aristotle's *Ethics* as well as a stoicism gained from Marcus Aurelius, whose Golden Rules he learnt by heart, and whose Meditations he would annotate and lend to admirers as he travelled on the veld. Brooding often on the lessons of Rome for Britain, he had the books which Gibbon used as sources for the *Decline and Fall of the Roman Empire* translated into English for his personal use at the cost of £8000.

Throughout his life, whilst Rhodes made his fortune in diamonds and gold, became Premier of the Cape and colonised Rhodesia, Oxford retained his regard and affection. Wherever you went, he used to reflect, although the Oxford system looks so impractical, you would find an Oxford man on top. Cambridge he considered, with its mathematics and science, limited one's outlook, whereas Oxford with its more philosophical training tended to broaden one's vision of the world. Public school education, Rhodes, the grammar school boy, considered behind the times, pointing to the imaginative qualities of Disraeli and Joseph Chamberlain who had been privately educated.[4] He liked to visit Oriel College when he came to England after he became rich and famous, because the Fellows never troubled him for advice on investments.

Rhodes's affection for Oxford, which was to bring such substantial benefactions after his death, survived a serious crisis in 1899, when he came to receive an Honorary Doctorate of Civil Law. A resolution conferring the degree had been passed in 1892, when he had been too busy to come. Meanwhile he had been discredited by the Jameson Raid. In a letter which the Vice-Chancellor refused to include in the *University Gazette*, but which was published in *The Times*, 88 members of Congregation expressed their regret that Rhodes was to receive the degree. Although the largest number of signatories came from Liberal Balliol, Conservatives and Unionists such as A. V. Dicey and C. G. Robertson were included, as well as H. A. L. Fisher, who was to become a Rhodes Trustee.[5] It was rumoured that the Proctors, both Liberals, would protest during the Encaenia Ceremony. Some friends advised Rhodes not to come: but Lord Kitchener, with all the prestige of the Victor of Omdurman, threatened not to receive his degree if Rhodes could not, and the occasion became a triumph for the latter.

'You have compared me with Clive and Warren Hastings', he said at a dinner in Oriel on the same day. 'Even some of these men, greater men than I, have not escaped calumny and have been tried before their peers for alleged misconduct. But they were acquitted, though I do not deny that I have made mistakes and there are certain events in my life which, if they occurred again, would be ordered differently. In the greater number of professions, as in law and medicine, men who adopt them are guided by precedents and by rules; in the profession which I have adopted, that of making additions to Her Majesty's Empire, I have no precedents and no rules. Can you be surprised if I sometimes make mistakes?'[6]

RHODES' WILL AND THE SCHOLARSHIPS

Flushed by his triumph, Rhodes promised Butler, who sat next to him at this dinner, to provide in his Will for the augmentation of the salaries of the Fellows and for the expenses of High Table, which were threatened through the curtailment of College rents during an agricultural depression; though the Fellows when they read the Will may not have appreciated the public advice that 'as the College authorities lived secluded like children', they should consult his Trustees about investments.

The Oriel Benefaction of £100,000 was a relatively small item in an estate which was worth £4 million. Rhodes's Will was in his mind as an instrument of Empire right from his undergraduate days, when in a first version he left his as yet unearned millions for the establishment of a secret society for the furtherance of the British Empire and recovery of the United States. There were several later versions. Lord Rosebery remembered how Rhodes would describe his Will as his companion. 'When I find myself in uncongenial company or when people are playing their games or when I am alone in a railway carriage, I shut my mind and think of my great idea . . . it is the pleasantest companion I have.'[7]

The final Will was much more sophisticated than that of 1877. The Empire and Anglo-Saxon influence were to be advanced not through a secret society, but by cooperation in education. The bulk of the estate was left to a Trust out of which colonial Scholarships were to be financed for 'young Colonists, to give breadth to their views for their instruction in life and manners, and for instilling in their minds the advantage to the Colonies as well as to the United Kingdom of the retention of the unity of the Empire'. To these were added Scholarships for the United States with the object of fostering a Union of the English-speaking peoples. By a final codicil, Scholarships were added for Germans in order that a good understanding between Britain, Germany and the United States should secure the peace of the world.

Under the original Will 60 Scholars were to be appointed from the Empire of which 24 would come from South Africa, 21 from Australasia, six from Canada, six from the Atlantic Islands (Newfoundland and Bermuda) and three from Jamaica. In addition 90 were allocated to the United States and 15 to Germany.

Rhodes was determined that his Scholars should not be 'bookworms'. As he dictated his Will to Hawksley he suggested a system of points, '4/10 for the element which I call "smug" and which means scholarship. Then there is brutality which stands for 2/10. Then there is tact and leadership 2/10 and then there is unctuous rectitude 2/10.' Hawksley and Rosebery polished up these frank phrases, so that under the final Will it was suggested that the marking system should provide 3/10 for scholarship, 2/10 for manly sports, 3/10 for qualities of manhood, truth, courage, devotion to duty, sympathy for the protection of the weak, kindliness, unselfishness and fellowship, and 2/10 for character and leadership. These qualities would be determined by a ballot of the candidates' schoolmates and by headmasters' reports.[8]

In the last year of his life Rhodes feared that he would not leave enough money to finance the Scholarships and stopped construction work on his seaside home at Muizenberg, where he spent his dying days in a hot and airless cottage.

The publication of the Will in 1902 caused almost as much consternation as gratification in Oxford, where Rhodes had consulted no one on it. The reaction of contributors to the *Oxford Magazine* has been seen in Chapter 1,[9] and C. R. L. Fletcher the historian expressed apprehensions lest arguments about the 'growing and altering needs of Empire, and such flabby-minded stuff' would lead to the abandonment of Greek and Latin as compulsory subjects, first for the Rhodes Scholars and then, insidiously to their abandonment for every one'.[10]

None of the Trustees appointed by Rhodes had academic connections with Oxford, except Milner who was in South Africa for the first few years of the Trust's existence. That the University's cooperation was obtained was mainly due to the appointment of George Parkin as Organising Secretary and of Francis Wylie as Oxford Secretary.

The Canadian, Parkin, was a brilliant speaker on Empire, inspired by, and capable of inspiring others with Rhodes's idea of a Great Imperial University. His main task was to visit the countries from which the Scholars were to come, and to establish selection procedures. Wylie was a Fellow and tutor of Brasenose College, aged 37, who had obtained a First in Mods and Greats at Balliol, rowed in the College Eight and tutored Lord Rosebery's children. He was exactly the right choice to obtain the individual agreement of each of the Oxford colleges to accept the Rhodes Scholars in the terms of the Will, which directed that the Scholarships be residential and not concentrated in a few Colleges, although in early years Balliol easily topped the list of College preferences expressed by the Scholars.

Some early decisions were crucial. Firstly, in light of the criteria set by Rhodes, the Scholars were appointed by interview rather than by examination, a notable break with English University and Civil Service tradition. Secondly, although Rhodes had envisaged Scholarship winners as schoolboys, the Trustees considered that more mature men would find it easier to adjust to Oxford's ways and standards of scholarship. It was decided that the Scholars should be appointed between the ages of 19 and 25 after two years at a University in their own country. Thirdly, a decision was immediately made to increase the number of Scholarships for Canada, so that each Province, and not only Ontario and Quebec, received an allocation; this established a precedent by which the Trustees felt able to provide Scholarships for countries or Provinces which were not included in the Will, provided that the original allocations were not diminished. The cooperation of the University was sweetened by an early hint from Rosebery, as Senior Trustee, that the Trust recognised that the arrival of the Scholars would increase the demands on the University's resources and would not forget this when it made its benefactions.

In the 77 years between 1903 and 1980 there were only three Oxford Secretaries. Sir Francis Wylie (1903–31) was succeeded by Sir Carleton Allen (1931–52) a former Rhodes Scholar from Australia, Fellow of University College and Professor of Jurisprudence. Allen was succeeded by Sir Edgar Williams (1952–80) who had been a Fellow of Merton and Balliol and was for a considerable period a Member of the Hebdomadal Council. He had also served as General Montgomery's Senior Intelligence Officer in the Second World War. In his time the post of Secretary of the Rhodes Trust was combined with that of Warden of Rhodes House, by which title the Oxford Secretary had been known since the building was erected.

Apprehensions as to the academic ability of the Scholars disappeared when three of the first batch were elected to College Fellowships on graduation. This foreshadowed a trend by which many Scholars, particularly from Australia and New Zealand, stayed on in Britain. Whilst this brain drain might have been deplored by the Founder, he would have been delighted that so many of the Scholars went on to work in other countries of the Empire, including before 1954 37 who held appointments in the Colonial Service, mainly in Africa.

Whether he would have been pleased with the general pattern of the subsequent careers of his Scholars is more doubtful. Of the professions followed by the 2,571 former Scholars who were listed in 1953, by far the largest number, 746, were academics and teachers, followed by 488 lawyers. By contrast there were only 204 in Government and international Service, including the Colonial Service, 239 in business and banking and 60 in politics. Of the 23 Scholars who had become Fellows of Oxford Colleges, nine were Australians, including Howard Florey, the only Rhodes Scholar who had won a Nobel

Prize. There were three Quadruple Blues, 12 Triple Blues and 65 Rugby Football Blues.[11]

Parkin had hoped that the Scholarships would turn out what he considered to be Oxford's highest product – 'Literary Statesmen' in the line of Gladstone, Salisbury, Rosebery, Bryce and Morley. This hardly occurred.[12] Some commentators indeed felt that Oxford's enervating manners were not an appropriate qualification for the hurly-burly of American and colonial politics and that the returning Scholars lacked 'punch'.[13]

In early years a much higher proportion of the Scholars from the Dominions than from the United States studied Natural Sciences, although this decreased after 1947 as scientific studies developed in the Commonwealth; Philosophy, Politics and Economics (Modern Greats) later became the most favoured School.[14]

The influence of the Rhodes Scholars on Oxford is perhaps easier to try to assess than the influence of Oxford on them. L. S. Amery, a Trustee, considered in 1954 that they had caused 'what was the University of one particular country, and indeed largely of a limited class, to feel itself the University, not only of a nation but of the whole English speaking world'.[15]

As foreseen by the classicists, the coming of the Rhodes Scholars hastened the end of Greek and then of Latin as compulsory requirements for entry to the University. The pressure came more from the United States than from the Dominions, where the classics were well taught in private and grammar schools, often by Oxford men. The decline of the classics in Oxford was not more rapid than in other British Universites; had there been no Rhodes Scholars, it might however have been slower in view of the prestige of the Oxford Greats School.

A more positive contribution was in the development of graduate studies. Although B.Litt. and B.Sc. degrees had been established in 1895, there had been little demand for them until the arrival of the Rhodes Scholars. Many of the latter came with B.A.s from their home countries, and did not consider an Oxford first degree to be a very useful additional qualification. By 1908 15 out of the 20 students in the University reading for the Bachelor of Civil law (B.C.L.) degree were Rhodes Scholars, and the Rhodes Trust felt obliged to contribute to the salary of a Lecturer in Law to meet their needs. The natural desire of many of the Scholars to take postgraduate courses was in some ways unfortunate, for Oxford's system of supervision of graduate students was altogether looser and less conscientious than the role of thc College tutor who listened to the undergraduates' weekly essays. Later, after the First World War, when Commonwealth and American students were cut off from the German Universities, where they had been accustomed to go to obtain their doctorates, pressure from the Rhodes Scholars was partly responsbile for the establishment by Oxford of a doctoral degree in Philosophy.

Some of the Rhodes Scholars' impressions of Oxford, together with those of other students from the various countries of the Empire, are discussed in Chapter 13. These impressions were mixed. The Scholars were older than the undergraduates who were living in College with them, and it appears from their memoirs that both in term time and in vacation many of them chose to spend their time with their compatriots rather than with British students. R. B. MacCallum, in two articles in the *Oxford Magazine* in 1930, doubted whether mixing between Rhodes Scholars and British students took place on any effective scale. He attributed this to the 'Imperial provincialism' of the English Public School man. 'It is a very condition of his qualities as a supremely confident member of a social aristocracy, a governing class and an Imperial nation that he has no standards by which he can compare himself with others.' MacCallum asserted that the Scots, with more democratic traditions, were much more congenial to the men from the Dominions or the United States.[16]

C. K. Allen noticed that the Oxford climate, for scholars arriving in October, deprived of sun, caused a certain lowness of animal spirits, only to be dispelled by vigorous exercise. Allen believed that what the Scholars gained most from Oxford was tolerance and exposure to the multifarious intellectual vitality of Oxford, seasoned with a due modicum of frivolity.[17] A. D. Lindsay considered that the Rhodes Scholars helped to transform Oxford into a classless society.[18] On the other hand, there is evidence that the presence of some from South Africa and the Southern States of the United States spread racial prejudice.[19]

Whatever the concepts of 'a Great Imperial University', there was in general no attempt at Imperial indoctrination. When the egregious Farnell, Rector of Exeter College, wrote to an Afrikaaner Scholar elect to tell him what a Rhodes Scholar's attitude to the Empire should be, Wylie immediately wrote another letter to explain that there was no political creed to which a Rhodes Scholar was expected to subscribe.[20]

As for what the Scholars carried back with them, Lord Elton, the Secretary of the Rhodes Trust asserted proudly in 1958: 'An Oxford education, in whatever subject, can still claim to be an education in the deepest and fullest sense of the word, and never a mere technological training, so that an Oxford man should be equipped to do *anything* more effectively, thanks to what the University has taught him.'[21]

THE RHODES TRUST

The Trustees appointed under Rhodes's Will were the elder statesmen, Lord Milner, Lord Rosebery and Lord Grey; Alfred Beit and Dr Jameson, who had been Rhodes's colleagues in business and politics; Sir Lewis Michell, his banker, and Bourchier Hawksley, his solicitor. They were, and remained, a quite unacademic body. Milner, who was for long Chairman, stoutly opposed suggestions that the Trust be taken over by the University. 'The thing will never work as it ought to work or provide the effect which Rhodes intended it to produce', he wrote to Michell in 1915, 'if you get a lot of crusted old dons to run it.'[22] Later Trustees were largely representative of Imperial administration and politics, such as Lord Baldwin, Lord Hailsham, L. S. Amery, Lord Boyle, Lord Amory and Sir Archibald Nye. Geoffrey Dawson, Editor of *The Times*, was a Trustee, as was Rudyard Kipling, who, however, resigned as a protest against the appointment of the Liberal Philip Kerr as Secretary. The only academics to become Trustees before 1970 were H. A. L. Fisher who had also been a Cabinet Minister, and the Canadian, John Lowe, and the Australian, K. C. Wheare, both former Rhodes Scholars.

Apart from specific bequests, such as those for the Scholarships and for Oriel College, Rhodes left his money to be used at the discretion of the Trustees. 'You know what my ideas are,' he said, 'see that you carry them out. If you don't I'll come back to worry you.'[23]

Although he had not given actual instructions in his Will, Rhodes had given fairly clear guidance to the Trustees about his ideas on the use of the reserve fund after the cost of the Scholarships had been paid. In a letter to Lord Grey a few months before his death, he suggested that it be used for three purposes. First, 'To assist the most promising of your youths (the Rhodes Scholars) in their professions in after life, especially if they show indications of higher ideas and a desire to undertake public duties – the paramount object being the preservation and consolidation of the British Empire'. Second, 'if deemed advisable, formation of a Parliamentary Party who, without any desire for office, will always give their vote to Imperial purposes'. Third, 'The most dangerous portion of the Empire being Africa, the steady encouragement of emigration, especially women, and getting our people on the land. We shall never be safe in Africa until we occupy the soil equally with the Dutch.'[24]

The first Trustees made some attempts to follow these wishes. A special political fund or sub-trust was set up which financed the activities of Cape and Transvaal politicians. Amery and Curtis also drew on this fund, from which the Round Table was subsidised. Not much was achieved, however, in promoting British migration to South Africa, the means by which Rhodes and Milner vainly hoped to bring about British predominance.

One of the main considerations for the Trustees was to make Oxford a fit place for Rhodes Scholars. Thus substantial grants were made to the University for the study of Law, Medicine and Forestry. Perhaps uneasy because the Will confined Scholarships to males, the Trustees also gave money to the impoverished women's Colleges to finance teaching posts and buildings. New areas of study were financed, as in 1936, when £100,000 was given to the University to support research into Social Studies, with special reference to the problems of modern Government in the British Commonwealth and the American Republic. The city of Oxford benefited by grants to the Radcliffe Infirmary and to the Oxford Preservation Trust.

Outside Oxford South Africa was naturally the principal beneficiary. Before 1910 money was given to promote South African Union, and native schools and Colleges as well as those for whites were supported. Important Imperial institutions such as the Imperial College of Tropical Agriculture in Trinidad and the Kitchener Memorial College in Khartoum were assisted.

The Trust before 1939 was closely linked with the Round Table, members of which who served as its General Secretary being Edward Grigg (later Lord Altrincham), Geoffrey Dawson and Philip Kerr (later Lord Lothian). The last General Secretary before the function was taken over by the Warden of Rhodes House was Lord Elton.

Lothian who was Secretary from 1925 to 1939 was, as has been seen, a man of wide contacts and interests. He liked to say that the office of the Trust in Waterloo Place in London was at the heart of the Empire. In his time imaginative initiatives were taken. Among them were the Rhodes Travelling Fellowships, which were instituted in order to enlarge the horizons of dons and tutors and so that in the Colleges there would be senior members with knowledge of the home countries of Rhodes Scholars. Through this scheme the career of Margery Perham as an Africanist was launched, to the indignation of Grigg, then Governor of Kenya, who wrote to Lothian to complain 'that Rhodes's money should be spent on people who arrive in Africa with ready made opinions and return to England to defeat the most cherished of his hopes'. Lothian, in circulating this to his Trustees described the protest as 'absurd', in implying that the Trustees before awarding a Research Fellowship should satisfy themselves that the candidate's political opinions were in accord with Mr Rhodes's views of 30 years earlier.[25] About the same time the Rhodes Memorial Lectures were founded, which brought to lecture in Oxford men as distinguished and diverse as Smuts and Einstein. Rhodes's interest in the United States had a particular appeal for Lothian, and one of his unachieved ambitions was to hold a great debate in Oxford on 'Wilson versus Rhodes – or League of Nations versus Commonwealth.'[26]

RHODES HOUSE

When Parkin died in 1922, his friends wished to commemorate him by a gift of books to the University. Shortly afterwards Milner died and the Trustees wanted to set up a memorial to him. They had always intended to provide a house for their Oxford Secretary; So eventually Rhodes House came to be erected, with three purposes. Firstly, to provide a library of books on the history and politics of the Empire and the United States; secondly, as the headquarters of the Rhodes Scholarship system and residence of its Oxford Secretary; and, thirdly, as a permanent memorial to Rhodes and those who had carried out his Will.

The work was almost inevitably entrusted to Sir Herbert Baker, Rhodes's architect, and equally inevitably it was the third purpose which came to dominate the design, so that the building became a Valhalla for Rhodes and his companions, each of whom was commemorated by a room. Baker had come a long way since he built houses in South Africa from local materials for Rhodes. Rhodes had sent him to study the great Greek monumental architecture in

Athens, Paestum and Agrigento; and he had designed Government houses in Pretoria and Nairobi and had been joint architect with Lutyens of New Delhi. Much of this experience found exuberant expression in Rhodes House.

The rotunda by which it is entered is a shrine for Rhodes. Round the dome of its cupola, above his bust, are inscribed the words of Aristotle, urging the pursuit of excellence, which so deeply influenced the founder's life. On the floor beneath this is a stone quarried from the Matopo Hills near Rhodes's grave, inlaid with 'a brass symbol of the spirit which amidst outward calm heats and quickens the creative mind'.[27] On the walls are the names of Scholars from the Empire, the United States and Germany who died in the First and Second World Wars, and in the vestibule outside, like mediaeval knights attending their dead King, are the busts of Milner and Parkin who together launched the appeal for Imperial Federation in the Oxford Union in the year when Rhodes first came to Oxford. Over the door is written '*Non Omnis Moriar*' – 'I shall not wholly die', lines from that ode of Horace which Rhodes used to express his desire for undying fame, and which commenced '*Exegi Monumentum Aere Perennius*' – 'I have fashioned a monument more enduring than bronze'.

Beyond this is the great Milner Hall, on whose walls hang portraits of later Trustees and Secretaries, gravely dressed in business suits and academic dress, on whom the Founder, casually seated on some Rhodesian rock, looks down in his characteristic unbuttoned shirt and baggy trousers. The library, with its magnificent oak beams reminiscent of Groote Schuur, is named for Rosebery. There is a lecture room each for Jameson and Beit, and a gallery for Grey. A more modest office bears the name of Michell the banker, and a garret that of Hawksley, the lawyer. Such a shrine must have its martyr, and a posthumous portrait commemorates the young Rhodesian Rhodes Scholar, Kingsley Fairbridge, who wore himself out in the cause of child migration to the Empire; and perhaps the role of repentant disciple is fulfilled by the bust of H. A. L. Fisher, who signed the letter regretting the award of an Honorary Doctorate to Rhodes but became a Rhodes Trustee.

Overall, on top of the dome, on the flag, and gallery and staircase, is the bird, so strangely found carved in the ruins of Zimbabwe and which Rhodes believed to be of Phoenician or Egyptian origin, symbolising that link between Southern and Northern Africa which he sought to construct.

The library was to more than justify its existence in housing and providing comfortable access to the Bodleian's books on most parts of the Empire and on the United States and in eventually building up a unique manuscript collection of material on the colonial period. The Warden's house was also no doubt satisfactory, for Wylie, carried away by the Viceregal style, persuaded Baker to include eight bathrooms. The public rooms were used occasionally. There was a general feeling, however, that the building needed to have some broader purpose. When it was opened in 1929, with speeches by Sir Otto Beit and J. H. Hofmeyr and music by the band of the Grenadier Guards, the *Oxford Magazine* expressed the hope that with Rhodes House and its library as its 'powerhouse', Oxford would 'grow to be a real home for the study of Imperial problems in government and administration'.[28]

When the building was planned, H. A. L. Fisher, Warden of New College and one of the Rhodes Trustees, was asked by his colleagues to ascertain the University's ideas on the use of Rhodes House. Fisher reported that the University had four proposals: (1) that Rhodes House provide work rooms for professors, readers and students; (2) that a Rhodes Memorial Lectureship should bring a distinguished person into residence for a term each year; (3) that Rhodes Travelling Fellowships be established for dons; (4) that some rooms be used for learned and similar societies as a meeting place.[29] All these suggestions were accepted in principle by the Trustees.

Kerr's first thought, which he put to the Trustees in 1926, was that the building might become a centre for the training of colonial civil servants. In 1929, however, confronted with the reality of Baker's Rhodes House, he was inspired with a more ambitious idea which he expressed in a draft memorandum circulated to fellow members of the Round Table, Lionel Curtis, R. H. Brand, Geoffrey Dawson and Reginald Coupland: 'The most interesting experiment in government in the history of the world', he wrote, 'is now being made in the British Empire. For more than a century it has maintained the Pax Britannica within its confines, and has assured every citizen individual liberty under the law. No systematic study of the experiment is being made.'

It was essential, he suggested, that British public opinion should have the materials on which to found sound judgements about the method of encouraging political self-government by steady and peaceful means, instead of by war and revolution. The experience which was being gained should be subject to systematic study, together with that of other colonial powers.[30] He proposed that a postgraduate school of Government, and especially Government in tropical countries, be established in Oxford, based on Rhodes House.[31]

Meanwhile, Coupland, the Beit Professor of Colonial History, was urging that Rhodes House become a research centre whose Fellows should be given ample opportunity to travel within the Empire. 'Why should not Rhodes House', he asked Lionel Curtis, 'establish a kind of Collegiate individuality? It would be a pity if the new Rhodes House developments were cramped or spoilt by the Middle Ages.'[32]

The redrafted memorandum which Lothian submitted to the Rhodes Trustees, after receiving the comments of Curtis, Coupland and others, envisaged an Institute with an even broader purpose than in the first draft. It would not only study the problems of Government in the Empire but in the world as a whole. 'The future of Democracy among peoples of European origin' was now given equal emphasis with 'the good government of the Colonial peoples'. 'As long as Oxford does not provide adequately for the study of government', he wrote, 'she fails to give to the world at large the light and learning it is justified in expecting from her and she fails to furnish her own students with the intellectual food they want. It can scarcely be doubted what the opinion of Cecil Rhodes on the question would have been.' The memorandum proposed that an Oxford Institute of Government be created, with Departments of Public Administration, International Relations and Government of Coloured or Backward Peoples. The Institute would make use of the Rhodes House library and would, among other things, concern itself with the training of the I.C.S. and colonial probationers.[33]

At this point, General Smuts arrived in Oxford to give the Rhodes Memorial Lectures in the Michaelmas Term of 1929. Smuts made a strong plea that a thorough survey should be made of the problems of Africa as a whole, as the only method of preventing the growth of irreconcilable differences in different parts. In November 1929 he addressed a special conference on Africa which was held in Oxford with H. A. L. Fisher, the Warden of New College, in the Chair. It was attended by many of the important figures in the University, including Sir Michael Sadler, Master of University College, Gilbert Murray, A. D. Lindsay, Master of Balliol, and Coupland. Roy Harrod spoke for the economists; R. R. Marett for the anthropologists. Among the scientists were E. B. Poulton, Hope Professor of Zoology, A. G. Tansley, Professor of Botany and R. S. Troup, the Professor of Forestry. Among participants from outside Oxford were

1 Sir William Jones, monument by J. Flaxman (1794), in University College, Oxford, of which he was a Fellow before going out to India where his studies opened up Sanskrit learning to Europe.

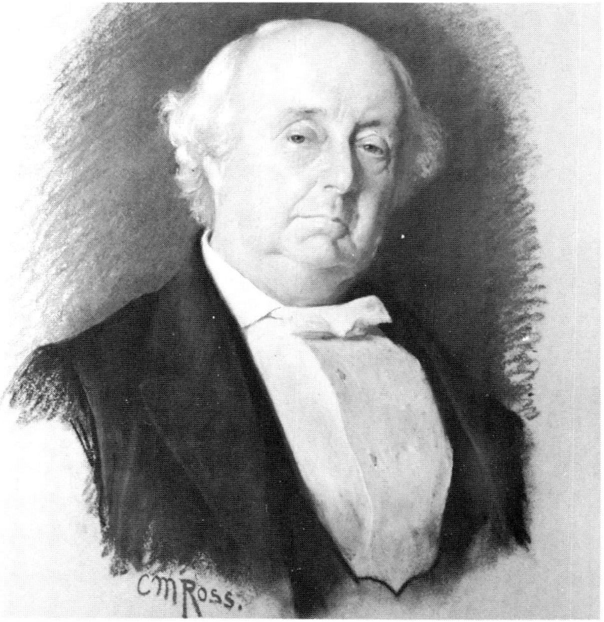

2 Benjamin Jowett, Master of Balliol, portrait by C. M. Ross (1892), in Balliol College, Oxford.

Jowett once wrote to Florence Nightingale, 'I should like to govern the world through my pupils.' Balliol men performed brilliantly in the system of competitive examinations for entry to government service which he helped to devise; his contacts also often gave them the first step in a political career.

3 George Nathaniel, Lord Curzon, as Viceroy of India (*c.* 1900).

One of three of Jowett's pupils who consecutively became Viceroy, Curzon was later an unusually energetic Chancellor of the University as well as Foreign Secretary. He attributed his failure to become Prime Minister to a cruel verse circulated about him at Balliol as an undergraduate.

4 Sir George Parkin, bust in Rhodes House by E. Whitney Smith (1928).

Parkin was the first Organising Secretary of the Rhodes Scholarship Scheme and the main proponent of Oxford's role as a Great Imperial University. It was said of him that he never got God and Oxford and the Empire wholly separated. He was a Canadian.

5 Alfred, Lord Milner, bust by Kathleen Scott in Rhodes House (1931).

One of Jowett's most brilliant pupils, Milner was converted to the cause of Imperial federation by George Parkin at the Oxford Union. Whilst High Commissioner in South Africa the staff which he recruited for reconstruction after the Boer War were all Oxford graduates. He was elected Chancellor of the University the day before he died.

6 Cecil Rhodes as an undergraduate at Oriel College (*c.* 1877).

Even at this time he made a will, leaving his still unearned fortune for the establishment of a secret society for the extension of British rule throughout the world. In its final version the will instead provided for the Rhodes Scholarships Scheme.

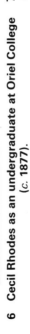

7 Miniature in University College, Oxford, of Goldwin Smith, Regius Professor of Modern History, 1858–68.

His proposals that the Empire should be dissolved caused Disraeli to describe him as 'a wild man of the cloisters and spouter of stale sedition' and his portrait to be removed from the Senior Common Room.

8 Milner's young men in South Africa (*c.* 1909).

This photograph was taken after Milner's departure. Standing (*from left to right*) R. H. Brand, H. Baker, L. Hichens; (*middle row*) H. Wyndham, R. Feetham, L. Curtis, P. Duncan, J. F. Perry, D. Malcolm; (*front row*) J. Dove, P. Kerr, G. Robinson.

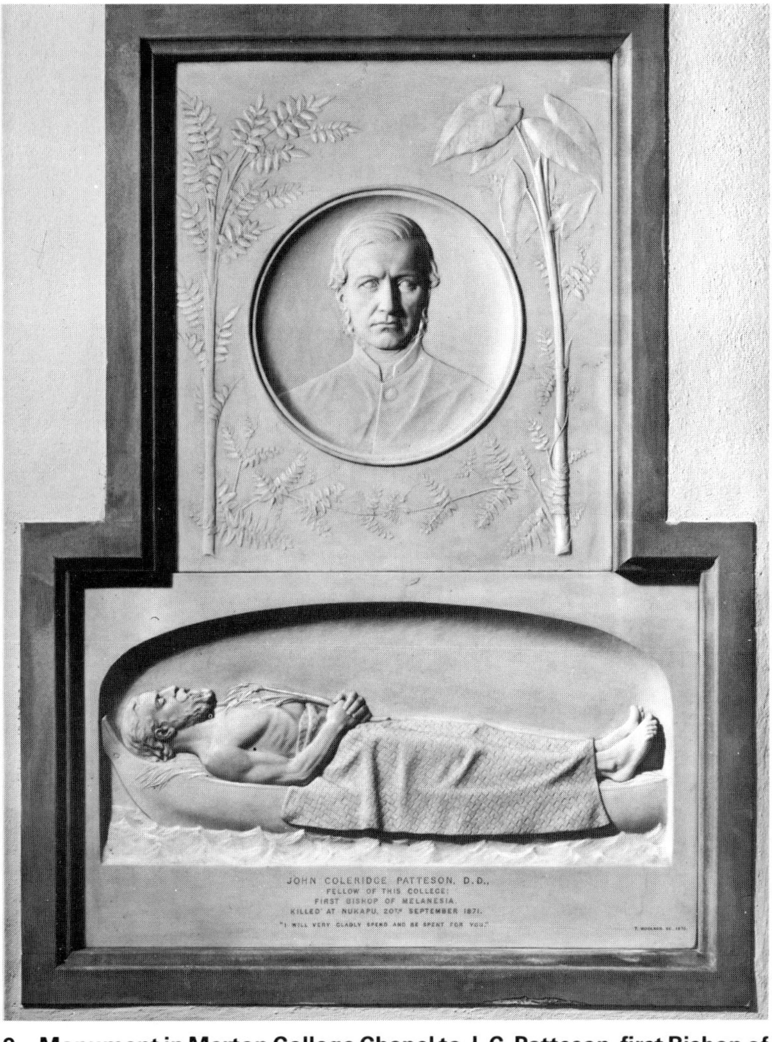

9 Monument in Merton College Chapel to J. C. Patteson, first Bishop of Melanesia by T. Woolner (1876).

The palm leaf found on his breast was tied in five knots by those who killed him, each signifying an islander who had been kidnapped by Blackbirders.

10 Stained-glass window in St Peter's College, Oxford, of James Hannington, first Bishop of Central Equatorial Africa.

He was murdered in 1884 whilst trying to open up a new road to Uganda from the coast.

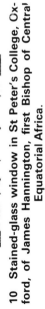

11 Weather vane on old Indian Institute, Oxford.

12 Boss in the Church of St Mary the Virgin of Mahatma Gandhi who visited Oxford in 1931.

13 Sir Monier Monier Williams, portrait by W. W. Ouless (1882), in the Indian Institute, Oxford, which he founded.

Although a much less eminent scholar, he was elected as Boden Professor of Sanskrit in a contest with Max Mueller because his religious views were considered sounder by the country clergy who were predominant in Convocation.

14 Rt Hon. Friedrich Max Mueller, P.C., portrait by Sir Herbert van Herkomer, All Souls College, Oxford (*c.* 1895).

After his defeat in the election for the Chair of Sanskrit he became Professor of Comparative Philology. He made the study of Eastern religions fashionable in Britain but his implacable hostility did much to frustrate Monier Williams' ambition of making Oxford, through the Indian Institute, the great centre of Indian studies in Britain.

15 Photograph from the album of Vincent Smith, Indian Civil Service.

After an early retirement Smith became Lecturer in Indian History and author of the *Oxford History of India.* Before 1914 far more members of the I. C. S. were recruited from Oxford than from any other university, although Smith himself was one of the few members recruited from Trinity College, Dublin.

16 Portrait of the Canadian, Sir William Osler, Regius Professor of Medicine, by S. Seymour Thomas, Radcliffe Science Library, Oxford (1909).

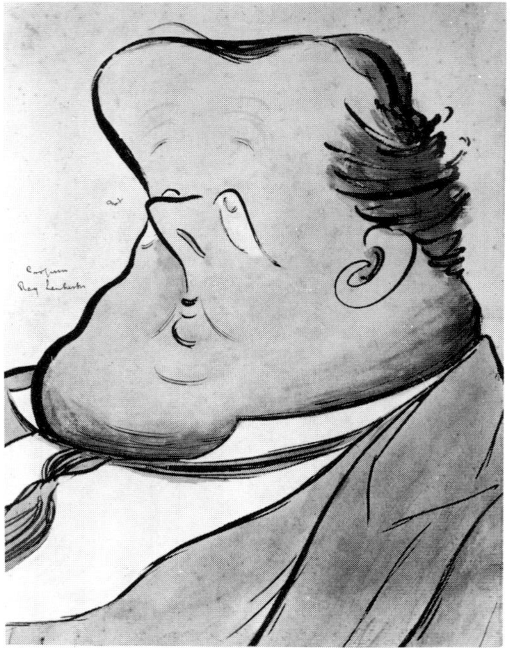

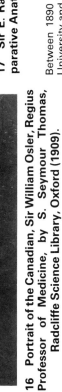

17 Sir E. Ray Lankester, Linacre Professor of Comparative Anatomy, cartoon by Max Beerbohm in Merton College (1907).

Between 1890 and 1914 Lankester repeatedly attacked the University and its classical graduates who governed the Empire for bringing it into mortal peril through neglect of science.

18 Sir William Schlich, Professor of Forestry (*c.* **1910).**

Schlich arranged for the probationers of the Indian Forest Service to be trained in Oxford so that they would later have greater prestige and influence with the Indian Government. His scheme was thwarted by the jealousy of Cambridge but eventually the Imperial Forestry Institute was established in Oxford.

19 Sir Halford Mackinder, sketch by W. Rothenstein (1933); copy in Oxford University School of Geography.

The post of Oxford's first Reader in Geography was financed by the Royal Geographical Society because of the ignorance of the subject among Imperial decision-makers. Mackinder's theories of Geopolitics, however, were to have more influence in Germany, as shown in Hitler's *Mein Kampf.*

20 Henry Balfour, Curator of the Pitt Rivers Museum, examining the first students to take the diploma course in anthropology which was established in 1906, mainly to meet the needs of colonial administrators and missionaries.

21 Kingsley Fairbridge, Rhodes Scholar from Rhodesia (1909–11),portrait by A. K. Lawrence (1952), in Rhodes House.

22 Revd Alek Fraser (1935), Principal of Trinity College, Kandy, and Achimota College, Gold Coast.

23 S. W. R. D. Bandaranaike, later Prime Minister of Ceylon, as an undergraduate at Christ Church (*c.* 1921).

24 Portrait in Rhodes House by Katherine Lloyd (1951) of J. H. Hofmeyr, Deputy Prime Minister of South Africa, who won a Rhodes Scholarship at 15.

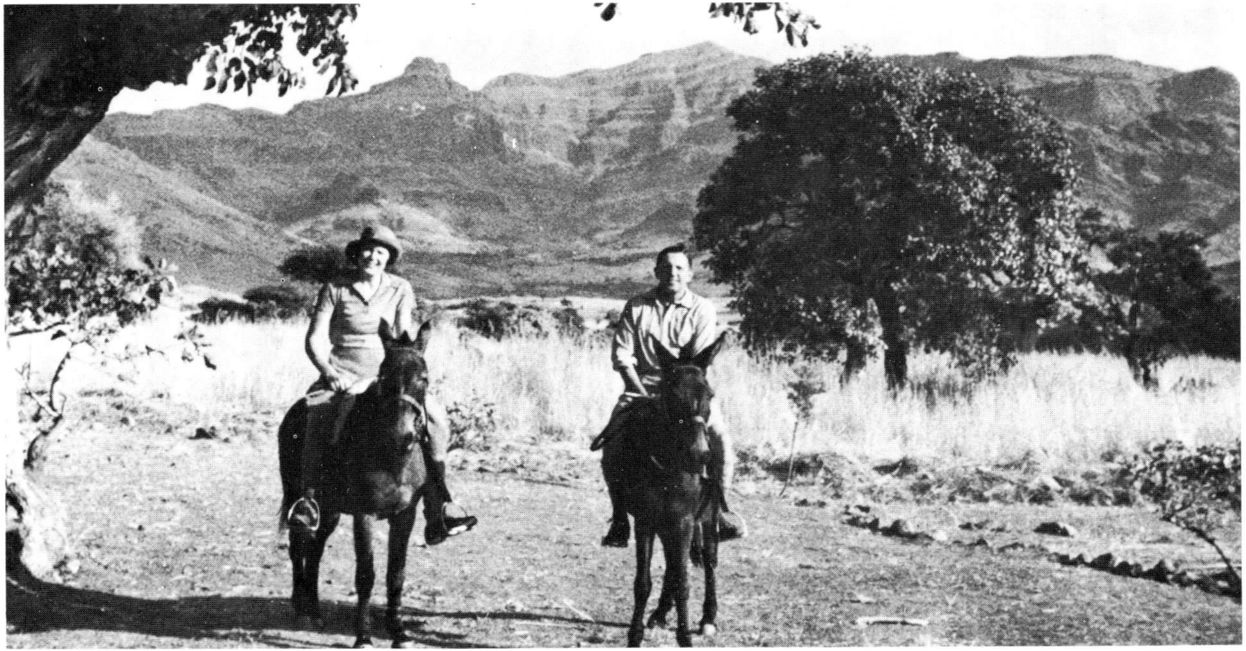

25 Margery Perham, in Darfur, Sudan, with District Commissioner J. E. H. Boustead (*c.* 1939).

Her extensive first-hand knowledge of Africa gave her as Reader in Colonial Administration a unique influence both with colonial officials and future African nationalists who studied at Oxford (photograph in Perham MSS, Rhodes House, Oxford)

26 Somerville College group (1890).

Before 1914 more women from Somerville than any other Oxford women's college worked in the Empire. The group includes the earliest Indian women to study at Oxford. Cornelia Sorabji is on the right and the two Princesses Duleep Singh in the front row.

27 Sir Ralph Furse, portrait in Commonwealth Forestry Institute, Oxford, by Barry Craig (1950).

Between 1918 and 1950 Furse, a Balliol man, was in charge of recruitment for the Colonial Services, which was made mainly from Oxford and Cambridge on the recommendation of a secret list of trusted College tutors.

28 Dripstop on the Bodleian Library of Sir Kenneth Wheare, the Vice-Chancellor, and kangaroo (*c.* 1964).

Wheare was one of many Australians and New Zealanders who remained in Oxford after graduating.

L. S. Amery, the former Colonial Secretary, Stephen Tallents from the Empire Marketing Board, and J. H. Oldham for the missionaries.

The report of the conference throws considerable light on how Oxford teachers saw the potential contribution of their disciplines to Empire in 1929. Smuts commenced by telling the members of the conference that their purpose should be to get the African problem out of the political atmosphere and away from sentimentalists and to let science speak. There must be a general staff to think out African problems as one coordinated whole. 'If Oxford would, as it were', he said, 'turn from the Greeks to the Negroes, it would help as nothing else could and we might found an Institute which might in fifty years time become one of the greatest things in Oxford.'

Smuts's proposal for an Institute of African Studies was warmly welcomed by the participants in the light of their individual interests. Harrod saw the mutual advantages for Oxford and Africa of advanced economic and statistical work at the Centre. Oldham and Marett spoke of the importance of study of the human factor. Troup saw possibilities of cooperation between foresters, historians, meteorologists and anthropologists. Fisher saw the Institute as serving the needs not only of postgraduate studies but those of undergraduates who planned to go out as administrators and missionaries. Amery reflected that 'the more rapidly the native standard of living was raised, the less effective would be his competition, and the bigger the field for European immigration'. Lothian also spoke of the need to study immigration problems. The Labour Commissioner of Tanganyika, Orde Brown, thought that the Centre might consider such questions as the condition of the African mine workers, who were better fed than their compatriots but acquired subversive ideas. 'Which was better, a sick savage or a healthy Bolshevik?' he pondered.[34]

A committee under Fisher's Chairmanship was set up to prepare a plan for an African Institute or Centre in Oxford; the Oxford scientists formed their own committee which reported on ways in which they could cooperate with the Institute. The University Hebdomadal Council approved the initiative. The Rhodes Trustees agreed to build an extension to Rhodes House which would provide accommodation either for a Centre of African Studies or an Institute of Government, on condition that £10,000 a year could be found elsewhere.[35]

Neither the British Government nor the Empire Marketing Board, though both were friendly, were able to accept the recurring financial responsibility. It was decided therefore with Smuts's help to approach the Rockefeller Foundation, to whom a printed proposal for the establishment of an African Centre was submitted by Fisher on behalf of the committee. The proposed Centre would be based on Rhodes House, whose Trustees would administer its funds in close cooperation with the University. It would consist of four departments: (1) History and Government, including the Treatment of Backward People (as exemplified by the British Trusteeship pattern) and India; the 'Equalitarian School' in France, and the idea of the Mandate; (2) Science; (3) Economics; and (4) 'the African himself'. Each department would be headed by someone of professorial rank, and there would be associates from the University and other institutions.[36]

Lothian, with his characteristic enthusiasm for fresh ideas, abandoned his plan for an Institute of Government and wrote to Curtis that the African Centre 'would not only revolutionise the future of Africa but create that nucleus of constructive thinkers about contemporary economic and political problems which is essential if Oxford is to keep its standing among the great Universities of the world'.[37]

Whilst the request was being prepared, Julian Huxley wrote to Lothian to propose an Ecological Department as part of the Oxford African Centre. The major problems in Africa, he urged, were biological, and Oxford's ecologists and foresters were well qualified to organise studies on such questions as linkage between locust migration and meteorological cycles, or between fluctuations in wild animal population and rinderpest.[38] Coupland wrote optimistically to Lothian that 'with £1,500 a year for this project of Huxley and another £1,000 for Margery Perham, we should have the core of our African scheme at work.[39]

Lothian cheerfully absorbed these ideas as they came in. He wrote to Lord Passfield, the former Sydney Webb, who was at the time Secretary of State for the Colonies:

> I am not afraid that the Institute will become 'Imperialist' in its sympathy. I am much more afraid that it will become Exeter Hall, for the key to the African problem to my mind is for the whites in Africa and Britain to gain that confidence in each other's integrity and purpose and to avoid that misunderstanding and rancour which wrecked South African history in the nineteenth century, and was in my view the ultimate cause of the Boer War and the failure of Great Britain to win South Africa to a more liberal point of view in dealing with the native. One of my hopes is that the

> Oxford Institute will help to bring the common understanding or a far sighted policy into being.[40]

He corresponded with Smuts about the appointment of a Director. Smuts proposed Sir Edward Grigg, the retiring Governor of Kenya. Lothian considered Grigg too identified with the settler point of view and preferred the South African Justice Richard Feetham, of the old Milner Kindergarten, or Sir Arnold Wilson who had administered Iraq.[41] He reached agreement with Lord Lugard and J. H. Oldham on a division of work between the Oxford Institute and the International Institute for African Languages and Culture, which was also applying to Rockefeller for support. The latter as an international body would collect information; the Oxford Centre with its academic freedom would be better placed to make use of the material in published studies.[42]

In spite of the confidence of Smuts however, the Rockefeller Foundation in May 1930 refused the Oxford application, though it made a grant to the International Institute;[43] the African survey which Smuts had proposed as part of the Oxford Centre's programme was eventually carried out by Lord Hailey on behalf of the Royal Institute of International Affairs.[44]

It seems curious that Lothian did not now revert to his scheme for the establishment of an Institute of Government which had been approved by his Trustees as an alternative use of Rhodes House. This may have been partly because Fisher considered that the teaching of government should be a responsibility of the University rather than of the Rhodes Trust. But at this time Lothian had taken on arduous external responsibilities in relation to Indian constitutional reforms. As Secretary of the Trust he became mainly interested in what it could do to help create a better climate for an Indian political settlement though, as has been seen in Chapter 6, not much was in fact done to further this purpose in his time.

Years later, in 1961, the Trustees tried to give Rhodes House, except the library, to the University as an official residence or office for the Vice-Chancellor. The University authorities finally decided that it was unsuitable, perhaps feeling that such Imperial surroundings could have embarrassed the Vice-Chancellor's receptions at a time when the 'wind of change' was blowing hard and decolonisation was well on the way.[45]

What, it may be wondered, would Rhodes have thought of the way in which his money was spent? Rhodes House would have delighted him. His foible, as Milner noticed, was size. 'I like the big, simple and barbaric', he told Baker, and used to say that it was through art that Pericles taught the laziest Athenians to believe in Empire.[46]

It is hard to imagine that the bachelor who found it difficult to forgive his friends for marrying would have approved of his Trustees' action in obtaining Parliament's sanction to make women eligible for his Scholarships. Indeed, Rhodes, as a law student, was probably taught the familiar tag that 'Parliament can legislate for everything except to make a man a woman.'

Whether he would have approved the extension of his Scholarships to Asians and Africans is difficult to say. He stood for 'equal rights for all civilised men'; but there is no evidence that he had any idea or wish that the British Empire would turn into a multiracial Commonwealth.

He would probably have been disappointed in the degree to which his Trust was able to contribute to the consolidation and expansion of the Empire, the unity of the Anglo-Saxon races, and British predominance in South Africa, which were the central themes of all his Wills from 1877 until his death. The results were hardly impressive even in relation to Parkin's translation of the founder's vision 'to make Oxford a nursery of leaders, the energising source of Empire, and the womb of a thousand years of peace for mankind'.[47] The second generation of Trustees, even as committed Imperialists as Kipling and Amery, found it almost impossible to identify activities to be supported in accordance with the Founder's philosophy in an Oxford, a nation and a loose alliance of States which were turning their back on Empire.

OXFORD AS THE GREAT IMPERIAL UNIVERSITY

Rhodes's magnificent bequests stimulated discussion outside as well as inside Oxford on her role as a great Imperial University. In 1908 a meeting on 'Oxford and the Empire' took place at the Royal Colonial Institute. An uninspiring paper was read to a distinguished audience by Egerton who raised two main questions, how far was Oxford worthy to play the role intended for it by Mr Rhodes, and what would be the effect on it of the Rhodes Scholars. He threw little light on either question and steered a cautious course between the demands of teaching and research and between the claims of the

Colleges and of the University. He also warned against the dangers of an educated proletariat. His audience may have had difficulty in discerning any meaning in his peroration which concluded 'Oxford, we may be sure, has before her many generations of vigorous life. Her position as an omphalos of the Empire has been secured to her. That she will rise to the height of her Imperial responsibilities, that she will make good her claim to be the Ruler of ten cities, must be the fervent prayer of every loyal Oxonian.'

After this, various hobby-horses were exercised. The Chairman, Sir Thomas Brassey, one of Oxford's substantial benefactors, seized the opportunity to demand a powerful Imperial Navy. Sir William Anson, M. P., Warden of All Souls, asserted the traditional view that Oxford should only teach the theoretical side, and not the practical work, of science, law and medicine. Sir Thomas Raleigh thought that India and the Empire would get better men for their Civil Services if selection were not made entirely through competitive written examinations.

As so often, it was the Canadian George Parkin who raised the level of the discussion by speaking passionately but practically about the role of Oxford as a great Imperial University. Its Law School, he said, must be able to provide the teaching required by men from any part of the Empire, whether English, French, Dutch, Roman or Islamic law. The University should become the great Imperial teacher of history, and send men trained to deal with historical documents to every colony of the Empire. It should establish a strong Imperial Geography School from which trained geographers would go out to deal with the vast problems of the Empire. It should improve its teaching of oriental and modern languages to remedy the linguistic weakness of the ruling class. Above all it was better placed than anywhere else in the world to establish a great School of Government with students from an Empire in which every kind of constitutional experiment was in process of being worked out.

'If Oxford were to accept the role of an Imperial University,' he pleaded, 'and say we are going to establish the best Imperial Law School, the best School of Geography and Language and Government the world has ever seen, I believe the British world would rise up to assist her forward with the ideal.'[48]

Curzon, who whilst Chancellor of the University gave an Address on Oxford and the Empire in 1909, was less precise than Parkin. He expressed the hope that there might be 'a perpetual stream circulating between the Colonies to Oxford and Oxford to the Colonies carrying to and fro upon its bosom the best of character and intelligence, of loyalty and patriotism, that either can give'. He referred to what Oxford was doing to train the governors and administrators and judges, the teachers and preachers and lawyers of Empire, but his only new idea for the future was for the education of journalists, whom he described as 'the live rails, connecting the outskirts of Empire with its heart'.[49]

After the First World War a Royal Commission on Oxford and Cambridge Universities, chaired by H. H. Asquith, was appointed in 1920 to consider their applications for financial assistance. Some witnesses, notably the Vice-Chancellor of Liverpool, J. G. Adami, who had taught in Canada, and C. K. Webster, the historian, suggested that the ancient Universities should keep the numbers of their undergraduates low and should devote their main attention to bringing graduates from other British Universities and from the Empire for postgraduate studies. The India Office also made a plea that Oxford and Cambridge should provide more places for Indian students.[50]

Such ideas would have led to a very different College life to that described by L. R. Phelps, the Provost of Oriel, who told the Commission how the entrants to his College came from a small group of middle-class schools, an occasional member of a different class being welcome. 'It is to this fact', he said, 'that the College system owes its charm. A body of men brought up under similar conditions and the same ideas, educated at schools of the same type, develops a corporate life, intimate, wholesome and moderately industrious.'[51]

Though the Commission's Report suggested that Oxford and Cambridge should open their doors more widely to poor students, it was somewhat grudging in recognition of the needs of Empire. It did not consider that the ancient Universities should largely become postgraduate institutions, and stated that it might fairly be contended that they should give preference as undergraduates to applicants domiciled in Britain, though Rhodes Scholars and Government probationers from India were special cases.

After the death of Parkin, though the educational needs of Empire continued to be discussed, particularly by members of the Round Table, the idea of Oxford as the cultural centre of the Empire seemed gradually to lose support. The view which prevailed was eloquently argued by Alfred (later Sir Alfred) Zimmern. Zimmern had obtained a First in Mods and Greats at New College and established his reputation with a book on the Greek Commonwealth. In 1930 he was to become the first Montague Burton Professor of International Relations at Oxford. Although he was a member of the Round Table, after the First World War he had an equal if not greater commitment to the League of Nations and for many years ran its Summer School in Geneva; in *The Third British Empire* published in 1926, he tried to reconcile the British Empire with the League of Nations.

In the passage quoted at the head of this chapter he strongly dissented from the idea that Oxford should be used to promote cultural Imperialism, to impose or dictate or inculcate English standards as universal standards. If this came about, he continued 'there would be a real Empire, with provinces, and everything outside of England would be incurably provincial. And to be provincial is to be dissatisfied, to have your eyes on the centre.' 'The bond between Oxford men', he concluded, 'is not of a common culture. It cannot be so. Nor is it that of politics, because that is outside the sphere of the University. It is simply personal. It is a bond between individuals.'[52]

Part III
Oxford Overseas

10 A Share in the Appointments

I cannot conceive a greater boon which could be conferred on the University than a share in the Indian appointments. . . . It would give an answer to the dreary question which a College Tutor so often hears . . . What line of life shall I choose, with no calling to take orders and no taste for the Bar and no connexions to put me forward in life?

Benjamin Jowett to W. E. Gladstone (1853)

It is not easy to estimate what proportion of Oxford men and women served in the Empire. Only three of the former men's Colleges, Balliol, Keble and St John's, have published information about the careers of their graduates over the whole period covered by this study. Of these neither Balliol, which had a great preponderance in the I.C.S. before 1914, nor Keble, a high proportion of whose graduates become clergymen under the terms of its foundation, were at all typical of other Colleges.

From Table A.1 in the Appendix it will be seen that the percentages of matriculates who worked for at least two years in the Empire between 1874 and 1913 were Balliol 27.1, Keble 20.4 and St John's 16.7. Between 1918 and 1937 the percentages were Balliol 18.2, Keble 20.0 and St John's 15.3; there was thus a decrease in all three Colleges after the First World War.

When the figures are broken down by professions (see Table A.2 in the Appendix) by far the largest number are seen to have become Government officials, missionaries and teachers. After 1918 the Colonial Service replaced the I.C.S. as a principal employer; the proportion of missionaries decreased, whilst that of lay educators increased. The proportion who worked in the private sector doubled after 1918 in Balliol and St John's but decreased in Keble.

All five of the former women's Halls or Colleges tried to record information on the careers of their alumnae in their Registers, three of which have been published. This was done partly because, being without endowments, they needed to keep in touch with prospective benefactors, but also because a close family spirit was developed when the Halls were new and small. Often, however, women who married ceased to respond to questionnaires and the number of women whose career information is not available is so large that it is hardly possible to make a valid calculation as to the proportion who served in the Empire. Of the Colleges whose records are least incomplete, those of Somerville show 8.5 per cent of the entrants between 1874 and 1913 as working in the Empire and 6.7 per cent for the period between 1918 and 1938. The corresponding figures for St Hugh's are 10 per cent for 1886–1913 and 8.9 per cent for 1918–38. However, the overall numbers are much fewer than those of the men's Colleges. They might be substantially higher if information were available and included on careers of women who went out as wives but often also worked as teachers or in social service.

In this and the following two chapters, Oxford's role will be considered in the three professions in which its alumni were most numerous in the Empire: Government Services, missionary work and education.

THE INDIAN CIVIL SERVICE

No positions in the Empire had greater prestige than those held by the Indian Civil Service. 'Such a power as that which Collectors have in India over the people', Macaulay told the House of Commons in 1853, 'is not found in any other part of the world possessed by any class of functionary.'[1] The emoluments and pensions were handsome: an I.C.S. official as a prospective husband, mothers would tell their daughters, was worth £1,000 a year, dead or alive. Until 1853, candidates for the Service were nominated at the age of 15 or 16 through the patronage of the Directors of the East India Company and then sent for training at the Company's College at Haileybury; thus the Service was not open to University men. Although Parliament in 1853 decided that future recruitment should be by open competition, it was still assumed that the candidates would continue to be selected at 16 and sent to Haileybury.

When Jowett wrote the letter quoted above, Gladstone was M.P. for Oxford University, and the letter ended 'You love Oxford too well not to do what you can for it.'[2] Jowett was determined that recruitment to the I.C.S. should be opened up to men from the Universities as part of his great plan, as he explained to Gladstone in another letter: 'To replace Oxford in its true relation to the country'.[3] He lobbied Ministers, obtained the support of headmasters of the great Public Schools, and was made a member of the Committee on the Examination of Candidates for the Indian Civil Service, which was appointed by the Government, with Macaulay as Chairman, in 1854. The Committee recommended that candidates for the Service should in future be selected by a written competition at the age of 22. The examination, they proposed, should be such as to enable the candidates to show 'the extent of their knowledge of our poets, our wits and philosophers, and their skill in Latin verses';[4] it was assumed that those successful would be among the cleverest University graduates of their year. The proposal was accepted and remained in force after the British Government took over direct responsibility for the Government of India from the East India Company in 1857. Haileybury was closed as redundant.

In the first few years of operation of the new arrangements, it seemed that Jowett had won his campaign. University graduates obtained most of the places, of which Oxford men won 33 per cent between 1855 and 1859; in response, the University appointed a teacher of Hindustani in 1859 and a Reader in Indian Law and History in 1861. The upper age limit for candidates was, however, now lowered first from 23 to 22 and then from 22 to 21 in order to enable the officers to arrive in India at a younger age. As a consequence the candidates had insufficient time to obtain University degrees and on leaving school were educated by crammers instead. The percentage of Oxford men among the entrants fell to 12 per cent in the period 1874–8 and three per cent between 1878 and 1882.[5]

There was considerable criticism in India of the quality of the 'Competition Wallahs' selected under the new system. Almost everyone concerned in the Government of India, the India Office and the Civil Service Commission considered that it was desirable that the entrants to the I.C.S. should be University men. There was disagreement however as to whether the candidates should be recruited at the age of 18–19 and then put through a special probationary course at a University; or, on the other hand, recruited after graduation and given a shorter period of probationary training. In 1876 when Lord Salisbury, the Secretary of State for India, consulted Oxford and Cambridge, a Committee set up by the Hebdomadal Council and chaired by Liddell, the Dean of Christ Church, suggested the former alternative whilst Jowett recommended the latter.[6] The Government eventually decided to reduce the maximum age to 19, followed by a two-year probationary period at a University. This was an unfortunate compromise as it did not enable the probationers to remain long enough at a University to graduate. Consequently there was a decline in the number of candidates and initially no interest among the Oxford and Cambridge Colleges in receiving the probationers, except at Balliol.

There was still a feeling among members of the Council of the Secretary of State, themselves mostly Haileybury men, that something important had been lost when the probationers ceased to live under one roof: an *esprit de corps* had then been formed, they argued, which had been invaluable in a Service whose members would subsequently be scattered all over the Indian sub-continent. In 1874 the Secretary of State, therefore, raised the possibility that a single College might be established at Oxford or Cambridge for the probationers. Max Mueller suggested that they should be concentrated in All Souls, which was then in search of a role, being under severe attack from the Oxford University Commission for its indolence. Max Mueller's advice however carried little weight in that sociable College, where he never came to dine between October and March for fear of exposure to the noxious night airs of Oxford.[7]

No single College was established, but Jowett wrote to every successful candidate in the I.C.S. examination to offer him a place at Balliol. Consequently in the first three years of the new scheme half of all the probationers in the country were at Balliol, where Arnold Toynbee was appointed as their special tutor. Jowett used Balliol's preponderant position in two ways. On the one hand it enabled him within the University successfully to support Monier Williams's initiative for the establishment of an Honour School of Oriental Studies and to persuade the India Office to allow those probationers who enrolled in the School's degree course to remain at Oxford for a third year. At the same time he was able to insist with the India Office that the official curriculum of the probationers include not only Indian law and history, but agriculture, economics and some knowledge of sanitation; in drafting this curriculum he was advised by Florence Nightingale. When the India Office refused to pay for instruction in agricultural chemistry, he paid himself or found the money from a private source.

To the probationers whom Jowett invited to stay with him in

Malvern during vacations he would point out, as he had to Lansdowne, that India offered more opportunity for doing great and permanent good than any department in England and that study by them now of the principles of agricultural science could result in better-fed cultivators.[8] His protégé Toynbee was remembered by his pupils as 'one of the most brilliant exponents of the new humanitarian school of Economics which was then battering against the frigid materialism of the Manchester School'.[9]

The long and bitter controversy between economists and human beings, Toynbee taught, had ended in the conversion of the economists. The era of free trade and free contract was gone and the era of administration had come, in which India should be governed in the interests of its dim multitudes of peasants.[10]

Jowett wrote of Toynbee's work after his death:

> As tutor of the Indian students he lectured to them in classes in Political Economy and some Indian subjects. He also saw them individually and became their adviser and friend. He felt that the future of India would in a great degree depend on what could be made of these young men in the course of years. Recognising the vastness of the field, he at once commenced the study of the excellent Blue Books and Reports published by the Government.
>
> He knew how much India had suffered from crude application of Ricardo and Mill to a state for which they were not adapted. He would try to make his pupils understand that they must learn political economy after the old orthodox fashion but that the theory must be applied to an Oriental or uncivilised country with a difference. He was very desirous to inspire them with just and humane attitudes towards the natives. If they went to India they were to go there for the good of her people on one of the noblest missions in which an Englishman could be engaged.[11]

By 1888 the reluctance of other Oxford Colleges to admit the I.C.S. probationers had been overcome; they were now enrolled in 17 colleges which jointly appointed teachers for them. Sir William Markby of Balliol, Reader in Indian Law and a former Vice-Chancellor of Calcutta, was appointed by the University as supervisor of the probationers in succession to Toynbee. In 1883 the University inaugurated the School of Oriental Studies, within which a B.A. degree course could be taken either in Semitic or Indian Studies. The latter included Sanskrit, Vernacular Indian History,

Economics, Land Tenure and Religions. The students enrolled in it were almost all I.C.S. probationers, and the numbers were small; five took honours in 1887, seven in 1888, three in 1889 and three in 1890. Among them were some notable Firsts such as A. M. T. Jackson who as a Sanskrit scholar was said to have had no equal in the Province of Bombay, and Sir Nicholas Beatson Bell, who became the first Governor of Assam.[12]

In the late 1880's, however, the question of the age limits for competition for the I.C.S. again came under discussion, mainly as a result of complaints that the upper age limit of 19 years gave little opportunity for Indian candidates to prepare themselves for the entry examination. Oxford was once more consulted by the India Office. Its representatives now urged unanimously that the age limits should be raised in order to enable graduates to be recruited. More and better candidates would be obtained, they said, 'When a man's university career is just over and he looks around him and sees how the professions are crowded in Britain'.[13] Although Jowett signed this statement, he was considerably worried lest the higher age of recruitment would imply a curtailment of the period of probation and thus would lead to the collapse of the degree course in Indian Studies, which could not be taken by the probationers in less than three years. His fears were justified: in 1892 the age limit for entry to the I.C.S. was raised to 23 and the probationary period was reduced to a year. The broad degree course in Indian Studies was discontinued in 1895, although it was still possible to study Sanskrit.

Now began the period of Oxford's greatest success in the I.C.S. Examination. Oxford obtained 52 per cent of the places between 1892 and 1894, compared with 20 per cent obtained by Cambridge, whose tutors complained bitterly that the system of marking unduly favoured Oxford,[14] because a man who read Classical Moderations and Greats, a four-year course, could compete for a far higher number of marks than a man who took one of the Cambridge Tripos three-year courses. The matter came to a head in 1904 when the Civil Service Commissioners and India Office consulted the Universities about the marking system.

After Jowett's death Oxford's strategy in relation to the I.C.S. was managed by J. L. Strachan Davidson, who was Master of Balliol from 1907 to 1916. Unlike Jowett, Strachan Davidson was not much interested in India itself or in its Government. His great concern was that the examination system should strengthen and not harm the Oxford Greats School. Even with an upper age limit of 23, a number of men neglected their last year's study of Greats in order to cram instead a variety of subjects which would gain them marks in the I.C.S. Examination. In the negotiations with the Government, the Civil Service Commissioners and the other Universities, Strachan Davidson had three objectives. Firstly, he sought to limit the maximum number of marks which could be obtained in the competition, thus diminishing the need for a man reading Greats to cram additional subjects. Secondly, he hoped that the maximum age of candidates would be raised from 23 to 24 in order to enable a Greats man to take his degree before having to prepare for the I.C.S. Examination. Thirdly, he wished to increase the allocation of marks for philosophy which was the central theme of the Greats Course.[15]

Oxford succeeded, in agreement with the other Universities, on the first two points. On the third, the allocation of marks for philosophy, there was a bitter dispute with Cambridge which instead was seeking to obtain more marks for Latin and Greek verses. Strachan Davidson sent the Chancellor of the University, Lord Goschen, a former Cabinet Minister, out to lobby, telling him that 'nothing will really please Cambridge unless it injures Oxford . . . . Cambridge will doubtlessly consent to lose one eye provided Oxford can be deprived of both.'[16]

Fortunately for Oxford, but by no means fortuitously, the Secretary of State for India, St John Brodrick, and his Permanent Under Secretary, A. D. Godley, were Balliol men, as was the Chief Civil Service Commissioner, S. D. Courthorpe. Each of them was expected by Strachan Davidson to help to counter the advantage that Cambridge enjoyed in having one of her graduates, A. J. Balfour, as Prime Minister. To the Chief Civil Service Commissioner, Strachan Davidson wrote bitterly 'You are like the elephants and don't know your own strength and I fear you will ruin Oxford with a light heart.' Courthorpe, in reply, told him that he was ungrateful. Sir William Anson, the Warden of All Souls, who was M.P. for the University and Parliamentary Under Secretary for Education, shocked Strachan Davidson even more by pointing out that Oxford's difficulties arose only because its combined Mods and Greats course lasted four years instead of three. This caused Strachan Davidson to write to Godley that if Oxford's course of classical studies were reduced to three years 'a great system of education will be condemned to extinction, not on its own merits but because it will not be compatible with the I.C.S. competition'.[17]

Although the marks for philosophy were not, in the end, raised by as much as Strachan Davidson had hoped, Oxford retained both its four-year classical course and its predominance in the I.C.S. competition. Between 1892 and 1914 Oxford obtained 48.2 per cent of the places, Cambridge 29.5 per cent.[18] In due course this pattern was reflected at the top. In 1938, the last normal year of British Rule before the Second World War and Independence, of the eight provincial Governors who were members of the I.C.S., six were Oxford men, all of whom had read Greats and taken their degrees between 1897 and 1910: of the remaining three Governors, who were appointed from outside the Service, two were Oxford men.[19]

Each year the *Oxford Magazine* published a table and commentary, compiled or inspired by Strachan Davidson, analysing the results. From this exercise Strachan Davidson noted complacently that the Oxford classical Mods and Greats course was the best of all training for the entry competition. Indeed some Oxford dons grumbled that the form of the examination was affecting the balance of studies in the University by causing men to read Greats instead of Modern History. The Civil Service Commissioners considered one reason for Oxford's preponderance was that Oxford sent its best men as candidates, whereas many of Cambridge's best men, a much greater proportion of whom studied science and engineering, preferred other careers.[20]

It would not be fair to suppose that the Civil Service Commissioners in designing the entry examinations for the Indian and Home Civil Services, were deliberately favouring Oxford. Sir Stanley Leathes, indeed, who was First Civil Service Commissioner from 1910 to 1927, was a Fellow of Trinity College Cambridge where he had taught Modern History. In an Address to the Congress of Universities of the Empire in 1912 he insisted that the essential qualification for the public service was knowledge of human nature. The study of mathematics and science, he explained, tended to create an unreal world in which reason reigned supreme. As for economics this was not a subject which young men were fit to learn, 'A light top dressing of political economy stimulates the weeds and chokes the crops.' The study of law, he maintained, did not deal with human nature direct but through the medium of rules and formulae; the administrator was often at liberty to deal with the special case upon its merits, the lawyer rarely or never. Having thus dismissed the subjects which happened to be more widely studied in Cambridge than in Oxford, he concluded that the nearest approach to the ideal education for administrators in the Empire was in classics and history, which were subjects studied by a much higher proportion of undergraduates at Oxford than at Cambridge.[21]

From 1896 the I.C.S. examination was combined with that for the Home Civil Service and from 1906 with that for the Eastern appointments to Ceylon, Hong Kong and Malaya. Quite often candidates at the top of the list preferred India to the Home Service, but hardly anyone preferred the Eastern appointments, for which men were usually taken who had failed to obtain places in the Home or Indian Services. In 1910 the Government of India complained to the India Office that the one-year period of probation was causing new I.C.S. recruits to arrive in India with inadequate knowledge of law. The remedy considered was once more to lower the age of recruitment and extend the period of probation. A Royal Commission under Lord Islington was appointed in 1913 to consider the whole question of recruitment and training for the public service in India. H. A. L. Fisher of New College was a member.

The Commission was as much interested in the recruitment and training of Indians as of Europeans. The witnesses from Oxford, however, seemed little concerned with this aspect. Sir Herbert Warren, President of Magdalen, blandly explained 'Our experience is that the fellows we would most like to see in India are the scholars from the Public Schools, more particularly the Classical scholars, and scholars in History.'[22]

The Islington Commission recommended a return to the system of recruitment at the age of 19, followed by a three-year probationary course. These recommendations were never implemented. Under the Montagu Chelmsford reforms of 1919 50 per cent of the places in the I.C.S. were reserved for Indians. Recruitment of graduates, both British and Indian, continued, followed by a course at a British University which lasted two years for the Indians and one year for the British. After 1919 the number of British candidates fell off on account of the uncertainty of India's future and the financially unattractive conditions of service. As early as 1912 one member wrote back to Oxford to say that the Service was no longer an eagle in the East, as described by Lord Selborne, but rather a pelican in the desert, feeding an unprofitable progeny with a rich and indigestible diet and being supplanted by the progeny it had raised. The teaching of ideals and methods to Indian successors was, he said, a much more tedious task than the untramelled pursuit of them.[23]

Oxford now lost its overwhelming predominance. Between 1921 and 1941, 170 successful candidates came from Oxford, 158 from

Cambridge and 77 from other Universities.[24] In some years an insufficient number of qualified candidates sat for the I.C.S. Examination and the British quota had to be filled by nomination. Some dons were relieved that the curriculum of classical studies was no longer dominated by the I.C.S. Examination. Percy Gardner, Professor of Classical Archaeology, who for years had been unable to get archaeology into the Greats course because it carried no marks in the I.C.S. Examination, was able to do so in 1921.[25]

At Oxford, the probationers' course struggled on until 1939, often with very small numbers. Even though Lord Halifax, a former Viceroy, was brought to Oxford to lecture on 'The I.C.S. as a Career', the inducement which he put forward of 'plenty of shooting and sky black with duck' seems to have been ineffective as compared with those of the Colonial Service which appeared to offer more security, and entry to which required no written examination to be passed.[26] The recollections of former members of the I.C.S. regarding their probation period were sought in a survey in 1979. For most of the British members the Oxford course seems not to have been very useful. One probationer in 1934 never set eyes on the gentleman in charge of his studies. There was criticism of the fact that no use was made of Indians as language teachers. There was a general impression of lack of imagination, a lack of realisation that the I.C.S. in its last stage had become an agent of change. Little was taught about village economics. 'Marking time' and 'just adequate' are descriptive phrases. An officer who took the course in 1938–9 considered that no one could have called his British contemporaries on it the élite of their generation, but that the Indians might have been so described.[27] For the Indians indeed, about to serve a British Raj, the acquaintance with British life and institutions provided essential self-confidence. But the course never recovered the glow of the period when men of the calibre of Jowett and Toynbee and Markby saw it as among the most important activities of the University and its members could make a serious study of Indian culture and economic problems through the degree course in Indian Studies.

THE EGYPTIAN AND SUDAN POLITICAL SERVICE

Most of the first British officials in the Sudan were Kitchener's Army officers; in 1904 however the Service was opened to civilian graduates, recruited by interview from Universities. Athletic distinction was given considerable weight so that Sudan became known as the territory 'where blacks were governed by blues'. In Oxford the University Appointments Committee was asked to handle both recruitment applications and the training of probationers for Egypt and Sudan; Cromer used the Professor of Arabic, Margoliouth, to identify potential candidates.

The Appointments Committee arranged for the probationers to be instructed in first aid, surveying and accounting. In 1908 the Governor General of the Sudan asked for anthropology to be included, and Marett, with Balfour's assistance, set up a course in the ethnology of the Sudan. The Egyptian Government on the other hand asked for surveying and accounting to be replaced by French which was the official language of the Secretariat but in which the new recruits were incapable of conducting routine correspondence.[28]

Whilst recruitment for Egypt soon came to an end, that for the Sudan continued for 50 years. The pattern of recruitment by interview, followed by a year's probation studying Arabic at a University, was to serve as a precedent for the Colonial Service. The Sudan Service was the only one which for constitutional reasons came under the Foreign Office rather than the India Office or Colonial Office. The greater independence from Whitehall which it enjoyed, the participation in recruitment by serving officers who were on leave in Britain, and sometimes even of the Governor-General himself, its provision of annual leave, the romance of its civilising mission and its predilection for athletes, made it an attractive Service in Oxford. Between 1899 and 1952 Oxford provided 180 recruits compared with 103 from Cambridge and 29 from other Universities. Of the Oxford entrants, 14 had First Class degrees, 83 had Seconds, 64 had Thirds and four had Fourths. Fifty-five had read Classics and 46 History.[29]

THE LEVANT CONSULAR CORPS

Rivalry between Oxford and Cambridge for posts in overseas Services or as hosts to their courses became fierce at the turn of the century. It has been seen how Cambridge criticised the I.C.S. marking system as being loaded in Oxford's favour and how it succeeded in causing Government support to be withdrawn from the Indian Forestry courses at Oxford. Cambridge, also, with what Strachan

Davidson characterised as their 'low rat-catching cunning', captured the Levant Consular Service course. This was transferred from Constantinople to Oxford in 1893, when a two-year course was organised for the student interpreters at the Indian Institute. Cambridge, however, first persuaded the Foreign Office to hold the course alternately in Oxford and Cambridge; and having done this, next succeeded in retaining all the courses on the grounds that it was extravagant to hold them in two places.[30]

THE COLONIAL SERVICE

The exceptional procedure of the Sudan was to inspire Sir Ralph Furse in the reorganisation of the recruitment of the Colonial Service, for which he was responsible from 1910 to 1948. Furse was educated at Eton and Balliol, where he took a Third in Greats. Service in the cavalry in the First World War, however, left an even greater impression and he described his object as to achieve a Colonial Service which would be a *corps d' élite* like a crack cavalry regiment.[31] Before Furse became responsible for recruitment of the Colonial Service, the appointments had been somewhat casually arranged by the Patronage Secretary in direct responsibility to the Secretary of State for the Colonies. Under the old procedures, Oxford men had frequently been appointed to senior posts. One of the most remarkable careers had been that of Sir George Bowen (1821–99), a classical scholar and Fellow of Brasenose College who had been appointed as President of the new University of Corfu at the age of 26. Thanks to this experience he was made Chief Secretary of the Ionian Islands in 1854 and K.C.M.G. at the age of 35. He then served as a colonial Governor continuously for 28 years in Queensland, New Zealand, Victoria, Mauritius and Hong Kong. No one was ever to match this record; although Corpus obstinately states on Lord Hailey's memorial that he was a Governor for 40 years, it was actually 11. Bowen's despatches were full of classical similes, as when he described the squatter question in Queensland as a revival of the strife between patricians and plebeians in Rome over the allocation of public lands.[32]

Furse introduced a systematic procedure. His *corps d'élite* was to be recruited as far as possible from the Public Schools and from Oxford and Cambridge. He never allowed the Service to be recruited by the Civil Service Commission through a competitive written examination, as was done for India and the Home Civil Service. His appointments were made on the basis of interviews which took place after consultation with a network of headmasters and College tutors. As he described the process in his memoirs, there was 'a secret list of Oxford and Cambridge tutors in order of reliability of their reports on undergraduates and a close connection with headmasters of schools . . . . We learnt to eschew publicity and rely on personal contacts in the most fruitful quarters . . . . Our methods were mole-like, quiet, persistent and indirect.'[33] Furse succeeded in obtaining control of the selection through this method of the candidates for Ceylon, Hong Kong and Malaya, who had previously taken the I.C.S. Examination, as well as of the other appointments which had never been conducted by examinations.

In 1926 Furse persuaded L. S. Amery, the Colonial Secretary, to override his senior officials and start courses at Oxford, Cambridge and London Universities for probationers destined for tropical Africa. He regarded these courses as not only useful for what they would teach but, by providing the inducement of an extra year at a University, as likely to improve the quality of candidates, which it had done for the Sudan Service. The inducement was needed. In 1908 the Oxford University Appointments Committee indeed had placed 28 men in Colonial Service appointments in British East Africa, Uganda and Northern and Southern Nigeria, and 13 in the following year.[34] The repeated warnings in the *Oxford Magazine* against the poor conditions of service, however, suggest that only those who could not get into the Home, Indian and Sudan Services before 1914 were likely to accept colonial appointments.

Furse's early supporters in Oxford were R. R. Marett, Reader in Social Anthropology, and later Rector of Exeter College, W. G. S. Adams, Professor of Government and Warden of All Souls, and A. L. Smith, the Master of Balliol. Later, as his recruitment network was established, his most enthusiastic collaborators were W. T. S. Stalleybrass, Principal of Brasenose College, Sir John Masterman, Provost of Worcester, and P. A. Landon of Trinity. Landon described to the American historian Robert Heussler how the recruitment process started. On the basis of his own impressions or those of other Fellows he would chat with a potential recruit at a sherry party and, if favourably impressed, invite him to a meal. On the basis of this he might write a note to Furse. The man normally had to be of good family and ideally to have gone to one of the better Public Schools, although exceptionally a brilliant athletic or social record at Oxford could compensate for this. Adequate mental equipment was insisted upon but 'the spectacled chap' was not considered suitable. Good judgement and good sportsmanship were the qualities sought, and 'character' was measured by Landon and Furse by whether a man looked you in the eye and how he shook hands.[35]

Stalleybrass was Oxford's leading missionary to the public schools, where he haunted the cricket and Rugby football grounds, presented prizes for classics, and spotted entrants for his College and later for the Colonial Service. His main concern was to provide a University education and a career to the sons of impoverished members of the professional classes. Furse himself would frequently visit Oxford and Cambridge to dine in College with his contacts and discuss their candidates. The best of these were invited to the Colonial Office for interview and, if successful, were enrolled in a probationary course at Oxford or Cambridge for a year after they took their degrees. Some of Oxford's most senior teachers were not included in the network; for example, Furse placed A. D. Lindsay, the Socialist Master of his old College, Balliol, at the bottom of his list of reliability in reports on undergraduates.

The system imposed a strain on the consciences of some College Tutors. As one of them wrote plaintively in the *Oxford Magazine* in a verse called 'The Testimonial':

> He has asked my support which I own I regret,
> And my mind is not wholly made up;
> For its ticklish to find a good home for a pet
> And not sell the public a pup.[36]

The Colonial Service type recruited by interview, most often a History graduate, very seldom with a First Class degree but usually with a good sporting record, was recognisably different from the Balliol men with Firsts in Classics whom the I.C.S. had recruited from Oxford in its heyday. The conditions were different. The I.C.S. were to work in a country which had a culture, as Burke once pointed out, when we were still in the trees, whereas in tropical Africa colonial officials were to work in much more primitive societies. The scholarly traditions of the I.C.S. were rather seldom found in the Colonial Service except in the Eastern colonies though there were some Oxford men who developed anthropological interests in Africa and occasionally managed to return and take the Oxford diploma in Anthropology.

Furse's object of recruiting the Colonial Administrative Service from the Universities was almost totally achieved by the 1930's, the great majority coming from Oxford and Cambridge. Oxford had a slight preponderance, but not sufficient to arouse the hostility of Cambridge. The courses at Oxford continued for some 40 years under different names and with different clients. Originally limited to tropical Africa, in 1934 they were broadened to include the whole Colonial Administrative Service. Margery Perham taught the probationers' course at Cambridge as well as Oxford and found 'an astonishing difference' between the two – 'Oxford so hypersophisticated and blasé, Cambridge so young and so keen and so polite'.[37]

The Colonial Office was much more generous than the India Office in financing additional posts in the University to cover the teaching needs of the courses. The courses were also more imaginatively organised than those of the I.C.S. To plan them Furse set up a Joint Committee of the Colonial Office with each University. Although the Supervisor of the course was generally a retired Colonial Service official, the academic advisers were some of the most lively teachers in the University, notably Kenneth Bell of Balliol and John Maud of University College. These brought in many of the most eminent teachers in the University such as Maurice Bowra, Sir Reginald Coupland, Sir John Masterman, Dame Margery Perham and R. S. Troup. The curriculum included government, history, economics, anthropology, law and the French language, with options for specialisation. Although, like the I.C.S. probationers, the colonial course participants were attached to Colleges, a Colonial Service Club was also established whose atmosphere many of them found more mature and congenial than their College Junior Common Room.

How useful the course was is not altogether clear. One of its Supervisors in 1959 told Heussler that 'it did the men no special harm'[38] and Governors in the field were sceptical as to its value. One of the most curious aspects to a foreigner might have been how little attempt the course made to provide a rationale for colonial rule. Perhaps the teacher who came closest to doing this was Coupland, who regarded teaching on the course as his most important Oxford commitment and provided a coherent account of how the colonies were acquired and of the growth of the idea of Trusteeship.

LETTERS FROM THE FIELD

A particularly valuable record of the influence of Oxford on the colonial administrators and of the evolution of their views on Empire is found in their letters back to former tutors or friends and contemporaries at Oxford, because this correspondence sometimes extends over their whole careers. One such series of letters is that between Gilbert Murray and Sir John Maynard of the I.C.S. who had been undergraduates together at St John's in the 1880s. Maynard's first letters glow with benevolent despotism: 'No one could be here and remain other than an Imperialist' he wrote in 1887, 'It is grand to feel oneself a member of a nation which is the Queen and Champion of such myriads of alien blood at the opposite side of the world. . . . If you treat the ordinary native as an equal he will proceed to insult you unless he is sufficiently well bred merely to laugh at you behind your back. . . . The Englishman here is honestly the protector of the poor, before whom the dark-skinned tyrants of their dark-skinned brothers shrink and cower, who brings the mighty from his seat and raises up the humble and meek.'[39]

Twelve years later in 1899, doubts crept into his letters. 'The longer I live in a bureaucratic country,' he wrote, 'the more clearly I see that Government is a necessary evil, whose functions should be cut down to the minimum and that it develops character better and causes less petty vexation and annoyance for people to govern themselves badly than [for us] to govern well.'[40] In 1907 he attributed the 'agitation against British Rule' which looked like the beginning of rebellion, to the 'magnificent and machine like efficiency of Curzon, . . . so splendidly contemptuous of the educated native and his aspirations.'[41] Some of the letters from Milner's young men to H. A. L. Fisher of New College have been quoted in Chapter 9.[42] However, the most comprehensive impression of how Oxford men viewed their work in the I.C.S., Colonial and other Services of the Empire may be found in the remarkable correspondence of L. R. Phelps of Oriel between 1877 and 1936. Phelps was a Fellow of Oriel during this time and its Provost from 1915 to 1929. Among his correspondents were not only old Oriel pupils but former probationers from the I.C.S., Sudan and colonial courses to whom he had taught economics. Several hundred letters from them survive.

In these there is considerable initial nostalgia and loneliness. Thus, A. W. Facer of Rhodesia in 1915 wrote from 'a small round hut which shudders and groans in the strain of a tropical hurricane. Insects wind round my feet and my dog whines piteously in the corner. Yet these things are all to me as if they were not, for the *Oriel Record* lies open before me.'[43] G. W. James lived in a mud hut in Sierra Leone which he called 'Oriel Cottage', with the Oriel arms on the front door, from which he wrote in 1926 to offer the College the gift of a West African tortoise.[44] From India came memories of walks with Phelps among the bluebells around Oxford, talking of Ruskin and George Eliot, and from Sudan, local comparisons with memories of gypsies on Shotover.

The correspondents asked Phelps for news of Oxford and of Oriel's successes on the river and in Schools; in return for this they sent information on Oriel men in their colonies and provinces which Phelps incorporated in the *Oriel Record*. Many wanted books, which he sent them, and the political news and gossip of Britain. Phelps was a Liberal, and later a Socialist; he shocked J. W. Hose of the I.C.S. in 1901 by forecasting the decay of the Imperial idea;[45] and E. Campbell in the Sudan in 1923 by voting Labour.[46] All sorts of favours were asked. Eric Saxon wrote from Northern Nigeria in 1920 that he must resign from the Service to marry a wonderful girl and would Phelps get him a job in a preparatory school where the boys did not know too much.[47] The Dean of Umtata needed a retirement post. Congenial colleagues were sought; thus W. Egerton of the I.C.S. in 1892 enquired from Murshidabad if Phelps knew of an I.C.S. probationer coming out whom he could recommend socially to become his Assistant Collector;[48] and J. Richardson from Khartoum in 1922 asked if Phelps could find a Master for the Gordon College – 'A gentleman is essential, about a Second Class in Schools and if possible who plays a little soccer.'[49] Some asked for money for their charities, others for themselves. Some wrote books and sought publishers. Many had friends to be entered for Oriel, or introduced around Oxford, though far more of these protégés were British than natives of India or the colonies.

The letters often commence with news of sport: polo in Northern Nigeria, cricket and tennis in most places, and shooting of animals and birds. Then there would be accounts of famines and economic questions which might interest Phelps as an economics tutor, and lighthearted references to legal cases, such as one in Sierra Leone in which the judge, chief witness and both advocates found that they were Oxford men and organised a collection for the Oxford Preservation Trust.[50] And then, sometimes, may be found comments on the philosophy of Empire.

Often these were reflections on the regrettable effects on primitive peoples of advancing civilisation, of which F. Sanford in North Rhodesia wrote in 1932, 'One endeavours too late to rescue the unsophisticated negro from the toils of civilisation which it seems must kill before it builds up',[51] whilst J. Richardson in the Sudan about the same time brooded, 'Do we want progress? The native does not, but motor cars and aeroplanes give them and us no alternatives.'[52]

Most of the officials believed in their mission of Trusteeship. 'It is impossible', wrote W. Egerton, when a District Magistrate in Bengal in 1892, 'for anyone of decent instincts not to feel sympathy with the natives and try to do his best to ameliorate their condition. I think our Government does a lot in this way, though often maligned.'[53] Forty years later D. Newbold, then Governor of Kordofan in the Sudan, wrote 'We have much on our side, the faith, brains and guts of picked Englishmen, a simple and decentralised administration . . . it is difficult to strike the happy mean between a blatant imperialism and a timid defeatism. The objective is simple – the greatest good of the greatest number.'[54]

There were those who found themselves in situations intolerable to their standards. One was A. S. Walford in the Kenya Government, who was disgusted when areas in which gold had been discovered were excised from the native reserves. 'The old Indian Civil Service was an occupation for gentlemen,' he wrote in 1933, 'but it is expecting a lot if members of our Public Schools and older universities are to serve contentedly with a Government which apparently attaches no sanctity to the value of its own word . . . it is incidents such as these which seem to make the ultimate surrender of the Empire inevitable if not desirable.'[55] J. L. Penney too, who served in the Cairo Police in the early twenties, wrote that it went against the grain when the police force abandoned its neutrality in elections to assist the party favoured by the Government; he resigned shortly afterwards.[56]

The I.C.S. officers in the correspondence appear more conservative than those of the Colonial Service. This is partly, though not entirely, explained by the fact that their letters cover a longer and earlier period. They were usually fairly sceptical about the political reforms which were being introduced. Criticism of the Liberal Viceroy, Lord Ripon, was natural, but A. T. Scott in 1905 considered that even Curzon's Viceroyalty was marred by 'his attempt to try to set unequal races on equality. . . . He forgot what my father used to say, that they [the Indians] are children and had to be treated like children.'[57] In 1919 Phelps was told that the Amritsar shooting was justified because this firm action prevented the need for shooting elsewhere. Later Irwin was criticised for being too soft with Congress.

Sometimes Phelps's former pupils were so perplexed that they asked his views on broad policies. Thus P. Harvey wrote from Egypt, after a political assassination in 1910, that he had worked hard to help Gorst in his programme of emancipation of Egyptians, but asked whether Phelps considered that it had broken down – 'Must we become Milner-Curzonites?'[58]

The last word may be left with A. T. B. Pritchard, writing from Khartoum in 1931: 'Until I came here I never realised what an advantage Orielenses had over all other members of all other Colleges . . . the feeling of fellowship is due to you and your long association with the College. I hope in this way to produce something which will live longer than I shall. I mean that I shall be one of those who corresponded with you, and perhaps when your letters are published my name will be amongst those of your correspondents.'[59] Pritchard's desire for immortality has not yet been realised, although the Phelps papers have twice almost miraculously been rescued from the Oriel College coal cellars,[60] and are a rich potential source for historians of Empire.

11 The Missionaries

The work has not been arbitrarily chosen as Oxford work. It is work for which Oxford men have an aptitude, as others have not.

Oxford Magazine, on the Oxford Mission to Calcutta (26 October 1887)

Because for centuries Oxford was a clerical university in which, even at the end of the nineteenth century, the majority of senior members were in Holy Orders, there was a keen interest and strong participation in Christian missionary work in the Empire. Oxford men went out in such numbers as colonial Bishops, clergy and missionaries that no comprehensive account can be given. It seems best therefore to focus on certain missions in whose founding and subsequent work Oxford had a special responsibility and to consider some characteristics of Oxford men and women who went out as missionaries to Asia, Africa and the Pacific in the Imperial period.

THE CONVERSION OF INDIA

Of all Oxford's lost causes none received keener support over a long period than that for the conversion of India to Christianity. As early as 1681, Fell, who was Bishop of Oxford and former Dean of Christ Church, persuaded the East India Company (E.I.C.) to support four or more scholars annually at Oxford to study Eastern languages and Divinity and become chaplains of the Company. Fell also arranged for translation and printing by the University Press of the Gospels in the Malayan language. Neither initiative was very fruitful. The chaplains became too busy looking after their European congregations and in trading on their own account to devote much time to evangelisation; nor were Malayan Gospels of much use in Bombay, Madras and Bengal. Moreover, the Company's policy soon became one of excluding Christian missionaries, lest their work alienate Indian rulers or cause disaffection in areas which it governed directly.[1]

In 1813, however, the Company was obliged by Parliament to admit missionaries to its territories. In the Oxford University archives evidence of considerable interest in the conversion of India can be found about this time. Thus in 1804 the Revd Claudius Buchanan offered a prize to be awarded by the University for the best work in English prose on 'The Probable Design of the Divine Providence in Subjection of so Large a Proportion of Asia to the British Dominion, the Duty, the Means and Consequence of Translating the Scriptures into the Oriental Tongues, and of Promoting Christian Knowledge in Asia'. Despite the Vice-Chancellor's support, Convocation rejected this offer, but in 1840 accepted a prize given by an official of the E.I.C. for 'The Best Refutation of Hinduism, Together with a Statement of the Evidences of Christianity as may be most Suitable to the Mental and Moral Character of the Learned Hindus, including those Facts which the Perverted Conditions of the Hindu Intellect and its Want of Historical Information may Render Indispensable'. It was to further the conversion of India, as we have seen, that the Boden Professorship of Sanskrit was endowed in 1832.[2]

In 1839 the undergraduate John Ruskin ended his Newdigate Prize poem on *Salsette and Elephanta* on an optimistic note:

> Truth calls, and gladened India hears the cry,
> Deserts the darkened path her fathers trod
> And seeks redemption from the Incarnate God.[3]

To Reginald Heber, who was Bishop of Calcutta from 1822 to 1826, however, it never appeared that the conversion of India would be an easy task. Heber had been one of the most distinguished students of his time at Oxford, winning the principal prizes for Latin verse, English poetry and literature, and becoming a Fellow of All Souls. Strongly influenced by Sir William Jones, he wrote that 'A missionary needs to be a scholar and a man of cultivated mind, for in many of his hearers he will meet with a degree of knowledge and refinement which a parochial minister in England does not often encounter.'[4] Travelling widely, and recording all aspects of Indian life, he criticised the rudeness of the Company's officials, contrasting this with the memories left by the French, 'who, though often oppressive and avaricious, had a great advantage over us in the easy and friendly intercourse in which they lived with natives of rank'.[5] Heber would invite Indians to dinner, and his wife would present them with pan and rosewater when they departed.

In the year in which Heber had won the Newdigate Prize with a poem on Jerusalem, one of his successors, Daniel Wilson, had won the Chancellor's Prize with an essay on 'Common Sense'. Wilson (1778–1858) who had been Vice-principal of St Edmund Hall, was Bishop of Calcutta from 1832 to 1858 and the first Metropolitan of India. Though they were contemporaries at Oxford, whilst Heber had the wide cultural interests of the late eighteenth century, Wilson was a typical uncompromising evangelical of the period before the Oxford Movement; he detested the latter, describing Tractarianism as 'egregious, drivelling FATUITY'.[6] He attacked the Indian Government for showing favour to Mohammedanism, for countenancing the gross abominations of Hinduism, for not permitting Christian instruction in schools and for failing to respect the Sabbath. 'Jesus, Master, have mercy on us', he exploded in 1841, 'We have two Sunday newspapers to help on Satan's work.'[7] In his 'Humiliation Sermon' of 1857 he attributed the Indian Mutiny to the East India Company's tolerance of idolatry and of the opium traffic, their recognition of caste and neglect of the Lord's Day, and the prevalence of licentiousness and infidelity.[8]

A later evangelical was Thomas Valpy French (1825–91), Fellow of University College, who became the first Bishop of Lahore. He, too, found the Tractarians unsympathetic; Oxford's business, he considered, was in its proper studies. He had been a pupil of Arnold at Rugby and bore the Doctor's mark throughout his life. His friends noticed the tremendous energy with which he rode a horse or pulled an oar, and that he did not know what relaxation meant. At St John's College, Agra, which he founded, in addition to his teaching he studied five languages a day. When he retired from his energetic episcopate, he went on to Muscat in a solitary attempt to convert the Arabs to Christianity and thus diminish the trade of African slaves through Zanzibar to Arabia. He died of heatstroke while preaching to them, leaving eight children.[9]

One of the consequences of the Oxford Movement was the revival within the Church of England of celibate religious communities modelled on those of the Middle Ages. The earliest male community was the Society of St John the Evangelist, or Cowley Fathers. The Society was founded by R. M. Benson, a Christ Church man, with the object of establishing a devotional College in India, but its work was at first diverted by the Bishop of Oxford to the new suburb of Cowley on the outskirts of Oxford. From 1874, however, it also ministered to Eurasian and poor Indian Christians in Bombay. Although based in Oxford it had no particular connection with the University.[10]

THE OXFORD MISSION TO CALCUTTA

The University's most ambitious contribution to the conversion of India came through the Oxford Mission to Calcutta which was founded in Christ Church in 1880 by Talbot, Gore, Liddon, King and Scott Holland, all leading High Churchmen, in response to an appeal from the Metropolitan of India, who called upon the University to provide men to work among the students of Calcutta. The Oxford Mission was – and remains – a celibate Order, which claimed that 'if not officially, yet definitely and distinctly, it represents Oxford to India. Through it the University of Oxford ministers of its intellectual and spiritual wealth to the deep poverty of the University of Calcutta.'[11]

Just as early Christianity had spread through Jerusalem, Antioch and Rome, it was now argued that in India the critical point was Calcutta, its administrative and intellectual centre. On the Hindu side the Brahmo Samaj appeared to the first Superior of the Mission, E. G. Willis, a former Vice-principal of Cuddesdon, to provide a monotheism which could lead to Christianity. As for the Muslims, Father O'Neill, another of the first members of the Mission, believed that 'All Muhammedan nations are dying out through their own vices.'[12]

Rapidly the Mission established a hostel in Calcutta for students who, coming from lower middle-class Bengali village families, often lived in great poverty and squalor. The Christ Church connection caused the hostel to be named 'The House' and its yard 'The Meadow'. Its only rule was 'that those living in the home must behave like gentlemen'. A magazine, *Epiphany*, was specially directed at students, encouraging them to discuss religious, literary and social questions in its correspondence columns. By 1898 the Mission had established a complete system of boys' education from village school to industrial school to high school to University boarding house to theological class.

And yet as early as 1889 a certain disappointment with the results of the dialogue with the educated classes became apparent. 'An Englishman', one of the fathers wrote home sadly, 'will not readily open his mouth on a religious subject, but if he does he means it. The Bengali is always ready to talk about religion, but then one discovers that his interest is only intellectual and superficial, and that nothing is further from his thoughts than to accept responsibility for such truths as he is led to acknowledge.'[13]

By 1910, as the Hindu revival developed, it was admitted that 'the class which we hoped to influence are harder to guide towards the faith because they are now largely given away to political ideals'. The sights began to be lowered. 'Though the work has not led to direct conversion such as we hoped' one of the Fathers wrote in the Mission's history, 'indirect results have been obtained in the Christianisation of thought and character among those who are still not Christians.'[14]

About this time, the Bishop of Calcutta somewhat surprisingly diverted the main effort of the Mission to Barisal, a remote area of East Bengal where a few thousand Christians who had alternated between the Roman Catholic, Baptist and Episcopalian churches needed pastoral care. The flow of Oxford recruits then dried up and in later years the Fathers came mainly from Cambridge and London.

Yet the Oxford pioneers who served longest, Father Douglass of Christ Church, a moderate scholar but a good oar, and Mother Edith, who had been Vice-Principal of Lady Margaret Hall, left a vivid memory of this late flowering of the Oxford Movement. Their first priority was prayer, daily prayer for the conversion of India; educational and other good works never took precedence over this. Secondly, they sought to work through Indian Brotherhoods and Sisterhoods, which should as soon as possible become independent, living according to the principles of the Rule, but each with a separately adapted constitution and way of life. Thirdly, in Calcutta and in Behala, on its outskirts, they provided a rare atmosphere in which the Bengali middle class, ridiculed, despised and feared in British official and commercial circles, could discuss intellectual problems freely with British graduates.[15]

There was little in the High Church atmosphere of the early members of the Oxford Mission and of the Cowley Fathers of that tolerance of other religions or of Indian aspirations and culture shown by Jones and even Heber. Father Benson, Superior of the Cowley Fathers, compared the Taj Mahal unfavourably with Keble College.[16] The Oxford Mission assimilated Indian music but Father

Douglass described the *Bhagavad Gita* as 'abominable idolatry' and, as a privileged eccentric at the age of 80, even after Independence, removed a portrait of Netaji Subhas Bose from the hostel walls and hurled it into the fire.[17]

As for the conversion of India, Father Benson by 1895 had come to see merits in gradualism. The conversion of Clovis and his 3000 soldiers in the early Middle Ages had been too sudden, he considered, to promote a true understanding of the faith. Moreover, whilst the basis of Greek and Roman philosophy strengthened the early Christian Church, in India, on the contrary, missionary work was hampered by the Indians' experience of European unbelief and scepticism. Father Benson was content to calculate that at the present rate of progress the proportion of Christians in India would rise from 1 in 150 to 1 in 10 over the next 300 years.[18]

Towards the end of British Rule some younger missionaries were influenced by the Swaraj or Independence Movement, and became concerned that the Church in India should have a truly Indian character. E. J. Palmer (1869–1954), who was a Fellow and chaplain of Balliol when he became Bishop of Bombay in 1908, did as much as anyone to bring about the transformation of the Church of England in India into the independent Church of India, Burma and Ceylon in 1930. But this did not satisfy his Balliol pupil, Jack Winslow, who served in India as a missionary for the Society for the Propagation of the Gospel (S.P.G.) from 1914 to 1922. In 1922, with the encouragement of Bishop Palmer, he and a few Indian and British friends, of whom one was Verrier Elwin of Merton College, formed the Christa Seva Sangha or Christ's Service Society, whose members lived in Indian style and sought to 'reorientalise' Christianity. Winslow deplored the situation in which British congregations refused to have Indian priests in their pulpits and at their altars, and British missionaries refused to have Indian guests in their houses. He urged that 'missions' and 'missionaries' be brought to an end and merged in the Indian Church, whilst the chaplains paid by the Government remained part of the Church of England. He envisaged an Indian Church which clothed its teaching in Indian ideas and drew from the study of Hindu Scriptures, just as the Western Christian Church had made use of Greek philosophical ideas in building its own edifice of doctrine. 'Exalted passages' from the Hindu religious books could be used, he suggested, as the 'Old Testament' of Indian Christianity. Members of the community wore a saffron girdle to show their sympathy with the Hindu *sanyasis* and lived a life of great simplicity.

Winslow remained in the Church, though he returned to England in 1934 to work in the Oxford Group; whilst, as has been seen, Elwin eventually renounced his Orders and turned to social and anthropological work among primitive tribes in Central India.[19]

THE UNIVERSITIES MISSION TO CENTRAL AFRICA

In addition to the Oxford Mission to Calcutta there was another Mission for which the University felt a special responsibility. In 1857 David Livingstone made an eloquent appeal to the Universities of Oxford and Cambridge to establish missions in Central Africa. 'I go back to Africa', he said 'to try to make an open path for commerce and Christianity. Do you carry out the work which I have begun. I leave it to you.' He was warmly supported by Samuel Wilberforce, Bishop of Oxford, who saw this as the completion of the work which his father, William Wilberforce, had started with the abolition of the British slave trade.

At a great meeting in the Sheldonian Theatre, committees from the two Universities established the Universities Mission to Central Africa (U.M.C.A.). The Mission's first head, Frederick MacKenzie, was consecrated, it was said, as the Church's first missionary Bishop for 1000 years. The aim of MacKenzie, a Cambridge man who had served in South Africa, was no less than a chain of missions from the Cape to Cairo. Within a year, however, he was dead. After his death, at another meeting in the Sheldonian in 1862, his letters were read out, full of reference to the 'war' for the release of slaves which the Mission had conducted against neighbouring tribes around their settlement. It was a tale of guns and smoking villages which MacKenzie had lightened with references to the history of Troy and of Hannibal. Although the Professor of the History of War pointed out that attack was frequently the only method of defence, Dr Pusey carried the meeting with him in his indignation when he said that it seemed to him a 'frightful thing that the messengers of the Gospel of Peace should in any way be connected with the shedding of blood'.[20]

MacKenzie's successor as Bishop – W. G. Tozer of St John's College, Oxford – was appointed with a new policy. He gave the Mission an entirely pacific character by moving it to Zanzibar, where it was protected by a British consul, and concentrated on the education and training of liberated slaves for the Ministry. Tozer also gave the Mission a High Church and ritualist stamp which became permanent. H. M. Stanley in 1872 disgustedly described him 'in his crimson robe of office and in the queerest of all headdresses, stalking through the streets of Zanzibar or haggling over the prize of a tin pot at a tinker's stall' as 'the most ridiculous sight I have seen outside a clown show. I, as a white man,' he wrote, 'protest against the absurdity.'[21]

A novel characteristic of the U.M.C.A. was that a high proportion of its members were graduates. In the early nineteenth century many missionaries had been people of limited education, described by Sydney Smith as the 'didactic artisan' and the 'delirious mechanic'.[22] But the U.M.C.A., as Bishop Steere put it, 'must look to the Universities for officers, though we may get the rank and file from other classes'.[23] The new style set by Tozer fitted with that of Oxford nineteenth century churchmanship. Between 1860 and 1900 the Mission therefore attracted twice as many graduates from Oxford as from Cambridge, whereas by contrast in the more evangelical Christian Missionary Society (C.M.S.) over about the same period Cambridge men outnumbered Oxford men by three to one.[24]

The U.M.C.A. acquired under Tozer and maintained later an Anglo-Catholic paternalistic character, very similar to that in the contemporary parishes in the London slums whose clergy were High Church priests from Oxford. Its members were unpaid. About half of them were the sons of clergy. They put much less emphasis on industrial work than did most contemporary missions, and they were less interested in material progress. Indeed they insisted that the African priests whom they trained should not separate themselves from their congregations by adopting a superior way of life. They made a notable contribution by writing dictionaries and grammars of African languages, the publication of which was sometimes subsidised by O.U.P. The death rate was very high; before 1900 about 12 per cent of the missionaries died in their first three years of service[25] and in Oxford the Mission therefore enjoyed a considerable romantic appeal.

At one of Canon Christopher's Missionary Breakfasts in 1895 Bishop Maples stated, in appealing for volunteers, that one University man, owing to his tact, good sense, breadth of view and knowledge of his fellow man, was worth as much as four ordinary students from the missionary Colleges.[26] Why this was so can be seen in his own career and that of his friend W. P. Johnson. They both joined the U.M.C.A. in 1874 on seeing a scrap of paper posted in the

Oxford Union by Bishop Steere, the Head of the Mission, who was on furlough, asking men who might be interested in service with the U.M.C.A. to get in touch with him.

W. P. Johnson (1854–1928) had won a place in the I.C.S. which he now relinquished, to the despair of the Master of his College and the admiration of his contemporaries, in order to read Theology and prepare himself for missionary service. Maples had been reading Theology in a desultory way, more taken up with music and rowing, when he heard of Johnson's decision and decided to accompany him. Johnson's departure had to be deferred until after Henley Week, in which he stroked his College boat. He and Maples arrived and were ordained in Zanzibar in 1876, and shortly afterwards were sent into the interior, where the Mission had recently resumed its operations.

Chauncey Maples (1852–95) was a born leader, whose method of directing others was to work with them, whether in printing, building, baking or cookery. In taking choir practice he would sing energetically all four parts, tenor, alto, treble and bass, simultaneously playing the harmonium and working the bellows. Yet his letters home were full of self-criticism. Apart from the gift of leadership, he considered that his only accomplishments were cooking and the writing of hymn tunes. When Nyasaland was separated from the diocese of Zanzibar and he was approached, he wrote 'Never, never a Bishop. I am terribly lacking in spiritual gifts.' Indeed, but for Johnson, he thought that he would resign and go home.

The first Bishop of Likoma only lasted a year. Inevitably Maples succeeded him. When he was consecrated in England he asked for prayers that he be given the gift of patience because irritability was a great snare to the dwellers in Africa. Lack of patience was to lead to his tragic end. Hurrying back to Likoma from England, he arrived at Lake Nyasa to find no steamer available, and so took a sailing boat. When a storm arose he refused to run for shelter; the boat capsized. The African crew supported him on wooden boxes and implored him to take off his cassock, but he would not. The last words which they heard as he sank were 'Do not let me cause your death. It was my fault. Save yourselves.'[27]

Chauncey Maples, who was only 43 when he died, left a glowing memory. No one, it was said, had such influence with the Africans, because he would listen to them. Europeans were fascinated by the brilliance of his table-talk on history, music, poetry, philology, botany, geology and metaphysics; and by his ability to enter enthusiastically into their own interests. He would perform conjuring tricks for

Africans and write light verses for Europeans. He believed firmly that the East African peoples were in point of possible development and intellectual achievement, if given their opportunity, not one whit behind the white races.[28] The European missionary, he considered, must become an African to win Africans, adopting native food and eating in the native fashion.[29]

Johnson acquired the nickname of 'the man who never sits down'. In his early years he had two severe breakdowns. After the first he had to return to the coast. The second left him blind. Although he was operated on in England, he lost the sight of one eye and only recovered the partial sight of the other. When he returned to Africa, Maples had taken over his work and was Archdeacon in charge of the Mission's headquarters in Likoma Island. Johnson was happy to concentrate on preaching and teaching outside Likoma. Having to train teachers with no books, he organised a peripatetic College. By day his students were porters; in the evenings they learnt English and arithmetic and helped him with his translations. More and more of a solitary, he was described as an 'old blind elephant, pressing on through whatever might be in the track without paying much attention to the obstacles'.[30]

Johnson was to outlive Maples by 30 years and spend 47 years in Africa. Between him and Maples there had been the free expression possible between those who have grown up together. But after Maples's death he felt increasingly out of sympathy with Likoma with its great cathedral and European style of living. He grumbled at the expense of bringing out European personnel. 'I don't think our station life is a success,' he wrote, 'it means living apart from the natives.' His desire was to create a wholly native Church.[31]

In his old age, after the First World War, he wandered off alone to reopen work in former German territories. He was, his biographer says, 'angular, obscure, difficult, but a man of God'.[32] He had none of the charisma of Maples; was often vague and hard to follow. But to himself he was clear in his determination 'to do and have as little as possible that might increase the white man's difficulty in entering into the native mind and life'.[33] His most notable practical contribution was to translate the entire Bible into the Chinyanja language.

From the careers of these two men, then, it would appear that what was of great value in a contemporary Oxford education was the variety of interests which it inspired, and which could help Maples to cheer and stimulate a small group of his compatriots, living at close quarters in a trying climate, whilst it gave Johnson a self-sufficiency which enabled him to live alone with people of primitive cultures.

A distinctive feature of these nineteenth-century Anglo-Catholics was that they did not associate civilisation or technical progress with religion. Because they regarded the Church as a universal, not an English, organisation, they sought ways of building an African branch of it with roots in its own society. Bishop Tozer insisted that natives while being Christianised should not be Europeanised. Bishop Hine, Maples's successor, an Oxford graduate with a medical degree who led the U.M.C.A. from 1896 to 1909, even considered that primitive tribes might be more closely in touch with the spiritual powers in which the early Church had believed than were contemporary Europeans.[34]

The evangelicals and nonconformists were generally less tolerant of tribal institutions because they were more concerned with the relationship of the individual with God than that of the Church with God. The attitude of the Anglo-Catholic Oxford missionaries was in some ways analogous to that of the Oxford colonial administrators who supported Indirect Rule; and the same criticisms might be raised against them, that in their desire to prevent the Africans whom they trained from becoming separated from their people, they did not perhaps give them sufficient education to enable them to cope with the rapid changes in society which were inevitable.

THE DISCIPLES OF BISHOP GORE

Of the brilliant Balliol graduates of the 1870s, Charles Gore was to make as great an impact in the Church as Milner and Asquith were to make in the State. He reconciled the High Church to Biblical criticism and freed the Oxford Movement from its Tory associations, teaching that Christians had an unlimited social responsibility for those around them. As the first Principal of Pusey House he exercised from there almost as much influence as Newman had done from the pulpit of St Mary's. A combination of strong Anglo-Catholic views with an equally strong sense of social responsibility was the characteristic of Gore's disciples. This may be illustrated from the lives of two of them who were friends and contemporaries at Trinity College, Frank Weston and Arthur Shearley Cripps.

Frank Weston (1871–1924) was inspired by a sermon of Bishop Smithies in St Barnabas Church, Oxford, to offer his services to the U.M.C.A. Within a few months of his arrival in Zanzibar, where his task was to train Africans for Holy Orders, he wrote an open letter to the Bishop, criticising the way in which the Mission was run. From the beginning and throughout his life he stated that the great obstacle to the Mission's progress 'lay in that consciousness of race which is so characteristic of Englishmen'. Missionaries, he said, treated Africans as children and expected from them deference and service.[35] He saw that if a native Church was ever to grow, native priests must be treated as equals. In the tradition of W. P. Johnson he insisted that the College be simple and that the African priests should not be Europeanised. An enthusiastic innovator, he hired a merry-go-round for the school and introduced beatings into the prize-giving ceremony.

In 1908, at the age of 37, Weston became Bishop of Zanzibar, though he continued to spend nine months a year visiting mission stations, mostly on foot. He held very High Church views and caused a sensation by charging the Bishops of Mombasa and Uganda with heresy and schism because they celebrated Communion together with Presbyterians, Baptists and Methodists. On another occasion he posted a notice on the door of Zanzibar Cathedral to say that his diocese was not in communion with the Bishop of Hereford. His practical sympathy with Africans was shown in 1914. When he saw how brutally the British Army treated the porters whom they had conscripted, he raised his own corps of 2000 porters and commanded it with the rank of Major. The experience gave him an insight into the practice of forced labour on which he wrote a pamphlet called *Serfs of Britain*. After the war to the irritation of Milner, who was Colonial Secretary, he conducted a campaign in Britain against forced labour, which was favoured by his old targets, the Bishops of Uganda and Mombasa. Aided by J. H. Oldham, he persuaded Winston Churchill, Milner's successor, to issue a despatch restricting the practice to local community projects. In an oecumenical age Weston's ecclesiastical ideas may seem archaic. In his insistence, however, that the main problems of the day were colour and caste, and that the Church was betraying its principles by ignoring them, he was in advance of his time.[36]

Weston's Oxford friend, Arthur Shearley Cripps, became not a Bishop but a saint and a poet. He went out in 1900 to work for the Society for the Propagation of the Gospel in the village of Enkeldoorn in Rhodesia, and remained there for 50 years, ministering to Africans, helping them to build churches with his own hands, living in such a Franciscan style that he would give away not only his clothes but his cassock to those in need. His Bishop said it would be no use to give him a horse, because he would carry it when he thought it was tired and let it run on ahead when it was fresh. He was usually in the midst of controversy, writing pamphlets and corresponding with Lionel Curtis, Margery Perham and others back in Oxford on the land question and the hut tax; these activities caused him to suggest that the best qualification for a missionary would be a Law degree. Eventually he left the S.P.G. in order to be free to work in his own way; Bishop Paget of Southern Rhodesia, another Oxford man, allowed him great latitude for, he said, he knew a saint when he saw one. John Buchan found in Cripps's sacred verses 'a note which had been absent from English poetry since Christina Rossetti, the unmistakable note of ecstasy'.[37]

In 1892 Gore founded in Oxford the Community of the Resurrection in order to provide a home and encouragement to those Anglican priests in Britain and the Empire who intended to remain celibate. The early members were mostly Oxford men, who in the first years of the Community seemed somewhat in search of a role in and around Oxford. Then they moved to Mirfield in an industrial area of Yorkshire where they founded what was to become a famous theological College, and in 1903 sent out brothers to work in and around Johannesburg, where the Bishop invited them to establish a centre for the strengthening of the spiritual life of the diocese. The members of the Community at first worked separately on the European and African side, a separation which they justified by the need for Africans to develop their own Church traditions under their own leaders, and which was symbolized by the black Christ in the Church of Christ the King which they built in Sophiatown. The Community found a noble role in building churches and starting schools and in pastoral work among the Africans who lived in the mining compounds and later in the black urban areas. As disciples of Gore, they could not confine themselves to church and schoolroom. They were sent for whenever Africans were in trouble. They fought for the poor and the persecuted in the courts and police stations and Town Council, and inevitably came into political conflict with the authorities on social questions which they saw as moral as well as political. Father Raynes of Pembroke College, who directed their work in South Africa in the 1930s and became Superior of the Community in

1943, still retained the Anglo-Catholic opposition to intercommunion with other denominations, but eventually, when the Community had to move from the Johannesburg area because its work there became impossible under the legislation of Apartheid, this tradition softened in the oecumenical atmosphere of Lovedale.[38]

THE OXFORD EVANGELISTS OF 1892

Although the Anglo-Catholics were predominant in late-nineteenth-century Oxford, the evangelicals also recruited some remarkable men, notably in 1892 when Oxford was swept by the evangelical fervour of the campaign led by the American missionaries Mott and Speer. Undergraduates could be seen walking ten abreast down the High Street, singing hymns and shouting 'Hallelujah'. The slogan of the revival was 'the evangelisation of the world in this generation'. Among the undergraduates who took the pledge to become missionaries abroad were J. H. Oldham, Alek Fraser and Temple Gairdner, all of Trinity, and W. E. S. Holland of Magdalen. As an initiation they had to preach in the open air at the Martyrs' Memorial. The Movement was puritanical; 'We were prigs and smugs', reflected Holland long afterwards; Gairdner had to give up his piano and cover the nude Greek statuettes in his rooms with dusters; Fraser had to renounce his gold waistcoat buttons. Yet there was a happy intoxication, so that Gairdner would walk round the Trinity College gardens chanting 'O ye Delphiniums and Azaleas, Bless ye the Lord'.[39]

Three of these four friends were Scots; as they went out from Oxford to their very different careers they attached little importance to denominations. Fraser was only ordained into the Church of England when he was 40; Oldham remained a layman all his life, and his lack of commitment to a particular church was perhaps an asset when he became Secretary of the International Missionary Council.

J. H. Oldham (1874–1969) had hoped to enter the I.C.S. before he took the Missionary Pledge. Missionary service took him back all the same to India where he had been born; he worked with the Student Christian Movement, living almost entirely with Indians. Although he was invalided home after a few years, the experience left him with a lasting conviction that the missionaries had lost India by teaching converts to despise their cultural heritage, and he determined that the mistake must not be repeated in Africa. One of the great issues of history, he said in 1916, was whether the African races would create a characteristic life of their own or be the tool of others.[40] With this concern he promoted the creation of the Advisory Committee for African Education in the Colonial Office and that of the International Institute of African Languages and Cultures. He usually liked to work behind the scenes from his office as Secretary of the International Missionary Council, and when he made a public appearance, as in his influential book *Christianity and the Race Problem*, in the campaign to abolish forced labour in East Africa, and in his insistence on the paramountcy of African rather than of white settler interests, his statements were moderate and conciliatory. He was the great missionary statesman of his time. He was also one of the founders of the oecumenical movement; God is not, he liked to say, primarily interested in religion.[41]

Alek Fraser (1873–1962) was a Presbyterian who impulsively joined the C.M.S. in Uganda to follow a girl whom he wished to marry. He became a great colonial headmaster and his educational work is discussed in Chapter 12. He had also a prophetic role; he believed, and frequently said, that Christianity and Christian education must lead to national independence. As he got older it seemed to him that British attitudes to Empire were becoming coarser and harder and he expressed his indignation with none of the discretion of Oldham. In a sermon in Westminster Abbey in 1924 he proclaimed that 'There is war in our great Empire between Christ and Mammon. . . . The greed that roused us into passing the Factory Acts is not yet dead. . . . Never has the theory of domination and exploitation been more crudely preached.' He described the settlers' object in Kenya as government by a ring of employers of labour who had already shown by cruel labour laws how little they could be trusted.[42] The Kenya Legislature adjourned in protest against the pulpit of Westminster Abbey being used for the expression of such opinions; Oldham warned Fraser that he was risking the cancellation of his appointment as Principal of Achimota College, the first secondary school in the Gold Coast. 'We want to defeat the Delamere crowd' (of Kenyan settlers), he wrote, 'and not merely irritate them. You can do that most effectively by carrying through Achimota.' Sir Ralph Furse at the Colonial Office was also worried about the effect of the sermon on the Achimota appointment in which Fraser would be a Government servant. Fraser was adamant. 'I am not going to be bound, but free', he told Oldham, 'Otherwise I shall not accept any service under Government.'[43] Many years later, in the early days of the Second World War in 1939, he preached an even more sensational sermon in St Aldate's Church, Oxford, in which he said 'We blame Germany for the brutal destruction of Warsaw, but the Kraals of Lobengula and the Matabele were as dear to them as Warsaw to the Poles. The German has today exploited the Jew. But we today exploit the African. In East Africa the African may not trade in towns, may not buy or lease lands, cannot hope for the franchise, . . . is not free to leave his employment, . . . and has no more rights than the Jew in Berlin.' He went on to point out that in Northern Rhodesia in 1937 the copper mines paid £5 million in dividends and only £244,000 in wages; and that at the present rate of progress it would be 2000 years before the villages in all African colonies had schools.[44]

This prophetic figure carried round the world with him the characteristic flippancy, jesting and love of horseplay of an Oxford undergraduate of the 1890s. He would terrify his guests in Africa and Ceylon by putting a dressing-gown cord in their beds and pretending it was a snake. His manner and his unorthodox ideas made enemies. In Ceylon 50 fellow missionaries petitioned for his recall.[45]

W. E. S. Holland (1873–1951) served in India with the C.M.S. for over 30 years. Between 1900 and 1913 he set up and ran the Oxford and Cambridge Hostel at Allahabad, which Oxford supported with money and by the voluntary services of young graduates. The object of the hostel was to give the students social and moral protection and bring them under Christian influence. At first Holland had high hopes of conversion of boys so Anglicised that their fathers bought them *Chatterbox* and the *Boys Own Paper*; he wrote back to C.M.S. headquarters that 'the despairing death grapple of Hinduism was being witnessed', and that only Max Mueller's books caused educated Hindus to cling on to their religion. By 1908, however, he found that politics had completely usurped religion in men's hearts; and the missionary services in the villages were drowned by the Nationalist anthem, the *Bande Mataram*.[46]

After the first ten years, despite his discussion of religion every evening with individual students in their rooms, and the 51 periods a week of voluntary Bible reading, conducted by two young theological students from Corpus, there had only been one baptism; though there was some consolation in the fact that no one who had taken part in athletics had ever been condemned for sedition.[47] Holland's annual letters to C.M.S. headquarters show a gradual broadening of objectives from his initial concern with evangelisation. By 1908 he wrote of the privilege of being allowed to have a hand in moulding the character of future leaders of India, whose genius and capacities must mean so much for the spiritual and intellectual enrichment of mankind. In 1909 he welcomed the Morley–Minto reforms because in these at last Indians and British could work together for better things. In the same sense, 20 years later when he was Principal of St John's College, Agra, he was inspired by A. D. Lindsay, the visiting Master of Balliol, to envisage the College as a laboratory for study of the economic, educational and spiritual problems of the community.[48]

Looking back at his time at the Oxford and Cambridge Hostel he concluded 'I believe on grounds of sheer missionary efficiency, as an investment for future missionary usefulness, I would have done well a few years ago to have given up all my Bible reading with my men and to have given myself for six weeks to the nursing of a student down with smallpox instead of sending him to the hospital. That is an act the Indian would have understood and it would have added a new value to my Bible reading ever since.[49] He came to believe also that the reason for the weakness of Indian Christianity was its exotic roots and the dominance of Europeans. 'So many an Indian household has its tale of unjust treatment of grandfather or uncle by his missionary employer; promotion refused here, dismissal there.'[50] Throughout his life Holland kept in close touch with Oxford where he was for a time chaplain of Balliol and curate of the University Church. Less intellectual than Gairdner, less clever than Oldham, less forceful than Fraser, the sweetness of his disposition and directness of his character made him the most successful recruiter of missionaries in the Oxford of his time.[51]

Temple Gairdner (1873–1928) was the son of a Unitarian Scottish doctor and of a Church of England mother who brought him up as an Imperialist. He was inspired by the romantic image of General Gordon to serve with the C.M.S. in Egypt, to the distress of his friends who foresaw that this was an unrewarding country in which to labour for evangelisation in one generation. Like Holland, he was to work among students and the educated classes. Unlike Holland he had a first-class mind. He became a considerable Arabic scholar who changed the missionary studies from classical to colloquial Arabic, but he was too loaded with administrative duties to have much scope for scholarship. He produced Bible plays in Arabic in church for which he composed the music, modelled he said on Trinity 'drunks', until this practice was stopped by C.M.S. headquarters. His friends spoke of the inexhaustible treasures of his mind. He taught unpopular messages, to the British to understand and esteem the Egyptians, to the Egyptian Christians to love the Muslims. He remained a romantic Imperialist and hoped in 1914 that Imperial Federation would be an outcome of the war. He became a Canon of Cairo Cathedral, but it does not seem that the C.M.S. made imaginative use of his talents, nor was his work much noticed in Oxford. When he visited the University on leave, no don at his old college, Trinity, ever invited him within its gates.[52]

THE MARTYR BISHOPS

There was yet another type of missionary who went out from Oxford, the muscular Christian, of which the most notable example was Bishop James Hannington (1847–85), who is commemorated by a Festival Day in the Church of England's Alternative Service Book of 1980. Oxford beatified him earlier; above the High Table in the place of honour in the Hannington Hall of St Peter's College he is depicted in a huge stained-glass window; his halo is supported by a rhinoceros, a lion and an elephant; the spears with which he was killed are by his side, and at his feet are the martyr's palm and crown.

As an undergraduate at St Mary's Hall, Hannington was an indifferent scholar and a practical joker who would amuse himself by screwing up the doors of his more studious neighbours or pushing a friend down the High Street in a wheelbarrow. He failed his ordination examinations; when at length he got through them and became a curate he suffered from depression until a friend sent him a book which suddenly gave him the faith and confidence of an evangelical religion. In 1882, although married with three children, he offered himself to the C.M.S. for five years' service in Uganda. On his first visit he was invalided home before reaching Uganda. In 1885 he went out again as first Bishop of Eastern Equatorial Africa. This time he tried to reach Uganda from the coast by the eastern route which led through the plains and was shorter and less unhealthy than the southern route through the forests. He was unaware (though the missionaries in Uganda were aware) of the suspicion and fear with which all visitors from the north and east were regarded by the Baganda. He made a worse and fatal mistake in arriving at lake Victoria at a different point from that at which he had asked the missionaries to meet him, and of which they had notified the Kabaka.

He was arrested at the border and after a few days' imprisonment was murdered on the orders of the ruler.[53]

Hannington had a gift for human relations. He danced with the Africans, had a high regard for their capacity, and foresaw a time when they would be trained not only as clergy but doctors. He also had a strong sense of publicity. It was understood between him and the C.M.S. that his letters to the Secretary would be 'doctored' and placed in the press.[54] In the *Life of Hannington* which appeared shortly after his death, his last words were related as 'I am about to die for the Baganda and have purchased the road to them with my life.' This was to be an invaluable quotation in the great campaign which the missionaries and Lugard launched a few years later in order to persuade the Liberal Government to bring Uganda under British Rule and construct a railway to it from the coast. Whatever the British public believed, some fellow missionaries were somewhat sceptical of the legend of Hannington, who spent hardly more than a year in Africa, as the martyr Bishop. R. P. Ashe of the C.M.S. in Uganda not only hinted in his memoirs at doubts as to the authenticity of the dying words, but found surprising discrepancies between the published text of Hannington's last diaries and a copy of the manuscript which he had made.[55]

When the diaries appeared, there was uneasiness too, not only in missionary circles, at accounts of the 'hearty thrashings' administered by the Bishop to his porters – 'Men very noisy,' recorded the diary, 'up twice and boxed some of their ears.'[56] Surely it was not thus, some pondered, that Livingstone had managed his caravans?[57]

A less controversial Oxford colonial martyr for commemoration in the new prayer book would have been John Coleridge Patteson (1821–71), Bishop of Melanesia. Patteson was at Eton and Balliol before becoming a Fellow of Merton. He was a High Churchman and friend of Keble. He was recruited in 1854 by Bishop Selwyn to work with him in New Zealand and in the Pacific and in 1861 became the first Bishop of Melanesia. Much of his life was spent in training boys from the islands as teachers and catechists. He was a remarkable linguist, speaking 23 languages and preparing grammars in 17 of them. He maintained close links with Oxford, corresponding with Max Mueller on philological questions and keeping up with Tylor's early anthropological work.

As time went on Patteson lost many of the prejudices which he had brought with him. In 1857 he had written of his colleagues 'Nothing but a good Public School (and I am bound to think of Eton) education can give a fellow things that can hardly be taught since they come from association and the discipline of boys of good feeling among themselves.'[58] But six years later he considered that 'some would come out with the notion that England and English clergymen were born to set the Colonies right. I can get the material cheaper and made to my own hand here.'[59]

On race, Patteson expressed himself emphatically at a time when the natives of New Zealand and Tasmania were being treated with insensitivity and brutality – 'The pride of race which prompts a white man to regard coloured people as inferior to himself is strongly ingrained in most men's minds and must be wholly eradicated before they will ever win the hearts and the souls of the heathen. . . . I never yet saw a New Zealand missionary who did not in some way or other make a Maori feel that he or she was not regarded as quite fit to be a companion, friend or associate for his own boys and girls. This is fatal to success.'[60]

He regretted that 'We seek to denationalise these people, whereas we ought surely to change as little as possible, only what is incompatible with the simplest form of Christian teaching and practice.'[61] He did not approve of making Melanesians wear clothing, as they were so much more graceful without it.

Patteson spent much of his time visiting the islands, taking off boys to his headquarters in Norfolk Island and returning them as trained teachers or catechists. But in the 1860s Melanesia began to be raided by 'blackbirders' from Australia who provided what was in effect slave labour to the Queensland planters who could no longer rely on the supply of convicts from Britain.

The Bishop did all he could to protect his people, and wrote a memorandum to his old Balliol friend Sir George Bowen, Governor of Queensland, on the measures which needed to be introduced. But the 'snatch-snatch ships' which kidnapped the islanders were followed by the even more ruthless 'kill-kill ships' which collected not slaves but skulls to be bartered with head-hunting tribes.

Patteson was killed while visiting the island of Nakupu. His body was returned, and is thus depicted in a memorial in Merton College Chapel, bearing five wounds on the breast, on which a palm branch was placed, tied in five knots, as an indication that his death was in revenge for the kidnapping of five islanders by blackbirders. His dramatic death, and the life written by his relative, Charlotte Yonge, did much to cause the British Parliament to pass an Act for the control of blackbirding, though this took many years to become effective.

THE MISSIONARY SETTLEMENT FOR UNIVERSITY WOMEN

Among the students at Oxford and elsewhere who took the Missionary Pledge in 1892 were a number of women. Some went out to serve with the C.M.S. and other missions. Others found scope in the new settlements such as Toynbee Hall in East London, where University men and women served and endeavoured to uplift the working-classes. It was from this settlement background that the women came who determined to go out, not as auxiliaries to male-dominated missions, but to found their own interdenominational Missionary Settlement for University Women in Bombay in 1893. Their principal object was to bring the Gospel to the future women leaders of India, such as doctors, lawyers and teachers, and above all to the Parsees who had made Bombay the most advanced centre of women's education in India. The founders considered that the conservatism of Indian women was the greatest obstacle to the conversion of India to Christianity, and, like the contemporary Oxford Mission to Calcutta, the Missionary Settlement for University Women (M.S.U.W.) believed that conversion could be achieved by infiltration from the top.[62] A secondary object was to create a network of 'Home Members' in the British Universities 'in sympathy and support for their representatives sent forth from their own homes, to battle with ignorance and vice'.[63]

Among the first missionaries were two from Oxford, Una Saunders from Somerville and Agnes de Selincourt, who had studied both at Cambridge and at Somerville. On their arrival in Bombay they called at the homes of Parsee families with lists of subjects which they could teach. Progress was slow. The missionaries insisted that no lessons would be given without the inclusion of Bible reading. This alarmed the Parsees; one lady said she could not allow her daughters to study the Bible because it was so beautiful that they would not want to study their own religion after it.[64] 'How hardly shall they that have riches enter the Kingdom of God' wrote Una Saunders early in 1898. Magic lantern exhibitions of the *Pilgrim's Progress*, with terrible representations of Satan and the various hobgoblins were appreciated, but the Parsee girls, 'so eager to begin a fresh thing, seemed to have no perseverance'.[65]

All sorts of tactics were tried to win the trust of the girls, through music, through tennis, and by coaching them for their University examinations, with a little Ruskin and Browning thrown in along with the Acts of the Apostles. In several of the Annual Reports, however, there was a note of acute disappointment. The missionaries still believed that 'in the Last Great Day many Parsees will be among the white robed multitude who sing before the throne'[66] but in the first 20 years there were only two converts. The first was rushed away by her family and never seen again; the second was prudently installed as the Mission's housekeeper. Meanwhile it was distressing to see the Parsees becoming theosophists instead of Christians.

Gradually and without any apparent formal change of policy the campaign of evangelisation was replaced by social and educational work. In 1905 the Settlement opened a hostel for girls attending the University, 'to provide a bracing atmosphere in which they may develop into high principled Christian gentlewomen'.[67] Non-Christians as well as Christians were admitted and required to attend prayers, but not to kneel. From 1918 the list of workers at the Settlement was headed 'Staff' instead of 'Missionaries'. Marjory Moinet, who arrived from Somerville in 1917, became the first woman professor in the University, where she taught History; she also carried out social surveys for the Government and started a branch of the Workers' Educational Association. Margery Huckett from L.M.H. taught French in the University. In 1930 the Settlement started a school of social workers.

The objectives of the Mission were restated several times. In 1920, after the Amritsar massacres, the Annual Report suggested that one of the best and most necessary tasks for missionaries in India was to be peacemakers and that the Settlement could help in healing bitterness by providing a place where Indians and English could be together.[68] In 1927 the Settlement's main responsibility was seen as 'to try and bring the contribution of constructive Christian thought to the modern problems of Indian Life'.[69] In 1929 the Report stated that 'to bring together people of different communities to work for the good of the great masses of outcastes and poor is an effort which brings nearer the Kingdom of God'.[70]

The Mission and its hostel passed through periods of considerable tension. Phyllis Harley of Somerville, who was in charge in 1930, wrote in the Annual Report how impressed she was with the idealism of the students in the Congress Movement, with whom she could sympathise in light of her own experience in the British women's suffrage movement. She boldly told British supporters of the Settlement that 'our work here is only of value if it is supported by people who are sympathetic and who want India to be herself and free'.[71]

In 1942 the students were out again in support of the Quit India Movement but the rioting was in the Colleges not in the hostel; and the Annual Report could say 'the one thing that has stood the test of these trying days is friendship'.[72] As to whether the Settlement's work caused many Parsees to be among the white-robed multitude singing a new song on the Last Great Day it would be imprudent to speculate, but the last day of the Indian Empire in 1947 was marked by a moving secular occasion. It was the students who took charge of the arrangements in the hostel for celebration of Independence. The verandah was transformed into a fairyland with garlands and flags and flowers lighted by little oil lamps. Everyone had supper on the roof. At midnight the youngest student hoisted the new flag. Then staff and students sang the *Gitanjali* of Tagore together with the familiar Christian hymn *Make Me a Captive Lord, and I Shall be Free* and finally a new hymn, which they learnt specially for the occasion, *I Vow to Thee My Country*.[73]

In terms of conversions, missionaries in Africa and the Pacific were richly rewarded, even in their lifetimes. In India, on the other hand, Christians numbered only 2 per cent of the population at the end of two centuries of British Rule. The missionaries could pride themselves that they had been a little ahead of the Government in creating an independent Church before there was an independent India. Beyond that, there could be the intangible benefit of the civilising influence which Christianity had exerted on Hinduism and to a lesser extent on Islam, though it could be maintained that this influence was as much due to the secular message of liberalism and the inculcation of Public School virtues. There was even sometimes a retransmission of values, as when Fraser, preaching in Oxford, quoted Gandhi, the Hindu who was so much influenced by Christianity, 'I could not be leading a religious life unless I identified myself with the whole of mankind, and this I cannot do unless I take part in politics.'[74]

After the end of the Indian Empire it became impossible for British missionaries to obtain work permits in the successor States unless they had technical skills, and some of those who retired may well have wondered what their lives had achieved and what they had left behind. A tribute came from a source which might not have been expected to be particularly sympathetic. In 1959 a Committee set up by the Ministry of Education of Independent India made a report on Religious and Moral Instruction in Educational Institutions. The members were the Governor of Bombay, two Vice-Chancellors and the Joint Secretary of the Ministry of Education. The Committee found that in a secular State freedom from moral restraints had led to a sad loss of all sense of values in schools and Colleges, and to indiscipline, frustration, rioting and even murder. In the Christian schools, on the other hand, the self-sacrificing spirit of the teachers, their close and friendly relations with their pupils and their moral influence caused indiscipline and strikes seldom to occur. The Committee said that they would have liked to see the atmosphere of these institutions extend to all Colleges and schools in the country.[75]

The Oxford missionaries of whatever denomination enjoyed the great advantage of the prestige which an Oxford or Cambridge education carried both with the local people and with the Imperial or colonial administration. The common social background which they shared with the senior administrators sometimes enabled them to act with a degree of independence which was affectionately accepted as eccentricity. Further, as will be seen in the next chapter, they became indispensable to the colonial Governments in providing schools and Colleges which trained local staff for the Government Services.

On the whole, the Oxford missionaries, with their background of classical history and philosophy seem to have been as good – perhaps better – at understanding new societies and cultures as those from elsewhere. Whether High Church or evangelical, most of them regarded racial prejudice as one of the worst of sins, and were not afraid to say so. The Anglo-Catholic missionaries, many of whom were celibate, found it easier to live in the style of the local people than did the evangelicals. The natural faults of the former were exaggerated paternalism and an undue preoccupation with outward forms, so that in the most critical period in Uganda, Bishop Hine was attacking Bishop Tucker for the use of banana wine in the Communion service because it was not 'fruit of the vine'. Some of the evangelicals, on the other hand, were inclined to impatience of, or show scorn for, native institutions and, when they became Bishops, like Wilson of Calcutta, to a fondness for palaces. As for the churchmen who remained in Oxford, the relationship of Church and Empire was always something of a puzzle. Perhaps the most ambitious statement came from the Warden of Keble College, Revd W. Lock, in 1907 in a book on *Church and Empire*, 'The British Empire is itself an expression of the Christianity which the Church has to guard, and Christians have now not only to teach that the powers to be are ordained of God, but see to it that they act as powers so ordained.'[76]

12 The Oxford of the Southern World and Education in the Empire

Queen of the South: Which the mighty Pacific
Claims for its Britain in ages to be,
Bright with fair visions and hopes beatific,
Glorious and happy thy future I see. . . .
Even if Britain's decay be down-written
In the dread doom book that no man may search,
Still shall an Oxford, a London, a Britain
Gladden the South with a Home and a Church.

Martin Tupper, 'Poetic Offerings in the Nature of a God-speed to the Canterbury Colonists' (1850)[1]

Oxford took a benevolent interest in the new Colleges and Universities of the Empire, which were often headed by her alumni. Gifts of books were made and maternal messages sent. From the end of the nineteenth century there was a procedure by which Universities in the Empire could be granted 'privileges' which entitled their graduates to a remission of part of the time required to read for an Oxford degree; a list of the Universities thus recognised was published in the annual *Oxford University Calendar*. But sometimes a broader cooperation was sought. Oxford was asked to take a leading part in the founding of University Colleges in New Zealand, Ceylon, East Africa and Rhodesia.

THE FOUNDING OF CHRISTCHURCH, NEW ZEALAND

The most enthusiastic attempt to found an Oxford overseas was in Christchurch, New Zealand, although the University's role was largely unofficial. In 1847 Edward Gibbon Wakefield persuaded J. R. Godley to take the lead in the establishment of an Anglican Church settlement in New Zealand. Wakefield, the great theorist of systematic colonisation of the time, was led by his reading of seventeenth-century American history to believe that a cohesive party of settlers of the same religious denomination had the best chance of establishing a new colony: the Church of England was one among several potential vehicles. Wakefield himself, who had once been imprisoned for abducting an heiress, did not inspire public confidence; he preferred, therefore, to work behind the scenes.

J. R. Godley (1814–61) had exactly the qualifications which Wakefield required to lead the venture. As an undergraduate at Christ Church he had been outstanding in his generation and was described by Gladstone as a 'Master Mind' and 'Prince among men'. As an Irish landlord he had studied and written about emigration as a solution to pressure on the land. He was a barrister and well known as a journalist. Most important of all, he was a member of the Oxford Movement, which had fallen into sad disarray as a result of the Gorham Judgement, which confirmed the State's control over the rites of the Church of England, and of the defection of Newman, Manning and others to Rome. For Godley and his friends the new Anglican colony appeared to provide the opportunity of putting Oxford Movement principles into practice, untrammelled by the State, in a country remote from the unhealthy attractions of Rome. Godley and Wakefield proceeded to form the Canterbury Association of whose 50 subscribers 30 were Oxford men, 16 of them from Christ Church: the Bishop of Oxford, Samuel Wilberforce, was Chairman of the Managing Committee. At its first meeting the Association resolved that the proposed settlement be called Canterbury and its chief town Christchurch. The settlement was to be modelled on an English country, with its cathedral city, its famous University, its Bishop, its aristocracy, its yeoman farmers and its few necessary tradesmen. There would be no popery and no dissent; for the colonists were to be recruited exclusively among Anglicans by the parish clergy of the Church of England, a high proportion of whom were Oxford graduates.

Whilst Wakefield was influenced by the history of New England, Godley reflected more often on that of Greece, where colonies which hived off from Athens and Corinth had carried with them their gods, their rites, their festivals and their educational system. In Canterbury land was to be sold for £3 per acre (a much higher price than in other colonies in Australia and New Zealand) out of which £1 was to be used for religious and educational foundations. At the apex was to be the cathedral with a University College built around it, as at Oxford.

The Charter of the Association stated that the object of the undertaking was to found a settlement according to the principles of the Church of England. Particular importance was attached to sending out the Bishop, together with his flock, in the first boat. The designation of a Bishop, in consultation with the Government and the Archbishop of Canterbury, was among the first decisions, although formal appointment had to await the consent of Bishop Selwyn, the Primate of New Zealand. The choice fell on the Revd Thomas Jackson of St Mary's Hall, Oxford, Principal of the Battersea Training College, and one of the most eloquent public speakers and money raisers of the time. At public meetings the Bishop-designate spoke 'as one who takes his wife and children to Canterbury, there to live and there to die'. He wanted his children, he said, to be faithful and true-hearted sons of the Reformed Church of England, to enjoy that old Grammar School education, followed by that venerable discipline and training which had raised generation after generation of English gentlemen. This was not to be, he promised, a colony 'where slang will be substituted for conversation nor where men drink but do not dress for dinner. . . . I trust that I may live to hear Horace quoted by many a boy born in Canterbury before I shall be gathered to my Fathers.'[2]

The Association appealed to the University of Oxford both for advice and material help. 'Founded under such auspices,' the Association wrote, 'a College in the Canterbury Settlement may tend to perpetuate the principles of which your Venerable University is now established, even when your own destinies have been fulfilled and the hand of change may have passed over you.'[3]

Affected, perhaps, by this sombre speculation about its future, the University replied with a scheme in which Jackson, who was to be Warden of the College as well as Bishop, probably collaborated; for it seemed closer to the spirit of the Battersea Training College than to that of Oxford. The College proposed would have a lower division organised along the lines of an English grammar school, and an upper division of University level. The upper division was to be organised into four departments. The Department of Theology would teach students who intended to take Holy Orders, and these would be required to teach for one hour every day in primary schools. The Classical Department would include all students. The Department of

Civil Engineering would give an elementary course of instruction in physics and industrial mechanics, especially as applicable to the needs of a new country. This would include practical application of the mechanical powers, the strength of materials, especially of New Zealand stone and woods, construction of roofs, bridges, canals, locks, windmills and watermills, as well as the theories of lighting and ventilation. Finally, there would be a Department of Agriculture, adapted to the soil and climate, where the students would aid with their own hands in tending cattle and working a small farm of arable land.[4] It was a surprisingly vocational, if overambitious plan to emerge from mid-nineteenth-century Oxford. As well as advice, Oxford University gave books and small endowments towards two professorial posts.

Although the press, especially *The Times*, and public opinion generally welcomed the project, there was some scepticism, notably expressed by Sydney Smith, who was curious to know how economists expected a settlement to thrive which at its outset threw away a third of its whole capital on idlers and non-producers, namely the clergy. 'Have nothing to do with this Canterbury,' he urged his readers, 'its beginning is radically unsound and it will end in failure and folly. Bishops, Archdeacons and parsons are not settlers. After they have amassed a competency they will carry it away from the Colony.'[5]

Sydney Smith's apprehensions were justified. The Bishop-designate, even before he set out, had embarrassed the Association by being unable to produce accounts for the money which he had raised. When he arrived in Canterbury he was horrified to find no palace and no roads on which to exercise his carriage and pair, and returned forthwith to England. Ten of the 20 clergymen who went out with the Pilgrims also left the colony. Godley remained in Canterbury for three years as the Association's agent. Desperate for money, he was obliged to sell land to squatters of any religious denomination or none who came in to run their sheep on the rich Canterbury pastures. The subsequent influx of gold prospectors further weakened the Anglican character of the settlement. For years after the foundation stone of the cathedral was laid there was no money for its construction.

As for the College, it was founded in 1853 'for the propagation of the most Holy Christian religion and for the promotion of sound piety and useful learning', having under the Bishop as its Sub-warden, Henry Jacobs, a former Fellow of Queen's College and

Headmaster of Lancing School. It was not found practical to place it in the Cathedral Square, but it was established in Gothic buildings on a bend in the river a few hundred yards away. The upper division consisted for many years of only one or two men reading Theology. The proposed Departments of Engineering and Agriculture were not established. Eventually in 1872 the upper division amalgamated with the Canterbury Museum Library, which included a School of Technical Science, to become Canterbury College, affiliated to the new University of New Zealand. Within these arrangements, the old upper division found its role as a residential College, mainly for training in Theology. It always retained a recollection of Oxford. It was familiarly known as 'The House' and its magazine was called *The Chichelian* after Archbishop Chichele, the founder of All Souls College. Even in the mid-twentieth century, after Canterbury College became a University and moved to the outskirts of Christchurch, it remained all-male, specialising in Theology, with the Bishop as its Warden; and the students wore gowns when they dined in Hall.

The lower division was much more successful in the early days. By 1863 there was an enrolment of 83 boys who read Homer, Demosthenes, Livy, Juvenal and Tacitus. Between 1852 and 1965 11 of its 19 headmasters were Oxford graduates. It continues to flourish as Christ's College with 600 boys, and with the character of an English Public School of the epoch before uniforms were abolished and girls were admitted to sixth forms.[6]

The farcical Jackson was replaced as Bishop by the Revd Henry Harper of Queen's College, Oxford, who had been chaplain of Eton where he was comfortably installed in a parish nearby, surrounded by his 22 children, when, at the age of 52, he felt unable to resist the call of his old friend, Selwyn, the Metropolitan of New Zealand. Although he had never ridden a horse before, much of his episcopate of 36 years was spent in traversing roadless plains and unbridged rivers, in splendid contrast to the behaviour of Jackson, and during his time the cathedral was opened.

The Anglican settlement and the Anglican University were an anachronism; Oxford itself abolished religious tests in 1854. Godley, at the nadir of the colony's financial fortunes in 1850, received an instruction from the Secretary of the Association in London that the College should be capable of taking rank with similar institutions in Britain and should aim to serve the educational needs, not only of New Zealand, but of Australia and India, as the 'Oxford of the Southern World'.[7] The Association would have done better to heed the more practical advice of Bishop Selwyn who wrote to them: 'The academic life of a Colony is to work when you must and to read when you can. . . . Mark out a good extent of land and put a wooden building on it. People are very tolerant and will call it "The College". By degrees the plan will be developed. . . . Under active and judicious management teachers and pupils will flow in.'[8]

COLOMBO, MAKERERE AND SALISBURY

In addition to the needs of the Canterbury Pilgrims, Oxford's help was sought at various times for three other infant colonial Universities. In March 1914 the Board of Education of the British Government informed the Vice-Chancellor of Oxford that it had been decided to establish a College of University rank at Colombo in order to provide higher education generally, as well as courses in arts and science for teachers in training and preliminary training of medical students. The courses would lead to intermediate and final degrees of the standards of London University. Oxford University's assistance was requested in advice, staffing and in some form of association or affiliation which would guarantee the value of the degrees.

As a consequence, Convocation passed a decree in October 1914 authorising the Hebdomadal Council to appoint a committee for the purpose of cooperating with the Government of Ceylon in the establishment and maintenance of a College of University rank. The University College came into existence in 1921. In 1950 Sir Ivor Jennings, the first Vice-Chancellor of the University of Ceylon, wrote to the Registrar of Oxford University, Douglas Veale, to enquire about the committee's history. Veale discovered that the committee had seldom met, except twice in 1926, when it was resuscitated to meet the visiting Principal of the University College; it had never produced an Annual Report and had been discharged in 1930.[9]

The response to the next request, on behalf of Makerere, was hardly more fruitful. In 1937 Sir Philip Mitchell, the Governor of Uganda, met with Reginald Coupland and John Maud in the latter's rooms in Oxford and spoke of his dream that Makerere, still a secondary school, might develop into a University College serving the whole of East Africa, under the guidance of Oxford.[10] He wrote to remind Coupland of this two years later and Coupland took up the matter with the Registrar, Douglas Veale, suggesting that Oxford might be able to help if the old procedure of affiliation were revived. 'It would be a timely gesture on Oxford's part', he suggested, 'to take Makerere under its wing when the principles of our African policy are challenged, and when the Nazis have declared their counter-policy of barring Africans from higher education'.[11] Veale considered that 'association' not 'affiliation' was the correct term. The Secretary of State for the Colonies, Malcolm MacDonald, an Oxford man, expressed 'much satisfaction' with the idea,[12] and the Hebdomadal Council in January 1940 established an advisory committee for Makerere College to advise on the curriculum, examinations and administration of the College; and to nominate a representative to inspect and examine the work of the College and report to its Council. The committee would also arrange for lecturers from Oxford to visit Makerere, would advise and assist Makerere students who might continue their studies in the United Kingdom, and encourage interest in the University, particularly in so far as such work affected colonial development in Africa. George Turner, the Principal of Makerere and a graduate of Magdalen College, received news of this decision with enthusiasm. 'It is a remarkable thing', he wrote to Margery Perham, 'that in a time of war, people in Oxford have given time and thought, and now the effective promise of service, to our interest.'[13]

Turner's first request to the committee was for advice on the education of the young Kabaka of Buganda, who was coming to study at Makerere. The committee asked Margery Perham, one of its members, to advise. Miss Perham suggested that the ruler's studies should be so directed that he would pass from the known to the unknown. Thus he would proceed from examining the Lukiko, or Tribal Council of Buganda, to the Legislative Council of Uganda, thence to that of Kenya and on to the British Parliament. He would then look at the origins of Parliament in the Witan, mediaeval Parliaments and main phases since. Other economic and political questions could be treated on the same principle.[14] The committee recommended a modified Modern Greats course for the Kabaka, combined with practical training in the growth of cotton.

A shield of wood with the Oxford arms was presented to Makerere. Occasional advice was given on appointments; but the war prevented the committee from carrying out its broad terms of reference. In 1947, Margery Perham suggested to Veale that it be buried, since it was long since defunct and as the new Inter-university Council for the Colonies could fulfil all and more of the functions expected of it; it had never, she said, really carried out any duties except in the selection of books; so the committee was abolished.[15]

A later request for Oxford sponsorship for an African University had even less result. In 1953 Lord Swinton, Secretary of State for Commonwealth Relations, addressed an earnest appeal to Lord Halifax, as Chancellor of Oxford, for assistance to the new University of Rhodesia and Nyasaland. 'At all costs', he wrote, 'we must keep the Rhodesian University within the United Kingdom family. We must make a success of Federation. The future of Africa outside the borders of Rhodesia hangs on it; and the University lies at the heart of the problem . . . surely the Oxford people would have the imagination to see what is at stake and to take the new University of Rhodes, to whom they owe so much, under their wing.' At the official level, Sir Christopher Cox, Educational Adviser to the Colonial Office and a Fellow of New College, wrote to Veale to say how undesirable it would be to see the new University fall under South African influence. A London University relationship would not be appropriate, he considered, because it would be difficult to extend this to a College where the majority of students were Europeans.[16]

Halifax was impressed. 'The stakes are quite high', he wrote to the Vice-Chancellor, 'and it would be an imaginative stroke of rejoinder to the Rhodes Scholarships.' There was to be no imaginative rejoinder, mainly it seems, because Veale was anxious not to upset Sir Alexander Carr-Saunders, the Principal of London University; eventually the new College chose the London relationship, and a link with Birmingham for its Medical School.[17]

EMIGRANTS AS TEACHERS

Although the University's corporate record in fostering education in the Empire is unimpressive, the individual contributions of Oxford men and women were considerable. In the nineteenth century Oxford graduates went out to the colonies to teach for a number of reasons. Some went as missionaries, mostly of the Anglican Church, and one of the first tasks of missionaries was to educate local people for the Ministry. The Colonial Bishoprics Act led to the establishment in the new dioceses of 'Bishops' Colleges', to train the clergy; these were often initially staffed from Oxford or Cambridge, according to the antecedents of the Bishop. A number of Oxford men went out because they wished to marry, and would thus lose their College

Fellowships, but felt no vocation for the work of a parish clergyman at home. Some were radicals, escaping from the restrictions and conventions of Oxford and England into the more democratic society of the colonies of settlement. There were also Conservatives, many of them among the Canterbury Pilgrims, who fled from the threat of revolution which spread through Europe in 1848. There were many too who hoped to avoid in the colonies entanglement in the bitter theological controversies caused by the Tractarian Movement. A few went to South Africa, Australia and New Zealand for their health. Most of all probably set out because there were not enough attractive posts at home in the Civil Service, the Law, the Church, or in teaching to absorb Oxford's increasing output of graduates: salaries of colonial professors tended to be considerably higher than those at home.

A number of men who eventually became teachers and educational administrators originally went out to the old Dominions as farmers; when they failed as such, particularly in the agricultural depression of the late nineteenth century, education was the only profession for which their Oxford degrees in Classics and History were a qualification. Most went out young and remained permanently in the colonies of settlement, though more in Australasia than in Canada for reasons of distance and climate. In India and tropical Africa, whether they went as missionaries or to teach in Government Service, the expatriates expected to return to Britain.

Oxford men were most likely to be found in Church of England Colleges and as teachers of classics, whilst Cambridge predominated in the teaching of mathematics. Nevertheless, in the early heroic days of schools and Colleges, the principals and professors who came out with degrees in Classics might have to teach many other subjects. Individual Colleges and schools developed particular connections with Oxford, and even when local people began to replace the expatriates as professors or teachers, these too were often Oxford graduates.

AUSTRALASIA

The earliest University to be established in Australasia was not in Canterbury but in Sydney. Its first principal was the Revd Dr John Woolley, who at its inauguration ceremony in 1852, spoke of the founding of his own *alma mater* with an historical recklessness only pardonable in a former Fellow of University College, Oxford:

> 980 years have passed since our glorious King Alfred provided amidst the fens and forests of Oxford a home of union and of refuge for the poor and scattered scholars who were, in those rude and uncertain times, with toil and danger watching before the pale and glimmering lamp of knowledge. Did his imagination dare her flight beyond the limits of his island home, and picture in the remotest corners of the earth the children of his race, nurtured in his own institutions, bearing forth the spirit and forms which they loved into a yet wilder solitude and a more inaccessible wilderness?

Sweeping into his peroration, Woolley hoped that 'the bays of Sydney Harbour will mirror many a reverend chapel and pictured hall and solemn cloister like those that gem the Isis and the Cam; whose memory like some choice perfume revives the spirit fainting under the cares and business of life'.[18]

Woolley was 36 when he arrived in Sydney as Principal and Professor of Classics. He had to resign his Oxford Fellowship on marrying and had been successively Headmaster of grammar schools at Hereford, Rossall and Norwich.

A close friend of A. P. Stanley, Dr Arnold's biographer, who was Secretary of the first Commission on the reform of Oxford University, Woolley was a brilliant classical scholar and educational planner whose philosophy of religion and education was based on the liberal Christianity of Arnold. He welcomed new discoveries in science, saying 'Each fetter that falls from the mind of man raises his face towards his Maker.'[19] Nevertheless, he saw the nucleus of the new University's teaching as a liberal education in classics and mathematics. 'The soundest lawyers', he said in his inaugural speech, 'come from schools in which law is never taught. The most accomplished physicians are nurtured where medicine is but a name.'[20]

As a Platonist he considered that the purpose of the University should be to prepare leaders for the Church, professions, public service and commerce, and that entry to this élite should be open to youths of all walks of life through a system of State primary and secondary schools. The founders of Sydney University intended to model it on London as an examining University in which the teaching would be done in affiliated Colleges. Woolley persuaded them instead to adopt the reformed Oxford model, in which the professors lectured in the University; in Sydney attendance at their lectures was made compulsory. He also enhanced the influence of the professors by insisting that they be made members of the Senate. As a liberal, he successfully opposed a proposal that a certificate of attainment in religious studies should be required by the University from the Colleges as a condition of graduation.

Although Woolley worked with great earnestness, not only within the University, but outside it to establish the grammar school and an adult education network, he was attacked on many sides. Religious interests considered his system godless; the Colleges resented compulsory University lectures; in general, he was criticised because between 1859 and 1865 the University only produced 50 graduates. His bold assertion that the purpose of the University was to offset the materialism which was threatening to overwhelm society offended the businessmen of Sydney, who also disliked his insistence on high standards and opposition to vocational studies. His lectures on Aristotle were attacked as instilling philosophical and political notions which might ripen into vulgar and rampant radicalism; even the Chancellor of the University, Sir Charles Nicholson, wrote that 'he has genius, learning and great amiability of character and yet in some of his actions and sayings evinces an entire absence of common sense'.[21] Woolley died an unhappy and disappointed man in a shipwreck whilst returning from a visit to England in which he had tried in vain to obtain another post.[22]

Woolley's successor, the Revd Charles Badham of Wadham College, was one of the finest Greek scholars of his time and an editor of Euripides and Plato but he was a friend of F. D. Maurice, and his advanced religious opinions prevented him from obtaining any post in England other than as a school headmaster; he adapted more easily to Sydney than Woolley, and was a pioneer of Australia's tradition of University correspondence courses. Walter Scott, who succeeded Badham on his death in 1885, was another distinguished Oxford classicist, who had a First in Greats and had won the Ireland, Craven and Derby Prizes.

When a separate Chair in History was established, Walter Scott asked A. L. Smith, Balliol's Modern History tutor, to recommend a candidate. This was Arnold Wood who was 26 when he arrived in Sydney to hold the Chair for nearly 40 years. Wood came from a nonconformist family. After taking a First in Modern History at Balliol he had read Theology at Mansfield College in order to prepare himself to be a University teacher 'engaged in a cure of souls'; but his studies caused him to doubt the historical evidence of the Gospels, and he was a reluctant agnostic when he went out to Australia in 1891.

He brought with him from Balliol, however, a high sense of moral purpose in the tradition of Jowett, Green and Toynbee. 'The purpose of the study of history', he asserted in his Inaugural Lecture, 'is to enable the student in his turn to make history, and history which it will be worth the while of future generations to study.' 'History', he maintained, 'should be studied primarily as the history of the human spirit in its noblest manifestations. The study of history . . . is the study of noble ideas.' He expressed his contempt for 'the wise criminals turned out by dozens in each year by our great English universities, who take their first classes, are elected to Fellowships, pass into their Common Rooms, and the world knows them no more. And meanwhile the foolish world outside the Common Room is left to solve the problems of life in its own foolish way, unhelped and unguided.'

A professor who proclaimed that the duty of the historian was to find a lesson for the present in the study of the past was unlikely to avoid involvement in political controversy. Although Wood described himself as an ardent Imperialist, he strongly opposed the Boer War, believing that 'the greatness of the British Empire has been founded on principles of righteousness' and that 'an unjust war . . . cannot fail in the long run to bring disaster to the Empire'. He was rebuked by the University Senate, which resolved that his articles and public speeches were unworthy of a Professor of History, and he might have been compelled to resign if the war had not ended at this time.

Throughout his career Wood wrote for the *Manchester Guardian*, supporting Irish Home Rule and opposing Imperial Federation. His liberal fervour encompassed Australian history; he described the English politicians, lawyers and Bishops of 100 years earlier as atrocious criminals whose innocent victims were sent out as convicts and founded Australian democracy. But he had little time to write books, wearing himself out in trying to apply Oxford's personal tutorial system in a situation in which he had to supervise several hundred students.[23]

For the grammar schools more rugged and less scholarly qualities were needed, such as those of A. B. Weigall, who was Headmaster of Sydney Grammar School from 1866 to 1912. At Brasenose College, Oxford, he had been a devoted pupil of T. H. Green who, he said, had been an inspiration to men who felt what he meant, even when they did not understand his philosophy. Weigall experienced no call to take Orders and hoped to become a diplomat; but he injured his health whilst working for his degree and was sent on a long sea voyage to recover. In the course of this he heard that the family solicitor had embezzled the estate, so he took a teaching post in Australia in order to support his sisters. He brought into Sydney Grammar School two other Oxford men as assistant masters and together they introduced most of the institutions of the English Public Schools – interschool cricket and football, an annual athletics meeting, prefects, school magazine and debating society. Weigall married the daughter of the bank manager and died in harness at the age of 72. There were 53 pupils when he arrived and 696 when he died.[24]

Oxford played a smaller part in Melbourne, where the University opened in 1852, in an atmosphere which was more secular and less preoccupied with Oxbridge traditions than Sydney; and where the three founding professors came from Ireland. In 1891, an unhappy professor there, Edward Jenks, wrote to the *Oxford Magazine* to warn Oxford men that the University was controlled by a council of laymen who did not tolerate academic freedom.[25]

Adelaide University was founded in 1874, largely through the efforts of the Anglican Bishop Augustus Short, who had been Gladstone's tutor at Christ Church, Oxford. Although he was a High Churchman, Short had been long enough in South Australia, 'the paradise of dissent', to realise that the Oxford model would be quite unacceptable, and instead Adelaide University adopted the Scottish non-residential pattern. In his Address as Vice-Chancellor at the inaugural ceremony, Short, however, described the purpose of the Universities in terms which contemporary Oxford would have heartily approved, as

> directing the studies and forming the character of the governing classes, they help to elevate the middle-class to higher civilisation, the result of a more intellectual education. They afford quiet retreats for students of literature and the theoretical parts of science and philosophy. Finally they award literary and scientific honours.[26]

Adelaide recruited its professors of classics from Cambridge, but of its first eight professors of history, between 1900 and 1970, seven were Oxford men. The first of these was G. C. Henderson, the son of a New South Wales coal miner, who went to Balliol on a scholarship in 1894 and came back inspired with ideals which would have delighted Woolley. He taught that poetry had a message for democracy and that love of nature should be cultivated as an antidote against the scramble to outdo one's fellow in material possessions. His lectures were so popular that they had to be transferred from the University to the Town Hall; and the Governor and Premier of South Australia would send telegrams of apology if they were unable to attend.[27]

In the eventual emergence of Canterbury, New Zealand, as a University College and finally as a University, a notable part was played by an Oxford man with very different ideas to those of the founders of the Canterbury Association. John MacMillan Brown who, between 1875 and 1935, was successively Professor of Classics and English, Vice-Chancellor, and Chancellor, as has been seen in Chapter 2, had studied under Jowett at Balliol, to which he came from Glasgow University. He had no desire, however, that the College at Canterbury should be a nursery for statesmen, for whom he expressed contempt. He aimed rather to spread the University's influence through society by means of the public education system. One of his most interesting achievements was to make Canterbury the earliest University in Australasia to confer degrees on women, and he married Canterbury's first woman graduate. He carried to Canterbury that Balliol charisma which Henderson brought to Sydney; his English lectures were delivered with such emotion that students emerged as if from a sacrament.[28]

CANADA

The idea that Oxford might decay and be reproduced within the Empire was a recurring one to those bred within its crumbling walls and nourished on classical history. Thus, the historian of Toronto University quotes an unknown Oxford poet, who wrote in 1760, in a lament on the death of George II:

> There may arise
> Another Oxford on the Atlantic shores
> Still fond, a thousand ages hence, to chant
> Some future hero born of Brunswick's line.[29]

There was little place, however, for Oxford traditions in the earliest Canadian Colleges which were established in the late eighteenth century by American Loyalists who brought the educational methods of New England with them. Even Bishop Strachan who founded Canada's first major University, McGill, in 1821, preferred the models of Scotland or Germany to those of Oxford and Cambridge, 'where', he said, 'the professors seldom lecture more than once a week and the atmosphere of opulence is far beyond our reach'.[30]

Oxford men were more likely, in the early days, to be found in small Colleges or Universities in the Anglican tradition such as Bishop's College at Lennoxville, which was founded to train future clergy and 'to offer to the country at large the blessings of a sound and liberal education upon reasonable terms'. When J. H. Nicolls, who was its first Principal from 1843 to 1877, arrived, there were only ten pupils. He had to raise money, buy books, obtain a University Charter and teach Latin, Greek, history, rhetoric and Divinity. Nicolls had been an undergraduate at Oriel at the height of the Tractarian Movement and later a Fellow of Queen's College. He remained a High Church man and conservative, firmly opposed to American ideas and institutions, but sensible enough to remain on good terms with leading politicians of various hues. His University survived, but it was always small, mainly because Greek and Latin were required for entry. Even in 1922 it only had 60 students.

Whilst Nicolls was establishing the University, the grammar school which fed it was being built up by two Oxford men, James Williams of Pembroke and W. H. Walker of Wadham, who succeeded Williams as Headmaster when he became Bishop of Quebec. They introduced the prefect system and an atmosphere so gentlemanly that the school became known as 'the Eton of Canada' and attracted the sons of the defeated Confederates after the American Civil War, including the son of Jefferson Davies.[31]

It was in Toronto, however, that Oxford was to be most influential, notably in two institutions into which Canadians, rather than Englishmen, imported Oxford traditions. Upper Canada College (U.C.C.) is of particular interest because quite different Oxford influences were successively introduced there. The College had been founded in 1829 by the Government as a reformed grammar school whose masters were recruited from Oxford and Cambridge. In 1895 George Parkin became Principal. Parkin had been profoundly influenced by his student year at Oxford. Later he had written the life of Thring, the great Headmaster of Uppingham. Under Parkin's regime at U.C.C., the stress was on character, Christian principles and loyalty to Empire. From Oxford he also brought the tradition of academic freedom, and succeeded in raising enough money to make the school independent of Government before he returned to England to organise the Rhodes Scholarships.

Parkin's son-in-law, W. L. Grant, said of him that 'He never got God and Oxford and the British Empire wholly separated.'[32] Grant himself studied at Balliol and taught history at Oxford before becoming Principal of U.C.C. in 1917. A true son of Balliol, he sought to make scholarship, instead of ability to pay, the qualification for entry. 'He saw the college', says its historian, 'as a living being which he intended to make supreme in scholarship, games and drama. It was doing the will of God.'[33] But Grant's view of Canada was wider than Toronto; he considered that all Canadians should be bilingual and the sympathy which he expressed for French Canadians caused his *History of Canada* to be withdrawn from the high schools of British Columbia as being pro-French and anti-British.

If Grant brought liberal traditions from Oxford, Terence MacDermot, a former Rhodes Scholar, who was Principal from 1935 to 1940, had acquired sympathies there with Socialists and pacifists. He wanted, he said, to 'stir up the boys to an awareness of their own country and continent . . . they acquiesce, poor devils, in cricket, in Empire and in good form; in all the scaly fragments of an obsolete Victorianism'.[34] MacDermot, however, faced an impossible task in Toronto in working out his educational ideals in an environment dominated by business, Imperialism and Conservatism.

The other remarkable example of Oxford educational influence in Toronto was on the University's History Department, and through it on the Canadian Government's Department of External Affairs. George McKinnon Wrong (1860–1948), who set up and directed the History Department from 1894 to 1927, was descended from a family of United Empire Loyalists and was trained as a theologian. A sense of purpose pervaded everything that he did. Like his friend Parkin he spent only a short period in Oxford but he founded a department for which Oxford was the model, the British Empire the subject, and political and constitutional history the content.

Between 1904 and 1915 of 15 staff appointments to the department, six had B.A. degrees from Oxford and six had undertaken further studies there. Between 1920 and 1929, of 16 staff members appointed, 12 had studied at Oxford. Two Fellows of All Souls – Kenneth Bell and Keith Feiling – were among them. Previously, history had been taught mainly by theologians and written by journalists, doctors and lawyers. Wrong and his staff were the first full-time historians in Canada. They considered themselves obliged to teach not only in the classroom but in the country as a whole. It was necessary, Wrong wrote to Parkin, to get hold of every man who promises leadership and educate him to think Imperially. 'If young men could be imbued with the ideology of Oxford, they would just naturally think Imperially and would prevent Canada from becoming a second U.S.A.'[35]

The department was unique in Canada in using a tutorial system in small discussion groups to which students read essays. Wrong also founded a Historical Club, to which third- and fourth-year students were elected and at which papers were read on current issues. All the staff taught extension and correspondence courses.

Wrong always saw his department's object as training for the public service and it was thus the natural nursery for the Canadian Foreign Service when this was established after the First World War. Among the History Department's Oxonian staff who joined it were G. M. Wrong's son Hume who later became the first Permanent Under Secretary of the Department of External Affairs and Lester Pearson who subsequently became its Minister and eventually Prime Minister; critics said that Pearson carried with him an 'on-the-one-hand-but-on-the-other' attitude which was characteristic of a Toronto history professor. Another member of Wrong's staff, George Parkin Glazebrook, became Assistant Under Secretary for External Affairs. In 1958 out of 362 Foreign Service officials 83 were graduates of Toronto.[36]

There were Canadian Universities outside the Anglican tradition where Oxford men made an occasional mark. Of the first ten Principals of the Presbyterian Queen's University at Kingston, Ontario, nine came from Edinburgh or Glasgow. William Hamilton Fyfe, the exception, who was Principal from 1931 to 1936, was a classicist, a Fellow of Merton and a socialist. Fyfe deplored the football fever at Kingston which he attributed to 'the infantile enthusiasm of middle age among its graduates'. A University's commodity, he dourly insisted, was scholarship which crumbled to dust if adulterated; 'you get out of education exactly what you put in'.[37] Both for Fyfe and for Queen's University the association seems to have been stimulating if sometimes bewildering.

SOUTH AFRICA

Nowhere in the Empire did the pioneer educationists encounter more problems in the export of Oxford's standards and practices than in South Africa. The earliest College founded by the British there was the South African College, set up by Scottish Presbyterians in collaboration with the Dutch Reformed Church. When, however, the Church of England sent out its first bishops, two of them, Bishop Robert Gray of Cape Town and Bishop John Armstrong of Grahamstown, were Oxford men; each sent back to their University for principals who would establish Anglican Colleges which would both provide secondary education for Europeans and train candidates for the Ministry. Diocesan School, Rondebosch, opened in 1849, and was modelled on Radley. The first Principal, Revd Henry White, Fellow and tutor of New College, 'with that noble self-sacrifice which was the mark of the man' (according to the College's historian), 'gave up brilliant prospects at Oxford to come out to South Africa'.[38] His pupils were required to bring two silver knives and forks as well as their baptismal certificates, but this does not seem to have civilised boys who often spent their vacations in frontier skirmishes. Henry White returned to England after a few years, and was replaced by his brother, Revd Gilbert White of Lincoln College. Gilbert White only lasted a year before resigning because the profits from the school did not cover his promised salary. The numbers in the school were now down to 12, and the Bishop this time sought a man who was known and muscular; he found him in George Ogilvie who had only a pass degree from Wadham but had taught in Buenos Aires and in South Africa. Ogilvie tamed the young colonists by introducing a form of football which combined the forms played at Winchester, Eton and Harrow, and he became known as the 'Arnold of South Africa'. Ogilvie's successor, Sedgwick, however (another Oxford man) encountered a revolt by senior boys against the incompetence of his teaching which brought about his dismissal.

The story was similar at St Andrew's, Grahamstown, founded in 1855, where five out of the first ten Headmasters were Oxford men, all in Holy Orders. J. F. Bankes, the first Headmaster, resigned after four years, telling the Bishop 'the colonists do not yet know the value of education as compared with the acquirements necessary in order to make £.s.d.'[39] Another Oxford man, Gould Ross, who was Headmaster from 1875 to 1881, engaged in violent theological controversy with the Dean and so antagonised his senior staff that they left to start a rival school. St Andrew's was saved by the Rhodes Trust, which made substantial contributions after the Boer War and the First World War. The Trust no doubt felt an obligation to prevent the financial collapse of the four schools for which Scholarships were earmarked in Rhodes's Will, namely, Diocesan College, South African College, Victoria College and St Andrew's. Both Diocesan College and St Andrew's widened their recruitment after 1902. Botha sent his sons to Diocesan College and Milner arranged for sons of other Boer leaders to enter St Andrew's. The disciplinary problems became easier when the upper departments were taken over by Universities. By 1938 it even became possible to unlock the library books at St Andrew's.

St John's College, Johannesburg, was founded in 1898, when the city was only 12 years old, as a parish school which in 1904 became a diocesan school. Here a Headmaster from Oxford, Revd Fitzwilliam Carter, faced a different kind of problem, the antagonism of Milner, who saw no place for private schools in the reconstruction of the Transvaal. St John's, menaced by the competition of the free Government high school, described itself in its prospectus as 'wholly different in character, a school for gentlemen's sons'.[40] Gentlemen, however, were so few on the Rand, that its numbers were reduced to 49 before it was rescued by the Community of the Resurrection, most of the early members of which were Oxford men. The Community of the Resurrection provided 15 members of the staff of St John's between 1906 and 1934, including J. O. Nash of Hertford and Pusey House, Headmaster from 1906 to 1917, who is regarded as the College's second founder. The description of Nash in the College history is almost the ideal of the Edwardian Headmaster: 'A strong disciplinarian, dignified in bearing, a mature scholar in the best Oxford tradition, an enthusiast for games, drama and music, with a keen sense of humour, convinced yet conservative in religious outlook.[41] Despite Milner's initial hostility, Feetham and Robinson of his old Kindergarten became Trustees, and the Rhodes Trust and the Randlords gave substantial grants.

Under the constitution of Michaelhouse, Natal, which was founded in 1896 with the object of providing liberal instruction in accordance with the principles of the Church of England, its Headmasters had to be priests who were M.A.'s of Oxford or Cambridge. E. B. Hugh-Jones of Jesus College, who was its Rector from 1903 to 1910, believed that as Natal emerged from being a pioneering society, intellectual values required emphasis; but he imprudently neglected to watch football matches and thus became so out of touch that his senior boys took off without consulting him to join a regiment in the Bambaia Rebellion. Later when the Church Colleges no longer required their Principals to be clergymen, Oxford provided a new type, South African Rhodes Scholars such as R. F. Currey who after graduating at Oxford taught at Rugby and returned to be successively Headmaster of Michaelhouse and of St Andrew's.[42]

The early problems encountered by English clergymen in controlling young South African colonists, or even in attracting them to their schools, were not confined to those from Oxford. Colenso, the first Bishop of Natal, was a Cambridge man, and successive Headmasters who he brought out from his old University to set up Hilton College, Pietermaritzburg, found the task beyond them. Here the saviour was the Municipal Inspector of Nuisances, Henry Vaughan Ellis, who had no degree but had studied under Arnold at Rugby, and had been a schoolmaster before becoming toughened by digging for gold on the Rand. Ellis, who introduced the prefect system and Latin classes before breakfast, made Hilton into Natal's leading public school, whilst under the Headmastership of C. C. Pritchard of Brasenose College, Oxford, the rival Bishop's College, whose boys wore Eton suits and mortar boards, only survived from 1872 to 1880.[43]

The glossy histories of the South African public schools, with their photographs of magnificent buildings, often designed by Sir Herbert Baker, show substantial achievements to which Oxford men contributed, once the adjustment between their temperaments and those of their pupils was made, even though more space is devoted to sport than modern Oxford might consider appropriate, and there is usually a diplomatic absence of information or comment on their attitudes to race. Records of educational work of Oxford men among black or coloured Africans and Asians are hard to find. The early schools for black Africans were mostly staffed by Scottish missionaries. Scotland also provided the impetus for the University of Fort Hare, which was the only one to provide higher education for Africans and Asians in the period before it ceased to be independent of Government. The most notable contribution made by Oxford to the education of black Africans was through the Community of the Resurrection which at the beginning of the twentieth century built up African education in the Transvaal almost from nothing, and whose St Peter's School was known as 'the Black Eton' before it was closed as a consequence of apartheid.[44]

From 1873 to 1918 there was only one University in South Africa –

the Cape of Good Hope – an examining and degree-giving University modelled on London. Of its constituent Colleges, Rhodes University College at Grahamstown, later to become Rhodes University, had the closest links with Oxford in its origins. It grew out of the upper department of St Andrew's, and those in Grahamstown who were responsible for its founding played skilfully on Imperialist enthusiasm and nervousness after the Boer War. Thus Parkin, when visiting the school, was induced to refer, in his report to the Rhodes Trustees, to the very strong British influence that Grahamstown might be expected to exercise. Dr Jameson, working his way back into politics from prison, was assured of a seat in Parliament in Grahamstown, and in return for this – or simultaneously – he promised £50,000 from the Rhodes Trust to start the University College, which the trustees described 'as designed to extend and strengthen the Imperial idea in South Africa, Stellenbosch being under notoriously anti-Imperialist influence'.[45] Heartily expressing these sentiments, perhaps with tongue in cheek, was the prime mover in the campaign for a University, Selmar Schoenland, the Curator of the local museum, who had taught at Oxford but was a German national. Rhodes University, as it became in 1951, always retained Oxford connections. Ironically, its earliest women's hostel, Oriel House, is named after Rhodes's old College, which was to be the last in Oxford to continue to refuse admission to women.

Oxford, and in particular Balliol, influence was strong in the University of Witwatersrand after it was transformed from being a School of Mines. Its young first Principal, the former Rhodes Scholar, J. H. Hofmeyr, urged it in 1919 to face 'the native problem . . . the eternal problem of the reconciliation of justice and apparent expediency' on which South Africa's University Colleges 'had hitherto been almost entirely silent'.[46] Among those who helped it to do so were the first Professors of Philosophy, Hofmeyr's Balliol friend John MacMurray and his successor R. F. L. Hoernlé, also from Balliol, who became the first Chairman of the South African Institute of Race Relations. Other Oxford men were I. D. MacCrone, Professor of Psychology, who wrote a standard textbook on race attitudes in South Africa; T. J. Haarhoff, Professor of Classics who, although a great champion of the Afrikaans language in which he wrote poetry, became a critic of apartheid; and W. M. MacMillan, Professor of History, whose role as a critic of Empire has been seen in Chapter 5. Indeed in the 1920s and 1930s Oxford men made a major contribution to the emergence of the University of Witwatersrand as South Africa's leading centre of liberal thought.[47]

TROPICAL AFRICA

Some of the early educational work of missionaries in tropical Africa has been mentioned in Chapter 11. Higher education developed late, partly as a reaction to what most British officials regarded as the disastrous consequences of the policies in India, where thousands of poorly educated students were turned out without prospects of employment. A very small University College in Sierra Leone had been affiliated to Durham University since 1876, but it was primarily a theological College. Apart from this, two Government secondary schools, designed to become University Colleges, were established between the First and Second World Wars. The first Principals of both were Oxford men; Alek Fraser at Achimota and George Turner at Makerere. Gordon College, Khartoum, which had been established earlier, and which was working towards University College status, was also headed by an Oxford man, Christopher Cox, and later by an Australian Rhodes Scholar L. C. Wilcher. Paradoxically, Turner, who had been appointed as a successful Headmaster of Marlborough, is mainly remembered at Makerere for dismantling the public school apparatus with its prefects and strict regulations in order to prepare for the free atmosphere of a University College.

Fraser as a missionary has been considered in Chapter 11. He was perhaps the greatest colonial Headmaster of his time. King's School, Budo, in Uganda, where he started his career, was a C.M.S. College for chiefs. Trinity College, Kandy, in Ceylon, where he was Principal from 1908 to 1914 was also a C.M.S. institution: but Achimota in the Gold Coast was a Government College founded by the Canadian Sir Gordon Guggisberg, most imaginative of British colonial Governors, to produce the future leaders of the nation, in whose competence he had greater faith than most of his contemporaries. Here, therefore, Fraser as Principal became a civil servant. He hated racism such as that of the missionaries in Kandy who said that the Ceylonese must never be allowed beyond the verandah in case they got swollen heads. He believed that Christianity and Christian education must lead to national independence. A College fails, he said, if it produces men who are isolated from their own people by ignorance of their language and thought. This led him to urge that Latin and Greek and most of higher mathematics should be dropped in favour of local languages at Trinity, Kandy – to the horror of the Anglican Conference in Ceylon, who said that this would result in the loss of the Government grant. Similarly, in Achimota, he insisted that the British teachers acquired a knowledge of the vernacular, studied

African history and traditions, and based their mathematics and science on African problems and conditions. He also introduced co-education there, in spite of the misgivings of the local experts.

He was a muscular Christian, but not a fanatic about games. In Uganda he carried swamp clay on his head for the building of the cathedral. In Ceylon he marched his boys from Kandy to Colombo to prove in wartime that the Ceylonese were as tough as Indians or Europeans. He saw no need for boy scouts: but involved his schools in social services instead. His boys in Ceylon built shelters for rickshaw men, and in the Gold Coast carried out village surveys. He had no sense of diplomacy and did not endear himself to the Gold Coast Ministry of Education by his favourite quotation from Kierkegaard – 'There is nothing so repellent to God as an official, for God is personal and the official is the negation of personality.'[48] He ruined his relationship with Guggisberg by writing a pungent minute in a file which he came across by chance and which did not belong to his department. He had a violent temper and saw issues in black and white – never grey. Yet men of great distinction volunteered to work under him. Aggrey, the black Afro-American educator, asked to be his deputy at Achimota. N. P. Campbell, whom Balliol College considered the most brilliant scientist they had ever produced, joined him after hearing him speak at a meeting in England and went out to Ceylon to teach science and lead the boys in cleaning out drains in the slums.

INDIA

In India, though Oxford men went out as chaplains to the East India Company from the seventeenth century, few were involved in education before the nineteenth century except in teaching European children in primary schools. Most of the pioneers in Indian education were nonconformists, often Scots. In the nineteenth century Oxford men could be found both in missionary and Government Colleges, though the salaries and prestige of the Indian Educational Service made it unattractive to British Oxford graduates as compared with the I.C.S. Oxford had a long connection with St John's College, Agra, named after the St John's Colleges both at Oxford and at Cambridge and founded by the C.M.S. in 1850 as 'an educational institution of such a kind as to win the confidence of the upper classes'. Its first Principal, Thomas Valpy French, mentioned in Chapter 11, who had a tall and stately presence and the sound of whose boots used to cause a hush through the school, courageously carried the school through the Mutiny before becoming Bishop of Lahore. One of the last European Principals, as has been seen, was W. E. S. Holland.

Of all Oxford men who taught in India, it was, however, a layman, Edwin Arnold (1832–1904), who endeared himself most widely to the Indians and Ceylonese because of his affection and admiration for their culture, with which he made the West familiar through his *Light of Asia*, a prose poem on the life of the Buddha, and other works. Arnold spent only four years in India as Principal of the Deccan Sanskrit College in Poona. When he returned to England in 1860 at the age of 27, he wrote in a letter to his successor: 'It is certain that we shall not always retain India, and equally certain that our business is to deal with her as honest tenants.' He had no illusions about the attitudes of Indians to English education, which they endured as the route to clerkships; nor indeed, as to the attitudes of many of his compatriots in India, such as the Brigadier who asked him 'What the devil is the good of teaching the niggers, Sir? You taught Nana Sahib, you did, and he learned to read French novels and to cut our throats.'[49]

The first Indian Universities at Calcutta, Bombay and Madras, were established in 1857, the year of the Mutiny, and were modelled on the University of London as affiliating and examining, but not teaching bodies. Latin and Greek had little place in the curriculum and few British teachers were found in the affiliated Colleges except in those run by missions or as Principals of large Government Colleges. In Calcutta, the Vice-Chancellorship in the nineteenth century was usually held on an honorary basis by a member of the Viceroy's Council, or by a senior judge. Four of these Vice-Chancellors in succession were Oxford men, all with Balliol connections: Sir Arthur Hobhouse, Sir William Markby, Sir Courtenay Ilbert and Sir Thomas Raleigh. The first three were Liberals. Hobhouse took a keen interest in the education of women, who were able to take degrees in Indian Universities long before they could do so in Oxford. Markby, who was a judge, taught classes for Indian lawyers in his spare time, and did much to enable Indians to qualify for high judicial office. On his return to England, as has been seen, he became Reader in Indian Law at Oxford and Supervisor of the I.C.S. probationers. Raleigh was Legal Member of Curzon's Council and Curzon appointed him as Vice-Chancellor, seeing a unique opportunity for educational reform in India whilst the Viceroy and Vice-Chancellor were both Fellows of All Souls.

One reason why Oxford men did not make a greater contribution to education in the dependent territories was that if they were capable, they were often taken into administrative posts. In India, a notable example was Rushbrook Williams, who only served a few years as Professor at Allahabad University before being taken first into the Government of India office which was dealing with constitutional reforms and then into its Department of Information.[50] The Sudan Government, in which Oxford men were preponderant, had a deliberate policy of recruiting teachers from the Gordon College into the Political Service; similarly in Egypt, although it was Cromer's policy to bring out young men from Oxford and Cambridge to teach in English – not in Arabic – many of these went on to better-paid posts in the Government.

No account of Oxford's influence on education in the Empire can omit some reference to the family of Dr Arnold of Rugby. The Doctor himself, sometimes despairing of a political system in England which could tolerate the barbarous Game Laws, had purchased land in New Zealand with the idea of emigrating. His son, Tom, although he gained a double First at University College and could have obtained a Fellowship, became a sceptic and radical and went out to farm the family's New Zealand estates. Unsuccessful in this, he started a school in Nelson and then went to Australia as Schools Inspector in Van Dieman's Land. He resigned his post on becoming a Roman Catholic and returned to teach at Oxford.

Tom's younger brother, William, abandoned an Oxford career because he was out of sympathy both with the High Church and with evangelicals and went out to India as an officer in the East India Company's Army. In an autobiographical novel, *Oakfield*, published in 1854, he wrote that 'The obvious work of every Englishman in India seems to me to be to justify his title to a position in a country not his own by trying to civilise it.' 'The Indians', he said, 'are a deplorably inferior race, but I do not consider them hopelessly so.'[51] Later he became the first Director of Public Instruction in the Punjab, where he successfully opposed the attempt of Sir John Lawrence to introduce compulsory Bible reading into Government schools, because, he said, that this was unfair on the Hindu and Muslim parents whose taxes paid for the schools.

From this brief survey, some pattern may perhaps be discerned.

Oxford University itself had a constitution which was too decentralised to enable it to respond effectively to requests for corporate assistance to education in the Empire. Many of the achievements in the later run-up period before Independence, which will be discussed in Chapter 14, were of peripheral and semi-autonomous bodies such as Ruskin College, the Extra-Mural Delegacy and Queen Elizabeth House.[52]

As for the individual Oxford men, hundreds of whom worked in Universities, Colleges and schools in the Empire, those who went out in the middle years of the nineteenth century were mostly in Holy Orders, and sound scholars, whose grounding in the Oxford classical school enabled them to take up and teach other subjects rapidly and effectively. Some of their defects and unhappiness had their roots in the morbid preoccupation of Newman's Oxford with forms of religion which they often brought with them.

They and their successors carried out to the colonies a strong, even obstinately held view that it was not the business of a University or of a grammar school to provide vocational education. This was often to bring them into conflict with leaders of colonial opinion. On the other hand when, in the latter part of the nineteenth century, Oxford ceased to be a clerical University, the men who went out from Jowett's Oxford – who had also often been at Arnold's Rugby – were mostly laymen of great earnestness, believing that a national education system, though aimed at producing an élite, should be open to the ablest boys from all ranks of society. A number of them also brought from Oxford a zeal for extra-mural education and a talent for popular exposition which gave them considerable influence in the colonial communities, notably in Australia and New Zealand.

From the end of the century, two streams can be distinguished: one preaching, like Parkin, that God, Oxford and Empire were indistinguishable from one another, and the other, like Fraser, that education would and should lead to national independence.

OXFORD WOMEN AND COLONIAL EDUCATION

In 1879 the first women's Colleges, or Halls as they were then called, opened in Oxford. Somerville, Lady Margaret Hall (L.M.H.) and the Oxford Home Students (O.H.S.) were followed by St Hugh's in 1886 and St Hilda's in 1893. As the first generation emerged they felt a spirit of adventure, liberated as many of them were from the prospect of purely domestic lives; they also felt a duty towards the pioneers of women's education and as they looked around for a worthy use to make of their trained minds, many of them found it in the Empire, in which three-quarters of those who went out served as teachers. Before 1914 by far the largest number served in India, followed by South Africa and Rhodesia, Canada and tropical Africa. After 1918 they were more evenly distributed betwen tropical Africa, South Africa, India, Australasia and the Middle East (see Tables A.4 and A.5 in the Appendix).

From the letters written back to their Colleges, it seems that the behaviour of their kith and kin in the old Dominions caused more of a shock to the Oxford women than that of pupils in India, where attitudes were expected to be different and where many of them had family connections with missionaries and the I.C.S. Mabel Cartwright, who had been taught by Arnold Toynbee, wrote from St Hilda's House, Toronto, of which she was Warden, in 1908 that the 'holy spirit of Discipline' was lacking, and that 'the free conditions of colonial life tempted the unwary with many entertainments'. Eventually she introduced discipline; the shy and timid were developed and the careless and frivolous were sobered and deepened. Though she was conscious of 'how far short we fall of the high standards of work and duty set to all her daughters by L.M.H.; yet in the remembrance of the lessons learnt there is a constant stimulus and encouragement to become more and more worthy of the ideal that was and is there shown forth'. [53] Hilda Oakley in the Royal Victoria College in Montreal in 1900 considered that the social spirit was more developed than in Oxford but that it was very rare to find a student capable of working on her own.[54] In New Zealand in 1912, W. H. Waller of St Anne's found her pupils always in tearing high spirits, with an absolute lack of self-control and a peculiar sense of humour.[55]

Most of the Oxford women who went to South Africa were teaching whites. Lorna Biden at St Anne's, Natal, wrote sadly in 1913 that the girls, most of whom learnt rifle shooting, 'have all the appearances and appliances of civilisation but so often very little of the grit and perseverance that has produced it'.[56] Alice de Boulay from 1905 to 1919 was nominally Inspectress of Needlework for the Transvaal Department of Education, but saw her most important duty as to visit and cheer all the women teachers, caged in small towns on the great endless veld, unable or not allowed like their male colleagues to ride on horseback. In the Cape Cart with four mules in which she travelled around .she carried picturebooks to stimulate interesting talks with lonely teachers in lonely places. She wrote in 1909 to ask for the prayers of L.M.H. for teachers who were making such a brave attempt to keep up a high standard of thought and living amidst circumstances which tended so little to encouragement.[57] The attachments of the L.M.H. women to their old College were particularly strong. G. M. Edwardes, suddenly called upon to direct a sizeable African domestic staff as Warden of a women's hostel at Rhodes College, Grahamstown, wrote that 'what I learnt years ago at L.M.H. is worth everything else put together'.[58]

They were robust and versatile. Eleanor MacGregor from St Hugh's who taught chemistry at the University of Witwatersrand, was a leading spirit in the African Girl Guides and founded an African primary school and crèche, kept herself up to the mark by hanging a board in her office with the motto 'Don't tell them to do it. See that it is done'.[59]

In India before Gandhi discipline was seldom a problem. So Sarah Williams of Somerville is found in 1898 introducing singing, the study of music and tennis in His Highness the Maharajah's College for Girls in Trivandrum;[60] Ethel Romanes of L.M.H., who became Sister Ethelred of the Wantage Sisters, wrote in 1915 that in the School for Anglo-Indian Girls at Poona she was able to introduce the Public School spirit and the cultivation of *esprit de corps*.[61] Even in 1938 A. Percival of St Hilda's found in Women's Christian College, Madras, that by contrast with Oxford the shy girl was shyer, the keen girl showed her enthusiasm more freely, and the studious girl was more devoted to her work.[62] There was often sympathy with Indian Nationalism. As G. M. Madge of L.M.H., who was teaching with the Young Women's Christian Association, wrote in 1922 'we watch eagerly for any signs of independence of thought – if Gandhi has done nothing else he has roused the student body of India as never before'.[63]

There was a sense of family loyalty to their old Colleges or Halls, in the spirit in which the original prospectuses had described them, L.M.H. as 'a Christian home' and Somerville as an 'English home'. So it was possible for Mother Edith to write back confidently to L.M.H., where she had been Vice-Principal, for volunteers to set up a boarding school for the Syrian Christians of South India and in response Amelia Holmes, though over 50, gave up her post as Headmistress in a leading English girls school, and went out with another L.M.H. colleague to take up the task.[64] The loyalty was stimulated by the intellectual challenge, such as that thrown out by Dora Addy who wrote back to St Hugh's from Central Africa in 1910, asking for Oxford women to come and teach and help to solve such problems as: how can Froebelian principles be applied to African education? How can the great truths be taught to the very ignorant? How is the Christian idea of marriage to be formed in a polygamous country?[65]

Their letters seldom complain; they bubble with enthusiasm at the almost unlimited scope which they have to use their education. Their own struggle for women's rights causes them to sympathise with emergent Nationalism. Perhaps if the attitude of Oxford women to their work in the Empire had to be summed up in one word it might be that used in the L.M.H. *Brown Book*, in an obituary to describe Margaret Benson, daughter of the Archbishop of Canterbury who died in Egypt in 1916 – 'eager', 'eager in every direction, in work and friendship, in religion, in philosophy no less than in games and sport'.[66]

13 Nursing Mother of the Elect

Just because much is demanded of her, Oxford may be able to rise to the heights of the future opened out, and become the nursing mother of the elect of the kindred peoples.[1]

H. E. Egerton, Beit Professor of Colonial History (1908)

In the three previous chapters the Empire has been observed mainly through the eyes of Oxford men and women who served in it as officials, missionaries and teachers. In this chapter the opposite picture will be considered – how Oxford appeared to people from the Empire.

When Egerton made the remark quoted above in a flatulent peroration to a lecture at the Royal Colonial Institute, he had in mind the Rhodes Scholars. Yet the impact of Oxford on students from the 'kindred peoples' of the white Dominions, often only removed by a generation from their British origins, was less vivid than that made on Asians, Africans and West Indians, for whom the experience of Oxford was much more exotic, and more likely to be recorded in their memoirs; it is therefore with the impressions of the latter that this chapter commences.

INDIANS

The most numerous accounts are those of the Indians, the earliest of whom entered Oxford in 1871, when students who matriculated were no longer required to be members of the Church of England. Between then and 1893, 49 Indians matriculated, of whom 22 were at Balliol and 16 were non-collegiate. A high proportion were Hindus from Bengal and Bombay and Parsees, but over 20 per cent were Muslims. About half of them became barristers; six entered the I.C.S.[2]

One of the most interesting members of this early group, though she came at a time when women were not yet formally matriculated, was the first Indian woman student at Oxford, Cornelia Sorabji, a Parsee whose parents were Christians. From a very early age she determined to qualify as a lawyer in order to devote her life to helping women in purdah, who were often cheated of their rights because they were unable to consult male lawyers. She obtained the highest marks of her year in graduating from Bombay University. The student who did this was normally awarded a Government scholarship to a British University, for which she was disqualified because she was a woman. Lord Hobhouse, who had been Law Member of the Viceroy's Council, was a member of the governing body of Somerville College, where he obtained a substitute scholarship for her. He also introduced her to Jowett, who had been his contemporary at Balliol. Jowett arranged for her, quite exceptionally for a woman, to attend lectures at All Souls as well as Balliol, and persuaded Congregation to pass a special decree enabling her to sit for the B.C.L. examination in 1892 although she was not able to collect the degree until 30 years later when women became full members of the University.

At Jowett's parties Cornelia Sorabji met leading politicians, including Gladstone, Balfour and Asquith, as well as professors and men of letters, such as Max Mueller, Froude and Freeman. She was even presented at Court. She wrote to her parents that 'next to home there is no place like Somerville', and that working in All Souls, where she was taught by Dicey, was 'bliss'. She stayed in vacations with the Romanes and the Markbys and took the little Spooners for walks in the Parks. Only Sir William Hunter offended her by asking in a loud voice, when he met her in the quad, if she lacked the moral courage to get married.[3]

Best of all, she said in her memoirs, she learnt at Oxford that difference of opinion need not affect friendship or personal appreciation, that one can be a zealot and yet open-minded, could gain in breadth without losing intensity.[4] Jowett sent her to see Florence Nightingale with a note which said 'Miss Sorabji is starting on a mission something like your own fifty years ago and you may perhaps feel a sympathy for her.'[5] The mission was triumphantly achieved. On her return to India, Cornelia Sorabji not only did invaluable work herself for purdah women, but her example eventually brought other Indian women into the legal profession.

In the early twentieth century two Government committees reported on the situation of Indian students in Britain. The first in 1907, under the Chairmanship of Sir W. Lee Warner, found that Indian students at Oxford were happier and more popular than those in Cambridge. At this time there were only 32 Indians at Oxford, whilst there were 87 at Cambridge. The difference in numbers was due to the fact that although since 1884 Indians had been allowed to offer Arabic and Sanskrit instead of Latin and Greek as an entry requirement at Oxford, they still had to pass an examination in a classical language as undergraduates, which they need not do at Cambridge. The problems at Cambridge were attributed to the fact that the Indians were concentrated in three Colleges, in which they formed cliques.[6]

By the time the second committee, chaired by Lord Lytton, reported in 1922 relations between Indian and British students appeared to have deteriorated both at Oxford and Cambridge. The spectacular murder in 1909 of Sir Curzon Wylie, the student adviser of the India Office by an Indian student at a reception at Imperial College, London, caused such revulsion that several Oxford and Cambridge Colleges closed their doors to Indians. Further, during the First World War, Scotland Yard had compiled dossiers on Indian students suspected of pro-German sentiments.

Oxford had now exempted Indians from examinations in Latin and Greek and their numbers had risen to 144, compared with 145 at Cambridge.[7] Two representatives of the Oxford Indian Majlis Society, M. C. Chagla and P. N. Sapru, in their evidence referred to the 'notoriously unsatisfactory relations that obtain between English and Indian students of this, and we presume of any other university in the United Kingdom'. English undergraduates, they said, were not cordial by temperament, but in the case of the Indians there was something more than lack of cordiality. Another Oxford Indian Majlis Society representative, Tara Chand, however, considered that the majority of Indian students were quite happy and had many Indian friends.[8]

The Secretary to the Delegacy for Oriental Students, S. M. Burrows, stated in his evidence that the chief difficulty was the race prejudice inculcated by American and South African Rhodes Scholars in Colleges where they came in large numbers.[9] This was confirmed by the Master of University College, which had 26 Rhodes Scholars, and by the Senior Tutor of Queens. Three Colleges, Magdalen, Corpus and University, refused to take any Indian students, and the Vice-Chancellor, L. R. Farnell of Exeter, went so far as to suggest that if a College acquired a reputation for taking a great many Indian students, the English students would avoid going there. A much more cheerful account was given by A. L. Smith, the Master of Balliol, which altogether had taken 60 Indian students; although ten of these had been recorded as unsatisfactory, on the whole it had been a very favourable experience. Neither Burrows nor the Principal of Somerville considered that there were racial problems in the women's Colleges, where Indian women had got on well with their English counterparts.[10] The 1922 report concluded that more racial prejudice was apparent at Oxford and Cambridge than at provincial Universities, not only because of the presence of Rhodes Scholars, but because of the preponderance of Public School men among whom there existed 'a certain pride of class which tended to keep them aloof from men of a different race as well as a different class'.[11]

The period immediately following the First World War was a particularly difficult one. Most of the Indian students had little in common with the men who returned to Oxford from the trenches N. B. Bonarjee who entered Hertford in 1919 had been at an English Public School and played Rugby football for the College. He nevertheless felt that all coloured people were regarded as 'wogs' and that Indians were not popular, although Oxford knew in her heart, he said, on the basis of her own Hellenistic tradition, that she ought to be more international in outlook.[12] His contemporary, K. P. S. Menon, who had a brilliant career, ending with a First in History and the top place in the I.C.S. Examination, loved his College, Christ Church, but nevertheless felt an uneasiness resulting from a complex between the ruler and the ruled. The complex was made deeper by the Amritsar massacre and Gandhi's non-cooperation movement.[13] The Indian students' suspicions were such that those who read Modern History refused to take the optional special subject about Warren Hastings because it was believed that the papers were sent to the India Office to be checked for evidence of disloyalty.[14]

Another irritation was the presence at the Indian Institute of an official appointed by the India Office as adviser for Indian students who, in some cases was designated as their guardian and controlled their finances. After a campaign organised by the Suhrawardy brothers, the official, S. M. Burrows, was transferred to the University as Secretary of a new Delegacy for Oriental Students where he continued, however, to be an object of suspicion.[15]

In 1921 Lord Curzon, who was both Foreign Secretary and Chancellor of the University, wrote to L. R. Farnell, the Vice-Chancellor, to express his disquiet at the disloyal attitude of some Indian students. The Vice-Chancellor responded by summoning all Indian students to a meeting in the Hall of Exeter College. The meeting was abortive, as the Hall was set on fire by the participants. At an adjourned meeting, with suitable precautions, Farnell described in his memoirs how he looked down on 400 eyes, gleaming from brown faces like panthers, and stated categorically that 'Anyone who comes here to sow discord and cause disruption is a traitor to our academic fellowship; we must here preserve the peace of God.'[16] A few years later, in 1926, Lord Birkenhead as Secretary of State for India wrote to Heads of Colleges asking them to take action against British Communist students who were influencing Indians. Merton and Queen's refused to take disciplinary action and the Vice-Chancellor intervened to exact promises from the students concerned that they would have nothing further to do with Communism. The incident led to a resolution of protest in the Oxford Union which was reversed in a subsequent debate attended by a large number of clergymen who were life members. The majority of Indian students supported the Vice-Chancellor, resenting the implication that they were involved.[17]

Those who drew up the University Examination Statutes remained sublimely indifferent to the question of the loyalty of the Indian students to the Empire. When the Indians in 1908 were exempted from offering either Latin or Greek in the first public examination, they were required instead to read Milton's *Areopagitica*, whose subject was freedom of the press, Mill on Liberty and Byron's *Childe Harold*. In place of Holy Scripture, they were examined in Burke's *Thoughts on Present Discontents* and *American Taxation*. It would have been hard to concoct a more explosive cocktail for the young intelligentsia of a country under foreign rule.[18]

In spite of initial social problems, the Indians of the inter-war generation often came to feel at home in Oxford through the Union debates. H. C. Gupta, on arriving at New College, felt 'the cold and severely aloof atmosphere of God's own Englishmen'; but later he marvelled at 'the phenomenal standard of the speeches in the Oxford Union debates, the delicate wit and humour, the fair hearing accorded to contestants, the rapier thrusts of argument and matchless repartee'.[19]

K. P. S. Menon used to rehearse his Union speeches to his sister as they walked around Christ Church Meadow. M. C. Chagla would pace up and down the quad, waiting for the *Isis* to arrive with news of the debates. Chagla indeed had been inspired to come to Oxford by reading Morley's life of the greatest of all Presidents of the Union, Gladstone. He failed to obtain a place at Gladstone's College, Christ Church, and so entered Morley's College, Lincoln. The eloquence which Chagla learnt at the Union was to be an asset in his varied career as a politician, lawyer, ambassador and Cabinet Minister.[20] In 1935 another Lincoln man, D. F. Karaka, was the first Indian to be elected President of the Union. He became a writer and journalist, Oxford remaining for him 'mentally, morally, spiritually and physically an inspiration'.[21]

For the Indians who were too shy to speak in the Union there was their own Majlis Society founded by Mohamed Ali and others at the beginning of the twentieth century. Here they would discuss India's political future. Between then and Independence in 1947 most Indians and Ceylonese belonged to the Indian Majlis Society, whose meetings began by the singing of the Congress anthem, *Bande Mataram* and ended with a hymn by the Muslim poet Iqbal. No one had the temerity, K. M. Pannikar recollects, to argue for anything less than Independence for India.[22] Among the members were men who hoped to enter the I.C.S. or were already I.C.S. probationers. Several of them recollect that they found nothing incongruous between the deep distrust of the British which they expressed in the Majlis and their desire to enter the service of the British Raj. Whilst membership of the Majlis was restricted to Indians, Burmans and Ceylonese, there was also a Lotus Club which included students from other countries who were interested in India.

In general the Indians express admiration, even affection, for their teachers at Oxford. Tutors and professors, says Pannikar, treated pupils as friends and were always active to advance their careers. When he obtained a First in History in 1917, the Dean of Christ Church wrote to him 'I am sincerely glad that you achieved this distinction as a Christ Church man; but I am also extremely happy at the success of a friend'.[23]

Even during the most difficult period, the experiences of both Indians and Ceylonese at Oxford varied greatly as can be illustrated from the memoirs of two of them. S. W. R. D. Bandaranaike, the future Prime Minister of Ceylon, was at Christ Church from 1919 to 1923, choosing to come to Oxford after reading *Tom Brown at Oxford* and *Mr Verdant Green*. His first year was a disappointment. He felt that he was simply not wanted. 'It is terribly wounding, after laboriously patching up an acquaintanceship with one's neighbour at dinner in Hall or at lectures, to be passed by in the street as though he had never seen one, or, still worse, to see him hurry off with a hasty nod.'

Eventually he learned that this conduct sprang not so much from prejudice, as from the shyness and reserve of Public School men who had their own cliques. Brooding in a damp, grey, sunless and depressing winter, Bandaranaike concluded that in light of the feeling of race superiority which even the best Englishmen held towards orientals, it would be easier to win their respect rather than their friendship. 'Before I am their equal I must be their superior.' He set out assiduously to obtain a place in the College tennis team and the Treasurership of the Union. He now made many friends, one in particular: 'The achievement of which I am proudest is the friendship of Edward Marjoribanks. In whatever part I am called upon by fate to play in the relations between my country and his, I shall not easily forget the fact that Marjoribanks was an Englishman.'

As a Ceylonese, Bandaranaike's comments on the Indians at Oxford are unusually interesting. He regretted that the Indians lived a life of their own and created an Indian Oxford within Oxford. The fault was not solely on either side but had its roots in the different psychology of the British and Indians. He used to attend the Majlis and was bored with the endless bickerings there and the whispered allegations that some members were in the pay of the Indian Institute. But a sense of humour usually sufficed to smooth things over, and his memory of his Indian friends at Oxford, with all their weaknesses and all their impulsive kindness, was a tender one.

He concluded that the disadvantages outbalanced the advantages of an English education for the Indians. A few Indians, he considered, should be sent to study in Britain, selected by a committee, rather along the lines of the Rhodes Scholarships, for intellectual ability and aptitude for games. The rest should be encouraged to study at home and then be given two years supervised travel in Britain, the United States and France. Bandaranaike read Classical Moderations and Law. He took back with him a passionate love of

Homer, inspired by Gilbert Murray. When he became Prime Minister, as leader of a socialist or populist party, there seemed some echo of Oxford behind his praise for the Commonwealth for its features of a democratic form of Government, an independent judiciary and an administrative service free from undue political influence.[24]

Very different were the memoirs of his contemporary G. K. Chettur who was at New College from 1918 to 1921 and wrote a book about his Oxford life which he called *The Last Enchantments*. He read English and was thrilled to meet W. B. Yeats, the Irish poet, John Masefield, the Poet Laureate, and Arthur Symons, all of whom read and criticised Chettur's own poems. He took the visiting Nobel Prize-winner, Rabindranath Tagore, on a punt on the Thames. He recorded joyfully the Spoonerisms of the Warden of New College, Dr Spooner himself, who complained 'it is empty work preaching to beery wenches' but was reassured by the fact that 'Our Lord is a shoving leopard'. He became President of the Indian Majlis, whose exclusivity he criticised, and went on Canon Streeter's reading parties with English students – men and girls – who without exception he found very courteous. By contrast with an Indian University, he wrote, the student at Oxford merged naturally into the system instead of being in continual conflict with it.

Yet even on Chettur, delighted with life and literature, humiliation could suddenly descend. He went to see a play by Ian Hay, *Tilly of Bloomsbury*, in which the character of an Indian student was depicted in a thoroughly contemptuous fashion. He rushed out of the theatre and ran all the way back to his tutor's rooms to pour out his indignation. His tutor helped him to write a letter to the Vice-Chancellor to ask him to exercise the authority which he then had of censorship of plays in the city. The Vice-Chancellor pointed out that the Scots were daily ridiculed on the English stage without offence being taken, but he took action, and the offending scenes were omitted for the rest of the time that the play appeared in Oxford.[25] And so Chettur returned to India to teach English literature and write English poems and to remember from time to time the Oxford way of life and outlook 'at once comely and liberal', and 'the place where I suffered the enchantment under which I live and move and have my being'.[26]

Between about 1905 and 1920 a number of Muslims from Aligarh College who were afterwards to play an important part in politics in India and Pakistan were at Oxford. Liaquat Ali Khan, Pakistan's first Prime Minister, studied Law at Exeter College, where K. P. S.

Menon remembered him as kindly and friendly but somewhat detached from Indian circles.[27] One of his successors, H. S. Suhrawardy, was a non-collegiate student. The brothers Mohammed and Shaukat Ali, who were to be prominent in the anti-British Khilafat Movement when they returned to India, were at Lincoln. Other Aligarh men were A. R. Siddiqi and Shoaib Qureshi. The connection with Oxford is somewhat puzzling as the British teachers at Aligarh almost all came from Cambridge. Lionel Curtis, who visited Aligarh, may have had something to do with it, as might the high reputation among Muslims of Margoliouth, the Laudian Professor of Arabic; or it may be, in light of the tempestuous history of Aligarh, that the preference for Oxford was a reaction against Cambridge teachers.

The 1930s seem to have been happier than the 1920s. Most of the Indians were then members of the Labour Club and made British friends, marching in demonstrations about the Spanish Civil War and other causes. J. D. Shukla, who entered Corpus in 1936 as an I.C.S. probationer, wrote: 'It was so pleasant to be in Oxford. The wind of socialism blew strong. It speaks a lot for the British tradition of freedom and the confidence in their society that they exposed us, the civil servants of an Empire, to the free and academic atmosphere of a great University rather than a Government institution.'[28] Corpus was a College too small for cliques, where everybody was involved in everything, but Mangat Rai, who entered Keble in the same year, was equally happy. The College gave him preference in admission because he was a Christian. He made two particular British friends, one of whom went into the Colonial Service and the other went to teach at Bristol University.[29] Indira Gandhi was at Somerville for barely more than a year in 1938, during which her interests were diverted by political questions such as the Spanish Civil War and by a fiancé at the London School of Economics. She had to be removed to Switzerland for medical treatment before completing her studies.

As well as those who hoped to enter the I.C.S., Indian students came to Oxford because its degree commanded a higher salary in India than a local one. The Indian Education Service was almost entirely recruited from men with British degrees. The qualification of barrister-at-law, which could be obtained simultaneously with an Oxford degree course, also led to substantial rewards. There were, too, subjects taught in Oxford which could not be studied in Indian Universities, including Anthropology, Mineralogy, and Geology. Consequently, from about 1910 onwards, the demand for places greatly exceeded the number available in the Colleges. Partly for this reason, and partly to avoid College fees, about half the Indians at Oxford were usually non-collegiate students, and this accentuated their tendency to spend most of their time with their compatriots.

Few Indians came to teach at Oxford before Independence, since when Indian, Pakistani and Bangladeshi economists and historians have made a considerable contribution. From the memoirs of I.C.S. probationers, it would seem that the collaboration of Indian teachers at an earlier time could have much improved the course. The great exception before Independence was S. Radhakrishnan, the first incumbent, from 1936 to 1952, of the Chair of Eastern Religion and Ethics at All Souls, founded by Henry Spalding. He was an impressive lecturer, always wearing a turban, who could rise to great heights of eloquence, as when during one of the civil disobedience campaigns he launched an attack on the British Raj based on a text from the Prophet Ezekiel: 'I will overturn, overturn, overturn it, and it shall be no more until He come whose right it is, and I will give it to Him.'[30] The University was proud to have such a distinguished and exotic scholar, even though puzzled by the gap between his philosophy and that of Greece and Rome. Radhakrishnan later became President of India.

WEST INDIANS

The sons of West Indian planters often came to be educated in Oxford. One of the most generous was Christopher Codrington (1668–1710), son of the Captain-General of the Leeward Islands, who, after a distinguished career as a soldier and Fellow of All Souls, left his money to endow the magnificent College library as well as to found Codrington College in Barbados. In Merton College the memory of a number of men from Barbados who studied there in the eighteenth century is commemorated by the silver which they gave to the College.

Under Rhodes's Will an annual Scholarship to Oxford was provided for Jamaica and Bermuda. Some West Indian Governments, such as Trinidad and Barbados, also provided a scholarship to Britain each year which could be held by coloured people. To obtain these, great application was required. As Eric Williams described it, three hurdles had to be overcome: first the Government exhibition from primary to junior secondary school; then another scholarship to pay for senior secondary school teaching, and thirdly, an Island Scholarship to Britain.[31] Three West Indians who later became Prime Ministers were to leap these hurdles and study at Oxford.

Grantley Adams of Barbados was the son of a primary school Headmaster who coached him into winning an exhibition to secondary school and continually held the lure of an Island Scholarship to Oxford before him, making him read a hundred lines of Homer each day before breakfast. He entered Oxford on the Barbados Government scholarship in 1919 as a non-resident student at St Catherine's Society, where he read Classical Moderations and Law. He came under the influence of Gilbert Murray from whom he learnt 'the standard of values taught by the ancient world, the clear mellow lights that radiated from its rarer spirit, their appreciation of the joy of life, their sense of balance and proportion'.[32] He specialised in Ecclesiastical Law, sitting at the feet of T. R. Glover, whose doctrine that religion and the practical affairs of the world were vitally related made an irresistible appeal.[33] He played cricket zestfully for St Catherine's. He was President of its Junior Common Room and became an active member of the Liberal Party, inspired by a speech by Asquith at the Union and by the Party's achievements in social legislation. It would seem to have been an active, happy life; but his close friends were not British; they were West Indians, a Nigerian and a Greek.

Adams's Jamaican contemporary at Oxford, Norman Manley, came from an even poorer background. His father died when he was young, and he grew up, he said, as a 'bushman', cleaning pastures and chopping log-wood on and around his mother's farm.[34] He was withdrawn from secondary school when his mother could no longer afford to keep him there, but later was able to attend another school, whose Headmaster was shocked by his ambition to become a Rhodes Scholar; then R. M. Murray, a former Rhodes Scholar, to whom he 'owed all the rest of my life', coached him privately. He won the Rhodes Scholarship and came up to Jesus College in 1914, liberated, he said, by the writings of Samuel Butler.

His studies were interrupted from 1915 to 1919 by service in the ranks of the Royal Field Artillery. The Army recruiting authorities did not send him to an officer's course although he was a member of the Oxford Officers' Training Corps; in the ranks he served happily with his Cockney fellow soldiers. When he returned to Oxford, however, he wrote to his sister: 'I have not made a single friend here. I haven't fallen in with any set or tradition. I have been an alien first and last. I cannot get behind the barrier that is always there; I feel chained. The case is different when I meet any of the many West

Indians that I know. I feel with them an altogether different person.'[35] This was a time of depression, following the strain of the war in which his brother had been killed beside him. He recovered to make friends through athletics and to become excited by modern art. He won the Lee Prize with an essay on Samuel Butler and took a Second Class degree in Law. After qualifying as a barrister he returned to the Bar and politics in Jamaica.

The third future Prime Minister, Eric Williams of Trinidad, who was at Oxford ten years later than Adams and Manley, has left a vivid and highly critical account of the experience. His father was a postal clerk, determined that his son should have the educational advantages that he had missed. Under relentless pressure from his father, Williams jumped the first hurdle on the first attempt, the second on the second attempt, and won the Island Scholarship at his third try.

The Director of the Education Department of Trinidad wrote to the Master of University College Oxford in 1937 to commend Williams for a place in the College. 'Mr Williams', he wrote, 'is not of European descent, but is a coloured boy, though not black. He comes of a good family and bears an excellent reputation as to his character and conduct in this Colony. He is about the average as an association footballer and is quite a good cricketer. I think you would find him acceptable as a member of your College.' This testimonial, in which the brilliant scholar is hardly discernible, was passed to St Catherine's where, like Adams, Williams became a non-resident student.[36]

On his arrival in Oxford, he found the British students supercilious, and in his memoirs mentions no friends except for some of his tutors and a Siamese student. The only society which he attended regularly was the Indian Majlis. In church he recalled that ladies would move from beside him and kneel elsewhere when he went to the altar rail. He read Modern History, engaging his tutor with his heated but amiable arguments that Aristotle was a dyed-in-the-wool reactionary, that Hobbes had a Fascist mentality, and that only a Briton could see democracy in the Witanegamot.

He obtained a brilliant First. 'I had come and seen and conquered Oxford; what next?'[37] His tutor advised him to take a second degree and apply for a Fellowship at an Oxford College, rather than take a Diploma of Education and return to Trinidad to teach in a secondary school. Eventually he took a D.Phil. in History with a thesis on 'The Economic Aspect of the Abolition of the West Indian Slave Trade and Slavery'. In this he was conscientiously and sympathetically guided by Vincent Harlow, but he was contemptuous of Coupland's views on the idealist motives of the British in abolishing slavery; this was exacerbated by the fact that Coupland was a Fellow of All Souls. Williams's failure to win an All Souls Fellowship left a lasting bitterness. 'No native, however detribalised', he wrote in his memoirs, 30 years later, 'could fit socially into All Souls.'[38] He recalled how the 40 Fellows round the table jeered at him when he made a mistake in oral French, and how a Fellow, who was one of Britain's leading author–politicians, stopped and glared at him in the street.

He obtained a doctorate, but could find no job with it. The Dean of his College on seeing him would say 'Are you still here? You had better go home. You West Indians are too keen trying to get posts here which take jobs from Englishmen.'[39] No one would publish his thesis; even Warburg, he recalled, who had published the works of Stalin and Trotsky, told him that he could not publish a book which maintained that the slave trade and slavery were abolished for economic rather than humanitarian reasons; this, they said, would be contrary to the British tradition. The Colonial Office told him that his qualifications were too high for a job at his old school in Trinidad. 'My 24 years preparation for an English degree had ended by unfitting me totally in the eyes of those best qualified for life in Trinidad.'[40] He wrote in vain to the Japanese and Sudanese Ambassadors to seek a University post in their countries. He even wrote to Gandhi for advice on employment in India.

Eventually he obtained an assistant professorship at Howard University in Washington, 'the Negro Oxford', as he called it, where he published his thesis and other books. He went on to work with the Caribbean Commission, to form a political party, and to become Prime Minister and then President of Trinidad, never losing his bitterness about Oxford. In a letter to Manley in 1954 he wrote, 'I was denied a Fellowship at Oxford – I have always been convinced that it was on racial grounds . . . they threatened to fail my Doctor's thesis because they didn't like my view.'[41] Ten years after this he visited Oxford as Prime Minister. He was entertained to dinner and then addressed an informal gathering of Oxford's teachers of Commonwealth history and politics. Now at last he was able to tell them direct what he had long waited to say, and, in order that the message should not be lost, an A.D.C. distributed to all those present copies of his works, including not only his thesis, but his ferocious, though not undeserved, attacks on the Oxford historians of the West Indies.[42]

AFRICANS

It has been suggested that Philip Quaque, who came from the Gold Coast in the eighteenth century to be educated and ordained and who returned there as a chaplain and preacher, was at Oxford; research by his compatriots however seems to indicate that there is no basis for this assertion.[43] Africans from coastal Nigeria, the Gold Coast and Sierra Leone began to come to Britain from the late nineteenth century onwards, most of them to read for the Bar in London and medicine in Edinburgh. Among them were the first Africans to take degrees at Oxford, two Creoles from Sierra Leone. Christian Cole, the son of a pastor, matriculated as a non-collegiate student in 1873 and graduated from University College with a Third in Moderations and a Fourth in Greats. He also read for the Bar and became the first African to practise in English courts. Cole published two tracts in verse in 1883, introduced with quotations in the original language from Horace, Heine and Dante. The theme of *Reflections on the Zulu War*, dedicated to Mr Gladstone, was

> The Blacks you have murdered
> You've murdered as Cain.
> O shame on you all
> Who've determined to wreak
> Vengeance bitter as gall
> On those who are weak.

A second poem in the same book, 'The Future of Africa', was dedicated to Bishop Colenso and looked forward to a time when Africans

> Will with stunning pride assert their claims
> And put to silence all opprobrious names.
> The world with eyes wide ope shall then exclaim
> Afric! Thy sons have won eternal fame.

Alas, there was to be no eternal fame for Oxford's first African graduate. He could not find employment in Sierra Leone, and went to practise law in Zanzibar, where he died at the age of 36.[44]

Cole's near contemporary, John Renner Maxwell, the son of a chaplain at Cape Coast, was more successful. He matriculated at Merton in 1876 and took a B.C.L. He returned to practise law in the

Gold Coast and ended as Chief Justice of the Gambia. Maxwell wrote happily of his time at Oxford – 'A resident for more than three years in one of the best Colleges in Oxford,' he says, 'I was not subjected to the slightest ridicule or insult on account of my colour or race from any of my fellow students – and never in my life I can forget the kindness extended to me by both tutors and students. The recollection of those days is one of the brightest of my life.' In West Africa, by contrast, he said, he had frequently met with sarcasm from Englishmen with regard to his physical appearance.[45]

One day in the Oxford Union Reading Room, he came across an article by Sir George Campbell on the advantages of miscegenation, or put more positively, 'homiculture', used in the same sense as 'oyster culture' or 'bee culture'.[46] Maxwell developed this idea enthusiastically in a book on *The Negro Question*. Negroes, he maintained, were not lacking in intellect, or immoral or inhuman, but their appearance would be improved by intermarriage with Asians and Europeans. He suggested that poor European women who might otherwise become prostitutes should be shipped out to Africa to further this purpose, and he himself set an example by marrying an Englishwoman.[47]

A remarkable black African from Zululand was Pixley Seme, who studied law at Jesus College from 1910 to 1912, having already been sent to take a B.A. at Columbia University by an American missionary. Seme founded an African Club at Oxford on behalf of which he wrote to Booker T. Washington, the American negro leader, to enlist his support. 'Here are to be found', he said, 'the future leaders of African nations, temporarily thrown together, and yet coming from widely different sections of that great and unhappy continent, and these men will return each to a community that eagerly awaits him and perhaps influence its public opinion.' The Club's purpose, he explained, was for interchange of ideas; violence had no place in its programme. Washington, however, when he visited England at this time, refused to involve himself in national causes or to lend his support to the Club, and urged Seme to devote himself to educational work in his own country.[48] He qualified for the Bar but had to return to South Africa without a degree when his money ran out. He has been described as 'able, ambitious, impatient, humorous, but a bit of a snob. Oxford gave him polish and a taste for nobility.'[49] To such a man it must have been particularly humiliating to find on his return that on the railways he had to ride in a cattle truck, and that on the streets he was not allowed to walk on the pavement. At Oxford he had dreamed of rebuilding the Zulu nation: now he was provoked into thinking in wider terms and became one of the founders of the African National Congress.

The first African woman to take a degree in Oxford was Aina Moore, who was at St Hugh's, Margery Perham's College, from 1932 to 1935. She was a Yoruba, born in Lagos, whose father, mother and grandfather had been educated in England. She herself attended a girls' boarding school in Reading and would have preferred to return to Nigeria for teacher training. At first she was unhappy and bewildered by Oxford, 'tossed in a sea of intellect with highly earnest students who were themselves occupied in trying to emerge from the surging whirl . . . but gradually I discovered that we were all aground on dry land and that I was among a sympathetic crowd'. There was a thirst for information among students, so that she received more invitations to coffee parties than other first-year students in order to answer questions about Nigeria and the political relations of its people to Britain. She found herself in a group of friends from various countries, reading different subjects, whose common ground was music. She joined the Labour Club, the African Society and the English Club. Although her brother, who was darker, had great difficulty in finding accommodation in London, she herself did not experience racial prejudice, except in sometimes being regarded as a curio, rather than as a human being. She wished that more African girls could enjoy the liberal education of Oxford.[50] On her return home, she married Sir Adetokunbo Ademola, a Cambridge graduate who became Chief Justice of Nigeria.

Many of the Ghanaians who came to Oxford had been educated at Achimota. Among them was K. A. Busia, who after reading P.P.E. in 1939 to 1942, became one of the first Africans to be admitted to the Administrative Service of a British colony. He preferred academic life, and returned to Oxford as a Nuffield Research Fellow to take a D.Phil. and then became the first African to hold a Chair at the University of Ghana. But a third career now commenced in politics. Despairing however of any prospects of change whilst Leader of the Opposition to Nkrumah's Government, he went into exile as a professor in the Netherlands and at St Antony's College in Oxford. Briefly he found himself Prime Minister of Ghana on Nkrumah's downfall, but with a further turn of the wheel of fate he was overthrown by an Army coup and returned to Oxford where he died in 1978.

Whilst Busia was Prime Minister, another Oxford man, Edward

Akuro-Addo was President of Ghana. His career also had its ups and downs. He first trained as a catechist, then took a degree in Mathematics at St Peter's Hall and qualified as a barrister at the Middle Temple. Before his brief Presidency, he had been Chief Justice of Ghana but was dismissed by Nkrumah for acquitting journalists who were prosecuted by the Government.

Seretse Khama from Bechuanaland came up to Balliol in 1945 where he read Law. At first he found the College inhospitable but eventually he derived from Oxford an affection for the British people which survived his deposition by the British from the Paramount Chieftancy when he married an English girl. He also acquired at Oxford an ability to laugh at himself which he never lost, even when he became the Chief of State in Botswana.[51] Also from Southern Africa came King Moshoeshoe of Lesotho to study Modern Greats at Corpus.

Ruskin College, which was set up to educate trade unionists, was in some ways the most congenial place in Oxford for mature Africans with limited academic attainments. Its courses were flexible, the average age of its students was about 30, far higher than in other Colleges. Some 20 per cent of its students came from overseas, and it was usually arranged for them to share rooms with British students. One of the earliest Africans to study there was P. G. Mockerie of Kenya, a schoolteacher who was sent with Jomo Kenyatta by the Kikuyu Central Association to represent them before the Joint Select Committee of Parliament on Closer Union in East Africa, and then spent a year at Ruskin 1931–2.

A more well-known member of Ruskin was Tom Mboya, who spent a year there in 1956 on a scholarship financed by the Workers' Travel Association, studying political science and economics and specialising in industrial relations. He had only obtained permission to leave Kenya by attending a Moral Rearmament conference on the way. His main interest was in discussions with Ruskin lecturers and with Margery Perham. In his memoirs he appears almost as the ideal Ruskin student from overseas. 'I feel', he wrote, 'that Oxford played a major part in my life, giving me a year of unhurried thought to help me decide what line of policies would be effective in our struggle. The year at Oxford gave me more confidence in myself. It gave me time to read more. It taught me to look to books as a source of knowledge. It led me to take part in intellectual discussions, sometimes of a very provocative nature.' His special study of industrial relations proved highly relevant when he became Minister of Labour in Kenya.[52]

Another notable Ruskin student was Siaka Stevens who was to become President of Sierra Leone, and who recalls the year which he spent at Ruskin in 1948 at the age of 40 as one of the pleasantest of his life. Intending in light of his previous experience of Europeans in Africa to be stiff and reserved , he responded instead to the cordiality and helpfulness of both staff and students and even found an Oxford butcher who used to give him more than his entitled meat ration. Like his compatriot Maxwell, 70 years earlier, he asked himself again and again 'How is it that Europeans here are so different to those in the colonies?' What changes them so? Do they realise the harm they are doing?' This led him to speculate about the roles not only of the colonial élites but of the African élites who succeeded them. In his studies at Ruskin he was comforted to find that the average trade unionist in England was as inclined to leave his union to be run by élites as he was in West Africa.[53]

One factor which may have been important in the adjustment to Oxford of the Africans, as compared with the Indians, was religion. Few of the Indians were Christians, and those who were seem to have made more British friends than those who were not. Many of the Africans, on the other hand, had church affiliations and through these were introduced to British families.

AUSTRALIANS

Of the 'kindred elect', it was perhaps the Australians who made most impact on Oxford. 'These Australians had sunshine in their veins; they bubbled with ready fun; they blew into the antiquity of Oxford, with the challenge of their own and their country's youth' – so Ernest Barker remembered them in the 1890s.[54]

The Australians who had brilliant Oxford academic careers tended to remain there; whilst the Canadians could take posts over the border in America, the Australian Universities were isolated. Among those who stayed on were Gilbert Murray, Hugh Cairns and Howard Florey, whose careers have already been noticed. Others were Sir Carleton Allen who was lecturer and Professor of Jurisprudence from 1920 to 1929, and Warden of Rhodes House from 1931 to 1952; and Sir Kenneth Wheare who was lecturer in Colonial History from 1935 to 1944, Gladstone Professor of Government from 1944 to 1957 and Rector of Exeter College from 1956 to 1972. However long they stayed, they seldom lost their rugged qualities. As an Exeter College obituary wrote of Wheare, 'He brought the right degree of toughness, even ruthlessness in running our affairs.'[55]

Sir Keith Hancock, who called his memoirs *Country and Calling*, was one Australian who moved continuously between Britain and Australia. Coming to Balliol as a Rhodes Scholar in 1922, he considered at first that the Oxford arrangement of a separate entrance and staircase for each block of six rooms favoured the Englishman's cliquishness, as compared with the long passages at Melbourne University which were suited to the natural gregariousness of Australian youth. Then he found that the cliques were all open to him and that life was thus so crowded and various at Balliol that he had neither time nor inclination to seek additional entertainment outside. He worked with fiery concentration to please three 'grand men': A. L. Smith, Humphrey Sumner and Kenneth Bell. He took seriously the intention of the Rhodes Scholarships that the men who were privileged to enjoy them should make an appropriate return in duty performed. Although elected to an All Souls Fellowship, he returned to take the Chair of Modern History at Adelaide. He came back to Britain to teach at Birmingham University, to write a Survey of Commonwealth Affairs for Chatham House, and to be the first Director of the Institute of Commonwealth Studies at London University; but when the Australian National University was opened, he was persuaded to head one of its departments. Hancock brought an Antipodean freshness to Commonwealth Studies. Politicians and professors, he said, infused too much sweetness and light into the picture of the Commonwealth, acclaiming *ad nauseam* Lord Durham's Report on Canada and the Statute of Westminster and seeing all the territories marked red on the map as keeping their appointed places in a triumphant procession to the finishing post of self-government. As a young Fellow of All Souls, he was carried off by Curtis to meetings of the Round Table, but later escaped from the spell.[56]

A contemporary of Hancock at Balliol was W. R. (later Sir William) Crocker, who was also taken up by Curtis. Crocker's Balliol world was quite different from that of Hancock. Through A. D. Lindsay's introductions, he frequented Liberals and radicals such as J. L. Hammond, Lord Parmoor and Gilbert Murray, though eventually he was to conclude that Lindsay ruined Balliol through his unfortunate appointments.[57]

Crocker joined the Colonial Administrative Service when Amery opened this to men from the Dominions, and, serving in Northern Nigeria, asked the unpardonable question: 'How are you going to develop these Emirates, which you have turned into mediaeval monarchies, into modern states of communities?'[58] before he resigned and wrote a critical book on British colonial policies. In a varied life, which included being an official of the United Nations and of the International Labour Organisation and an Australian Ambassador, he continued in true Balliol Socratic style to ask awkward questions until he ended in the ornamental post of Governor of an Australian State.

G. V. Portus, an Australian Rhodes Scholar who came up to New College in 1907 and later taught history at the University of Adelaide, recollected three aspects of Oxford above all. Firstly, there was the manner in which his tutor H. A. L. Fisher made coaching a kind of contest of wits and transformed history from being just a subject into an intellectual excitement. Secondly, Oxford was the most democratic society to which he had ever belonged. 'I have never lived in any other society where a man could utter any opinion, however revolutionary or unconventional, without being snubbed or sat on.' As a corollary, scattered through the University were clubs and societies for all kinds of interests and opinions. He himself used to attend both the Socialist Club and the Society of King Charles the Martyr. Thirdly, the British undergraduates were generally shy, because of the monasticism of Oxford; shyness led to apparent aloofness. The Australians' reaction to this was bumptious, but by the second year, most of them recognised, and some of them even admitted, that the British Empire existed because of, and not in spite of, Britain.[59]

The New Zealanders were even more reluctant to return home than the Australians; generations of them stayed on to work for the Oxford University Press, and it is hard to imagine what scope would have been found in New Zealand for a classical scholar as eminent as Sir Ronald Syme who, after taking a First in Greats at Oriel, remained in Oxford for 40 years as a Fellow and as Camden Professor of Ancient History.

CANADIANS

Two of the Canadians on whom Oxford made the deepest impression were there for a very short time and their subsequent work in education has been discussed in the previous chapter. George Parkin spent a year as a non-collegiate student in 1873–4 whilst on leave of absence from his post as Headmaster of a Canadian school. He was already a mature 27. If Parkin made a notable impact on Oxford by introducing the Imperial idea among students, the influence of Oxford on a young man who had grown up in the backwoods of Canada, nurtured on English history and literature, was equally great. He breakfasted with Ruskin and worked on his road at Hinksey. He listened to preachers as different as Pusey and Stanley. He was inspired by the philosophic idealism of T. H. Green and fascinated to hear Max Mueller talk on Indian literature. He was conscious of living among the cream of English youth, who were destined to have a large share of ruling the Empire, and his biographer describes him, gazing round at Oxford's noble spires from the top of the Radcliffe Camera, quoting an earlier visitor 'It is like the new Jerusalem.'[60]

Parkin's early career was to alternate between that of a schoolmaster and a propagandist of Empire. Rosebery called him 'The Bagman of Empire', and Buckle, the Editor of *The Times*, said that he 'had shifted the mind of England'. With Rosebery as the Chairman of the Rhodes Trustees, Parkin was a natural choice as the first organiser of the Rhodes Scholarship scheme, in which position, according to his tactful biographer, 'he grew slowly into an honest regard for Cecil Rhodes';[61] Rhodes perhaps was somewhat lacking in moral earnestness, a quality cherished by Parkin, who found it in Oxford but sought it in vain on his travels in Australia. It was sad for him not to be able to live in his beloved Oxford at last. Wylie persuaded the Trustees, however, that Parkin's presence as a senior partner would embarrass him in his dealings with the University, and Parkin had to settle in Goring-on-Thames, 25 miles away.

G. M. Wrong was to become such an enthusiastic supporter of Oxford and its contribution to the Empire that it is strange to find that although he appeared in the Canadian *Who's Who* as 'educated at Oxford' he only spent one Long Vacation there and was never enrolled in the University.[62]

From Parkin and G. M. Wrong sprang a remarkable Oxford–Toronto dynasty of historians and diplomats. One of Parkin's daughters married Vincent Massey and another married W. L. Grant, both of whom went to Balliol along with Wrong's sons Murray and Hume, whose sister was at Somerville. All these taught History at Oxford or Toronto or both, although Massey and Hume Wrong went on into diplomacy. Murray Wrong married one of the seven daughters of A. L. Smith, the Master of Balliol, and thus acquired as brothers-in-law several leading members of the British Establishment. In the next generation, Grant's daughter, the granddaughter of Parkin, married George Ignatieff, a Canadian Rhodes Scholar who, after serving as Ambassador in several countries, became Provost of Trinity College, Toronto.

Vincent Massey has left a record of the Canadians at Oxford just before the First World war. Massey was the heir to the Massey Harris agricultural equipment fortune. Even before he came to Oxford he had founded a Hall at Toronto University in memory of his grandfather, and he already had a Toronto degree. The two years at Balliol were the happiest of his life.

A. L. Smith, who taught him history, told him that he was not in Oxford to gain First Class honours, but to get all he could out of the experience. Talks in Sligger Urquhart's rooms meant as much to him as lectures and essays. He fell under the spell of Lionel Curtis, 'the most persuasive and magnetic of men', and, with his fellow Canadians, started an undergraduate journal, *The Blue Book*, in which he expounded Liberal Imperialism and chastised the Tory Imperialism of Mafeking Night. He helped to found the Ralegh Club. He observed, like the Indian students, that people he had dined with the night before looked straight through him next day; unlike some of the Indians he deduced that in Oxford you did not address anybody unless you had something to say, and concluded that this was a time-saving habit. Back in Canada he parted company with Curtis, deploring his use of the Round Table to propagate a particular set of ideas and his ability to turn a very sharp corner in debate. In his subsequent diplomatic career Oxford contacts were usually at hand. In the critical period before and during the Second World War, whilst Massey was Canadian High Commissioner in London, he had two other Oxford men, Lester Pearson and George Ignatieff on his staff. Later he was invited to be Master of Balliol, but became Governor-General of Canada instead.[63]

Lester Pearson, the future Prime Minister of Canada, who was at St John's from 1921 to 1923, came from a much poorer background, and worked as a sausage packer and as clerk in a fertiliser factory before taking a History degree at Toronto University where Massey was his tutor. He came on a scholarship from the Massey Foundation with a romantic picture of Oxford, derived from the *Boy's Own* paper and *Chums*, and found it all that he had hoped for and dreamed of. He played hockey and lacrosse for the University, dined with the King Charles Club, which had been founded by Prince

Rupert, and took a Second Class degree, which enabled him to join the History Faculty of Toronto University. This was not the end of the family's Oxford connection. His son Geoffrey was to win the same Massey Scholarship and read P.P.E. at New College.[64]

While Balliol and Lionel Curtis were confirming Massey in his Imperialist convictions, his compatriot Frank Underhill was becoming a Socialist and anti-Imperialist. Underhill had studied history at Toronto University under G. M. Wrong and obtained a scholarship to Balliol where A. D. Lindsay was his tutor: in the old Oxford anti-Imperialist traditions he found that the works of Goldwin Smith provided the key to understanding Canadian history. He returned to teach history at Toronto and to write about political issues, and was one of the founders of the Cooperative Commonwealth Federation – in effect the Socialist Party of Canada. His anti-Imperialism caused him to oppose Canadian entry into the Second World War, and the Board of Governors of Toronto University demanded his resignation. He survived, like Goldwin Smith before him, to become a national institution, and Lester Pearson, the Prime Minister, attended his eightieth birthday party.[65]

After Parkin's time, the Canadians, unlike the Australians, mostly went home when they had taken their degrees at Oxford. Although two of them in succession – John Lowe and C. A. Simpson – occupied the position of Dean of Christ Church between 1939 and 1969, they had both taught theology in Canada and in the United States between graduating at Oxford and returning there.

The blissful existence of Massey's generation of Canadians at Oxford was not universally approved. The journal of Victoria University, Toronto, in 1914 deplored the failure of Oxford to turn out as many of the 'earnest men' who Canada needed as she ought. 'In Oxford', the Editor wrote sadly, 'earnestness is discouraged, in fact probably the most striking feature of Oxford life is its utter irresponsibility. It is the creepers which cling upon the ancient University which give to it its picturesqueness and beauty. Remember however that they only began to flourish when the stone began to crumble.'[66]

Stephen Leacock, the Canadian humorist, who was financed by the Rhodes Trust to undertake 'Imperial missionary work',[67] drew a different picture of the crumbling stones. 'Oxford is a noble university', he wrote in *My Discovery of England* in 1922.

> It has a great past. It is at present the greatest university in the world, and it is quite possible that it has a great future. Oxford

> trains scholars of the real type better than any other place in the world. Its methods are antiquated. It despises science. Its lectures are rotten. It has professors who never teach and students who never learn. It has no order, no management, no system. Its curriculum is unintelligible. It has no President. It has no state legislature to tell it how to teach, and yet it gets there. Whether we like it or not, Oxford gives something to its students, a life and a mode of thought which in America as yet we can emulate but not equal.[68]

SOUTH AFRICANS AND RHODESIANS

Most of the English-speaking South Africans and Rhodesians who came to Oxford were only first- or second-generation settlers whose impressions were little different from those of the British. There were many who conformed to the heavy Rugby-playing, unimaginative, unpolitical image. But there were others on whom Oxford's idealism was to make its mark.

One of the first Rhodes Scholars from South Africa was W. M. MacMillan who was chosen at Stellenbosch as runner-up to the first man selected, an Afrikaaner who hotly disapproved of Rhodes. Arriving at Merton in 1903, he was at first bewildered in a College dominated by 'bloods', so idle and riotous that only 19 out of 38 entrants who arrived in 1903 survived their first two years. His Scottish connections, however, led to friendships with Sir James Murray, the Editor of the *Oxford English Dictionary*, and his large family as well as with a young tutor in his College, W. H. Fyfe, who was to become prominent as a Socialist as well as an educationist. MacMillan felt at home with the Congregationalists at Mansfield College but kept clear of the evangelical student groups whom he and his friends regarded as 'good in the worst sense of the word'.

In the long run the greatest influence on him came from the lectures of A. L. Smith on 'Political and Economic Questions'. They comprehended population, poor law, federations and, notably, the historical development of the Socialist movement; from them MacMillan acquired a permanent interest in the understanding of social questions of the past and also of the importance of the historical approach to the contemporary world. Both were to involve him in controversy when he returned to teach History in South Africa,[69] where his subsequent career has been discussed in Chapter 5.

One of MacMillan's students in South Africa was Margaret Hodgson who came up to Somerville in 1914 and later, as Margaret Ballinger, fought a long and lonely battle for the rights of Africans whilst she was representing the natives in the South African Parliament. In this she was supported not only by Barnes and MacMillan but in particular by her Somerville friend, the novelist Winifred Holtby, who devoted her royalties to enabling Margaret Ballinger and her trade unionist husband to be financially independent.

A different kind of idealist, social rather than political, was Kingsley Fairbridge, who came up to Exeter College on a Rhodes Scholarship from Rhodesia in 1908, already possessed by the vision of settling the children from the slums of England in the uncultivated lands of the Empire; but before he could launch his campaign from Oxford, he needed to be known and liked. To achieve this he won a Blue for boxing, played in every kind of game, and attended wine clubs, debating societies and card parties until he was on speaking and dining acquaintance with perhaps as many men as anyone in the University. Then he was invited to address the Colonial Club about child emigration. Fifty men turned up; he faced the bull-necked sturdiness of a New Zealander, the ingenuous gaze of a South African Rugby Blue, the wide untroubled look of a Newfoundlander. He told them that Imperial unity was not a phrase or an artificial thing; Great Britain and Greater Britain were interdependent. Britain had over 60,000 orphans being brought up in institutions; whilst the colonies had a superfluity of land. Here and now, he said, let us found a society to take as many of these children as possible overseas, to train them in the colonies for farm life. His speech was effective. The Society for Furtherance of Child Emigration to the Colonies was formed on the spot. Fairbridge started its first school in Australia, supported by the members of the Oxford committee until most of them were killed in the First World War.[70]

In the next generation, Patrick Duncan's career carried on the tradition of Balliol idealism. He was the son of the Governor-General of South Africa of the same name who had been one of Milner's Kindergarten: but whilst Oxford had helped to turn his father into an Imperialist, it caused the son to question the racial policies of the South African Government. It was a very individual questioning. At Oxford he resigned from the Labour Club because he found it hysterical. He joined the British Colonial Service and served in Basutoland, which he loved, and on whose laws and customs he wrote a book; but he resigned from the Service to enter South African politics. 'My destiny was to give everything I could to the one cause, ending the Colour Bar.' He earned a precarious living as a bookseller and journalist. When he was prosecuted for his publications, he quoted the Aristotle and Cicero which he had learned at Oxford to plead that unjust law is not law. Deprived of South African citizenship, he moved around Africa, impetuous, impatient and sometimes absurd, as when he described Ghana as 'the nearest thing to Utopia that I have seen'. An agnostic, he became representative in Algeria of a Christian Aid Committee. Yet his name is likely always to be cherished by black South Africans for the sacrifices which he made on their behalf.[71] Abram Fischer, who was a Rhodes Scholar at New College from 1932 to 1934 moved even further to the Left. After many years as defence lawyer in South African political trials, he was himself gaoled for life under the Suppression of Communism Act.

Of the Afrikaaners, the most interesting was J. H. Hofmeyr, the prodigy who graduated in South Africa at the age of 15, whilst still wearing short trousers and who, while marking time before becoming old enough to take up his Rhodes Scholarship, acquired another B.A. in Natural Sciences as well as an M.A. and wrote a biography of his politician uncle. When at last he came up to Balliol in 1913, his mother accompanied him. Hofmeyr disliked the coldness of his Public School contemporaries, but found congenial friends among the evangelicals who conducted open-air services at the Martyr's Memorial. He was shocked by the moral tone of Oxford and even more shocked to find an Indian next to him at table, and to be invited by another Indian to breakfast. Before he went down, however, he had made a good Indian friend in John Matthai through their Christian social work activities.

Inevitably, Hofmeyr easily took Firsts in Mods and Greats. All his life he was a devoted Oxford man. In a remarkable political career which took him to the position of Deputy Prime Minister under Smuts, he was the great hope of the South African liberals. That his liberalism was partly acquired in Oxford was undeniable, though it did not prevent him from comparing Mussolini favourably with the Emperor Augustus and believing that it was the destiny of the highlands of Rhodesia, Tanganyika and Kenya to be settled and developed by Europeans.[72]

Oxford had no such liberalising influence on Albert Hertzog, son of the Prime Minister of South Africa, who left Leyden University because they made fun of his Dutch accent and became a non-collegiate student at Oxford. Later the well-meaning Haldanes got him into New College where he was less happy.[73] On his return to South Africa he entered politics and resigned from the Nationalist Party because its attitude to the admission of coloured sports teams was not sufficiently strict. He then founded a new Party whose aim was to establish Afrikaaner hegemony under which English would be relegated to a second-language status. Perhaps, however, Oxford left a certain mark, for his obituary described him as combining fanatical political views with enormous personal charm and courtesy in his private dealings,[74] and all through his life he sent back to Oxford for blazers and ties. Like the Australians, a number of South Africans settled in Oxford; among them were Herbert Frankel, the first Professor of Colonial Economics, and, more briefly, Max Gluckman, the anthropologist.

Coming from such different backgrounds, the visitors' perception of Oxford was yet broadly similar in three aspects: the warmth and intellectual challenge of their relationship with their tutors; the tolerance and eclecticism of undergraduate society; and the difficulty of breaking through the English reserve. Some never achieved the breakthrough and made their friendships with other expatriates. Those who succeeded, whether, white, black or brown, often did so through rowing in boats, playing games, debating in the Union or enlisting in a wide variety of undergraduate clubs.

Perhaps of greatest interest is what their reminiscences do not say. On the one side, despite the individual enthusiasms of Curtis and C. R. L. Fletcher, they did not have the impression that the University, through its courses or in any other way, tried to inculcate loyalty to Empire. This was quite different to the experiences of those who had attended English preparatory schools where there was no jam for tea when the school team lost a match and 'let down the Empire', or Public Schools where military training was compulsory. On the other side, despite the discussions in the Majlis and the Labour Club, and the apprehensions of the India Office, Oxford – unlike London – never really became a centre where the incipient Nationalisms of Asia, Africa and the West Indies struck sparks from each other.

14 Epilogue

From 1919 to 1939 . . . there was a fairly even balance between those . . . who hated the Empire, whether on moral grounds or as a class symbol, and those who . . . would defend it and liberalise it . . . Now there is no longer an Empire to glorify or hate, there are no longer natives to be governed and slowly educated to some degree of freedom. There are nations and races to be treated as equals.

Oxford Magazine, Editoral article (1967)[1]

COLONIAL STUDIES

It was only when the end of Empire was imminent that Oxford set up a Committee and Institute for Colonial Studies. That it did so, according to Sir Douglas Veale, was largely due to a partnership between Margery Perham in the University and Sir Ralph Furse in the Colonial Office.[2] In fact, Veale himself was the essential third partner. A graduate of Corpus, he had served as Private Secretary to successive Ministers of Health before he returned to Oxford where he was Registrar of the University from 1930 to 1968. Through his long service he came to exercise great influence in a system of rotating Vice-Chancellors in which the Registrar's position could become as important as that of a Permanent Secretary in Government. His experience fitted him admirably for insuring cooperation between the University and the Government on new ventures, often launched through carefully planned lunches. Among his main interests were medical education and colonial or Commonwealth studies. He travelled widely in the Commonwealth as a representative of Oxford or of the Inter-University Council.

By 1940 Lord Nuffield was pressing the postgraduate College which he had founded in Oxford to show something for his money. Margery Perham, who was a Fellow of Nuffield College, seized the opportunity to set up two research projects which could be pursued in wartime and did not involve travel abroad. One was a series of studies on colonial Legislatures and the other was an examination of the economic problems of Britain's largest colonial territory, Nigeria. Margery Perham had collected a considerable quantity of unpublished material on Africa, and her flat became the virtual headquarters of the projects. As the work went on, she found that she and her colleagues were being pushed by circumstances into wider activities and were becoming Oxford's unofficial centre for people interested in current colonial research; they also became not only the liaison point between Oxford and colonial Governments but also with students from outside Oxford, in response to a greatly increased interest in colonial affairs during the war in the United States as well as in Britain. Margery Perham felt that if the centre were to develop further, it would be more appropriate for it to be a University Institute rather than to continue to be attached to Nuffield College, which could not expect to have a monopoly in such a broad field.[3] This was one initiative which led to the establishment of a University Committee for Colonial Studies and an Institute for Colonial Studies in 1943–4, with Margery Perham as the Director of the latter.

COLONIAL SERVICE TRAINING

At about the same time Sir Ralph Furse, the Director of Recruitment in the Colonial Office, wrote a prescient memorandum in 1943 on post-war training for the Colonial Service. In this he pointed out that after the fall of Singapore the British Empire would never be the same again. One of the great dangers, he said, was 'that Britain would lose confidence in itself as a colonial power', and her young officers would need to be fortified against this and against ill-informed defeatist criticism.

He also suggested that, 'as the educated native moved to the centre of the stage', more sensitivity would be required by British colonial administrators, more of the ancient Greek spirit, instead of the Roman preoccupation with the *Pax Britannica*; more interest in the artistic and spiritual life of colonial peoples.[4] The new generation of administrators must also expect to spend more of their time on economic and social development work. He proposed that after the war administrative officers should attend new kinds of courses in response to the new situation, both when first appointed and again in mid-career. His original idea was that a Colonial Staff College should be established; he was dissuaded, however, by Margery Perham and Veale who saw how desirable it was to link colonial research and colonial training at Oxford.

To consider Furse's memorandum the Government set up a committee under the Duke of Devonshire on which Oxford was represented by Margery Perham and Veale. The Committee endorsed Furse's main recommendations, and two kinds of one-year 'Devonshire Course' were established at Oxford, Cambridge and London Universities; Course A was for probationers; Course B was for men in mid-career and allowed them considerable time for research.[5] In Oxford the Committee for Colonial Studies was responsible for the University's cooperation in the courses and thus coordinated the needs of training and of research.

The new courses were influenced by the Report of representatives of Oxford, Cambridge and London who visited Nigeria in 1946 to examine training needs. Veale represented Oxford and the key recommendations seem to show his hand. For the probationers, the Report suggested, knowledge of the methods of anthropologists was more important than knowledge of anthropologists' conclusions; economics must be recognised to be a developing science in the application of which to the practical problems of Government the lay administrator must be ready to trust the expert, but without surrendering his judgement; there should be more emphasis on the history of Local Government. A recommendation that in the teaching of colonial history there should be more emphasis on the actual achievements in recent years was less easy to fit into Oxford's free-ranging teaching methods.[6]

The courses for Colonial Service officers which were revived in 1946 had gone through various phases. The first in 1926 had been a 'Tropical African Services Course' and was attended by probationers for the Administrative Service in West and East Africa. In 1934 the title changed to 'Colonial Administrative Services Course' to include officers posted to Ceylon, Hong Kong and Malaya. The two 'Overseas Services Courses' run from 1946 for probationers and mid-career officials were eventually consolidated as the Overseas Course in Government and Development. Throughout all these courses, Government, history, economics, anthropology, law and languages were taught, together with various options, but in the later period there was more stress on Local Government and economic development.

Whilst participants in the early courses had all come from Britain or the Dominions, after the Second World War officials born in the colonies were admitted, as colonial Governments became aware of the need for localisation of the Civil Service. The last British cadets, those destined for Fiji and Bechuanaland, came to Oxford on the Course in Government and Development of 1962–3, though this course continued until 1968–9 for the indigenous officials.[7] The last Supervisor, E. G. Rowe, a former official in Tanzania, in his reflections on the Oxford Overseas Courses concluded that in the later phase their main value had been in helping men such as those from Northern Nigeria who lacked formal education but were being suddenly promoted to succeed the departing British. 'The University's patient response to this situation was magnificent', he wrote. 'The reward of much dedicated teaching of poorly qualified material was that the Civil Services of many a less developed region got a shot in the arm at a vital time – perhaps a greater if less exciting achievement than putting a further polish on flyers quite capable of gaining distinction without going near a tutor.'[8]

QUEEN ELIZABETH HOUSE

In 1954 Queen Elizabeth House (Q.E.H.) was founded by Royal Charter not as part of, though closely associated with, the University, almost it seemed in fulfilment of the hopes of Parkin and Lothian; indeed it was first planned to build it in the grounds of Rhodes House. The idea came from Sir Charles Jeffries in the Colonial Office and Veale in Oxford. The House was intended to be a residential centre for the study of social, economic and political problems of the colonies both by British people who were going out there and by public servants and community leaders from the dependent territories; it was also to organise conferences and courses. What the Colonial Office wanted was an atmosphere which was politically acceptable and would strengthen the British connection with colonies and former colonies; they were anxious, however, that the initiative should appear to come from the University, so that the centre would not be regarded as neocolonialist by African and other Nationalists. Veale, on the other hand, found it easier to present the project to Council and Congregation as a Government initiative. The result was an ambiguity about ultimate financial responsibility which was to cause constant embarrassment to Q.E.H. The University provided a site; the Colonial Office paid for the construction of the building, and the South African Sir Ernest Oppenheimer paid for the running costs for the first ten years. After that, Q.E.H. was in a state of frequent financial crisis. The founders had expected that it would receive generous contributions from companies with interests in the colonies. The unforeseen speed of decolonisation, however, probably made private companies less interested in contributing than had been expected.[9]

The Institute of Commonwealth Studies moved into Q.E.H., and from 1968 the same person was Warden of the House and Director of the Institute. The central plan was that the Institute would be responsible for studies leading to degrees or diplomas, whereas Q.E.H., which was not part of the University, would sponsor the visits of people who wanted an opportunity to study without enrolling for degrees and would organise conferences for people both inside and outside the University.

The activities of the Institute and of Q.E.H. are beyond the scope of this book, yet in general the late fifties and the early sixties can be recollected as a golden age for African and Colonial Studies in Oxford. The Colonial Office was generous in funding posts. In addition to those officials and probationers who came on the Colonial Office courses, which later became the responsibility of the Overseas Development Ministry, many students came on grants from other sources, and the expanding American interest in Africa was reflected in the number of American graduates to be found in seminars. To mention only the dead, there seemed hardly a day in term time without a well-attended seminar held by Margery Perham, George Bennett or Thomas Hodgkin, and one of the most unorthodox and stimulating of all contemporary Oxford teachers, Jack Gallagher, the Beit Professor of Commonwealth History, was living in Q.E.H.

SPECIAL COURSES

It was not only in the Institute of Commonwealth Studies and Q.E.H. that Oxford gave more attention to the needs of the colonies than ever before or since. In 1952 the copper companies of the Rhodesias endowed a Chair of Race Relations to commemorate the hundredth anniversary of Rhodes's birth, though not without some anxiety being expressed in the University lest a Chair of this kind 'should stir up trouble amongst nationalist minded natives'.[10] The Department of Education organised a special International Course for teachers and educational administrators. The Department of Agriculture organised vacation courses for volunteers who were going out to teach in Commonwealth countries. More colonials came to take diplomas at Ruskin College. Perhaps most impressive of all was that after Independence the Governments of Ghana, Ceylon and Pakistan each asked for a special course to be set up in Oxford to train their civil servants.

The time and effort devoted by Oxford to all these special courses was viewed by the Editor of the *Oxford Magazine* with some misgivings lest the needs of 'practical people' who did not enrol for degree courses might cause too great a demand on academic time which could more profitably be spent on ordinary teaching and research. 'Though the course may be made to measure', he urged in 1957, 'yet the material should be made of standard Oxford cloth. A high academic qualification should be insisted upon and the contents of the course should be of a good honours standard.'[11] Such admonitions, perhaps fortunately, did not prevent the I.C.S. and Q.E.H. from organising special crash-courses when men and women who were about to become ministers, ambassadors and senior civil servants, sometimes with only a primary education, came to Oxford for what preparation they could get whilst decolonisation proceeded at its final hectic pace. Despite the carping of the *Oxford Magazine*, Oxford teachers responded with zest to the challenge of devising teaching methods for people who often had a very limited basic education, could only spare a few months to study, but were about to become leaders of their countries.

Among the most imaginative were two courses of four months' duration, organised by Q.E.H. and financed by the Ariel Foundation, just before Zambia became independent, for senior officials of Kenneth Kaunda's party. Most of them had never completed secondary education but were destined to become Parliamentary Secretaries, Permanent Secretaries, Ambassadors, or for other high posts. It was fascinating to observe how the initial suspicions of men who had never met a British national except in a situation of political confrontation relaxed in the atmosphere of croquet and academic freedom, though the crash-training in diplomacy did not seem to have been wholly successful when shortly after attending the course one of the former participants, on being designated as Zambia's High Commissioner in London, was reported as describing the British Government as 'toothless bulldogs'.[12]

Yet although much of the best talent of the University participated in the courses and despite the unique asset of the Rhodes Scholarships, now extended to non-white countries of the Commonwealth, the *Oxford Magazine* in 1954 speculated that the Commonwealth Universities perhaps felt more affinity with the newer British Universities. Veale put his finger on the cause. The University's administration, he wrote in 1950, was particularly ineffective in dealing with outside bodies because its representatives under Oxford's democratic form of Government were nervous lest they be repudiated by their principals.[13] In the newer British Universities a permanent Vice-Chancellor usually found it easier to take rapid decisions.

This handicap and the appeal of some of the new Universities was illustrated when the Government decided in 1964 to set up and finance a new institution for training officials from developing countries in economic and administrative questions. To Oxford this seemed an admirable solution to the financial problems of Q.E.H. which could be used as the premises of the new institution. The Government's Advisory Council for Training in Public Administration unanimously recommended that the Institution be located in Oxford. Instead the Institute of Development Studies was placed at the University of Sussex. Among reasons which have been suggested were the cramping effect of existing institutions at Oxford, the tendency in Oxford 'for a sort of other worldly brilliance to be esteemed and therefore cultivated' and the fact that the Minister concerned had found Oxford snobbish and out of touch with social realities when she was a student there.[14]

As the pace of decolonisation accelerated, 'colonial' became an embarrassing word and a change of title was sought for the Committee and Institute, despite rumblings from Furse about premature abandonment of its trust by the colonial power. Various titles were suggested, according to the interests of the members of the Committee; 'Institute for Comparative (Overseas) Social Studies', 'Institute of Asian and African Affairs', 'Institute of Underdeveloped Countries', 'Institute for Studies in Colonisation and Development'; even ingeniously the 'Coupland Institute' was proposed, which could have covered any activities. Eventually in 1956, 'Commonwealth' was substituted for 'colonial', a somewhat misleading change, for the Institute did not study the old Dominions.[15]

Sometimes the *Oxford Magazine* wondered whether it was appropriate for the ancient University to seek so eagerly to keep up with the times. In 1957 it published a note entitled 'A Retreat from Empire', criticising the decision to change the title of the Beit Professorship and Lectureship from 'Colonial' to 'Commonwealth' History, since the Beit Professor and Lecturer would continue to spend most of their time on the study of the overseas possessions of the British Crown in that period when they had constituted the British Empire. This brought a sharp reply from V. T. Harlow, the Beit Professor, inviting the author of the note to attend his lectures and learn about the evolution of the Commonwealth, to the delight of the Editor who revealed that the note had been written by Max Beloff, Gladstone Professor of Government.[16] Behind these donnish exchanges lay a real question, what share of various resources should be devoted to the study of the history of the British Empire, and what share to study of the contemporary problems of the Third World.

As time went on Q. E. H. became gradually less of a centre for study of the Commonwealth and more one for the study of problems of economic development in the Third World. Without endowments, it could only remain solvent by following the fashion, which made this the area for which funds were most easily available from the Government and other sources.

As for the Commonwealth it was hard to foresee in the fifties and sixties whether it would survive and with what membership. It was only gradually that it became generally recognised that Britain's membership of the Common Market could be reconciled with membership of the Commonwealth and that the latter still had a future with its own Secretary General and Secretariat.

For some years after India became independent, Indian Studies received less consideration than before. In 1959 G. F. Hudson pointed out in the *Oxford Magazine* that the end of British Rule had led to abolition of arrangements for teaching Hindi, Urdu, Bengali and Tamil, though these were the languages of 400 million people in the Commonwealth.[17] The eviction of the Indian Institute from its old premises, built with the contributions of Indian Princes, was viewed by many as a symbol of the decline of interest in Indian Studies since the time of Max Mueller and Monier Williams. The setback was temporary. In due course the history of the Indian National movement found a place in the Modern History syllabus and in 1983 a Centre for Indian Studies, funded initially by the Indian Government on the personal initiative of Indira Gandhi, was established at St Antony's College.

ST ANTONY'S COLLEGE

When Q. E. H. was founded, the *Oxford Magazine*, whilst wishing it success, observed that the Oxford climate was much more friendly to Colleges than to other institutions: that this was so was illustrated by the success of St Antony's College, which was working to some extent in the same field. St Antony's was founded as a graduate College in 1948 with a benefaction from the French businessman Antonin Besse who had made his fortune in the British colony of Aden. From the beginning it concentrated on study of other countries and regions, whether in political, economic, historical, cultural or other fields. It had a much firmer financial base than Q. E. H. in its endowment and in the fees of its students, who were registered for postgraduate degrees, and the majority of whom came from abroad. It set up small regional centres for Asian, Latin American, Middle Eastern, African, Russian and East European, and West European Studies. Success bred success, so that visiting Fellowships were established by the Foreign Office, the Indian Government, the Volkswagen Company of Germany, the Nissan Company of Japan and other sponsors.

Although the Oxford Course in Government and Development closed in 1969, whilst the parallel course in Cambridge continued, two other courses, each of one year, were being run even up to the time of writing. A Foreign Service Course for officials from developing countries was held at Q. E. H. in which about half the participants came from the Commonwealth. Another course was run for administrators from the Hong Kong Government. Queen Elizabeth House, though it never had the resources to become 'a Commonwealth All Souls', as some had hoped, also administered short individual Fellowships for senior Government officials, notably from India, who wished to come and 'recharge their batteries'.

The needs of the 1950s and early 1960s were unique. Oxford dons not only taught on the courses but went out to teach and carry out research in the new Universities which were set up in Africa, Asia and the West Indies. Nothing like this had been needed in India whose Universities had existed for 90 years before Independence, and whose administrators and specialists had been trained for years to take over from the British when they left. The *Oxford Magazine* noted in 1955 that far more money was being spent on the study of Africa than on all other continents put together and that dons were no longer to be found in vacations on the banks of the Seine and Arno but by those of the Niger, Zambesi and Limpopo.[18]

The benefits for Oxford were considerable, particularly in bringing to its African studies, which had hardly existed before 1939, teachers and postgraduate students with a rich first-hand experience of the continent. In the countries of the Commonwealth the courses were particularly appreciated by the small nations, whose officials not only gained from the broadening experience and the wealth of Oxford's teaching and libraries but from the international background. The Governments of the West Indies found that a valuable contribution was made in bringing about mutual knowledge and understanding between the officers who came to Oxford from the different islands. Former participants recollected how much they had learnt from each other informally in the Commonwealth Services Club. Above all what they remembered was, as one wrote in a letter to E. G. Rowe, 'the love and humility of my tutors'.[19]

As for the study of the history of Empire, one of Oxford's most eminent practitioners has described how the missionary fervour for 'Commonwealth' barely survived into the 1950s. The secularisation of Imperial history, he recollected, released levity at seminars unthought of 30 years earlier and strengthened the resolve to discover and to understand historical facts as they appeared to the actors on the global stage at the time, rather than with eyes conditioned by retrospective foresight, theory or theology.[20]

15 Conclusions

It may be that . . . by good government we may educate our subjects into a capacity for better government, that, having become instructed in European knowledge they may in some future age demand European institutions. Whether such a day will ever come I know not. Whenever it comes it will be the proudest day in English history. . . . The sceptre may pass away from us but . . . there is an Empire exempt from all natural causes of decay. . . . The imperishable Empire of our arts and our morals, our literature and our laws.

T. B. Macaulay, Debate in the House of Commons on the East India Company Charter (1833).[1]

Was the Empire Oxford's last lost cause? The cause of Rhodes and Milner, that of a great Union or Federation of the Anglo-Saxon race, had been lost even before Milner died. The hopes of the later Round Table and indeed of the critics of Empire, for a multiracial Empire–Commonwealth based on mutual belief in the rule of law and of democratic, Parliamentary institutions were also to be disappointed in many of the new States.

Parkin's vision of Oxford as a Great Imperial University, which he attributed to Rhodes but which became increasingly his own, only partially became a reality. The Rhodes Scholarship scheme indeed has been Oxford's unique contribution to cooperation between Britain and the Dominions, and with the United States, through mutual understanding between statesmen, diplomats, civil servants and professional bodies. The influence of the network, an open society instead of the secret society originally envisaged by Rhodes, has probably been decisive in more crises than will ever be known. It is a self-perpetuating society, for in order to avoid political patronage, Parkin arranged that it would be committees of former Rhodes Scholars in each country who would select the candidates for future Scholarships.

Beyond the Scholarships, however, it will be recollected how

Parkin had urged that Oxford should make itself the great Imperial teacher of history and geography, establish Schools of Law and Languages which would serve the whole Empire, and above all should organise the greatest School of Government which the world had ever seen.

In his lifetime Oxford became the leading University in Imperial Geography with a high sense of its political relevance, but by the time of his death, the geographers were already losing their Imperial fervour. The colonial historians in Parkin's time were also imbued with the moral significance of Empire, and they did, as he hoped, play a leading part in setting up History Departments in other Universities of the Empire, such as Toronto, Adelaide and Sydney. The teaching of the languages of the Empire however came to be carried out more conveniently in London, whose linguistic resources were far greater than those of Oxford. In law, perhaps, the Empire did as much for Oxford as Oxford did for the Empire, through the Rhodes Scholars who stayed on in Oxford to teach.

The anthropologists in the high period of Indirect Rule worked closely with Whitehall and with colonial Governments, but towards the end of Empire suffered a crisis of conscience lest their academic integrity be diminished by this collaboration. Conversely the Empire did little to stimulate the study of economics at Oxford until in the last phase the Colonial Development and Welfare Acts led to a need for advice and training on the preparation of development plans and aid programmes.

Yet none of these activities were anything like as important in the eyes of Parkin, Lothian and Curtis as study and teaching about Government within the Empire, in which they believed that Oxford could have a unique role in light of the orientation of its Greats and Modern History Schools, of the presence and needs of the Rhodes Scholars, and of the special relationship of All Souls with the decision-makers of Empire. Oxford's contribution in this field was to be by no means insignificant. The Gladstone Professorship of Government was founded in 1912; W. G. S. Adams and K. C. Wheare, who held the Chair, gave considerable attention to Imperial and Commonwealth questions; Margery Perham and her successors in the Readership of Colonial (later Commonwealth) Government, were leading scholars in the subject; Rhodes House Library assembled one of the most comprehensive collections in the world of relevant publications and documents. Yet the great School of Comparative Government of the Empire was never quite achieved. By the time that the Institute of Commonwealth Studies and Q.E.H. were founded, even had funds been available for these kinds of studies, it would have been too late.

For history seems to have shown Parkin and Lothian to be right. The excellent work done in the courses organised by Oxford on administration and development was often to be fruitless because political stability, which is the prerequisite for economic and social development, was lacking in many of the successor States of Empire, whilst others failed to build political institutions which would enable a change of Government to take place in any way except through *coups d'état* and revolutions. If there had been an Institute of Government on the lines desired by Parkin and Lothian there might have been more time and opportunity for reflection on the kind of political and administrative institutions which could best serve new nations in which tribal, religious, regional and linguistic loyalties were strong. Oxford, which had served the Tudors and later suffered for its belief in the Divine Right of Kings, should not have found it difficult to understand the reasons for, and the philosophy of, the one-Party State. In fact, it was more in the old Dominions, in throwing light on relationships between Federal and Provincial Governments, that Oxford teaching seemed to have proved of practical use.

Perhaps it was Jowett whose aspirations were best fulfilled. Oxford obtained a lion's share of the I.C.S. appointments, carrying the idealism of the Greats School and of T. H. Green throughout the Indian Empire. Yet almost alone among his classical Oxford contemporaries, Jowett saw that an alternative to a classical education might have been more appropriate. Unlike other colonial powers, Britain, after the East India Company's College at Haileybury was closed, did not maintain a special training institution for colonial administrators. Even within the University, however, it was possible to devise a degree course in which the cultural, historical, economic and social characteristics could be studied of the regions where the future administrators would serve, instead of those of Ancient Greece and Rome. Oxford opinion preferred the latter, and Jowett's degree course in Indian Studies lasted for too short a time for the effect on the careers of I.C.S. graduates to be adequately compared with that of Greats on their contemporaries. Such evidence as has been found suggests that the knowledge of Sanskrit and of Indian traditions which the graduates in Indian Studies acquired opened doors which helped them considerably in their work. The content of the one-year courses which were subsequently run for I.C.S. and colonial probationers do not seem to have made much impact on most the British participants, though they were valuable for the probationers from overseas.

In the next generation Furse achieved for a time his ambition of recruiting a colonial administrative Service which was less intellectual and more athletic than the I.C.S. almost exclusively from amongst Oxford and Cambridge men who had attended Public Schools. In his old age however he watched with dismay the attacks on élitism and colonialism prevail and his work 'bedevilled at home by those death watch beetles who have worked all my life to rot the noble fabric bequeathed to us by our ancestors'.[2]

Jowett's achievement of making hard work fashionable at Oxford was to have a profound influence on the future colonial administrators, British or indigenous, who came to study there. If there is any group of heroes in the story of Oxford and Empire it is the College tutors to whom the colonial students, alone or in pairs, would read their weekly essays and who would shock and stimulate them with unorthodox comments. Their kindness, tolerance and encouragement emerge from the memoirs of almost all colonials who studied in Oxford, even of those who complain of the attitudes of fellow undergraduates. The wise and lasting relationship is seen in letters which their former pupils wrote back to them from all over the Empire. In the days when College Fellows had to be bachelors, these pupils were in a sense the sons they never had; later generations of married tutors, like A. L. Smith and Kenneth Bell, would bring the colonials into their large and sometimes tumultuous families.

The tutorial system or relationship was one of the characteristics of the educational methods which Oxford men tried to carry with them to the new Colleges of the Empire which they helped to establish. It was an expensive system, only practicable within an élitist society. But on the whole it was not the educators but administrators and politicians who chose to create aristocratic schools and Colleges for the sons of Chiefs in India and Africa or for the rich in the white Dominions. Jowett's disciples, wherever they were, sought to hang out ladders of scholarships to enable talented youths of whatever background to join the élite.

Sometimes the exported Oxford traditions of the pre-eminence of classical studies, segregation of sexes, wearing of gowns and enthusiasm for organised games lasted longer than in Oxford itself. Elsewhere they were radically transformed in the period immediately before and after Independence when American funds and technical assistance became lavishly available for higher and secondary education.

For the missionaries the Empire had opened up or facilitated vast areas of work, though in the end some of them had found colonial rule an embarrassment. It has been seen how their achievements in terms of conversions were much more tangible in Africa and the Pacific than in India. The Oxford influence tended to be conservative in the broadest sense. As Stacey Waddy of Balliol wrote about Africa on the occasion of the hundredth anniversary of the Oxford Movement in 1933:

> Our prayer is that of the teachings and customs of the ancient past they may throw nothing away that is good. Are not the ideas of a corporate tribal life, of the dead as still living, of careful initiation into the tribal life and culture which characterise an African people, rich material to be transmitted into Christian conceptions and to find fulfilment in the offered life with the Catholic Church?[3]

Such an approach fitted smoothly into colonial systems of Indirect Rule. It was likely to have to adapt drastically after Independence, however, to the aspirations of societies or their political leadership who were determined on rapid modernisation and industrialisation.

A few threads which run through this study may be drawn together. One is the role of Oxford women in the Empire. Something has been seen of the work as teachers and missionaries in which most of them were engaged because they were almost entirely excluded from the administrative and professional services in which so many Oxford men found their careers.

The first two generations of women to be admitted to the new Halls for women at Oxford from the 1880s were of outstanding ability and intelligence, for the demand for places greatly exceeded the supply. At a time when equal status for women in the University had not yet been achieved, they were sternly trained to work hard and keep a low and modest profile. There were a few who broke through the barriers which confined them in the Empire to teaching and social work. Perhaps the most notable was Gertrude Bell (1868–1926) who became one of the best-known figures in British administration of the Middle East. At L.M.H. she was the earliest Oxford woman to achieve a First in Modern History. She then spent years travelling in the Middle East and Arabia, learning Arabic and Persian. Hogarth brought her to Cairo in the First World War to work in the Arab Bureau. Later she worked as Oriental Secretary in the Iraq Government, where her knowledge of the tribes made her invaluable. She edited an Arabic newspaper, was Honorary Director of Archaeology, and charmed Iraqi notables into serving as Ministers under the British Mandate, making no secret of her hopes for early political independence for the Arab peoples.[4]

Another traveller with a purpose was Ella Sykes of L.M.H. who wrote her first book *Through Persia on a Side Saddle* for the benefit of other women ' who felt the wanderlust but were unable to gratify their longing for adventure'. Later, in 1912, she was impressed by a letter in *The Times* on 'What To Do with Our Unmarried Daughters' which discussed the openings which might exist in the Empire for Britain's million surplus women. Impulsively she went out to Canada to investigate the possibilities, working as a hired help in remote prairie farms, scrubbing floors and cooking for dozens of farm-hands. She wrote a book on her experiences, calling on British women to come out to Canada as nurses, teachers and secretaries and 'do their part in building the Empire and standing for higher ideals than the almighty dollar'.[5]

The intellectual quality of the early Oxford women, together with the courage, patience and devotion with which they sought to make good use of their rare education suggest that their talents might profitably have been used more widely if those who ruled the Empire had possessed the imagination and courage to do so.

Little has been said about the role of Oxford men and women in industry and commerce, for in the high period of Empire this was slight. Curzon whilst Chancellor observed how businessmen considered Oxford graduates to be ill-equipped to enter their firms and he urged in vain that a diploma course be established in Business Education,[6] but it has been seen how the proposal was rejected by Congregation in 1914. The Asquith Commission in 1920 deplored Oxford's lack of interest in the research needs of the Empire in industry and commerce as compared with that shown by the Universities of Germany and Japan.[7] As can be seen from Table A.2 in the Appendix the proportion of Oxford men in the Empire who worked in the private sector rose somewhat after 1919 but even up to 1939 there was a prejudice amongst undergraduates against going into 'trade' which was one reason why the University was found to be such a fruitful field of recruitment for the colonial administrative Service.

From time to time this study has touched on the attitude to race of Oxford administrators, missionaries, dons and undergraduates. Yet it is far from clear what the influences were which caused eminent Oxford men to express themselves so insensitively on the subject in the late nineteenth century. If Curzon's Viceregal speeches were patronising and irritating, the remarks of Lord Salisbury, who was Chancellor of the University as well as Prime Minister, were brutal. Opposing Home Rule for Ireland, he observed in 1886 that 'you could not confide free representative institutions to Hottentots, and that self-government only worked well when confided to people of Teutonic race'.[8] When the Parsee Dadabhai Naoroji ran for Parliament in a London constituency in 1892, Salisbury's election message to his opponent was that 'we had not got to the point where a British constituency would elect a black man'.[9] For Salisbury's conviction that only Teutonic races could work democratic institutions Oxford historians had some responsibility. Theories of Social Darwinism, by which nations and races were classified in order of evolution, originated outside Oxford but were widely held by Oxford men, with the notable exception of the missionaries. One difficulty is that different people used 'race' in different senses. For Max Mueller the 'Aryan race' usually meant the Indo-Europeans whose languages shared a common origin. Sometimes the reference to race was used to describe the unity of the British people wherever they might settle. This is what Lord Rosebery meant when in his Rectorial Speech at Glasgow University in 1900, he asked rhetorically 'What is Empire if it is not race?'[10] The British in fact were an amalgam of races, and their settlement overseas could create problems for, and even lead to the extermination of, the indigenous inhabitants, but used in a patriotic sense, as Milner used it, the expression of devotion to the British race did not necessarily imply a contempt for or hostility towards other races. Indeed, a characteristic of Oxford colonial administrators was to admire the noble savage and prefer him to the urban élite.

The critics of the exponents of British racial superiority in Oxford never gave up; what is not clear is why their views came so suddenly to prevail. The conversion of Curtis, Lothian and some other members of the Round Table from the arrogant attitudes of racial, national and indeed Oxford superiority which they held in South Africa into those which they came to express after 1918 is particularly striking.

The influence of Oxford on the Empire cannot be assessed without taking into account the influence of the Public Schools on the men who came up to Oxford. This made itself felt in several ways: it led to a class-consciousness, which sometimes but not always was associated with race-consciousness, and to the formation of cliques which students from other parts of the world found discouraging. In the colonial Empire the experience of the prefect system fitted conveniently either into systems of Direct or Indirect Rule.

The sense of Oxford superiority which men coming up from Public Schools acquired at the University on top of their existing feeling of class and race superiority often exasperated foreigners. Allied to it was a quality which critics might call facetiousness and friends might call whimsy and which was one of Oxford's peculiar characteristics in the Imperial period. The effect on a bewildered foreigner of Oxford's style of solemn teasing is seen in a book by Jacques Bardoux, a Frenchman who spent a term in Oxford in 1895 at the age of 21. He was appalled by the way in which lectures were given by men who had not learned how to teach; he deplored the general lack of intellectual curiosity, but admired Oxford as a school for political success. When, however, he tried to enter into a serious discussion of colonial disputes between France and Britain, he was gravely asked, 'How can we ever be friends with the French? Why, you are always laughing at the size of our women's feet!' Among the information which he passed on to his French readers was that unpopular students were put on top of bonfires at Bump Suppers, and that abandoned women were imprisoned by the Vice-Chancellor.[11]

Once a man had held office in the Oxford Union, he was liable to lapse into its frivolous style at any time in later life. Even A. V. Dicey, the eminent Professor of Constitutional Law, would tell his bewildered pupils, many of them from the Empire and the United States, that it was better to be flippant than dull.[12]

The late nineteenth and early twentieth centuries were the great period for hoaxes and practical jokes among undergraduates, some of whom never grew out of the habit. All over the Empire stories were told of the eccentricities of Oxford men. This was not necessarily unfortunate; it was a safety valve for an independence of spirit which questioned and even laughed at the unimaginative instructions based on precedent which were churned out of great bureaucratic machines like the Government of India. Even Curzon's minutes show a strong sense of the ridiculous which helped to maintain his sanity as he fought a losing battle with the files.

Although this study is concerned only with Oxford and Empire, it may be borne in mind that the influence on and of the United States was also considerable. In 1958 there were three places called Oxford in Canada, one each in Australia and New Zealand, and 20 in the United States.[13] As many Rhodes Scholars came from the United States as from the whole of the Empire, and it was pressure on behalf of American Rhodes Scholars quite as much as of those from the Empire which was exerted on behalf of abolition of compulsory Greek and Latin and of the expansion of graduate studies.

Some Cambridge views on Oxford and Empire have been mentioned in the Introduction. In general Cambridge had little understanding or use for Oxford's romantic attitude to Empire. R. E. Robinson has recently described how the high moral tone of Oxford's historians of Empire and their penchant for presenting the Imperial record teleologically in terms of an ideal end appeared from Cambridge to offer more faith than science.[14] On the other hand the Utilitarians who dominated Cambridge in the late nineteenth century were mostly lawyers whose concern for law and order caused them to resist the demand for relinquishment of British Rule in India and Egypt;[15] thus they had little sympathy with the Oxford critics of Empire. Despite occasional expressions of jealousy, Cambridge appeared less interested in the Empire and its governance than Oxford. Its representatives, for example, seldom bothered to attend the meetings of the Devonshire Committee on the postwar training of the Colonial Administrative Service.

At the end of Empire, as in one country after another the Union flag was lowered at midnight, there were often Oxford men present at the Independence ceremonies, both British and local, who may have reflected on Oxford's contribution to what Macaulay had foreseen as the proudest day in English history, and to his 'imperishable Empire of our arts and our morals, our literature and our laws'. Oxford made no great contribution to the arts of Empire. Though Ruskin's insistence that the Gothic style was fit for every purpose resulted in some bizarre Imperial public buildings, including railway stations, the prolific architects of Government Houses and Legislatures, such as Lutyens and Baker, were not Oxford men. As for literature, few of the major Victorian novelists, the commentaries on whose work were studied with such lamentable results by Indian failed B. A.s, were from Oxford either. In any case, the subject of 'Commonwealth Literature' had to be invented after Independence to help the new but English-speaking States to escape from the continuing burden of cultural colonisation. Partly as a consequence of Empire, English was to become the foremost world language, but despite the authority of the *Oxford Dictionary* it was increasingly the American version which prevailed.

The laws and constitutions which the British left behind were often superseded by American, French, Islamic or Marxist models. If

Macaulay's reference to morals implies a moral code, though the immediate successors to the British, a considerable number of whom had studied at Oxford, shared the traditions of Civil Service impartiality and of academic freedom, it seemed doubtful whether these would persist in later generations within the one-Party States.

It is in none of these aspects that the Oxford legacy seems important, but in an influence which is less easy to define.

Although Bright used to refer to Oxford as the home of dead languages and undying prejudices, in fact what made most impression on those who came to study there from the Empire was the atmosphere of amiable tolerance in which every kind of opinion could be expressed, and almost any kind of behaviour tolerated, so long as it was not antisocial. Perhaps, as Zimmern observed, what Oxford did not seek to do was as important as what it did in the Imperial context. Most visitors were happy, some were unhappy; but in hardly any of the memoirs which they left is there a suggestion of a conscious attempt by their teachers to indoctrinate them with a philosophy of Empire or with the civilising mission of Britain. Curtis indeed was a proselytiser, but only held a University appointment for a year. C. R. L. Fletcher too gave up his University career in order to concentrate on his writing. Freeman's lectures might have racial tones, and Egerton's perorations sometimes wandered into a mystical Imperialism, but undergraduates needed no more to express agreement with them than with any of the wide variety of sermons, High, Broad and Low Church, which they could sample on Sundays. Attendance at lectures was not even compulsory, and a First Class degree was obtained not for the candidate's opinions but for the skill with which he marshalled his arguments. In short, Oxford prided itself that it taught its students not what to think but how to think.

Yet despite this, there was a belief, inspired both by Oxford's Anglican and classical traditions, that the study of history, ancient and modern, was most important for its moral lessons, and that man's highest form of activity was to be found in Government and in the service of his fellows. This was often implicit rather than explicit, but it was what made first Jowett and Toynbee, later Coupland, Hancock and Margery Perham, devote so much care to the education of I. C. S. and colonial probationers.

Oxford confirmed among its undergraduates attitudes of responsibility for weaker members of society which, at its best, had been inculcated in the prefect system of the Public Schools; and it was no accident that the high period of Empire coincided with the University's involvement in settlement work in the slums of East London, nor that Oxford men were so successful in the early paternal stage of Imperial and colonial rule. But the urban poor eventually became capable of standing on their own feet; the fags progressed to become prefects themselves. So too inexorably the ethic of Trusteeship led to acceptance that all the peoples of the Empire, at various paces adapted to their level of development, were destined at some time to exercise self-government. The acceptance may have been eased by the lessons of the impermanence of Empires derived from study of the history of Athens and Rome.

In a sense it is too early to try to assess Oxford's influence on Empire, for the history of Empire can often only be understood in light of the history of the Commonwealth which succeeded it, and for the latter the records are not yet open: indeed we are still too close even to the Imperial period for objectivity to be easy. At a later time Oxford may bring to the study of that period the same broad approach as it has to the history and civilisation of Greece and Rome. If it does so, the story of its own connections with Empire may usefully point the way to broader themes.

Meanwhile, looking back to the period between the mid-nineteenth and mid-twentieth centuries, it appears that there were a succession of controversies in which those in Oxford who favoured the Empire – Commonwealth idea were generally on the losing side. Firstly, dreams of Imperial Federation were shattered not by opposition at home but by the refusal of the Dominions to place control of their foreign policy and defence in the hands of an Imperial Parliament. Next, after the First World War, in what Lothian saw as the debate between the spirits of Woodrow Wilson and Cecil Rhodes for the loyalty of those who formed public opinion, the former on the whole prevailed and eventually even Curtis and Lothian subordinated their Imperial sentiments to broader associations. Then after the Second World War British Governments forsook the role of cultural centre of the Commonwealth for the cause of European integration, signalising this by instructing the Universities to charge students from the Commonwealth fees which were two or three times as high as those paid by Europeans.

Finally, interest in the Commonwealth was largely submerged in the broader enthusiasm for studying the problems and helping the countries of the Third World, symbolised by Oxfam, based in Oxford itself. As this book goes to press, the University's Committee and Institute for Commonwealth Studies as well as the Commonwealth

Forestry Institute all appear to be about to shed the Commonwealth name.

The Commonwealth has shown unexpected resilience, and whatever the bias of Government in favour of European cultural links, Oxford appears likely for the foreseeable future to retain its special relationship through the Rhodes Scholarships. As for the cause of Empire, the last word may be left with the Australian, Sir William Crocker, whose long career as a British colonial official, with the United Nations and as his country's High Commissioner to several Commonwealth countries has already been seen. As he looked back to his days as an undergraduate at Balliol when Lionel Curtis had captured him for the cause of Empire, 'Lost causes', he wrote in his memoirs in 1981, 'are too often taken for causes which never had a case or a chance. The winning causes are not necessarily the best causes; or indeed the only causes which could have won. . . . What is clear now, but was not clear then, is how much those interested in, let alone concerned about the Empire were in a minority, and a small minority.'[16]

Appendix

TABLES ON NUMBER, PROFESSION AND COUNTRY OF WORK OF OXFORD MEN AND WOMEN WHO WORKED IN THE EMPIRE

In all tables periods of less than two years and military and diplomatic postings are excluded. India includes what became Burma and Pakistan. Sudan is shown under Middle East. St John's commences 1875/6.

Sources: men's Colleges, published Registers of Balliol College of 1934, 1952, 1969, 1983; of St John's, 1981; of Keble, 1970. These are the only men's Colleges to have published Registers covering the whole period. Women's Colleges, published Registers of L.M.H., 1970; Somerville (n.d.) covering the period 1879–1971; St Hilda's, 1977; unpublished Registers of St Hugh's and O.H.S. (later St Anne's).

When a person worked in more than one country, only the longest period is included.

TABLE A.1 *Number and percentage of Balliol, Keble and St John's Colleges matriculates known to have worked in the British Empire outside U.K. shown by year of matriculation*

	Balliol	*Keble*	*St John's*
Number of matriculates 1874/5–1913/14	2,208	2,160	1,541
Number of these who worked in Empire	600	441	257
Percentage who worked in Empire	27.1	20.4	16.7
Number of matriculates 1918/19–1937/38	1,683	1,318	1,158
Number of these who worked in Empire	306	264	177
Percentage who worked in Empire	18.2	20.0	15.3

TABLE A.2 *Percentage of Balliol, Keble and St John's Colleges matriculates known to have worked in the British Empire outside U.K. shown by profession*

	Balliol		*Keble*		*St John's*	
	1874/5–1913/14	1918/19–1937/8	1874/5–1913/14	1918/19–1937/8	1875/6–1913/14	1918/19–1937/8
Religious	4.0	4.2	43.3	31.4	29.2	12.4
Education	12.7	30.1	14.5	22.3	15.6	18.7
Indian Services	50.0	13.7	7.7	6.4	19.8	10.7
Colonial Services	10.9	17.0	13.3	23.1	16.3	26.7
Dominion Services	1.7	7.2	0	0.4	0.8	4.5
Private sector	9.3	16.0	13.0	8.7	8.2	19.2
Law	8.8	9.1	4.0	4.2	7.8	4.0
Medicine	1.3	2.6	2.3	0.4	2.3	4.0
Unknown	1.0		1.8	3.0		

TABLE A.3 *Percentage of Balliol, Keble and St John's matriculates known to have worked in the British Empire outside U.K. shown by country of work*

	Balliol		*Keble*		*St John's*	
	1874/5–1913/14	1918/19–1937/8	1874/5–1913/14	1918/19–1937/8	1875/6–1913/14	1918/19–1937/8
India	58.4	22.2	21.0	18.6	37	20.6
S. Africa and Rhodesia	6.7	8.7	25.5	14.4	9.5	11.9
Canada	8.0	11.6	11.8	5.7	8.6	13.9
Australia and N.Z.	9.8	18.3	15.3	12.9	12.5	6.7
W. Indies	1.5	2.1	3.3	6.1	7.3	5.1
Africa (ex. S. Africa and Rhodesia)	6.1	19.6	10.4	22.3	9.9	20.6
Asia (ex. India) and Pacific	3.8	9.5	10.4	13.3	7.8	10.8
Middle East and Mediterranean	4.1	7.9	2.6	6.8	7.3	10.3

TABLE A.4 *Number of women who entered Oxford between* 1879/80 *and* 1913/14 *and are known to have worked in the Empire outside U.K., by profession*

	Somerville	*L.M.H.*	*St Hugh's*	*St Hilda's*	*O.H.S. (St Anne's)*	*Total*
Education	47	21	19	9	26	122
Religious	6	14	7	4	6	37
Social work	7	1	1	1	1	11
Medicine Health	2	1		2	3	8
Administration	1	1		1		3
Secretarial	1		2			3
Law	1					1
Other	1					1
TOTAL	66	38	29	17	36	186

N.B.: for note on data see Table A.5.

TABLE A.5 *Number of women who entered Oxford between 1879/80 and 1913/14 and are known to have worked in the Empire outside U.K., by country of work*

	Somerville	*L.M.H.*	*St Hugh's*	*St Hilda's*	*O.H.S. (St Anne's)*	*Total*
India	29	19	5	9	27	89
S. Africa and Rhodesia	19	6	14	4	5	48
Canada	9	4	4	1	1	19
Australia and N.Z.	3	3		2	3	11
W. Indies			1	1		2
Africa (ex. S. Africa)	2	1	3			6
Asia (ex. India)	3		2			5
Middle East and Mediterranean	1	5				6
TOTAL	66	38	29	17	36	186

NOTE Somerville and L.M.H. statistics commenced in 1879; St Hugh's in 1889; St Hilda's in 1893; O.H.S. in 1888. College Registers are deficient in information on professions in the early years.

Most of the 'religious' were also engaged in education.

TABLE A.6 *Number of women who entered Oxford between* 1918/19 *and* 1938/9 *and are known to have worked in the Empire outside U.K., by profession*

	Somerville	*L.M.H.*	*St Hugh's*	*St Hilda's*	*O.H.S. (St Anne's)*	*Total*
Education	49	36	65	37	61	248
Religious	3	4	6	4	7	24
Social work	1		7	2	4	14
Medicine/Health	1	1	3		2	13
Government/Admin.	3	2	1	2	2	7
Secretarial	3	1	3		2	9
Law	2		2		2	6
Journalism/Broadcasting	2					2
Scientific research	2	1	1		1	5
Librarian	1	1	2	1		5
Other and unknown	5	4	4	2		15
TOTAL	72	50	94	48	81	345

N.B.: for note on data see Table A.7.

TABLE A.7 *Number of women who entered Oxford between* 1918/19 *and* 1938/9 *and are known to have worked in the Empire outside U.K., by country of work*

	Somerville	*L.M.H.*	*St Hugh's*	*St Hilda's*	*O.H.S. (St Anne's)*	*Total*
India	14	12	12	5	16	59
S. Africa and Rhodesia	12	7	14	11	18	62
Canada	12	6	15	3	8	44
Australia and N.Z.	13	5	11	7	15	51
W. Indies	1		2	1	3	7
Africa (ex. S. Africa)	10	15	16	14	11	66
Asia (ex. India)	1	2	8	6	4	21
Middle East and Mediterranean	9	2	16	1	6	34
Unspecified (missionary)		1				1
TOTAL	72	50	94	48	81	345

NOTE The percentage of the women who entered Oxford and subsequently worked in the Empire is impossible to ascertain because information is unavailable on many careers. In the two Colleges with the most comprehensive records the percentage is shown as:

Somerville 1879/80–1913/14 – 8.5%;1918/19–1938/9 – 6.7%.

St Hugh's 1886/7–1913/14 – 10%; 1918/19–1938/9 – 8.9%.

This is certainly below the true figure.

Notes

NOTES TO THE INTRODUCTION

1. L. Stephen, *Studies of a Biographer*, vol. II (London, 1898) pp. 125–7.
2. *Congress of Universities of the Empire*, Report of Proceedings (London, 1912) p. 10; G. C. Brodrick, *Memories and Impressions* (London, 1900) p. 214.
3. Anon., *Government by Mallardry* (London, 1932), in All Souls College Library.
4. C. T. Allmany, *Lancastrian Normandy in France* (Oxford, 1983) p. 113.
5. C. Grant Robertson, *All Souls College* (London, 1894) p. 3.
6. H. Hall, 'Origin of Lord Almoner's Professorship of Arabic', *Athenaeum* (16 Nov. 1889) p. 673.
7. W. W. Hunter, 'A Forgotten Oxford Movement', *Fortnightly Review*, vol. 65 (1896) p. 689.
8. Goldwin Smith, *Inaugural Lecture as Regius Professor of Modern History* (Oxford, 1859) pp. 3ff.
9. W. Stubbs, *Lectures on Medieval and Modern History* (Oxford, 1886) p. 5.
10. B. B. Misra, *Central Administration of the East India Co.* (Manchester, 1959) p. 383.
11. A. F. Madden, 'The Commonwealth, Commonwealth History and Oxford 1905–1971', in A. F. Madden and D. K. Fieldhouse (eds), *Oxford and the Idea of Commonwealth* (London, 1982) pp. 7ff.

NOTES TO CHAPTER 1: THE VIEW FROM THE SENIOR COMMON ROOM

1. E. Huws Jones, *Mrs Humphrey Ward* (London, 1973) p. 35.
2. *Oxford Magazine*, vol. 4 (16 June 1886) p. 253.
3. Ibid., vol. 10 (10 Feb. 1892) p. 153; vol. 10 (24 Feb. 1892) p. 253; vol. 11 (15 Feb. 1893) p. 218.
4. Ibid., vol. 17 (7 June 1899) p. 406.
5. Ibid., vol. 12 (28 Nov. 1893) p. 125.
6. Ibid., vol. 21 (21 May 1903) p. 8.
7. Ibid., vol. 29 (20 Oct. 1910) p. 5 and vol. 15 (17 Feb. 1897) p. 197.
8. Ibid., vol. 28 (3 Feb. 1910) p. 171.
9. Ibid., vol. 5 (15 June 1887) p. 274.
10. Ibid., vol. 25 (28 Nov. 1906) p. 115.
11. Ibid., vol. 1 (5 Dec. 1883) p. 433.
12. Ibid., vol. 13 (6 and 13 Feb. 1895) pp. 196, 213.
13. Ibid., vol. 15 (18 Nov. 1896) p. 75.
14. Ibid., vol. 13 (23 Jan. 1895) p. 167.

15. Ibid., vol. 4 (16 June 1886) p. 254.
16. Ibid., vol. 18 (23 May 1900) p. 350.
17. Ibid., vol. 18 (30 May 1900) p. 370.
18. Ibid., vol. 18 (30 May 1900) p. 368.
19. Ibid., vol. 18 (6 June 1900) p. 389.
20. Ibid., vol. 20 (5 Feb. 1902) p. 189.
21. Ibid., vol. 20 (12 Feb. 1902) p. 208.
22. Ibid., vol. 20 (30 Apr. 1902) pp. 295–6.
23. Ibid., vol. 20 (30 Apr. 1902) p. 799 and in A. D. Godley, *Fifty Poems*, (Oxford, 1927) p. 32.
24. Ibid., vol. 20 (7 May 1902) p. 314.
25. Ibid., vol. 22 (2 Mar. 1904) p. 238.
26. Ibid., vol. 23 (8 Feb. 1905) p. 171.
27. Ibid., vol. 26 (21 May 1908) p. 319.
28. The Hon. Mrs Gell, *Under Three Reigns* (London, 1927) p. 162.
29. L. K. Haldane, *Friends and Kindred* (London, 1961) p. 187.
30. *Oxford Magazine*, vol. 27 (20 May 1909) p. 309.
31. Ibid., vol. 27 (19 Nov. 1908) p. 88.
32. Ibid., vol. 29 (9 Mar. 1911) p. 280.
33. Sir H. Newbolt, *My World as in My Time* (London, 1932) p. 96.
34. *Oxford Magazine*, vol. 24 (18 Oct. 1905) p. 2.
35. Ibid., vol. 24 (18 Oct. 1905) p. 2.
36. Ibid., vol. 32 (23 Oct. 1913) p. 22.
37. Ibid., vol. 6 (19 Jan. 1887) p. 3.
38. Ibid., vol. 8, (6 Nov. 1889) p. 52.
39. Ibid., vol. 9 (10 June 1891) p. 400.
40. Ibid., vol. 10 (7 Dec. 1892) p. 145.
41. Ibid., vol. 47 (5 Dec. 1894) p. 134.
42. Ibid., vol. 19 (22 May 1901) p. 360.
43. Ibid., vol. 32 (4 Dec. 1913) p. 133.
44. Ibid., vol. 36 (3 May 1918) p. 234.
45. Ibid., vol. 40 (22 June 1921) p. 447.
46. Ibid., vol. 19 (21 Nov. 1900) p. 96.
47. Ibid., vol. 28 (24 Feb. 1910) p. 234.
48. Ibid., vol. 32 (29 Jan. 1914) p. 162.
49. Ibid., vol. 33 (16 Oct. 1914) p. 9.
50. Ibid., vol. 34 (25 Feb. 1916) p. 208 and vol. 35 (15 Feb. 1917) p. 169.
51. Ibid., vol. 37 (8 Nov. 1918) p. 49 and p. 60.
52. Ibid., vol. 38 (31 Oct. 1919) p. 46.
53. Ibid., vol. 38 (18 June 1920) p. 398.
54. Ibid., vol. 40 (8 Dec. 1921) p. 146.
55. Ibid., vol. 41 (2 Nov. 1922) p. 38.
56. Ibid., vol. 43 (13 Nov. 1924) p. 101.
57. Ibid., vol. 43 (29 Jan. 1925) p. 224.
58. Ibid., vol. 48 (14 Nov. 1929) p. 194.
59. Ibid., vol. 48 (30 Jan. 1930) p. 392.
60. Ibid., vol. 45 (25 Nov. 1926) p. 147.
61. Ibid., vol. 63 (19 Oct. 1944) p. 7. He was R. E. T. Latham.
62. Ibid., vol. 55 (4 Feb. 1937) p. 354.

63. Cecil Headlam, *Ten Thousand Miles through India and Burma: An Account of the Oxford University Authentics' Cricket Tour in the Year of the Coronation Durbar* (London, 1903) pp. 94, 98, 169.

NOTES TO CHAPTER TWO: PROPHETS, CLASSICS AND PHILOSOPHER KINGS

1. Balliol College Library, Jowett–Nightingale MSS, B. Jowett to F. Nightingale (4 Dec. 1873).
2. J. MacMillan Brown, *Memoirs* (Christchurch, N. Z., 1974) pp. 36ff. and Winwoode Reade, *The Martyrdom of Man* (London, 1925 edn) pp. xxv, 430.
3. J. Ruskin, *Lectures in Art,* vol. 20: *Collected Works* (London, 1903) p. 41.
4. J. Ruskin, *A Knight's Faith* (1885), in *Collected Works*, vol. 31 (London, 1903) p. 505.
5. E. B. Poulton, *Viriamu Jones and Other Oxford Memories* (London, 1911) pp. 244–7.
6. J. A. Hobson, *Confessions of an Economic Heretic* (London, 1938) and *D.N.B.* article on J. A. Hobson by R. H. Tawney.
7. E. Abbott and L. Campbell, *Life and Letters of Benjamin Jowett*, vol. I (London, 1897) p. 170.
8. Ibid., p. 119.
9. M. Richter, *Politics of Conscience: T. H. Green and his Age* (London, 1964) p. 70.
10. Jowett–Nightingale MSS, Jowett to Nightingale (28 May 1888).
11. Abbott and Campbell, *Life and Letters*, p. 126.
12. Jowett–Nightingale MSS, Jowett to Nightingale (4 Jan. and 19 Mar. 1870).
13. Abbott and Campbell, *Life and Letters*, p. 165.
14. Richter, *Politics of Conscience*.
15. A. Toynbee, *Progress and Poverty* (London, 1883) p. 54.
16. *Oxford Magazine*, vol. 1 (18 Apr. 1883) p. 149 and (21 Nov. 1883) p. 384.
17. Jowett–Nightingale MSS, Jowett to Nightingale (19 Feb. 1872).
18. Abbott and Campbell, *Life and Letters*, vol. II, p. 161.
19. D. Forbes, *The Liberal Anglican Idea of History* (Cambridge, 1952) pp. 31–4.
20. L. Stephen, *Studies of a Biographer*, vol. II (London, 1898) p. 128.
21. Richter, *Politics of Conscience*, p. 144.
22. For example R. Braibanti, *Administration and Economic Development in India* (London, 1963) p. 9.
23. R. Jenkyns, *The Victorians and Ancient Greece* (Oxford, 1980) p. 337.
24. Sir George Schuster, *Private Life and Public Causes* (Cowbridge, 1979) p. 4 and *passim*, and in conversation with the writer.
25. P. Woodruff, *The Men Who Ruled India* (London, 1953).
26. E. Glyn, *Romantic Adventure* (London, 1936) p. 128.
27. W. T. Arnold, *Studies of Roman Imperialism* (Manchester, 1906) p. lxxix.

28. *Oxford Magazine*, vol. 7 (19 June 1889) p. 398.
29. C. P. Lucas, *Greater Rome and Greater Britain* (Oxford, 1912) p. 97.
30. J. Bryce, *The Ancient Roman Empire and the British Empire in India* (London, 1914) p. 41.
31. Ibid., p. 59.
32. Ibid., p. 2.
33. R. M. Ogilvie, *Latin and Greek* (London, 1964) p. 136.
34. N. Mitchell, *Sir George Cunningham* (London, 1968) p. 173.
35. Lord Rosebery, *Questions of Empire* (London, 1921) p. 246.
36. Oxford University Appointments Committee Papers, letter from Ministère des Finances, Cairo (Nov. 1910).
37. *Report of Royal Commission on Public Services in India*, vol. XI (London, 1914) p. 86.
38. See p. 18 above.
39. Lord Ronaldshay, *Life of Lord Curzon*, vol. I (London, 1928) p. 20.
40. J. Rennell Rodd, *Social and Diplomatic Memories*, vol. III (London, 1925) p. 393.
41. Lord Ronaldshay, *Life of Lord Curzon*, vol. I, p. 49.
42. India Office Library, Curzon MSS, Eur/111/128, Scrapbook.
43. G. N. Curzon, *Problems of the Far East* (London, 1894) title-page.
44. K. Rose, *Superior Person: A Portrait of Curzon and his Circle* (London, 1969) p. 96.
45. Lord Curzon, *Speeches as Viceroy and Governor-General*, vol. 3 (Calcutta, 1904–6) p. 123.
46. Ibid., vol. 1, p. 23.
47. Ibid., vol. 1, p. 245.
48. Ibid., vol. 2, p. 208.
49. Ibid., vol. 2, pp. 313–23.
50. Ibid., vol. 3, p. 262.
51. Ibid., vol. 3, pp. 262–70.
52. Ibid., vol. 4, p. 138.
53. University Education Committee Report (Delhi, 1949).
54. Rose, *Superior Person*, p. 354; also India Office Library, Curzon, 'Autobiographical Fragment'.
55. Rose, *Superior Person*, p. 49 and India Office Library, Curzon, 'Autobiographical Fragment'.
56. J. E. C. Welldon, *Forty Years On* (London, 1935) p. 119.
57. Rose, *Superior Person*, p. 345.
58. Ibid., p. 345.
59. D. Dilks, *Curzon in India*, vol. 1 (London, 1969) p. 105.
60. J. E. C. Welldon, *Recollections and Reflections* (London, 1915) p. 220.
61. J. E. Wrench, *Alfred, Lord Milner* (London, 1958) p. 47.
62. T. O'Brien, *Milner* (London, 1979) p. 36.
63. Wrench, *Alfred, Lord Milner*, p. 40.
64. O'Brien, *Milner*, p. 13.
65. Ibid., p. 105.
66. J. Buchan, *Memory Hold the Door* (London, 1940) p. 103.
67. J. A. Spender, *Sir H. Campbell Bannerman*, vol. I (London, 1923) p. 264.

68. Wrench, *Alfred, Lord Milner*, p. 182.
69. O'Brien, *Milner*, p. 150.
70. Lord Milner, 'Key to My Position', in *Questions of the Hour* (London, 1925) p. 211.
71. A. Milner, *England in Egypt* (London, 1892).
72. Royal Colonial Institute (R.C.I.), *Report of Proceedings*, vol. 39 (1907–8), Address by Lord Milner on 'The Two Empires', p. 332.
73. Sir A. Rumbold, *Watershed in India* (London, 1979) p. 55.
74. Curzon, *Speeches*, vol. 4, p. 84.
75. Lord Curzon, *Subjects of the Day* (London, 1915) pp. 17ff.
76. R.C.I., *Report of Proceedings*, pp. 332ff.
77. Lord Curzon, *The Place of India in the Empire* (London, 1909) p. 23.
78. Lord Milner, *The Nation and the Empire* (London, 1913) p. xxxviii.
79. Ibid., p. xxxii.

NOTES TO CHAPTER THREE: HISTORIANS AND SENTINELS OF EMPIRE

1. W. Stubbs, *Lectures on Medieval and Modern History* (Oxford, 1886) p. 5.
2. J. W. Burrow, *A Liberal Descent* (London, 1981) p. 208.
3. W. R. W. Stephens, *Life and Letters of E. A. Freeman*, vol. II (London, 1895) p. 179.
4. Ibid., vol. II, p. 364.
5. Ibid., vol. I, p. 242.
6. Ibid., vol. II, p. 279.
7. Ibid., vol. II, p. 236.
8. Ibid., vol. I, p. 144.
9. Ibid., vol. II, p. 428.
10. E. A. Freeman, 'Race and Language', in *Historical Essays*, 3rd series (London, 1879) p. 176.
11. *Oxford Magazine*, vol. 1 (18 Apr. 1883) p. 161.
12. H. Paul, *Life of Froude* (London, 1905) p. 215.
13. Cited in Eric Williams, *British Historians in the West Indies* (Trinidad, 1964) pp. 138–40.
14. W. E. Moneypenny and G. E. Buckle, *Life of Benjamin Disraeli*, vol. II (London, 1929) p. 1292.
15. *D.N.B., F. York Powell.*
16. L. S. Amery, *My Political Life*, vol. I (London, 1953) pp. 183–4.
17. H. E. Egerton, *Claims of the Study of Colonial History upon the Attention of the University of Oxford* (Oxford, 1906) p. 31.
18. Rhodes House, Oxford, H. E. Egerton, MS 'Lectures on British Colonies in the Nineteenth Century' (n.d.) Lecture I, p. 2.
19. Ibid., Lecture XIV, p. 31.
20. Ibid., Lecture XIV, p. 32.
21. Ibid., Lecture XV, p. 33.
22. Cited in J. Greenlee, 'A Succession of Seeleys', *Journal of Imperial and Commonwealth History*, vol. 4 (1975–6) p. 272.
23. Ibid., p. 266.
24. Egerton, Lecture XV, p. 33.

25. G. Battiscombe, *Reluctant Pioneer. A Life of Elizabeth Wordsworth* (London, 1978) p. 120.
26. Edward Thompson MSS, R. Coupland to E. Thompson (1 Sep. 1943).
27. R. Coupland, *The Empire in These Days* (London, 1935) p. 29.
28. Information from H. G. Alexander who was present.
29. Williams, *British Historians*, pp. 154–62.
30. Rhodes House, Oxford, R. Coupland MSS, Box 5, Address to Oxford Indian Majlis Society (25 Feb. 1931).
31. Coupland MSS, Box 6, review in the *Observer* (1 Mar. 1922).
32. V. Harlow, *The Historian and British Colonial History*, Inaugural Lecture as Beit Professor Colonial History, Oxford (Oxford, 1951) p. 4.
33. Ibid., pp. 8ff.
34. M. Perham, *Native Administration in Nigeria* (London, 1937).
35. Her collected articles were published as *Colonial Sequence*, vol. I (London, 1967); vol. II (1968).
36. Ibid., vol. I, p. 312.
37. M. Perham and L. Curtis, *The Protectorates of South Africa* (London, 1935) pp. 69ff.
38. M. Perham, *The Colonial Reckoning* (London, 1961) p. 154.
39. Ibid., p. 158.
40. Obituaries in *Oxford Magazine*, vol. 52 (10 May 1934) p. 662 and *The Times* (2 May 1934).
41. C. R. L. Fletcher, *Introductory History of England*, vol. V (London, 1904) p. 418.
42. P. Sutcliffe, *The Oxford University Press* (Oxford, 1978) pp. 158–60.
43. C. R. L. Fletcher and Rudyard Kipling, *History of England* (Oxford, 1911) p. 21.
44. Ibid., p. 226.
45. Ibid., p. 238.
46. Ibid., pp. 241–2.
47. Ibid., p. 242.
48. Ibid., p. 228.
49. Ibid., pp. 248, 242.
50. J. W. Bulkeley, *The British Empire, A Short History* (Oxford, 1921) p. 97.
51. Ibid., p. 180.
52. Ibid., p. 209.

NOTES TO CHAPTER FOUR: THE ROUND TABLE AND THEIR FRIENDS

1. B. De Bergerac, *Oxford Pageant of Victory* (Oxford, 1919) p. 1.
2. P. Sutcliffe, *The Oxford University Press* (Oxford, 1978) p. 101 and *New College Record* (1979) p. 15.
3. S. L. Nimocks, *Milner's Young Men* (Duke, U.S.A., 1968) pp. 22ff.
4. R. Stokes, *Political Ideas of Imperialism* (Oxford, 1960) *passim*.
5. Bodleian Library, H. A. L. Fisher MSS, Box 3, fol. 16, P. Kerr to H. A. L. Fisher (21 May 1905).
6. Ibid., Kerr to Fisher (23 Mar. 1906).

7. Ibid., L. Curtis to Fisher (25 Jan. 1909) and R. H. Brand to Fisher (15 Feb. 1909).
8. Bodleian Library, L. Curtis MSS, Box 1, L. Curtis to O. Fleming (24 May 1901) and *The Times of Natal*, Box 1, fol. 126 (n.d.).
9. J. E. Wrench, *Geoffrey Dawson and Our Times* (London, 1955) p. 51.
10. Curtis MSS, Box 1, Lord Selborne to Curtis (8 Feb. 1909).
11. Ibid., Box 2, Curtis to his mother (1 June 1910).
12. D. Lavin, 'Lionel Curtis and the Idea of Commonwealth', in A. F. Madden and D. K. Fieldhouse (eds), *Oxford and the Idea of Commonwealth* (London, 1982) pp. 104ff.; also D. Lavin, 'History, Morals and Politics of Empire', in J. Bossy and P. Jupp (eds), *Essays Presented to M. Roberts* (Belfast, 1976) p. 129.
13. *Oxford Magazine*, vol. 4 (8 Dec. 1886) p. 416.
14. R. A. Cosgrove, *The Rule of Law: A. V. Dicey, Victoran Jurist* (London, 1980).
15. L. S. Amery, *My Political Life*, vol. 1 (London, 1953) ch. 10.
16. J. E. Kendle, *Colonial and Imperial Conferences* (London, 1967) p. 73.
17. Bossy and Jupp, *Essays Presented to M. Roberts*, p. 19.
18. J. R. M. Butler, *Lord Lothian* (London, 1960) p. 69.
19. K. C. Wheare, *Constitutional Structure of the Commonwealth* (Oxford, 1960) p. 3.
20. Nimocks, *Milner's Young Men*, p. 160. Fabian Ware was the critic.
21. A. Toynbee, *Acquaintances* (London, 1967) p. 133.
22. Butler, *Lord Lothian*, pp. 38–9.
23. Ibid., p. 242.
24. Ibid., p. 91.
25. Ibid., p. 166.
26. *The Times, History of the Times*, vol. IV (London, 1952) p. 12.
27. Anon., *Government by Mallardry* (London, 1932), in All Souls Library.
28. J. D. B. Miller, *Richard Jebb and the Problem of Empire*, Commonwealth Papers, no. 3, University of London Institute of Commonwealth Studies (1956).
29. Sir George Schuster, *Private Life and Public Causes* (Cowbridge, 1979) p. 63.
30. A. F. Madden, 'The Commonwealth: Commonwealth History and Oxford' in A. F. Madden and D. Fieldhouse (eds), *Oxford and the Idea of Commonwealth* (London, 1982) p. 25.
31. L. Curtis, *With Milner in South Africa* (Oxford, 1951) p. 226.
32. Curtis MSS, Box 1, fol. 222 (27 Nov. 1906).
33. J. Dove, *Letters of John Dove* (London, 1938) p. 15.
34. M. Perham and L. Curtis, *The Protectorates of South Africa* (London, 1935) pp. 69ff. and Butler, *Lord Lothian*, p. 139.
35. E. Grigg, *Faith of an Englishman* (London, 1936) pp. 232, 246.
36. Toynbee, *Acquaintances*, p. 146.
37. Royal Commonwealth Society, London, Macolm Macdonald MS, Autobiography: 'Constant Surprise', p. 154.
38. H. V. Hodson, 'The Round Table 1910–1981', *Round Table* (Oct. 1981) no. 284, p. 31.

39. Lavin, 'History, Morals and Politics of Empire', p. 126.
40. On the Round Table generally, see Nimocks, *Milner's Young Men*, J. E. Kendle, *Round Table and Imperial Union* (Toronto, 1975); Hodson, 'The Round Table 1910–1981', p. 30.

NOTES TO CHAPTER FIVE: PROFESSORS, PRIGS AND PEDANTS – THE CRITICS OF EMPIRE

1. *Hansard*, 3rd series, vol. 169 (5 Feb. 1863) p. 6.
2. *D.N.B.* article on Goldwin Smith by Sir Sidney Lee and E. Wallace. *Goldwin Smith, Victorian Liberal* (Toronto, 1957) pp. 183, 10.
3. Goldwin Smith, *The Empire* (Oxford, 1863) p. 3.
4. Ibid., p. 8.
5. Ibid., pp. 9, 290.
6. Ibid., p. 13.
7. Goldwin Smith, *Inaugural Lecture as Regius Professor of Modern History* (Oxford, 1859) pp. 38–9.
8. *Oxford Magazine,* vol. 4 (2 June 1886) p. 220.
9. Goldwin Smith, *Reminiscences* (New York, 1910) p. 369.
10. Goldwin Smith, *Commonwealth or Empire* (London, 1902) pp. 34ff.
11. Balliol College Library, Jowett–Nightingale MSS, B. Jowett to F. Nightingale (20 May 1874).
12. *Oxford Magazine*, vol. 27 (16 June 1910) p. 393.
13. Ibid., vol. 9 (3 June 1891) p. 394.
14. Vincent Massey, *Canadians and their Commonwealth* (Oxford, 1961) p. 4.
15. F. Harrison, *Autobiographical Memories* (London, 1911) p. 85.
16. R. Congreve, *Gibraltar, or the Foreign Policy of England* (London, 1857) pp. 4ff.
17. R. Congreve, *India* (London, 1857) p. 5.
18. E. H. Pember, 'England and India', in R. Congreve (ed.), *International Policy*, 2nd edn (London, 1884) pp. 155ff.
19. E. H. Beesly, 'England and the Sea', in Congreve (ed.), *International Policy*, p. 113.
20. Harrison, *Autobiographical Memories*, p. 174 and *passim*.
21. M. B., *Recollections of J. H. Bridges* (London, 1908) p. 62.
22. F. H. Torlesse, *J. H. Bridges and his Family* (London, 1912) p. 181.
23. Ibid., p. 210.
24. Ibid., p. 213.
25. Ibid., p. 229.
26. R. Congreve, *Essays* (London, 1874) p. 240.
27. J. L. Hammond, *C. P. Scott* (London, 1934) pp. 12–22.
28. Ibid., p. 344.
29. J. A. Hobson and M. Ginsburg, *L. T. Hobhouse* (London, 1931) pp. 34–40.
30. L. T. Hobhouse, *Democracy and Reaction* (London, 1904) pp. 36ff.
31. J. A. Hobson, *Confessions of an Economic Heretic* (London, 1938) p. 26.
32. Ibid., p. 61 and J. A. Hobson, *Imperialism* (London, 1902).

33. *D.N.B.* article on J. L. Hammond by Gilbert Murray.
34. C. E. Montague, *Disenchantment* (London, 1922) pp. 212–13.
35. W. T. Arnold, *Studies of Roman Imperialism* (Manchester, 1906), Introduction by Mrs Humphrey Ward and C. E. Montague.
36. Bodleian Library, Gilbert Murray MSS, Box 484, Reminiscences.
37. F. Hirst, Gilbert Murray and J. L. Hammond, *Liberalism and the Empire* (London, 1900) pp. 123ff.
38. Bodleian Library, *Indian Magazine* (Oxford, 1914) p. 76.
39. Gilbert Murray, 'The Empire and Subject Races', *Sociological Review*, vol. III (July 1910) no. 3, pp. 227–32.
40. Sir D. Wilson, unpublished draft MS 'Gilbert Murray', G. Murray to J. Buchan (25 Apr. 1903) p. 103.
41. Murray, 'The Empire and Subject Races', p. 231.
42. Wilson, 'Gilbert Murray', p. 246.
43. M. Olivier, *Sydney Olivier, Letters and Selected Writings* (London, 1948) pp. 10ff.
44. Eric Williams, *British Historians and the West Indies* (Trinidad, 1964) pp. 162–3.
45. O. H. Ball, *Sydney Ball* (Oxford, 1923) p. 211.
46. R. Coupland, *The Empire in These Days* (London, 1935) pp. 6ff.
47. Norman Leys, *Kenya* (London, 1924) pp. 4ff.
48. S.O.A.S. Library, London, L. Barnes MS 'Let Them Scratch', pp. 16ff.
49. L. Barnes, *Empire or Democracy* (London, 1939) p. 97.
50. Ibid., pp. 172, 244.
51. L. Barnes, 'Radical Destination', unpublished MS biography in possession of Mrs L. Barnes (MS cited in note 48 above is shortened version) vol. II, pp. 118ff.
52. W. M. MacMillan, *My South African Years* (Cape Town, 1975) and Mona MacMillan, 'Champion of Africa – The African Concerns of W. M. MacMillan', unpublished MS in possession of Mrs M. MacMillan.
53. T. Hodgkin, *Nationalism in Colonial Africa* (London, 1956) p. 10.
54. Bodleian Library, Gilbert Murray MSS, Box 501, fol. 83, obituary address on Frederic Harrison by G. Murray, Wadham College, Oxford, 4 June 1923.

NOTES TO CHAPTER SIX: BENARES ON THE ISIS – INDIAN STUDIES AND THE INDIAN INSTITUTE

1. Hamayun Kabir, *Britain and India* (New Delhi, 1960) pp. 20ff.
2. S. Southwood, 'Thomas Stephens', *Bulletin, London School of Oriental Studies*, vol. 3 (1923–5) p. 231; also G. Schurhammer, 'Thomas Stephens', *The Month*, vol. 13 (1955) p. 199.
3. E. Terry, *Voyage to East India* (London, 1777 edn) p. 111.
4. Henry Lord, *Discovery of Two Foreign Sects in the East Indies* (1636; London, 1752 edn) pp. 341, 356.
5. S. N. Mukherjee, *Sir William Jones* (Cambridge, 1968).
6. *D.N.B.*, 'Halhed, N.', article by A. Gordon.
7. R. H. Gombrich, *On Being Sanskritic*, Inaugural Lecture as Boden Professor of Sanskrit (Oxford, 1978) p. 5.

8. Ibid., p. 9.
9. Ibid., p. 10.
10. Sir M. Monier Williams, *Memorials of Old Haileybury College* (London, 1894) p. 208; also G. D. Bearce, *British Attitudes to India 1784–1958* (London, 1961) p. 96.
11. *The Times* (29 Oct. 1860).
12. Unidentified newspaper clipping M. Monier Williams MSS, in possession of His Honour Judge E. F. Monier Williams.
13. G. Max Mueller, *Life and Letters of F. Max Mueller*, vol. II (London, 1902) p. 369.
14. *Oxford Magazine*, vol. 10 (10 Feb. 1892) p. 153.
15. Nirad Chaudhuri, *Scholar Extraordinary, the Life of F. Max Mueller* (London, 1974) p. 72.
16. *Oxford Magazine*, vol. 5 (9 Feb. 1887) p. 57.
17. J. Leopold, *British Applications of the Aryan Theory of Race to India*, vol. 89 (E.H.R., 1974) p. 578.
18. F. Max Mueller, *Life and Letters*, p. 357.
19. Indian Institute, Oxford, M. Monier Williams MS 'Notes on a Long Life Journey' (n.d.) p. 2.
20. Ibid., p. 361.
21. Ibid., p. 372.
22. M. Monier Williams, *Modern India and the Indians* (London, 1889) p. 349.
23. M. Monier Williams, 'Speech to National Indian Association 1877', in ibid., p. 349.
24. Indian Institute, Oxford, Anon., 'Record of Establishment of Indian Institute', (n.d.) pp. 28ff.
25. M. Monier Williams, *Modern India*, pp. 349ff.
26. Balliol College Minute Book (25 June 1878 and 9 Nov. 1878).
27. Balliol College Archives, B. Jowett MSS, B. Jowett to M. Monier Williams (4 Apr. 1879 and 15 Mar. 1881).
28. Monier Williams MSS, J. Ruskin to Monier Williams (5 Sep. 1875).
29. F. Max Mueller, 'Decree on Indian Institute', pamphlet and flyleaf, Bodleian, G.A. Oxon B139 (136a) (1880).
30. Max Mueller, *Life and Letters*, vol. II, p. 369.
31. 'Record of Establishment of Indian Institute', p. 48.
32. Ibid., p. 71.
33. M. Monier Williams, *Address on the Holy Bible and the Sacred Books of the East*, London Religious Tracts Society (n.d.).
34. India Office Library, Cornelia Sorabji MSS, Cornelia Sorabji to her father (10 Apr. 1890).
35. Bodleian Library, Oxford University Archives 11/m/1/3, confidential note by Lord Curzon (1909).
36. Bodleian Library, Oxford University Archives 1.1.m.1.4, minutes of Curators of Indian Institute.
37. S. J. Owen, *Occasional Notes on British–Indian Subjects* (Oxford, 1868) p. 116.
38. W. H. Hutton, *The Teaching of Indian History* (Oxford, 1914) p. 8.
39. S. J. Owen, *India on the Eve of the British Conquest* (Oxford, 1872) pp. iv–vi.

40. Hutton, *The Teaching of Indian History*, p. 20.
41. A. L. Basham, 'Modern Historians on Ancient India', in C. H. Philips (ed.), *Historians of India, Pakistan and Ceylon* (London, 1961) p. 272.
42. Vincent Smith, *Indian Constitutional Reform Viewed in the Light of History* (Oxford, 1919).
43. Sir V. Lovett, *History of the Indian Nationalist Movement* (London, 1920) p. 157.
44. Sir V. Lovett, *Britain's Work in India*, Inaugural Lecture as Reader in Indian History (Oxford, 1920) p. 11.
45. *Oxford Magazine*, vol. 38 (1919–20) p. 18; review by P. E. Roberts of the *Oxford History of India* by Vincent Smith. (Oxford, 1920).
46. Lady Markby, *Sir William Markby* (Oxford, 1917).
47. *Oxford Magazine*, vol. 5 (23 Feb. 1933) p. 478.
48. Balliol College Archives, note by A. D. Lindsay on M. K. Gandhi's visit to Oxford; H. G. Alexander, Oral information; Malcolm MacDonald, 'Constant Surprise', MS Autobiography, Royal Commonwealth Society, London.
49. Rhodes House Archives, File 2844, 'Indian Lectureship', E. Thompson to Lord Lothian (26 Apr. 1932).
50. Ibid., Lothian to Thompson (10 June 1932); Thompson to Lothian (23 May 1933).
51. Ibid., Lothian to Thompson (17 May 1933); Thompson to Lothian (23 May 1933).
52. *Oxford Magazine*, vol. 72 (21 Jan. 1954) p. 144. Obituary of H. N. Spalding.
53. Edward Thompson, MSS, H. N. Spalding to H. A. L. Fisher (20 Feb. 1940).
54. Ibid., Spalding to E. Thompson (17 Feb. 1938 and 2 Feb. 1938).
55. Bodleian Library, Oxford University Archives 1/1/6.
56. Rhodes Trust Archives, File 2844, Lord Elton to L. Curtis (21 Nov. 1939).
57. *Oxford University Gazette* (8 May 1941).
58. Rhodes Trust Archives, File 2844, Elton to Lord Hailey (2 Dec. 1939) and Elton to L. S. Amery (2 Jan. 1940).
59. Ibid., Thompson to Elton (30 June 1942).
60. Ibid., Elton to Amery (17 Oct. 1940).
61. Ibid., memorandum by H. A. R. Gibb (1945).
62. *Oxford University Gazette*, vol. 95 (1965) pp. 3240, 3243.
63. *Oxford Magazine*, vol. 20 (1901–2) p. 237; vol. 30 (1911–12) p. 47; vol. 49 (1930–1) p. 195.
64. Gombrich, *On Being Sanskritic*, p. 27.
65. 'Record of the Establishment of the Indian Institute'. p. 52.
66. A. N. Malan, *Solomon Caesar Malan, D.D.* (London, 1897) p. 371.

NOTES TO CHAPTER SEVEN: MUZZLED LIONS – THE SCIENTISTS AND EMPIRE

1. E. Ray Lankester, *Nature and Man*, Romanes Lecture (Oxford, 1905) p. 43.

2. G. Rolleston, *Scientific Papers and Addresses*, vol. 1 (Oxford, 1884) p. xxi.
3. W. J. Sollas, *Ancient Hunters and their Modern Representatives*, 2nd edn (London, 1915) p. 105.
4. *Report of Royal Commission on Oxford and Cambridge Universities*, CMD 1588, vol. 1 (London, 1922) Appendix 6.
5. E. B. Poulton, *Viriamu Jones and Other Oxford Memories* (Oxford, 1911) p. 217.
6. H. N. Moseley, *Notes by a Naturalist during the Voyage of H.M.S. Challenger* (London, 1879) p. 363.
7. *Oxford Magazine*, vol. 21 (1902–3) p. 112.
8. Oxford University Hope Department Files, E. Ray Lankester to E. B. Poulton (30 July 1899) and other undated letters.
9. E. Ray Lankester, *The Advancement of Science* (London, 1890) p. 190.
10. Lankester, *Nature and Man*, pp. 43ff.
11. E. Ray Lankester, Presidential Address, *Proceedings of the British Association for the Advancement of Science* (York, 1906) p. 36.
12. E. Ray Lankester, *Science from an Easy Chair* (London, 1911) p. 8.
13. Poulton, *Viriamu Jones*, pp. 258ff.
14. Ibid., pp. 257–79.
15. Ibid., p. 254.
16. Lankester, *The Advancement of Science*, pp. 183ff.
17. Bodleian Library, A. Milner MSS, Dep. 180, A. Milner to E. B. Poulton (11 Feb. 1901); Poulton to Milner (16 Nov. 1902); Milner to Poulton (16 Dec. 1902).
18. Sir E. Ray Lankester (ed.), *The Neglect of Science*, Report on Conference (London, 1916).
19. W. T. Stead, *The Last Will and Testament of Cecil James Rhodes* (London, 1902) pp. 23–4 and comments in footnote by 'a Fellow of Oriel' and by 'a distinguished Oxford professor'.
20. Oxford University Department of Zoology Archives, E. Ray Lankester, Lecture on 'Relation of the University to Medicine' (1878).
21. H. Cushing, *Life of Sir William Osler* (London, 1940 edn) p. 650.
22. Balliol College Library, Jowett–Nightingale MSS, B. Jowett to F. Nightingale (17 May 1865).
23. Cushing, *Life of Sir William Osler*, p. 728.
24. Ibid., p. 1065.
25. K. Dewhurst, *Oxford Medicine* (Oxford, 1970) p. 107.
26. Sir G. Jefferson, 'Memories of Sir Hugh Cairns', *Journal of Neurosurgery and Psychiatry* (1959) vol. 22, p. 155.
27. L. G. MacFarlane, *Howard Florey* (Oxford, 1979) p. 84.
28. St Antony's Middle East Centre, Richard Graves, unpublished Autobiography, p. 103. Graves was at Magdalen from 1899 to 1902.
29. Macfarlane, *Howard Florey*, p. 62.
30. Ibid., p. 64.
31. Ibid., pp. 397, 257 and 315.
32. Trevor Williams, *Florey: The Years after Penicillin* (Oxford, 1984) p. 276.
33. MacFarlane, *Howard Florey*, p. 229.

34. E. P. Stebbing, *The Forests of India* (London, 1923 and 1925) vol. II, ch. II; vol. III, ch. XIII gives a useful account of the early training of Indian Forest probationers, though biased by his animosity towards Oxford as Professor of Forestry at Edinburgh.
35. *Hansard*, 4th series, vol. 142 (7 Mar. 1905) pp. 531ff.
36. *Report of Royal Commission on Public Services in India* (Islington Report), vol. XV (London, 1917) p. 93. Evidence of F. C. Drake.
37. Ibid., p. 93. Evidence of F. C. Drake.
38. Ibid., p. 97. Evidence of Sir W. Schlich.
39. Ibid., p. 93. Evidence of F. C. Drake.
40. Ibid., p. 28. Evidence of Pandit Gokul Das.
41. Ibid., p. 97. Evidence of Sir W. Schlich.
42. See Chapter 10.
43. R. Furse, *Aucuparius* (London, 1962) pp. 134–5, 148–50.
44. E. P. Stebbing, *The Forests of India*, vol. III, ch. XIII.
45. M. V. Laurie, 'The Commonwealth Forestry Institute 1957–1967', paper presented to The Ninth Commonwealth Forestry Conference, 1968, Appendix 3, p. iii, in the possession of the Commonwealth Forestry Institute, Oxford.
46. Imperial Forestry Institute, *Annual Report* (1935–6) p. 5.
47. R. S. Troup, 'New Site for the Department of Forestry', *Journal of the Oxford Forestry Society* (1934) Second Series, no. 15, p. 5.
48. R. Symonds, *The British and Their Successors* (London, 1966) p. 145.
49. *Report of the Localization Committee* (Adu Report) (Zomba, Nyasaland, 1960) p. 22.

NOTES TO CHAPTER EIGHT: SUBURBS OF THE CELESTIAL CITY – GEOPOLITICIANS, ANTHROPOLOGISTS AND OTHERS

1. Quoted in D. I. Scargill, 'The Royal Geographical Society and the Foundation of Geography at Oxford', *Geographical Journal*, vol. 142 (1976) p. 438.
2. J. Steven Watson, 'Educating Statesmen', Address on the Occasion of the Centenary of University of Canterbury (1973), p. 1, MS in Christ Church Library, Oxford.
3. R. Hakluyt, *Principal Navigations, Voyages, Traffiques and Discoveries of the English Nation* vol. 1 (London, 1903 edn), pp. xviii, xix and R. Hakluyt, *A Particular Discourse Concerning Western Discoveries* (London, 1877 edn).
4. E. W. Gilbert, *British Pioneers in Geography* (Newton Abbot, 1972) pp. 30ff; also E. G. R. Taylor, 'The Original Writings of the Two Hakluyts', *Hakluyt Society*, series II, vol. LXXVI (London, 1935) p. 1.
5. *Oxford Magazine*, vol. 4 (27 Jan. 1886) p. 10; vol. 47 (28 Feb. 1929) p. 456.
6. H. J. Mackinder, *Britain and the British Seas* (Oxford, 1902).
7. H. J. Mackinder, 'The Geographical Pivot of History', *Geographical Journal*, vol. 23 (1904) p. 421.
8. Lord Curzon, 'Frontiers', Romanes Lecture (Oxford, 1907).

9. Brian W. Blouet, 'Sir Halford Mackinder 1861–1947', Research Paper 13, School of Geography, University of Oxford (1975) and the H. Mackinder MSS in the Oxford University School of Geography are the main sources on Mackinder, as well as W. H. Parker, *Mackinder – Geography as an Aid to Statecraft* (Oxford, 1982).
10. L. J. Day, 'A. J. Herbertson', *Geography*, vol. 50 (1965) p. 358.
11. O. G. S. Crawford, *Said and Done* (London, 1955) p. 42.
12. A. J. Herbertson, 'Geography and Some of its Needs', *Geographical Journal*, vol. 36 (Oct. 1910) p. 478.
13. The main sources on Herbertson are C. H. Firth, *The Oxford School of Geography* (Oxford, 1918) and E. W. Gilbert, 'A. J. Herbertson', *British Pioneers on Geography*, p. 313.
14. *Oxford Magazine*, vol. 46 (17 Feb. 1938) p. 401 and article by K. Mason, 'Geography in Oxford'.
15. Parker, *Mackinder – Geography as an Aid to Statecraft*, p. 74ff.
16. C. P. Lucas, *Historical Geography of the British Colonies*, vol. I (Oxford, 1900–10) p. 68.
17. Ibid., vol. I, p. 123.
18. Ibid., vol. III, p. 225.
19. Ibid., vol. IV, p. 325.
20. Hereford George, *Historical Geography of the British Empire* (London, 1904) pp. 4ff.
21. A. J. Herbertson and O. J. R. Howarth (eds), *Oxford Survey of the British Empire*, vol. I (Oxford, 1914) p. 361.
22. Ibid., vol. II, pp. 305–12.
23. Ibid., vol. II, p. 262.
24. Ibid., vol. II, p. 368; vol. III, p. 400.
25. Ibid., vol. III, p. 144.
26. Ibid., vol. V, p. 310.
27. Ibid., vol. V, p. 427.
28. Ibid., vol. IV, p. 200.
29. *Oxford Magazine*, vol. 1 (7 Nov. 1883) p. 352; also W. R. Chapman, 'Ethnology in the Museum', unpublished D. Phil. thesis, University of Oxford (1981).
30. J. L. Myres, 'The Science of Man in the Service of the State', *Journal of Royal Anthropological Institute*, vol. 59 (1929) p. 19; also in *Proceedings of 500th Meeting of Oxford University Anthropological Society* (1953) p. 7, in possession of Oxford University Institute of Social Anthropology.
31. H. H. Risley, *Tribes and Castes of Bengal* (Calcutta, 1891).
32. Sir H. H. Risley, 'India and Anthropology', *Man*, vol. X (1910) p. 163.
33. Sir H. H. Risley, *The People of India* (London, 1908).
34. *Proceedings of the Royal Anthropological Institute* (1967–8), obituary article on J. H. Hutton by C. von Furer Haimendorff, p. 66.
35. J. P. Mills, 'Anthropology as a Hobby', *Journal of the Royal Anthropological Institute*, vol. 83 (1953) p. 1.
36. W. V. Grigson, *The Maria Gonds of Bastar* (London, 1938), Introduction, p. xiii.
37. V. Elwin, 'W. V. Grigson', in *Man*, vol. 49 (Apr. 1949) p. 48.
38. R. H. Codrington, *The Melanesians, A Study in their Anthropology and Folklore* (London, 1891) p. vi.

39. Rhodes House Oxford, R. H. Codrington MSS, PAC 533, 3, unidentified obituary notices.
40. V. Elwin, *The Tribal World of Verrier Elwin* (Delhi, 1964) p. vii.
41. R. R. Marett and T. K. Penniman, *Spencer's Last Journey* (Oxford, 1931) p. 9.
42. Ibid., p. 46.
43. *Report of Royal Commission on Oxford and Cambridge Universities*, Cmd 1588 (London, 1922); MS Appendix, evidence of R. R. Marett.
44. Information on Rattray comes from N. Machin who is writing a book on him.
45. *D.N.B.* article on C. K. Meek.
46. A. Kuper, *Anthropologists and Anthropology* (London, 1973) pp. 59–81, and R. Firth, in obituary article on A. R. Radcliffe Brown, in *P.B.A.*, vol. 42 (1956) p. 287.
47. Lord Hailey, 'Role of Anthropology in Colonial Development', *Man*, vol. 43 (Jan. 1944) no. 5, p. 10.
48. Grigson, *The Maria Gonds*, p. xvii.
49. *D.N.B.* article on Lord Hailey by Philip Mason.
50. G. Lienhardt, 'E. P., a Personal View', *Man*, New Series, vol. 9 (1974) p. 299.
51. Mills, 'Anthropology as a Hobby'.
52. H. Merivale, *Lectures on Colonization and Colonies* (London, 1861).
53. C. E. Mallet, *History of the University of Oxford*, vol. III (London, 1927) p. 215.
54. A. Kadish, *Oxford Economists in the Late 19th Century* (Oxford, 1982).
55. *Report of Royal Commission on Oxford and Cambridge Universities*, MS appendix, evidence of E. Cannan.
56. Institute of Agricultural Economics, *Annual Reports* and Files; also E. H. Whetham, *Agricultural Economists in Britain, 1900–1940* (Oxford, 1981).
57. See p. 179 below.
58. Lord Curzon, *Subjects of the Day* (London, 1915) p. 11.
59. F. H. Lawson, *The Oxford Law School 1850–1965* (Oxford, 1968) p. 261 and *passim*.

NOTES TO CHAPTER NINE: RHODES AND THE IMPERIAL ATHENS

1. G. N. Clark, *Cecil Rhodes and his College* (Oxford, 1983) p. 3.
2. Ibid., p. 7.
3. J. Flint, *Rhodes* (London, 1976) p. 27, and B. Williams, *Cecil Rhodes* (London, 1938) p. 41. But see also C. Newbury, 'Cecil Rhodes and the South African Connection', in A. F. Madden and D. K. Fieldhouse (eds), *Oxford and the Idea of the Commonwealth* (London, 1982) p. 79.
4. Rhodes House, Oxford, E. A. Maund MSS AFR 229/IV fol. 172, p. 54.
5. Rhodes House, Oxford, MSS Misc. Africa S8 p. 40.
6. Rhodes House, Oxford MSS Africa, Cowen MSS, S229, 11 Box 2B Item 12C.
7. Lord Rosebery, *Speech at Rhodes Memorial at Oxford* (London, 1907) p. 5.
8. W. T. Stead, *The Last Will and Testament of Cecil James Rhodes* (London, 1902) pp. 38–9.

9. See p. 15 above.
10. *Oxford Magazine*, vol. 20 (7 May 1902) p. 314.
11. G. Elton (ed.), *The First Fifty Years of the Rhodes Trust and the Rhodes Scholarships* (Oxford, 1953) ch. V.
12. G. R. Parkin, *The Rhodes Scholarships* (London, 1913) p. 212.
13. F. Aydelotte, *The Oxford Stamp* (New York, 1917) p. 42.
14. Before 1915, 54 per cent of Dominions Scholars and 12.2 per cent of Americans studied Natural Sciences. The proportions were 68 and 14.7 per cent respectively between 1919 and 1925, but 35 and 16 per cent respectively in 1954. Elton, *The First Fifty Years*, p. 32.
15. Ibid., p. vi.
16. *Oxford Magazine*, vol. 48 (22 May 1930) p. 748; (29 May 1930) p. 783.
17. Elton, *The First Fifty Years*, pp. 144, 147.
18. *Balliol College Record* (Sept. 1949) p. 2.
19. See p. 259 below.
20. Elton, *The First Fifty Years*, p. 108.
21. H. W. Morison, *Oxford Today and the Rhodes Scholarships* (Toronto, 1958) p. vii.
22. Bodleian Library, Lord Milner MSS, Dep. 468, Lord Milner to Sir Lewis Michell (31 Dec. 1915); Newbury, in Madden and Fieldhouse, *Oxford and the Idea of the Commonwealth*, p. 90.
23. Parkin, *The Rhodes Scholarships*, p. 89.
24. Rhodes House, Oxford, misc. Afr. Rhodes MSS s8.40 C. J., Rhodes to Lord Grey (25 Aug. 1901).
25. Rhodes Trust Archives, File 'Reports 266' note by Lord Lothian (14 Sept. 1931).
26. J. R. M. Butler, *Lord Lothian* (London, 1960) p. 135.
27. Sir Herbert Baker, in anon (ed.), *Cecil Rhodes and Rhodes House* (Oxford, 1972) p. 17.
28. *Oxford Magazine*, vol. 47 (16 May 1929) p. 611.
29. Rhodes Trust Archives, Minutes of Public Purposes Trust (9 Mar. 1925).
30. Rhodes Trust Archives, File 'Oxford University Institute of Government', memorandum by P. Kerr (1 July 1929).
31. Ibid.
32. Ibid., R. Coupland to L. Curtis (6 Apr. 1924).
33. Ibid., memorandum by P. Kerr (1 July 1929).
34. Rhodes Trust Archives, File 'Oxford University Institute of Government', Report of Conference on Africa (Nov. 1929).
35. Rhodes Trust Archives, Minutes of Public Purposes Trust (16 Dec. 1929).
36. *A Proposed Institute of African Studies* (Oxford, 1930), copy in H. A. L. Fisher MSS, Bodleian Library, Oxford.
37. Rhodes Trust Archives, File 'Oxford University Institute of Government', Lothian to Curtis (28 Feb. 1930).
38. Ibid., J. Huxley to Lothian (28 Apr. 1931).
39. Ibid., Coupland to Lothian (Feb. 1931).
40. Ibid., Lothian to Lord Passfield (28 Mar. 1930).
41. Ibid., J. Smuts to Lothian, (6 Mar. 1930); Lothian to Smuts (26 Mar. 1930).

42. Ibid., Lothian to H. A. L. Fisher (11 Mar. 1930).
43. Ibid., Rockefeller Foundation to Fisher (8 May 1930).
44. See K. E. Robinson, 'Experts, Colonialists and Africanists', in J. C. Stone (ed.), *Experts in Africa* (Aberdeen, 1980) p. 63, and J. Hargreaves, 'History: African and Contemporary', in *Africa Research and Documentation* (1973) no. 3, p. 1.
45. *Oxford Magazine*, New Series, vol. 2 (1961–2) p. 1.
46. Sir Herbert Baker, *Cecil Rhodes by his Architect* (London, 1954) pp. 22, 14.
47. Elton, *The First Fifty Years*, p. 7.
48. Royal Colonial Institute (R.C.I.), *Report of Proceedings*, vol. 40 (1908–9) pp. 56–77.
49. Lord Curzon, *Subjects of the Day* (London, 1915) p. 10.
50. *Report of Royal Commission on Oxford and Cambridge Universities*, Cmd 1588, vol. I (London, 1922) p. 186 and MS Evidence, of J. G. Adami and C. K. Webster, Bodleian Library.
51. Ibid., vol. II, p. 149.
52. A. Zimmern, *The Third British Empire* (London, 1926) pp. 139ff.

NOTES TO CHAPTER TEN: A SHARE IN THE APPOINTMENTS

1. *Hansard* H. of C. Debates, Third Series, vol. 128 (24 June 1853) col. 746.
2. R. J. Moore, 'Abolition of Patronage in the East India Co.', *Historical Journal*, vol. VII (1964) no. 2, p. 246. B. Jowett to W. E. Gladstone (26 July 1853).
3. Ibid., Jowett to Gladstone (14 Dec. 1854).
4. *Report of Commitee on the Examination of Candidates for the Indian Civil Service*, vol. XL (*Parliamentary Papers*, 1854–5) p. 112 and *Correspondence Relating to the Age of Candidates for the Civil Service of India*, vol. LV (*P.P.*, 1876) p. 276.
5. C. J. Dewey, 'Education of a Ruling Caste', *Eng. Hist. Rev.*, vol. 88 (1973) p. 262.
6. *Papers Relating to Selection and Training of Candidates for the Civil Service of India*, vol. LV (*P.P.* 1876) pp. 8–9.
7. *University of Oxford Commmission, Minutes of Evidence*, vol. LVI (*P.P.* 1881) p. 215.
8. E. Abbott and F. Campbell, *Letters of Benjamin Jowett* (London, 1899) p. 122.
9. Sir M. O'Dwyer, *India as I Knew It* (London, 1925) p. 19.
10. A. Toynbee, *Progress and Poverty* (London, 1883) pp. 7, 23, 54 and A. Kadish, 'Arnold Toynbee', unpublished MS, p. 260.
11. A. Toynbee, *The Industrial Revolution* (London, 1896 edn), Introductory Memoir by B. Jowett, p. v.
12. Information from annual *Oxford University Calendars* and the *Brazen Nose*, vol. 1 (1909–14) p. 59.
13. Balliol College, Oxford, Jowett MSS, Box F, K 10, memorandum to Secretary of State for India signed by H. G. Liddell, B. Jowett, W. Markby and J. L. Strachan Davidson (26 Nov. 1889).

14. Information from annual tables in *Oxford Magazine*, vol. 11 (26 Oct. 1892) p. 22; vol. 12 (25 Oct. 1893) p. 23; vol. 13 (31 Oct. 1894) p. 37.
15. Balliol College Archives, J. L. Strachan Davidson MSS, *passim*.
16. Ibid., J. L. Strachan Davidson to Lord Goschen (6 Mar. 1904).
17. Ibid., Strachan Davidson to S. D. Courthorpe (3 Mar. 1904); Courthorpe to Strachan Davidson (15 Mar. 1904); Sir William Anson to Strachan Davidson (13 June 1904); Strachan Davidson to A. D. Godley (14 June 1904).
18. Figures from annual tables in *Oxford Magazine* and annual reports of Civil Service Commissioners'; see also *Report of Royal Commission on Public Services in India* (Islington Report), vol. x (London, 1917) p. 256.
19. The I.C.S. Oxford Governors were Sir H. Haig (United Provinces), Sir H. Craik (Punjab), Sir M. Hallett (Bihar), Sir R. Reid (Assam), Sir G. Cunningham (North West Frontier Province) and Sir L. Graham (Sind). The other Oxford Governors were Sir R. Lumley (Bombay) and Lord Erskine (Madras).
20. *Congress of Universities of the Empire* Report of Proceedings (London, 1912) p. 88.
21. Strachan Davidson MSS, note by Civil Service Commissioners (29 Mar. 1911).
22. *Report of Royal Commission on Public Services in India* (Islington Report) vol. XI (1914) p. 86.
23. *The Blue Book* (Dec. 1912), article by 'Indicus', p. 266.
24. H. A. E. Ewing, 'The Indian Civil Service 1919–1942', unpublished Ph.D. thesis, University of Cambridge (1980) p. 180.
25. P. Gardner, *Autobiographica* (Oxford, 1933) p. 59.
26. India Office Library, London, 'District Officers' Collection [material compiled by R. C. C. Hunt and J. Harrison for *The District Officer* (London, 1981)], MS notes by R. N. Lines.
27. Ibid., notes by H. B. Martin, H. O. Downing, J. E. Maher, E. A. Midgley and others.
28. Oxford University Appointments Commitee Minute Book and Files.
29. A. Kirk-Greene, *The Sudan Political Service: A Preliminary Profile* (Oxford, 1982) p. 15.
30. Strachan Davidson MSS, Strachan Davidson to Courthope (15 Mar. 1904) and *Oxford Magazine*, vol. 23 (15 Mar. 1905) p. 264; vol. 54 (1935–6) p. 313.
31. Rhodes House, Oxford, Sir R. Furse MSS, Brit. Emp. S415, memorandum by R. Furse (14 Apr. 1920).
32. D.N.B. article; also Sir George Bowen, *Thirty Years of Colonial Government* (London, 1889).
33. R. Furse, *Aucuparius* (London, 1962) p. 223.
34. *Oxford Magazine*, vol. 27 (4 Feb. 1909) p. 170; vol. 28 (3 Feb. 1910) p. 171.
35. R. Heussler, *Yesterday's Rulers* (London, 1963) p. 127.
36. Furse, *Aucuparius*, p. 223; *Oxford Magazine*, vol. 68 (1949–50) p. 165.
37. M. Perham, *Colonial Sequence*, vol. II (London, 1970) p. 270.
38. Heussler, *Yesterday's Rulers*, p. 126.

39. Bodleian Library, Gilbert Murray MSS, Box 1, fols 15–21, Sir John Maynard to G. Murray (20 Mar. 1887).
40. Ibid., Box 6, fol. 126, Maynard to Murray (25 June 1899).
41. Ibid., Box 12, fols. 118–9, Maynard to Murray (11 July 1907).
42. See p. 65 above.
43. Oriel College, L. R. Phelps MSS, A. W. Facer to L. R. Phelps (11 Sept. 1915).
44. Ibid., G. W. James to Phelps (11 Apr. 1926).
45. Ibid., J. W. Hose to Phelps (24 Sept. 1901).
46. Ibid., E. Campbell to Phelps (7 Feb. 1923).
47. Ibid., E. Saxon to Phelps (29 Mar. 1920).
48. Ibid., W. Egerton to Phelps (26 Sept. 1892).
49. Ibid., J. Richardson to Phelps (30 Nov. 1922).
50. Ibid., James to Phelps (21 Feb. 1928).
51. Ibid., F. Sandford to Phelps (10 Feb. 1932).
52. Ibid., Richardson to Phelps (17 Dec. 1929).
53. Ibid., Egerton to Phelps (26 Sept. 1892).
54. Ibid., D. Newbold to Phelps (29 Aug. 1932).
55. Ibid., A. S. Walford to Phelps (22 Jan, 1933).
56. Ibid., J. L. Penney to Phelps (n.d., probably 1924).
57. Ibid., A. T. Scott to Phelps (5 Nov. 1905).
58. Ibid., P. Harvey to Phelps (25 Feb. 1910).
59. Ibid., A. T. B. Pritchard to Phelps (9 Feb. 1931).
60. P. C. Lyon, 'Report on the Correspondence of Rev. L. R. Phelps 1877–1936', Oriel College (1939).

NOTES TO CHAPTER ELEVEN: THE MISSIONARIES

1. W. W. Hunter, 'A Forgotten Oxford Movement', *Fortnightly Review*, vol. 65 (1896) p. 689.
2. Bodleian Library, Oxford University Archives NW/16/1 and NW/16/6.
3. J. Ruskin, *Collected Works*, vol. 2 (London, 1903) p. 90.
4. Bishop R. Heber, *Lives of Missionaries* (London, n.d.) p. 169.
5. Ibid., p. 238.
6. J. Bateman, *Life of Rt Rev. Daniel Wilson*, vol. II (London, 1860) p. 144.
7. Ibid., vol. 2, p. 192.
8. Ibid., pp. 384ff.
9. H. Birks, *Life of T. Valpy French* (London, 1895).
10. H. E. W. Slade, *The Story of the Cowley Fathers* (London, 1970) and M. V. Woodgate, *Father Benson of Cowley* (London, 1953).
11. G. Longridge, *History of the Oxford Mission to Calcutta* (London, 1910) p. 137.
12. Fr. O'Neill, *Brahmoism, Is It For Us or Against Us* (Oxford, 1881) and E. G. Willis, *Letter to the Regius Professor of Theology* (Oxford, 1879). Both in the Pusey House Collection, Oxford.
13. Longridge, *History of the Oxford Mission*, pp. 88, 28.
14. Ibid., p. xiii.

15. *Father Douglass of Behala*, by some of his friends (London, 1952) and Sister Gertrude, *Mother Edith* (London, 1964).
16. R. M. Benson, *Letters* (London, 1916) p. 63.
17. *Father Douglass*, p. 150.
18. R. M. Benson, 'The Conversion of India', *Indian Church Quarterly Review*, vol. 8 (Apr. 1895) p. 97.
19. J. C. Winslow and Verrier Elwin, *The Dawn of Indian Freedom* (London, 1931), ch. IV; also J. C. Winslow, *Christa Seva Sangha* (London, 1930) pp. 1–12.
20. O. Chadwick, *MacKenzie's Grave* (London, 1959) p. 190.
21. H. M. Stanley, *How I Found Livingstone* (New York, 1872) p. 19. (The passage is omitted in later editions.)
22. D. Neave, 'Aspects of the University Mission to Central Africa', M.Phil. thesis, University of York (1974) p. 70.
23. Ibid., p. 89.
24. The numbers were U.M.C.A. 46 Oxford, 26 Cambridge in 1860–1900, according to Neave, 'Aspects of the University Mission to Cental Africa', and C.M.S. 79 Oxford, 241 Cambridge in 1825–1900, according to the Centenary Volume of *C.M.S. Mission for Africa and Far East* (London, 1902) p. 695.
25. Neave, 'Aspects of the University Mission to Central Africa', pp. 91ff.
26. *Oxford Magazine*, vol. 13 (1894–5) p. 425.
27. A.E.M. Anderson-Morshead, *History of Universities Mission to Central Africa* (London, 1909) pp. 1–12; also C. Maples, *Life of Bishop Maples By His Sister* (London, 1897) pp. 30–1, 363, 377.
28. Maples, *Life of Bishop Maples*, p. 223.
29. Ibid., p. 186.
30. R. H. Barnes, *Johnson of Nyasaland* (London, 1933) p. 81.
31. Ibid., p. 145.
32. Ibid., p. 10.
33. Ibid., p. 197.
34. H. A. L. Cairns, *Prelude to Imperialism* (London, 1968) p. 179.
35. H. Maynard Smith, *Frank, Bishop of Zanzibar* (London, 1926) p. 30.
36. Ibid., *Passim*.
37. D. V. Steere, *God's Irregular* (London, 1973) pp. 35, 59, 69.
38. N. Mosley, *Life of Raymond Raynes* (London, 1961) and A. Winter, *Till Darkness Fell*, Community of the Resurrection, Mirfield (n.d.).
39. C. E. Padwick, *Temple Gairdner of Cairo* (London, 1929) pp. 320–46.
40. *D.N.B.* article on J. H. Oldham by K. Bliss; N. Leys and J. H. Oldham, *By Kenya Possessed* (Chicago, 1976) p. 58; BBC Radio Programme, 'Six Christians of the 20th Century', (Nov. 1983).
41. J. H. Oldham, *Christianity and the Race Problem* (London, 1924).
42. Rhodes House, Oxford, A. Fraser MSS, Brit. Emp. s.283, File 3, sermon preached in Westminster Abbey (Apr. 1924).
43. Ibid., J. H. Oldham to A. Fraser (30 May 1924); Fraser to Oldham (1 June 1924).
44. Ibid., sermon preached in St Aldate's Church (12 Nov. 1939); W. E. F. Ward, *Fraser of Trinity and Achimota* (Accra, 1965) p. 146.
45. Ibid., p. 157.

46. Church Missionary Society (C.M.S.) *Annual Reports* of missionaries (London, 1900) p. 411; (1902) p. 279; (1908) p. 258.
47. Ibid. (1910).
48. Ibid. (1908) p. 258; (1909) p. 279; C.M.S. Archives unprinted report (May 1931).
49. C.M.S. *Annual Reports* (1912–13) p. 143.
50. W. E. S. Holland, *The Goal of India* (London, 1917) p. 226.
51. *The Times* (29 Mar. 1951), Obituary.
52. Padwick, *Temple Gairdner.*
53. E. C. Dawson, *James Hannington* (London, 1887) and H. B. Thomas, 'The Last Days of Bishop Hannington', *Uganda Journal*, vol. VIII (Sep. 1940) no. 1, p. 19.
54. Dawson, *James Hannington*, p. 326.
55. R. P. Ashe, *Two Kings of Uganda* (London, 1889) pp. 181, 185.
56. James Hannington, *Last Journals* (London, 1888) pp. 141, 173.
57. Cairns, *Prelude to Imperialism*, p. 41.
58. J. Gutch, *Martyr of the Islands* (London, 1971) p. 94.
59. Ibid., p. 153.
60. Ibid., p. 156.
61. Ibid., p. 171.
62. *History of the Missionary Settlement for University Women (M.S.U.W.)* (Bombay, 1923) p. 1.
63. M.S.U.W. *Annual Report* (1895–6).
64. M.S.U.W. *Annual Report* (1899).
65. M.S.U.W. *Annual Report* (1898).
66. M.S.U.W. *Annual Report* (1899).
67. M.S.U.W. *Annual Report* (1903).
68. M.S.U.W. *Annual Report* (1919–20).
69. M.S.U.W. *Annual Report* (1926–7).
70. M.S.U.W. *Annual Report* (1928–9).
71. M.S.U.W. *Annual Report* (1929–30).
72. M.S.U.W. *Annual Report* (1942–3).
73. M.S.U.W. *Annual Report* (1947–8).
74. Fraser, sermon preached in St Aldate's Church, Oxford, Fraser MSS, File 3.
75. *Report of Committee on Religious and Moral Instruction* (New Delhi, 1960) pp. 9–10.
76. W. Lock, *Church and Empire* (London, 1907) p. 11.

NOTES TO CHAPTER TWELVE: THE OXFORD OF THE SOUTHERN WORLD AND EDUCATION IN THE EMPIRE

1. M. Tupper, 'Poetic Offerings in the Nature of a God-speed to the Canterbury Colonists', in *Canterbury Papers* (London, 1850) p. 115.
2. Ibid., pp. 93, 94 and C. E. Carrington, *Godley of Canterbury* (London, 1950).
3. W. J. Gardner, E. T. Beardsley and T. E. Carter, *History of University of Canterbury* (Christchurch, N.Z., 1973) p. 19. There is some doubt as to whether this paragraph was included in the letter which was finally sent.

4. *Canterbury Papers*, p. 101.
5. Ibid., p. 69.
6. At the time of the author's visit in 1980.
7. *Canterbury Papers*, H. F. Alston to J. R. Godley (1 Oct. 1850) p. 233.
8. Ibid., p. 35. In addition to the *Canterbury Papers*, this account of Christchurch relies on the uncompleted Ph.D. thesis (n.d.) by Maurice C. Knight, 'The History of College House – the Collegiate Department of Christ's College' kindly made available by Rt Revd Bishop A. K. Warren of Christchurch, New Zealand.
9. Bodleian Library, Oxford University Archives, File VR/SF/CEV 1 'Ceylon University College'.
10. Ibid., File VR/SF Mak 1, Sir Philip Mitchell to R. Coupland (8 July 1939).
11. Ibid., Coupland to D. Veale (9 Jan. 1940).
12. Ibid., M. MacDonald to Vice-Chancellor (18 Jan. 1940).
13. Ibid., G. Turner to M. Perham (29 Feb. 1940).
14. Ibid., Perham to Turner (19 June 1940).
15. Ibid., Perham to Veale (12 May 1947).
16. Ibid., File UR/SF/COL/119 'Central African University', Lord Swinton to Lord Halifax (15 Sept. 1953); Sir Christopher Cox to Veale (9 Sept. 1953).
17. Ibid., Halifax to Vice-Chancellor (18 Sept. 1953).
18. H. E. Barff, *Short Historical Account of the University of Sydney* (Sydney, 1902) p. 30.
19. W. J. Gardner, *Colonial Cap and Gown* (Christchurch, N.Z., 1979) p. 46.
20. Ibid., p. 50.
21. Ibid., p. 52.
22. H. E. Barff, *University of Sydney*, pp. 2–76.
23. R. H. Crawford, *A Bit of a Rebel – The Life of G. A. Wood* (Sydney, 1975) pp. 132, 153.
24. M. W. McCullum, *A. B. Weigall* (Sydney, 1913) and C. Turney, *Pioneers of Australian Education* (Sydney, 1969) p. 115.
25. *Oxford Magazine*, vol. 9 (9 Mar. 1891) p. 232.
26. W. C. K. Duncan and R. A. Leonard, *The University of Adelaide* (Adelaide, 1973) p. 8.
27. M. R. Casson, 'G. L. Henderson', *South Australiana*, vol. III (1964) p. 22.
28. J. MacMillan Brown, *Memoirs* (Christchurch, N.Z., 1974) p. 111 and *passim*.
29. W. S. Wallace, *History of Toronto University* (Toronto, 1927) p. 1.
30. C. MacMillan, *McGill and Its Story* (London, 1921) p. 47.
31. D. C. Masters, *Bishops University* (Toronto, 1950).
32. R. B. Howard, *Upper Canada College* (Toronto, 1979) p. 106.
33. Ibid., p. 199.
34. Ibid., p. 230.
35. W. D. Meikle, 'And Gladly Teach – G. M. Wrong and the Department of History at the University of Toronto', Ph.D. thesis, Michigan State University (1977) p. 144 and *passim*.
36. Ibid., pp. 59, 166 and *passim*.

37. D. D. Calvin, *Queen's University at Kingston* (Kingston, Ontario, 1941) pp. 133, 169.
38. D. McIntyre, *Diocesan College, Rondebosch* (Cape Town, 1950) p. 8.
39. R. F. Currey, *St Andrew's, Grahamstown* (Oxford, 1955) p. 22 and *passim*.
40. K. C. Lawson, *Venture of Faith, St John's College, Johannesburg* (Johannesburg, 1968) p. 21.
41. Ibid., p. 150.
42. A. M. Barratt, *Michaelhouse* (Michaelhouse, Natal, 1969).
43. A. F. Hattersley, *Hilton Portrait* (Pietermaritzburg, 1945).
44. A. Winter, *Till Darkness Fell*, Community of the Resurrection, Mirfield (n.d.).
45. R. F. Currey, *Rhodes University* (Grahamstown, 1970) p. 12.
46. B. K. Murray, *Wits, The Early Years* (Johannesburg, 1982) p. 80.
47. Ibid., pp. 125–60.
48. W. E. F. Ward, *Fraser of Trinity and Achimota* (Accra, 1965) p. 284 and *passim*.
49. E. Arnold, *Education in India* (London, 1860) pp. 6, 8.
50. L. F. Rushbrook-Williams, 'Inside Both Indias', *Indo-British Review*, vol. IX (1982) no. 11, p. 3.
51. T. Bertram, *New Zealand Letters of Thomas Arnold the Younger* (Wellington, N.Z. 1966); W. D. Arnold, *Oakfield* (London, 1854) p. 118; F. Woodward, *The Doctor's Disciples* (London, 1954) pp. 180ff.
52. See p. 287 below.
53. L.M.H. *Brown Book* (1908) p. 522.
54. *Somerville Students' Association Report* (Oct. 1900) p. 20.
55. *The Ship* (1912) p. 31.
56. *The Ship* (1913) p. 23.
57. L.M.H. *Brown Book* (1909) p. 58.
58. Ibid. (1914) p. 33.
59. *St Hugh's College Chronicle* (1924–5) p. 31.
60. *Somerville Students' Association Report* (Nov. 1898) p. 72.
61. L.M.H. *Brown Book* (1915) p. 37.
62. *St Hugh's College Chronicle* (1938) p. 21.
63. L.M.H. *Brown Book* (1922) p. 78.
64. Ibid. (1925) p. 83.
65. *St Hugh's Club Paper* (1910) p. 26.
66. L.M.H. *Brown Book* (1916) p. 44.

NOTES TO CHAPTER THIRTEEN: NURSING MOTHER OF THE ELECT

1. Royal Colonial Institute, *Report of Proceedings*, vol. 40 (1908–9) p. 60.
2. J. Foster, *Oxford Men and Their Colleges* (Oxford, 1893) and *Alumni Oxoniensis* (Oxford, 1888).
3. India Office Library, C. Sorabji MSS, Eur. F. 165, letter from C. Sorabji to her parents (2 July 1890).
4. C. Sorabji, *India Calling* (London, 1934) p. 23.
5. Balliol College Library, Jowett–Nightingale MSS, B. Jowett to F. Nightingale (26 June 1892).

6. *Report of Committee on Indian Students* (Lytton Report), part I (London, 1922) Appendix IV, Lee Warner Report.
7. Ibid., p. 68.
8. Ibid., part II, pp. 30–3.
9. Ibid., part II, p. 19.
10. Ibid., part II, pp. 21, 30.
11. Ibid., part I, p. 18.
12. N. B. Bonarjee, *Under Two Masters* (London, 1970) pp. 72ff.
13. K. P. S. Menon, *Many Worlds* (London, 1965) p. 53.
14. Lytton Report, part II, p. 34.
15. Ibid., part II, p. 34; also *Report of Royal Commission on Oxford and Cambridge Universities*, Cmd 1588 (London, 1922); MS Appendix, evidence of S. M. Burrows, Bodleian Library.
16. L. R. Farnell, *An Oxonian Looks Back* (London, 1934) p. 298.
17. B. De, *Essays in Honour of S. C. Sarkar* (Delhi, 1976) pp. 13ff.
18. *Oxford University Examination Statutes* (1908) p. 36; (1902) p. 27.
19. India Office Library, London, 'District Officers' Collection (see note 26 to Chapter 10), notes by H. C. Gupta.
20. M. C. Chagla, *Roses in December* (Bombay, 1974) pp. 3ff.
21. D. F. Karaka, *Then Came Hazrat Ali* (Bombay, 1972) p. 55.
22. K. M. Pannikar, *Autobiography* (Delhi, 1974) p. 14.
23. Ibid., p. 22.
24. S. W. R. D. Bandaranaike, *Speeches and Writings* (Colombo, 1963) pp. 12–75.
25. G. K. Chettur, *The Last Enchantment: Recollections of Oxford* (Mangalore, 1934) p. 161.
26. Ibid., pp. 4–6.
27. K. P. S. Menon, 'Days at Oxford', in Z. Ahmed (ed.), *Liaquat Ali Khan* (Karachi, 1970) p. 15.
28. 'District Officers' Collection, notes by J. D. Shukla.
29. E. N. Mangat Rai, *Commitment My Style* (Delhi, 1973) pp. 33ff.
30. Hiren Mukerjee, 'As an Academician', in K. I. Dutt (ed.), *S. Radhakrishnan* (New Delhi, 1973) p. 20.
31. E. Williams, *Inward Hunger* (London, 1969) p. 30.
32. F. A. Hoyos, *Grantley Adams and the Social Revolution* (London, 1974) p. 16.
33. Ibid., p. 17.
34. R. Nettleford, *Manley and the New Jamaica* (London, 1971) p. xcviii.
35. P. Sherlock, *Norman Manley* (London, 1980) p. 61.
36. St Catherine's College Archives, letter from Director of Education, Trinidad to Master of University College, Oxford (8 Jan. 1937).
37. Williams, *Inward Hunger* p. 43.
38. Ibid., p. 45.
39. Ibid., p. 52.
40. Ibid., p. 53.
41. Ibid., p. 112.
42. The writer was present.
43. F. Bartels, 'Philip Quaque', *Transactions of Gold Coast Historical Society*, vol. 1 (1955) part V, p. 153.

44. C. Cole, *Reflections on the Zulu War and the Future of Africa* (London, 1883); also C. Fyfe, *Sierra Leone* (Oxford, 1962) p. 406.
45. J. Renner Maxwell, *The Negro Question* (London, 1892) p. 54.
46. Ibid., p. 87.
47. Ibid., p. 104 and Fyfe, *Sierra Leone*, p. 406.
48. L. R. Harlan, 'Booker T. Washington and the White Man's Burden', *American Historical Review*, vol. LXXI (1965–6) p. 463.
49. M. Benson, *The African Patriots* (London, 1963) pp. 25ff.
50. Aina Moore, 'The Story of Kofoworola Aina Moore', in M. Perham, *Ten Africans* (London, 1936) pp. 323ff.
51. Information from private sources.
52. T. Mboya, *Freedom and After* (London, 1963) pp. 56–8.
53. Siaka Stevens, 'A West African Looks at Ruskin', Ruskin College, Oxford, *New Epoch* (1948) no. 1, p. 3; also Siaka Stevens, *What Life Has Taught Me* (Kensal, 1984) p. 122.
54. E. Barker, *Age and Youth* (London, 1953) pp. 323–4.
55. Exeter College Association Register (1979) p. 8.
56. W. R. Hancock, *Country and Calling* (London, 1954) p. 55.
57. W. R. Crocker, *Travelling Back* (Melbourne, 1981) pp. 13ff.
58. W. R. Crocker, *Nigeria* (London, 1936) p. 216.
59. C. V. Portus, *Happy Highways* (Melbourne, 1983) pp. 89ff.
60. J. Willison, *Sir George Parkin* (London, 1929) pp. 27–34.
61. Ibid., pp. 28ff.
62. W. D. Meikle, 'And Gladly Teach: G. M. Wrong and the Department of History at the University of Toronto', Ph.D. thesis, Michigan State University (1977) p. 144.
63. V. Massey, *What's Past is Prologue* (London, 1963) pp. 28ff; also, C. T. Bissell, *The Young Vincent Massey* (Toronto, 1981).
64. L. B. Pearson, *Memoirs*, vol. I (1973–5) pp. 43ff.
65. N. Penlington (ed.), *On Canada. Essays in Honour of Frank H. Underhill* (Toronto, 1971).
66. *Oxford Magazine*, vol. 33 (1914–15) p. 137.
67. Rhodes Trust Archives, Minutes of Meeting of Trustees (16 Apr. 1907).
68. S. Leacock, *My Discovery of England* (New York, 1922) p. 81.
69. W. M. MacMillan, *My South African Years* (Cape Town, 1975).
70. K. Fairbridge, *Autobiography* (London, 1927) pp. 159ff.
71. P. B. Duncan and C. J. Driver, *Patrick Duncan: South African and Panafrican* (London, 1980).
72. A. Paton, *J. H. Hofmeyr* (London, 1964).
73. L. K. Haldane, *Friends and Kindred* (1961) p. 197.
74. *The Times* (8 Nov. 1982), Obituary.

NOTES TO CHAPTER FOURTEEN: EPILOGUE

1. *Oxford Magazine*, New Series, vol. 7 (20 Jan. 1967) p. 172.
2. Sir Douglas Veale, 'Colonial Studies', MS memorandum written for the 'History of Oxford University' (1969), copy in Rhodes House Library, R. Furse MSS.

3. M. Perham, 'The Institute of Colonial Studies – its Origins and Purpose', MS memorandum (1956) p. 1, in possession of R. Symonds.
4. *Report on Post-War Training for the Colonial Service* (Devonshire Report) (London, 1946) col. 198, pp. 20ff.
5. Ibid., p. 21.
6. J. T. Saunders, R. I. Turner and D. Veale, *Report to Nuffield Foundation on a Visit to Nigeria* (Oxford, 1946) p. 61.
7. E. G. Rowe, 'Reflections on the Oxford Overseas Services Courses', *Journal of Administration Overseas*, vol. 9 (1970) p. 205.
8. Ibid., p. 213.
9. Professor S. H. Frankel MSS, Lord Munster to Lord Halifax (28 Oct. 1953); Sir C. Jeffries to Sir Douglas Veale (12 Mar. 1954); note of conference between University and Colonial Office on 24 Feb. 1954 (ref. Col. 18).
10. Rhodes House, Oxford, D. Lindsay Keir MSS, Brit. Emp. 5393, Box 1 also Rhodes Trust Archives, File 'Oxford University Institute of Government', Lord Elton to Sir E. Peacock (10 Dec. 1951).
11. *Oxford Magazine*, vol. 73 (24 Feb. 1955) p. 225; vol. 75 (9 May 1957) p. 42.
12. The writer taught on these courses.
13. *Oxford Magazine*, vol. 69 (12 Oct. 1950) p. 8.
14. Dudley Seers, 'Conception, Birth and Early Years' in *Institute of Development Studies 1966–76*, University of Sussex (1977) p. 19.
15. Minutes of Oxford University Committee for Commonwealth Studies.
16. *Oxford Magazine*, vol. 75 (6 June 1957) p. 497; (13 June 1957) p. 524.
17. Ibid., vol. 77 (5 Feb. 1959) p. 219.
18. Ibid., vol. 73 (24 Feb. 1955) p. 275.
19. Rowe, *Oxford Overseas Services Courses*, p. 215.
20. A. F. Madden, 'The Commonwealth, Commonwealth History and Oxford', in A. F. Madden and D. K. Fieldhouse (eds), *Oxford and the Idea of Commonwealth* (London, 1982) p. 27.

NOTES TO CHAPTER FIFTEEN: CONCLUSIONS

1. *Hansard*, H. of C. Debates, Third Series, vol. 21 (10 July 1833) col. 536.
2. R. Furse, *Aucuparius* (London, 1962) p. 222.
3. Revd Stacey Waddy, 'The Oxford Movement in the Empire', in N. P. Williams and C. Harris (eds), *Northern Catholicism* (London, 1933), p. 128.
4. *D.N.B.* article by D. G. Hogarth on Gertrude Bell; also M. R. Ridley, *Gertrude Bell* (London, 1941).
5. Ella C. Sykes, *A Home Help in Canada* (London, 1912) p. 57.
6. Lord Curzon, *Principles and Methods of University Reform* (Oxford, 1909) p. 158.
7. *Report of Royal Commission on Oxford and Cambridge Universities*, Cnd 1588 (London, 1922) p. 44.
8. Lady G. Cecil, *Robert, Marquis of Salisbury*, vol. III (London, 1921) p. 302.
9. R. P. Masani, *Dadabhai Naoroji* (London, 1934) p. 263.

10. Lord Rosebery, *Questions of Empire* (London, 1900) p. 13.
11. J. Bardoux, *Memories of Oxford* (translation) (London, 1899) pp. 58, 60.
12. R. S. Rait, *Memories of A. V. Dicey* (London, 1925) p. 298.
13. *Times Atlas of the World* (London, 1958).
14. A. F. Madden and D. K. Fieldhouse (eds), *Oxford and the Idea of Commonwealth* (London, 1982) p. 42.
15. See R. Stokes, *Political Ideas of Imperialism* (Oxford, 1960).
16. W. R. Crocker, *Travelling Back* (London, 1981) p. 13.

Select Bibliography

I UNPUBLISHED SOURCES

Balliol College Minute Book, Balliol College.
Barnes, Leonard, 'Radical Destination', MS biography in possession of Mrs L. Barnes.
Barnes, Leonard, 'Let Them Scratch', shortened MS version of above, School of Oriental and African Studies, London.
Brand, R. H., MSS, Bodleian Library.
Carritt, E. F., 'Fifty Years a Don', MS, Bodleian Library (n.d.).
Chapman, W. R., 'Ethnology in the Museum', D.Phil. thesis, Oxford University (1981).
Church Missionary Society, *Annual Reports* of missionaries (London).
Codrington, R. H., MSS, Rhodes House Library.
College Registers, St Anne's and St Hilda's Colleges.
Coupland, R., MSS, Rhodes House Library.
Cowan, C., MSS, Rhodes House Library.
Curtis, Lionel, MSS, Bodleian Library.
Curzon, G. N., Lord, MSS, India Office Library, London.
Curzon, G. N., Lord, 'The Indian Institute', Confidential Report to Curators (1909), Bodleian Library.
'District Officers' Collection [material compiled by R. C. C. Hunt and J. Harrison for *The District Officer* (London, 1981)], India Office Library, London.
Egerton, H. E., MS, 'Lectures on British Colonies in the Nineteenth Century', Rhodes House Library (n.d.).
Ewing, H. A. E., 'The Indian Civil Service, 1919–1942', Ph.D. thesis, Cambridge University (1980).
Fisher, H. A. L., MSS, Bodleian Library.
Frankel, S. H., Papers, in possession of Professor S. H. Frankel.
Fraser, Alek, MSS, Rhodes House Library.
Furse, Sir R., MSS, Rhodes House Library.
Graves, R., unpublished autobiography, St Antony's College.
Hope Department of Zoology, Oxford University, correspondence of Professor E. B. Poulton and others.
Indian Institute, Oxford, 'Record of Establishment of Indian Institute', anon. (n.d.).
Indian Institute, Oxford, Minutes of Curators.
Jowett, Benjamin, MSS, Balliol College.

Jowett–Nightingale correspondence, letters between Benjamin Jowett and Florence Nightingale, Balliol College.
Kadish, A., 'Arnold Toynbee', unpublished MS in possession of Dr A. Kadish.
Keir, D. Lindsay, MSS, Rhodes House Library.
Knight, Maurice C., 'The History of College House, the Collegiate Department of Christ's College', uncompleted Ph.D. thesis, Christchurch, N.Z. (n.d.).
Lankester, E. Ray, lecture on 'Relation of the University to Medicine', Oxford University Department of Zoology (1878).
Laurie, M. V., 'The Commonwealth Forestry Institute 1957–1967', presented to Ninth Commonwealth Forestry Conference (1968), Commonwealth Forestry Institute, Oxford.
Lindsay, A. D., MSS, 'Notes on Visit of Mahatma Gandhi to Oxford', Balliol College.
Macdonald, Malcolm, 'Constant Surprise', MS Autobiography, Royal Commonwealth Society Library, London.
Machin, N., 'Life of R. S. Rattray', draft MS.
Mackinder, H., MSS, Oxford University School of Geography.
MacMillan, Mona, 'Champion of Africa – the African Concerns of W. M. MacMillan', unpublished MS in possession of Mrs M. MacMillan.
Madden, A. F., 'Commonwealth Government at Oxford, the End of a Chapter', Oxford University Institute of Commonwealth Studies Library (1984).
Maund, E. A., MSS, Rhodes House Library.
Meikle, W. D., 'And Gladly Teach – G. M. Wrong and the Department of History at the University of Toronto', Ph.D. thesis, Michigan State University (1977).
Milner, A., Lord, MSS, Bodleian Library.
Monier Williams, Sir M., 'Notes on a Long Life Journey', Indian Institute, Oxford.
Monier Williams, Sir M., MSS, in possession of His Honour Judge E. F. Monier Williams.
Murray, Gilbert, MSS, Bodleian Library.
Neave, D., 'Aspects of the Universities Mission to Central Africa', M.Phil. thesis, University of York (1974).
Oxford University Appointments Committee Archives.
Oxford University Archives, Bodleian Library.
Oxford University Committee for Colonial (later Commonwealth) Studies, Minutes and archives.
Oxford University Institute of Social Anthropology Archives.
Oxford University Press Archives.
Perham, M., 'The Institute of Colonial Studies – its Origins and Purpose', MS memorandum (1956), in possession of R. Symonds.
Phelps, L. R., MSS, Oriel College.
Queen Elizabeth House, Oxford, Minutes of Governing Body and Archives.
Ralegh Club, Minutes, Rhodes House Library.
Rhodes, Cecil, MSS, Rhodes House Library.
Rhodes Trust, Oxford, Archives and Minute Books.

Rowe, E. G., 'Report on West African Tour 1965' and 'Report on West Indian Tour 1965', in Oxford University Institute of Commonwealth Studies Archives.
Sorabji, Cornelia, letters, India Office Library, London.
St Catherine's College Archives.
Strachan Davidson, J. L., MSS, Balliol College.
Thompson, Edward, MSS, in possession of Dr. E. P. Thompson.
Veale, Sir Douglas, 'Colonial Studies', MS memorandum written for the history of Oxford University (1969), copy in Rhodes House Library, R. Furse MSS.
Warboys, M., 'Science and British Colonial Imperialism', D.Phil. thesis, University of Sussex (1979).
Watson, J. Steven, 'Educating Statesmen', Address on the Occasion of the Centenary of University of Canterbury (1973), MS in Christ Church Library.
Wilson, Sir Duncan, unpublished draft MS 'Gilbert Murray'.

II PUBLISHED SOURCES

Abbott, E. and Campbell, L., *Life and Letters of Benjamin Jowett* (London, 1897).
Abbott, E. and Campbell, L., *Letters of Benjamin Jowett* (London, 1899).
Ahmed, Z. (ed.), *Liaquat Ali Khan* (Karachi, 1970).
Allen, D., *Sunlight and Shadow* (London, 1960).
Allmany, C. T., *Lancastrian Normandy in France* (Oxford, 1983).
Amery, L. S., *My Political Life* (London, 1953).
Anderson-Morshead, A. E. M., *History of Universities Mission to Central Africa* (London, 1909).
Anon., *A Proposed Institute of African Studies* (Oxford, 1930), copy in H. A. L. Fisher MSS, Bodleian Library.
Anon., *Bishop Heber*, Lives of Missionaries Series (London, n.d.).
Anon., *Government by Mallardry* (London, 1932) in All Souls Library.
Anon., *Father Douglass of Behala, by some of His Friends* (London, 1952).
Arnold, E., *Education in India* (London, 1860).
Arnold, W. D., *Oakfield* (London, 1854).
Arnold, W. T., *Studies of Roman Imperialism* (Manchester, 1906).
Ashby, E., *Universities: British, Indian, African* (London, 1966).
Ashe, R. P., *Two Kings of Uganda* (London, 1889).
Aydelotte, F., *The Oxford Stamp* (New York, 1917).
Aydelotte, F., *The Vision of Cecil Rhodes* (London, 1946).
Baker, Sir Herbert, *Cecil Rhodes by His Architect* (London, 1954).
Ball, O. H., *Sydney Ball* (Oxford, 1923).
Bandaranaike, S. W. R. D., *Speeches and Writings* (Colombo, 1963).
Bardoux, J., *Memories of Oxford*, translated from the French edn (London, 1899).
Barff, H. E., *Short Historical Account of the University of Sydney* (Sydney, 1902).

Barker, E., *Age and Youth* (London, 1953).
Barnes, Leonard, *Caliban in Africa* (London, 1930).
Barnes, Leonard, *The Duty of Empire* (London, 1935).
Barnes, Leonard, *Empire or Democracy* (London, 1939).
Barnes, R. H., *Johnson of Nyasaland* (London, 1933).
Barratt, A. M., *Michaelhouse* (Michaelhouse, Natal, 1969).
Bateman, J., *Life of Rt. Rev. Daniel Wilson* (London, 1860).
Battiscombe, G., *Reluctant Pioneer: A Life of Elizabeth Wordsworth* (London, 1978).
Beaglehole, T., 'From Rulers to Servants', *Modern Asian Studies*, vol. 11 (1977).
Beal, J. B., *Pearson of Canada* (New York, n.d.).
Bearce, G. D., *British Attitudes to India 1784–1958* (London, 1961).
Benson, M., *The African Patriots* (London, 1963).
Benson. R. M., 'The Conversion of India', *Indian Church Quarterly Review*, vol. 8 (1895).
Benson, R. M., *Letters* (London, 1916).
Berger, C., *The Sense of Power* (Toronto, 1970).
De Bergerac, B., *The Oxford Pageant of Victory* (Oxford, 1919).
Berkeley, J. W., *The British Empire: A Short History* (Oxford, 1921).
Bertram, T., *New Zealand Letters of Thomas Arnold the Younger* (Wellington, N.Z., 1966).
Birks, H., *Life of T. Valpy French* (London, 1895).
Bissell, C. T., *The Young Vincent Massey* (Toronto, 1981).
Blainey, G., *Centenary History of University of Melbourne* (Melbourne, 1957).
Blouet, B. W., 'Sir Halford Mackinder 1861–1947', Research Paper 13, Oxford University School of Geography (1975).
Blue Book (periodical) (1913–14).
Bonarjee, N. B., *Under Two Masters* (London, 1970).
Bossy, J. and Jupp, P. (eds), *Essays Presented to M. Roberts* (Belfast, 1976).
Bowen, Sir George, *Thirty Years of Colonial Government* (London, 1889).
Bowman, H., *Middle East Window* (London, 1942).
Braibanti, R., *Administration and Economic Development in India* (London, 1963).
British Academy, *Proceedings*.
Brittain, V., *The Women in Oxford* (London, 1960).
Brodrick, G. C., *Memories and Impressions* (London, 1900).
Bryce, J., Lord, *Relations Between Advanced and Backward Races of Mankind*, Romanes Lecture (Oxford, 1902).
Bryce, J., Lord, *The Ancient Roman Empire and the British Empire in India* (London, 1914).
Buchan, John, *Memory Hold the Door* (London, 1940).
Bulkeley, S. W., *The British Empire: A Short History* (Oxford, 1926).
Burrow, J. W., *A Liberal Descent* (London, 1981).
Butler, J. R. M., *Lord Lothian* (London, 1960).
Butler, R. F. and Prichard, M. M., *St Anne's College: A History* (Oxford, 1930).
Cairns, H. A. L., *Prelude to Imperialism* (London, 1968).

Calvin, D. D., *Queen's University at Kingston* (Kingston, Ontario, 1941).
Canterbury Papers (London, 1850).
Carrington, C. E., *Godley of Canterbury* (London, 1950).
Casson, M. R., 'G. L. Henderson', *South Australiana*, vol. III (1964).
Cecil, Lady Gwendoline, *Robert, Marquis of Salisbury* (London, 1921).
Chadwick, O., *MacKenzie's Grave* (London, 1959).
Chagla, M. C., *Roses in December* (Bombay, 1974).
Chaudhuri, Nirad C., *Scholar Extraordinary, the Life of F. Max Mueller* (London, 1974).
Chettur, G. K., *The Last Enchantment: Recollections of Oxford* (Mangalore, 1934).
Church Missionary Society, Centenary Volume, *C.M.S. Mission for Africa and Far East* (London, 1902).
Clark, G. N., *Cecil Rhodes and His College* (Oxford, 1983).
Codrington, R. H., *The Melanesians: A Study in their Anthropology and Folklore* (London, 1891).
Cole, C., *Reflections on the Zulu War and the Future of Africa* (London, 1883).
College periodic publications: *Balliol College Record*, *The Brazen Nose*, *Christ Church Annual Reports*, *Exeter College Association Register*, *Keble College Record*, *L.M.H. Brown Book*, *Magdalen College Record*, *New College Record*, *Oriel Record*, *The Pelican Record* (Corpus Christi), *The Postmaster* (Merton), *St Edmund Hall Magazine*, *Queen's College Record*, *St Hilda's College Report*, *St Hugh's College Chronicle*, *St Peter's Annual Reports*, *The Ship* (St Anne's), *Somerville College Report*, *Trinity College Report*, *University College Report*, *Wadham College Gazette*.
College Registers of Balliol, Brasenose, Keble, L.M.H., Merton, St Hilda's, St John's and Somerville Colleges.
Congress of Universities of the Empire, Report of Proceedings (London, 1912).
Congreve, Richard, *Gibraltar or the Foreign Policy of England* (London, 1857).
Congreve, Richard, *India* (London, 1857).
Congreve, Richard, *Essays* (London, 1874).
Congreve, Richard (ed.), *International Policy*, 2nd edn (1884).
Convergence, vol. XI, H. Callaway, 'Conversation with Thomas Hodgkin, the Scholar and Revolutionary' (London, 1978).
Cordeaux, E. H. and Merry, D. H., *Bibliography of Printed Works Relating to the University of Oxford* (Oxford, 1968).
Cosgrove, R. A., *The Rule of Law: A. V. Dicey, Victorian Jurist* (London, 1980).
Coupland, R., *The Empire in These Days* (London, 1935).
Crawford, O. G. S., *Said and Done* (London, 1955).
Crawford, R. H., *A Bit of a Rebel: The Life of G. A. Wood* (Sydney, 1975).
Crocker, W. R., *Nigeria* (London, 1936).
Crocker, W. R., *On Governing Colonies* (London, 1946).
Crocker, W. R., *Travelling Back* (London, 1981).
Curry, R. F., *St Andrew's Grahamstown* (Oxford, 1955).
Curry, R. F., *Rhodes University* (Grahamstown, 1970).

Curtis, L., *The Problem of the Commonwealth* (London, 1916).
Curtis, L., *With Milner in South Africa* (Oxford, 1951).
Curzon, G. N., Lord, *Speeches on India* (London, 1904).
Curzon, G. N., Lord, *Speeches as Viceroy and Governor-General* (Calcutta, 1904–6).
Curzon, G. N., Lord, *Frontiers*, Romanes Lecture (Oxford, 1907).
Curzon, G. N., Lord, *Principles and Methods of University Reform* (Oxford, 1909).
Curzon, G. N., Lord, *The Place of India in the Empire* (London, 1909).
Curzon, G. N., Lord, *Subjects of the Day* (London, 1915).
Cushing, H., *Life of Sir William Osler* (London, 1940 edn).
Davies, H. W. C., *History of Balliol College* (London, 1963 edn).
Dawson, E. C., *James Hannington* (London, 1887).
Day, L. J., 'A. J. Herbertson', *Geography*, vol. 50 (1965).
De, B., *Essays in Honour of S. C. Sarkar* (Delhi, 1976).
Dewey, C. J., 'Education of a Ruling Caste', *Eng. Hist. Rev.*, vol. 88 (1973).
Dewhurst, K., *Oxford Medicine* (Oxford, 1970).
Dilks, D., *Curzon in India* (London, 1969).
Dove, J., *Letters of John Dove* (London, 1938).
Duncan, P. B. and Driver, C. J., *Patrick Duncan: South African and Panafrican* (London, 1980).
Dutt, K. I. (ed.), *S. Radhakrishnan* (New Delhi, 1973).
Egerton, H. E., *Claims of the Study of Colonial History upon the Attention of the University of Oxford* (Oxford, 1906).
Elton, Godfrey, Lord, *The First Fifty Years of the Rhodes Trust and the Rhodes Scholarships* (Oxford, 1953).
Elwin, V., *The Tribal World of Verrier Elwin* (Delhi, 1964).
Engel, A. J., *From Clergyman to Don* (Oxford, 1983).
Faber, G., *Jowett* (London, 1958).
Fairbridge, K., *Autobiography* (London, 1927).
Farnell, L. R., *An Oxonian Looks Back* (London, 1934).
Farnell, V., *A Somervillian Looks Back* (Oxford, 1948).
Feiling, Keith, *In Christ Church Hall* (London, 1960).
Firth, C. H., *The Oxford School of Geography* (Oxford, 1918).
Fisher, H. A. L., *James Bryce* (London, 1927).
Fletcher, C. R. L., *Introductory History of England* (London, 1904).
Fletcher, C. R. L. and Kipling, Rudyard, *History of England* (Oxford, 1911).
Flint, J., *Rhodes* (London, 1976).
Forbes, D., *The Liberal Anglican Idea of History* (Cambridge, 1952).
Fort, G. Seymour, *Alfred Beit* (London, 1932).
Foster, J., *Alumni Oxoniensis* (Oxford, 1888).
Foster, J., *Oxford Men and their Colleges* (Oxford, 1893).
Freeman, E. A., *Historical Essays*, 3rd Series (London, 1879).
von Furer Haimendorff, C., 'J. H. Hutton, Obituary', *Proceedings of the Royal Anthropological Inst.* (1968).
Furse, M., *Stand Therefore* (London, 1953).
Furse, Sir R., *Aucuparius* (London, 1962).
Fyfe, C., *Sierra Leone* (Oxford, 1962).
Gardner, P., *Oxford at the Crossroads* (London, 1903).

Gardner, W. J., E. T. Beardsley and T. E. Carter, *History of University of Canterbury* (Christchurch, N.Z., 1973).
Gardner, W. J., *Colonial Cap and Gown* (Christchurch, N.Z., 1979).
Gell, The Hon. Mrs, *Under Three Reigns* (London, 1927).
George, Hereford, *Historical Geography of the British Empire* (London, 1904).
Gertrude, Sister, *Mother Edith* (London, 1964).
Gibbs, M. E., *The Anglican Church in India* (New Delhi, 1972).
Gilbert, E. W., *British Pioneers in Geography* (Newton Abbot, 1972).
Glyn, Elinor, *Romantic Adventure* (London, 1936).
Gombrich, R. H., *On Being Sanskritic*, Inaugural Lecture as Boden Professor of Sanskrit (Oxford, 1978).
Grant Robertson, C., *All Souls College* (London, 1894).
Green, V. H. H., *Religion at Oxford and Cambridge* (London, 1964).
Greenlee, J. G., 'A Succession of Seeleys', *Journal of Imperial and Commonwealth History*, vol. 4 (1975–6).
Grigg, E., *Faith of an Englishman* (London, 1936).
Grigson, W. V., *The Maria Gonds of Bastar* (London, 1938).
Gutch, J., *Martyr of the Islands* (London, 1971).
Hailey, Malcolm, Lord, 'Role of Anthropology in Colonial Development', *Man*, vol. 34 (Jan. 1944) no. 5.
Hakluyt, R., *A Particular Discourse Concerning Western Discoveries* (London, 1877 edn).
Hakluyt, R., *Principal Navigations, Voyages, Traffiques and Discoveries of the English Nation* (London, 1903 edn).
Haldane, L. K., *Friends and Kindred* (London, 1961).
Hall, H., 'Origin of Lord Almoner's Professorship of Arabic', *Athenaeum*, vol. 16 (Nov. 1889).
Hammond, J. L., *C. P. Scott* (London, 1934).
Hancock, W. R., *Country and Calling* (London, 1954).
Hannington, James, *Last Journals* (London, 1888).
Hansard Parliamentary debates.
Harlan, L. R., 'Booker T. Washington and the White Man's Burden', *American Historical Review*, vol. LXXI (1965–6).
Harlow, V., *The Historian and British Colonial History*, Inaugural Lecture as Beit Professor of Colonial History (Oxford, 1951).
Harrison, Frederic, *Memories and Thoughts* (London, 1906).
Harrison, Frederic, *Autobiographical Memories* (London, 1911).
Hattersley, A. F., *Hilton Portrait* (Pietermaritzburg, 1945).
Headlam, Cecil, *Ten Thousand Miles through India and Burma: An Account of the Oxford University Authentics' Cricket Tour in the Year of the Coronation Dunbar* (London, 1903).
Herbertson, A. J., 'Geography and Some of its Needs', *Geographical Journal*, vol. 36 (Oct. 1910).
Herbertson, A. J. and Howarth, O. J. R., *Oxford Survey of the British Empire* (Oxford, 1914).
Heussler, R., *Yesterday's Rulers* (London, 1963).
Hewins, W. E. S., *Apologia of an Imperialist* (London, 1929).
Hine, J. E., *Days Gone By* (London, 1924).

Hirst, F., Murray, Gilbert and Hammond, J. L., *Liberalism and the Empire* (London, 1900).
Hobhouse, L. T., *Democracy and Reaction* (London, 1904).
Hobhouse, L. T. and Hammond, J. L., *Lord Hobhouse: A Memoir* (Oxford, 1905).
Hobson, J. A., *Imperialism* (London, 1902).
Hobson, J. A., *Confessions of an Economic Heretic* (London, 1938).
Hobson, J. A. with Ginsburg, M., *L. T. Hobhouse* (London, 1931).
Hodgkin, Thomas, *Nationalism in Colonial Africa* (London, 1956).
Hodson, H. V., 'The Round Table 1910–1981', *Round Table* (Oct. 1981) no. 284.
Holland, W. E. S., *The Goal of India* (London, 1917).
Hollis, C., *The Oxford Union* (London, 1965).
Howard, R. B., *Upper Canada College* (Toronto, 1979).
Hoyos, F. A., *Grantley Williams and the Social Revolution* (London, 1974).
Hunter, W. W., 'A Forgotten Oxford Movement', *Fortnightly Review*, vol. 65 (1896).
Hutchins, F. G., *British Imperialism in India* (Princeton, 1967).
Hutton, W. H., *The Teaching of Indian History* (Oxford, 1914).
Huws Jones, E., *Mrs Humphry Ward* (London, 1973).
Hyam, R., 'The Colonial Office Mind', *Journal of Imperial and Commonwealth History*, vol. VIII (1979).
Imperial Forestry Institute and Oxford University Institute of Forestry, *Annual Reports*.
Indian Magazine (periodical) (Oxford, 1914).
Iqbal, Afzal, *Life and Times of Mohamed Ali* (Lahore, 1974).
Jebb, R., *Studies in Colonial Nationalism* (London, 1905).
Jefferson, Sir G., 'Memories of Hugh Cairns', *Journal of Neurosurgery and Psychiatry*, vol. 22 (1959).
Jenkyns, R., *The Victorians and Ancient Greece* (Oxford, 1980).
Kabir, Hamayun, *Britain and India* (New Delhi, 1960).
Kadish, A., *Oxford Economists in the Late 19th Century* (Oxford, 1982).
Karaka, D. F., *Then Came Hazrat Ali* (Bombay, 1972).
Kendle, J. E., *Colonial and Imperial Conference* (London, 1967).
Kerr, P. (Lord Lothian), 'Political Relations between Advanced and Backward Peoples', in A. J. Grant (ed.), *International Relations* (London, 1916).
Kirk-Greene, A., *The Sudan Political Service: A Preliminary Profile* (Oxford, 1982).
Kitchen, G. W., *Ruskin at Oxford* (London, 1904).
Kuper, A., *Anthropologists and Anthropology* (London, 1973).
Lal Sud, Babu, *How to Become a Barrister and Take a Degree at Oxford and Cambridge* (Kapurthala, 1917 edn).
Langley, N., *Codrington and his College* (London, 1964).
Lankester, Sir E. Ray, *The Advancement of Science* (London, 1890).
Lankester, Sir E. Ray, *Nature and Man*, Romanes Lecture (Oxford, 1905).
Lankester, Sir E. Ray, *Science from an Easy Chair* (London, 1911).
Lawrence, Sir Walter, *The India We Served* (London, 1928).
Lawson, F. H., *The Oxford Law School 1850–1965* (Oxford, 1968).

Lawson, K. C., *Venture of Faith, St John's College, Johannesburg* (Johannesburg, 1968).
Leacock, S., *My Discovery of England* (New York, 1922).
Leopold, J., *British Applications of the Aryan Theory of Race to India*, vol. 89 (E.H.R., 1974).
Leys, Norman, *Kenya* (London, 1924).
Leys, N. and Oldham, J. H., *By Kenya Possessed* (Chicago, 1976).
Lock, W., *Church and Empire* (London, 1907).
Lockhart, J. G. and Woodhouse, C. M., *Rhodes* (London, 1963).
Longridge, G., *History of the Oxford Mission to Calcutta* (London, 1910).
Lord, Henry, *Discovery of Two Foreign Sects in the East Indies* (London, 1752 edn).
Lovett, Sir V., *History of the Indian Nationalist Movement* (London, 1919).
Lovett, Sir V., *Britain's Work in India*, Inaugural Lecture as Reader in Indian History (Oxford, 1920).
Low, Sydney, 'Organization of Imperial Studies in London', *P.B.A.*, vol. 5 (1912).
Lucas, C. P., *Historical Geography of the British Colonies* (Oxford, 1900–10).
Lucas, C. P., *Greater Rome and Greater Britain* (Oxford, 1912).
Lucas, C. P., *The British Empire* (London, 1915).
M. B., *Recollections of J. H. Bridges* (London, 1908).
McCullum, M. W., *A. B. Weigall* (Sydney, 1969).
MacDonald, K. C., *History of Waikaki Boys High School* (Christchurch, N.Z., 1958).
MacDonell, A. A., *India's Past* (London, 1927).
MacFarlane, L. G., *Howard Florey* (Oxford, 1979).
McIntyre, D., *Diocesan College, Rondebosch* (Cape Town, 1950).
MacKail, J. W., *J. L. Strachan Davidson* (Oxford, 1925).
Mackinder, H. J., 'The Geographical Pivot of History', *Geographical Journal*, vol. 23 (1904).
Mackinder, H. J., *Britain and the British Seas* (Oxford, 1902).
MacMichael, H., *The Sudan* (London, 1954).
MacMillan, C., *McGill and Its Story* (London, 1921).
MacMillan, W. M., *My South African Years* (Cape Town, 1975).
MacMillan Brown, J., *Memoirs* (Christchurch, N.Z., 1974).
Madden, A. F. and Fieldhouse, D. K. (eds), *Oxford and the Idea of the Commonwealth* (London, 1982).
Magnus, Laurie, *Herbert Warren of Magdalen* (London, 1932).
Malan, A. N., *Solomon Caesar Malan, D.D.* (London, 1897).
Mallet, C. E., *History of the University of Oxford* (London, 1927).
Mangat Rai, E. N., *Commitment My Style* (Delhi, 1973).
Maples C., *Life of Bishop Maples By His Sister* (London, 1897).
Marett, R. R., *Tylor* (London, 1936).
Marett, R. R., *A Jerseyman at Oxford* (London, 1941).
Marett, R. R., 'Obituary', *Proceedings of British Academy*, vol. XXIX (1943).
Marett, R. R. and Penniman, T. K., *Spencer's Last Journey* (Oxford, 1931).
Markby, Lady, *Sir William Markby* (Oxford, 1917).
Masani, R. P., *Dadabhai Naoroji* (London, 1934).

Massey, Vincent, *Canadians and Their Commonwealth* (Oxford, 1961).
Massey, Vincent, *What's Past is Prologue* (London, 1963).
Masters, D. C., *Bishops University* (Toronto, 1950).
Max Mueller, F., *Chips from a German Workshop* (London, 1867).
Max Mueller, F., *Inaugural Address to Aryan Section of International Congress of Orientalists* (London, 1874).
Max Mueller, F., *Decree on the Indian Institute* (pamphlet) (Oxford, 1880).
Max Mueller, F., *India, What Can it Teach Us?* (London, 1883).
Max Mueller, G., *Life and Letters of F. Max Mueller* (London, 1902).
Maxwell, J. Renner, *The Negro Question* (London, 1892).
Maynard Smith, H., *Frank, Bishop of Zanzibar* (London, 1926).
Mboya, T., *Freedom and After* (London, 1963).
Menon, K. P. S., *Many Worlds* (London, 1965).
Merivale, H., *Lectures on Colonization and Colonies* (London, 1861).
Miller, J. D. B., *Richard Jebb and the Problem of Empire*, University of London Institute of Commonwealth Studies (1956).
Mills, J. P., 'Anthropology as a Hobby', *Journal of the Royal Anthropological Institute*, vol. 83 (1953).
Milner, Lord, *England in Egypt* (London, 1892).
Milner, Lord, *Arnold Toynbee* (London, 1901).
Milner, Lord, *The Nation and the Empire* (London, 1913).
Milner, Lord, *Questions of the Hour* (London, 1925).
Misra, B. B., *Central Administration of the East India Co.* (Manchester, 1959).
Missionary Settlement for University Women, Bombay, *Annual Reports* (1895–6 to 1947–8).
Missionary Settlement for University Women, *History of the Missionary Settlement for University Women* (Bombay, 1923).
Mitchell, N., *Sir George Cunningham* (London, 1968).
Monier Williams, Sir M., *Modern India and the Indians* (London, 1889).
Monier Williams, Sir M. (ed.), *Memorials of Old Haileybury College* (London, 1894).
Monier Williams, Sir M., *Address on the Holy Bible and the Sacred Books of the East* (London, n.d.)
Montague, C. E., *Disenchantment* (London, 1922).
Moore, R. J., 'Abolition of Patronage in the East India Co.', *Historical Journal*, vol. VII (1964) no. 2.
Morgan, P., *Oxford Libraries outside the Bodleian* (Oxford, 1980).
Morison, H. W., *Oxford Today and the Rhodes Scholarships* (Toronto, 1958).
Morrell, W. P., *Memoirs* (Dunedin, 1979).
Moseley, H. N., *Notes by a Naturalist during the Voyage of H.M.S. Challenger* (London, 1879).
Mosley, N., *Life of Raymond Raynes* (London, 1961).
Mukherjee, S. N., *Sir William Jones* (Cambridge, 1968).
Murray, Gilbert, 'The Empire and Subject Races', *Sociological Review* (July 1910).
Murray, Gilbert, *Essays and Addresses* (London, 1921).
Murray, Gilbert, *Unfinished Autobiography* (London, 1960).

Myres, J. L., 'The Science of Man in the Service of the State', *Journal of the Royal Anthropological Institute*, vol. 59 (1929).
Nettleford, R., *Manley and the New Jamaica* (London, 1971).
Newbolt, Sir H., *My World as in My Time* (London, 1932).
Nimocks, S. L., *Milner's Young Men* (Duke, U.S.A., 1968).
O'Brien, T., *Milner* (London, 1979).
O'Dwyer, Sir M., *India As I Knew It* (London, 1925).
Ogg, D., *Herbert Fisher* (London, 1947).
Ogilvie, R. M., *Latin and Greek* (London, 1964).
Oldham, J. H., *Christianity and the Race Problem* (London, 1924).
Olivier, M., *Sydney Olivier: Letters and Selected Writings* (London, 1948).
O'Neill, Fr., *Brahmoism, Is It For Us or Against Us?* (pamphlet) (Oxford, 1881), Pusey House Collection, Oxford.
Owen, S. J., *Occasional Notes on British–Indian Subjects* (Oxford, 1868).
Owen, S. J., *India on the Eve of the British Conquest* (Oxford, 1872).
Oxford Magazine.
Oxford University Calendar (annual).
Oxford University Examination Statutes (annual).
Oxford University Gazette (published weekly in term time).
Oxford University Institute of Agricultural Economics, Annual Reports.
Oxford University Institute of Colonial (later Commonwealth) Studies, Annual Reports.
Oxford University Institute of Social Anthropology, *Proceedings of 500th Meeting of Oxford University Anthropological Society* (1953).
Padwick, C. E., *Temple Gairdner of Cairo* (London, 1929).
Palmer, E. J., *Challenge of an Indian Experience* (Oxford, 1933).
Pannikar, K. M., *Autobiography* (Delhi, 1974).
Parker, W. H., *Mackinder: Geography as an Aid to Statecraft* (Oxford, 1982).
Parkin, G. R., *The Rhodes Scholarships* (London, 1913).
Parliamentary Papers, England, *Report of Committee on Examination of Candidates for the Indian Civil Service*, vol. XL (1854–5).
Parliamentary Papers, England, *Papers Relating to Selection and Training of Candidates for the Indian Civil Service*, vol. LV (1876).
Parliamentary Papers, England, *Papers Relating to Admission of Natives to the Civil Service of India*, vol. LV (1878–9).
Parliamentary Papers, England, *University of Oxford Commission, Evidence*, vol. LVI (1881).
Parliamentary Papers, England, *Correspondence Relating to the Age of Candidates for the Civil Service of India*, vol. LXIV (1884–5).
Paton, A., *J. H. Hofmeyr* (London, 1964).
Paul, H., *Life of Froude* (London, 1905).
Pearson, C. H., *Memoirs* (London, 1900).
Pearson, L. B., *Memoirs* (London, 1973–5).
Penfield, W., *Something Hidden* (Toronto, 1981).
Penlington, N. (ed.), *On Canada: Essays in Honour of Frank H. Underhill* (Toronto, 1971).
Perham, Dame Margery, *Ten Africans* (London, 1936).
Perham, Dame Margery, *Native Administration in Nigeria* (London, 1937).
Perham, Dame Margery, *The Colonial Reckoning* (London, 1961).

Perham, Dame Margery, *Colonial Sequence* (London, 1967 and 1968).
Perham, Margery and Curtis, L., *The Protectorates of South Africa* (London, 1935).
Philips, C. H. (ed.), *Historians of India, Pakistan and Ceylon* (London, 1961).
Pollock, Sir F., *For My Grandson* (London, 1933).
Porter, A., 'Cambridge, Keswick and Late 19th Century Attitudes to Africa', *J.I.C.H.*, vol. 5 (1976–7).
Porter, B., *Critics of Empire* (London, 1968).
Portus, C., *Happy Highways* (Melbourne, 1983).
Poulton, E. B., *Viriamu Jones and Other Oxford Memories* (London, 1911).
Prestige, G. L., *Life of Charles Gore* (London, 1935).
Purchas, H. T., *Bishop Harper and the Canterbury Settlement* (Christchurch, N.Z., 1909).
Queen Elizabeth House, Oxford, *Annual Reports*.
Rait, R. S., *Memories of A. V. Dicey* (London, 1925).
Reade, Winwoode, *The Martyrdom of Man* (London, 1925 edn).
Rennell Rodd, J., *Social and Diplomatic Memories* (London, 1925).
Report of Committee on Indian Students (Lytton Report) (London, 1922).
Report of Committee on Religious and Moral Instruction (New Delhi, 1960).
Report of Conference on Neglect of Science, (ed.) Sir E. Ray Lankester (London, 1916).
Report of Royal Commission on Oxford and Cambridge Universities, Cmd 1588 (London, 1922). A typed copy of the unpublished evidence is in the Bodleian Library, Oxford.
Report of Royal Commission on Public Services in India (Islington Report) (London, 1914–17).
Report of the Institute of Development Studies at the University of Sussex on Its First Ten Years, University of Sussex (1977).
Report of the Localization Committee (Adu Report) (Zomba, Nyasaland, 1960).
Report on Post-War Training for the Colonial Service (Devonshire Report) (London, 1946).
Report to Nuffield Foundation on a Visit to Nigeria, by J. T. Saunders, R. I. Turner and D. Veale (Oxford, 1946).
Reynolds, J. C., *Canon Christopher* (Abingdon, 1967).
Rhodes, Cecil James, *Last Will and Testament*, ed. W. T. S. Stead (London, 1902).
Rhodes Trust, Oxford, *Cecil Rhodes and Rhodes House* (pamphlet) (Oxford, 1972).
Rhodes Trust, Oxford, *Register of Rhodes Scholars, 1903–81* (Oxford, 1981).
Richter, M., *Politics of Conscience: T. H. Green and His Age* (London, 1964).
Ridley, M. R., *Gertrude Bell* (London, 1941).
Risley, Sir H. H., *Tribes and Castes of Bengal* (Calcutta, 1891).
Risley, Sir H. H., *The People of India* (London, 1908).
Roberts, P. F., *History of British India* (London, 1921).
Robertson, C. Grant, *All Souls College* (London, 1899).

Robinson, K. E., 'Experts, Colonialists and Africanists', in Stone, J. C. (ed.), *Experts in Africa* (Aberdeen, 1980).
Rolleston, G., *Scientific Papers and Addresses* (Oxford, 1884).
Ronaldshay, Lord, *Life of Lord Curzon* (London, 1928).
Rose, K., *Superior Person: A Portrait of Curzon and His Circle* (London, 1969).
Rosebery, A. P., Lord, *Speech at Rhodes Memorial at Oxford* (London, 1907).
Rosebery, A. P., Lord, *Questions of Empire* (London, 1921).
Round Table.
Rowe, E. G., 'Reflections on the Oxford Overseas Services Course', *Journal of Administration Overseas*, vol. 9 (1970).
Rowse, A. L., *Oxford in the History of the Nation* (London, 1975).
Royal Anthropological Institute, *Proceedings*.
Royal Colonial Institute (subsequently Royal Commonwealth Society), *Reports of Proceedings*.
Rumbold, Sir A., *Watershed in India* (London, 1979).
Rupke, N., *The Great Chain of History* (Oxford, 1983).
Rushbrook-Williams, L. F., 'Inside Both Indias', *Indo-British Review*, vol. IX (1982) no. 11.
Ruskin College, *New Epoch* (1948).
Ruskin College, *Annual Reports*.
Ruskin, John, *Collected Works* (London, 1903).
Sadleir, M., *M. E. Sadler* (London, 1949).
Satthianadhan, S., *Four Years in an English University Together with a Complete Guide to Indian Students Proceeding to Great Britain* (Madras, 1893).
Scargill, D. I., 'The Royal Geographical Society and the Foundation of Geography at Oxford', *Geographical Journal*, vol. 142 (1976).
Schurhammer, G., 'Thos. Stephens, The First Englishman in India', *The Month*, vol. 13 (1955).
Schuster, Sir George, *Private Life and Public Causes* (Cowbridge, 1979).
Sherlock, P., *Norman Manley* (London, 1980).
Slade, H. E. W., *The Story of the Cowley Fathers* (London, 1970).
Smith, Goldwin, *Inaugural Lecture as Regius Professor of Modern History* (Oxford, 1859).
Smith, Goldwin, *The Empire* (Oxford, 1863).
Smith, Goldwin, *Commonwealth or Empire* (London, 1902).
Smith, Goldwin, *Reminiscences* (New York, 1910).
Smith, John (pseudonym), *Sketches in Indian Ink* (Calcutta, 1880).
Smith, Vincent, *Oxford History of England for Indian Students* (London, 1912).
Smith, Vincent, *Indian Constitutional Reform Viewed in the Light of History*, 2nd edn (Oxford, 1919).
Smith, Vincent, *Oxford History of India* (Oxford, 1920).
Sollas, W. J., *Ancient Hunters and their Modern Representatives* (London, 1915 edn).
Sorabji, Cornelia, *India Calling* (London, 1934).
Spangenberg, B., *British Bureaucracy in India* (New Delhi, 1976).

Spender, J. A., *Sir H. Campbell Bannerman* (London, 1923).
Stanley, H. M., *How I Found Livingstone* (New York, 1872).
Stebbing, E. P., *The Forests of India* (London, 1923 and 1925).
Steere, D. V., *Gods Irregular* (London, 1973).
Stephen, Leslie, *Studies of a Biographer* (London, 1898).
Stephen, R. H., 'The Rhodes Bequest', *The Oxford Point of View*, vol. 1 (1902).
Stephens, W. R. W., *Life and Letters of E. A. Freeman* (London, 1895).
Stevens, Siaka, *What Life has Taught Me* (Kensal, 1984).
Stokes, R., *Political Ideas of Imperialism* (Oxford, 1960).
Stubbs, William, *Lectures on Medieval and Modern History* (Oxford, 1886).
Sutcliffe, P., *The Oxford University Press* (Oxford, 1978).
Sykes, Ella C., *A Home Help in Canada* (London, 1912).
Syme, Sir Ronald, *Colonial Elites: Rome, Spain and the Americas* (London, 1958).
Symonds, Richard, *The British and Their Successors* (London, 1966).
Symonds, Richard, 'Powerhouse of Imperial Studies – the Early Search for a Role for Rhodes House', *Round Table*, vol. 288 (1983).
Taylor, E. G. R., 'The Original Writings of the Two Hakluyts', *Hakluyt Society* series II, vol. LXXVI London, 1935).
Terry, E., *Voyage to East India* (London, 1777 edn).
Thomas, H. B., 'The Last Days of Bishop Hannington', *Uganda Journal*, vol. VIII (Sept. 1940) no. 1.
Times Atlas of the World (London, 1958).
Times, The, History of the Times, vol. IV (London, 1952).
Torlesse, F. H., *J. H. Bridges and His Family* (London, 1912).
Toynbee, Arnold, I, *Progress and Poverty* (London, 1883).
Toynbee, Arnold, I, *The Industrial Revolution* (London, 1896 edn).
Toynbee, Arnold, II, *Acquaintances* (London, 1967).
Tozer, W. G., *Letters of Bishop Tozer* (London, 1902).
Troup, R. S., 'New Site for the Dept of Forestry', *Journal of the Oxford Forestry Society*, 2nd Series, no. 15 (1934).
Turner, F. M., *The Greek Heritage in Victorian Britain* (Yale, 1981).
Turney, C., *Pioneers of Australian Education* (Sydney, 1969).
Vogeler, Martha S., *Frederic Harrison: The Vocation of a Positivist* (Oxford, 1984).
Wallace, E., *Goldwin Smith, Victorian Liberal* (Toronto, 1957).
Wallace, W. S., *History of Toronto University* (Toronto, 1927).
Ward, G., *Letters from East Africa* (London, 1899).
Ward, W. E. F., *Fraser of Trinity and Achimota* (Accra, 1965).
Welldon, J. E. C., *Recollections and Reflections* (London, 1915).
Welldon, J. E. C., *Forty Years On* (London, 1935).
West, F., *Hubert Murray: The Australian Proconsul* (Melbourne, 1968).
West, F., *Gilbert Murray: A Life* (London, 1984).
Wheare, K. C., *Constitutional Structure of the Commonwealth* (Oxford, 1960).
Whetham, E. H., *Agricultural Economists in Britain, 1900–1940* (Oxford, 1981).
Whittington, F. T., *Augustus Short: First Bishop of Adelaide* (London, 1883).

Williams, B., *Cecil Rhodes* (London, 1938).
Williams, Barry, *The Franciscan Revival in the Anglican Communion* (London, 1982).
Williams, Eric, *British Historians and the West Indies* (Trinidad, 1964).
Williams, Eric, *Inward Hunger* (London, 1969).
Williams, N. P. and Harris, C. (eds), *Northern Catholicism* (London, 1933).
Williams, Trever, *Florey: The Years after Penicillin* (Oxford, 1984).
Willis, E. G., *Letter to the Regius Professor of Theology* (pamphlet) (Oxford, 1879). Pusey House Collection, Oxford.
Willison, J., *Sir George Parkin* (London, 1929).
Winslow, J. C., *Christa Seva Sangha* (London, 1930).
Winslow, J. C. and Elwin, Verrier, *The Dawn of Indian Freedom* (London, 1931).
Winter, A., *Till Darkness Fall*, Community of the Resurrection, Mirfield (n.d.).
Woodgate, M. V., *Father Benson of Cowley* (London, 1953).
Woodruff, P., *The Men who Ruled India* (London, 1953).
Wrench, J. E., *Geoffrey Dawson and Our Times* (London, 1955).
Wrench, J. E., *Alfred, Lord Milner* (London, 1958).
Yousif, A. A., *University Extramural Studies in Ghana and Nigeria* (London, 1968).
Zimmern, A., *The Third British Empire* (London, 1926).

Note. In addition to the above, there are official histories of all Oxford Colleges founded before 1937.

Index